635

THE GOSPEL OF GENTILITY

THE
GOSPEL
OF
GENTILITY

*American Women
Missionaries in
Turn-of-the-Century
China*

Jane Hunter

YALE UNIVERSITY PRESS
NEW HAVEN AND LONDON

Published with assistance from the
Frederick Jackson Turner Award of the
Organization of American Historians.

Designed by Sally Harris
and set in Goudy Old Style type by The Saybrook Press,
Old Saybrook, Connecticut.
Printed in the United States of America by
Murray Printing Company, Westford, Massachusetts.

Library of Congress Cataloging in Publication Data

Hunter, Jane, 1949–
The gospel of gentility.

Bibliography: p. 305.
Includes index.
1. Women missionaries—China.   2. Missions—China.
I. Title.
BV3415.2.H86   1984   266'.023'73051088042   83-16668
ISBN 0-300-02878-4

10 9 8 7 6 5 4 3 2 1

For
Elizabeth Morrison Hunter
and
Ralph William Hunter

CONTENTS

ILLUSTRATIONS

PREFACE

To American women, more than to any others on earth, is committed the
exalted privilege of extending over the world those blessed influences, which
are to renovate degraded man, and "to clothe all climes with beauty."
—Catharine Beecher, A *Treatise on Domestic Economy* (1842)

Catharine Beecher's practical guide for the nineteenth-century housewife
included this tribute to the glorious possibilities of the woman's sphere.
Woman's chores might seem menial and inconsequential, but she should
make no mistake: well executed in the proper spirit, they contained
enormous power. Through her improving influence on her husband and
children, she might reform American society. By introducing her special
qualities into the public arena, through schoolteaching or church work,
she might reform all peoples. Diffused beyond her home, woman's nurture
and refinement carried the miraculous potential to conquer and redeem
the entire world.

Even as Beecher wrote, the female voluntary societies of the Christian
benevolent empire were working to fulfill her mandate. Women's "cent"
and "mite" societies gathered housewives' extra pennies to add women's
subsidies to the support of the foreign missionary movement. Female
supporters thrilled to the courage and heroism of young missionary women
who accompanied their husbands to the jungles of Asia and Africa, and
who suffered and perished nobly there. After the Civil War, American
women founded agencies of their own to send unmarried female missionaries to the heathen in foreign lands. By 1890, the married women of the
general missionary boards and the single women of the women's boards
together composed 60 percent of the mission force.

Simultaneous with the feminization of the mission force, the movement
became important to a nation newly intrigued by the possibilities of
international expansion. Empire seemed to offer an appealing resolution
to the dissonance between growing industrial capacity and the limits of the

American frontier. It promised new markets for American goods, new challenges for the American spirit, new moral wildernesses for American civilization. The Spanish-American War inspired a burst of fresh support for the flagging foreign mission movement. Even after passions for territorial expansion had cooled, the mission movement would continue to tap a rich vein of American nationalism.

Throughout the nineteenth century, women's contributions to the American missionary impulse were unique both in style and substance. In accordance with their stations within American families, women relied particularly on "blessed influence" rather than on direct authority to win compliance from other peoples. Their approach was intimate and personal rather than directive. They associated their Christian mission with their domestic responsibility to instill moral character ("to renovate degraded man") and to breed refinement (to "clothe all climes with beauty"). As in their homes, women's moral and material responsibilities were closely connected. Their special concern with the details of domestic life made them both the most dedicated and the most successful emissaries of an entire civilization. As one of the celebrants of the missionary enterprise put it, "Every home they set up, every school they establish, is an object lesson in the art of living."[1]

But the changes which had encouraged the nation to look beyond its borders for future adventures had also challenged the possibilities of the American home. A female evangelism of love encouraged women to go out from their homes to reform the world; but in the context of labor unrest, urban crowding, and massive immigration, the home itself seemed increasingly vulnerable. In the late nineteenth century, many women turned inward rather than outward, reinforcing the family circle with the genteel rituals of a new leisure class. In fact, the woman's sphere now seemed to harbor two contradictory impulses: domestic outreach, embodied in social settlement work, and domestic retreat, embodied in the bourgeois family.

Female evangelists in the age of empire were caught between the confident ideology and the troubling vulnerability of the American home. Inspired by divine enthusiasm to travel halfway around the world to spread truth and refinement, women in the mission field seemed surprised to discover the myriad challenges presented to American domestic life by an alien environment. Throughout their lives, they balanced their initial loyalty to the evangelical mission of woman's sphere with their anxious efforts to reinforce its sacred core, the home. Their mediations between public and private responsibilities, between expansive and defensive commitments, were dramatic versions of the central tensions within American female culture at the time.

The Protestant women who volunteered for missionary service represented an important sector of the native-born population. Women of an appropriate background might gravitate toward mission service for any number of reasons, ranging from a divine call to a family death, from marriage to a male missionary to accommodation to spinsterhood. Like other American women of the late Victorian period, missionary volunteers participated in a national, feminine culture reinforced by church institutions, publishers of women's periodicals, and producers of domestic bric-a-brac. Missionary service represented a courageous decision but not an extraordinary one, and those who made it shared many values and attitudes with schoolteachers and ministers' wives at home.

Missionary lives, therefore, provide a valuable source for the historian interested in turn-of-the-century female culture. Unlike schoolteachers living at home, missionaries left an extensive record of their lives in the form of correspondences, sometimes continuing over decades, with families at home. Their letters contain descriptions of foreign life and life in the mission compound, confessions of cravings for home, reflections about their countrymen, and thoughts about themselves. The novelty of their circumstances provoked missionary correspondents to articulate loyalties, prejudices, self-doubts, and cultural certainties that would likely never have been recorded, perhaps never even entertained, at home.

Missionary women went to the field to work for all mankind, but they particularly focused their energies on converting their own sex, barred from the attentions of male missionaries. They believed that Christianity was responsible for the elevated status of Western women; in preaching the Gospel they were only sharing what they had received in such bounty. As one volunteer put it, it was both "the heinousness of heathen womanhood and gratitude for [their] own Christian womanhood" that inspired American women's service.[2]

With this conviction of Christianity's beneficence toward women, female missionary organizations were not self-consciously feminist and in fact were among the more conservative women's organizations at the turn of the century. Even those missionaries who addressed the problems of poverty and disease presented no challenge to their own society, for their efforts to improve the lives of the poor took place thousands of miles away.

Unlike such organizations as the Women's Christian Temperance Union, which advocated the vote and pitched the powers of womanly influence against the liquor interest, missionary women battled only alien forces and men of another society or a "lesser" race. The enrollments of single women in missionary work had never been higher than at the turn of the century, perhaps because the women's mission movement offered respectable careers even to the pious daughters of clergymen.

Nevertheless, the women who ventured alone overseas in ever-increasing numbers at the turn of the century took their place with their more rebellious sisters to constitute one of the most significant female generations in American history. The achievements of the boldest women of this generation, which in 1900 included the largest proportion of unmarried women over the age of twenty-five to date, are well known. Much literature documents the lives of Jane Addams, Emma Goldman, Charlotte Perkins Gilman, and others. Conservative, evangelical missionaries found the fulfillment overseas that more radical women found closer to home; in so doing they broadened the possibilities for women's lives and afforded new testimony to their potential. In their journeys to foreign fields, missionary women perhaps resembled empire seekers of other kinds. Much as proponents of economic empire saw Asia as a potential solution for the domestic problem of surplus goods, so certain women saw in missions a potential solution for a more personal problem—a tentative energy for which there was no acceptable home market.[3]

Based on the private papers of some forty women and on the archives of the Congregational and the Methodist Episcopal mission boards, this study explores the life patterns of female volunteers from initial commitment to veteran service on the China field. The first section (chapters 1 and 2) sets the stage for the study; chapter 1 in the histories of missions, American expansionism, and Chinese reform; and chapter 2 in the personal and demographic circumstances which led women to enlist for foreign service. Once in China, single women and married women experienced different dilemmas of identity, described in chapters 3 and 4. Single women came to discover social autonomy in shared spinsterhood, while married women struggled to balance their missionary vocation with maternal responsibilities.

Both found unexpected authority in their status as Westerners in colonial China. In their homes and in the foreign community (chapter 5), and in Chinese society itself (chapter 6), missionary women experienced imperial gratifications which undermined their habits of feminine subordination. Chapter 7 seeks to judge the women's missionary enterprise by looking at its results: what was the impact of women missionaries on their female students and converts? The Afterword speculates on the implications of the China mission experience for comparative American and Chinese women's history.

In a study which draws heavily on English-language accounts of Chinese people and places, it seemed sensible to preserve the Chinese orthography used in the original letters and journals. Since turn-of-the-century missionaries tended to use the Wade-Giles romanization system, if they used any at all, I have used the same system for my own translations from the Chinese.

ACKNOWLEDGMENTS

Grateful acknowledgment is made to the following persons for permission to quote from family manuscripts: Agnes McClure Alden for the Jeanie Graham McClure Papers; Helen C. Bassler for the Emma and Lizzie Martin Papers; Eunice Smith Bishop for the Grace Smith Papers; Mary Lacy Buckley for the Jessie Ankeny Lacy Papers; David N. Campbell for the Campbell Family Papers; Rachel Fish for the Lida Ashmore Papers; John H. Foster for the Clara Foster Papers; L. Carrington Goodrich for the Sarah Goodrich Papers; Donald C. Hendrick and Helen C. Votteler for the Monona Cheney Papers; Elsie Clark Krug for her papers; Gordon W. Manly and Jean Manly Bucciarelli for the Florence Manly Papers; Peter Kong-ming New for the Mrs. Way-sung New [Y. T. Zee] Papers; Christine H. Pickett for her memoirs "From the Rising of the Sun," and for our interview; Alice Reed for her papers; Charles A. Rowland for the Mildred Rowland Papers; Dorothy L. Walters for the Idabelle Lewis [Main] Papers; Theodore S. Wilder for the Gertrude Wilder Papers.

I would like to thank the following institutions for permission to quote from materials in their collections: Enid H. Douglass, Director, for the China Missionaries Oral History Project; Houghton Library, Harvard University, and the United Church Board for World Ministries, for the American Board of Commissioners for Foreign Missions Papers; the Presbyterian Historical Society for the Calendar of the Correspondence of the Board of Foreign Missions; Special Collections, University of Oregon Library, for the Lida Ashmore, Jessie Ankeny Lacy, Monona Cheney, and Idabelle Lewis [Main] papers; the Woman's Division, Board of Global

Ministries, United Methodist Church, for the Woman's Foreign Missionary Society Deceased File; Yale Divinity School Library for the China
Records Project.

Thanks also to the following publishers who generously allowed me to
quote from materials under their copyright: Abington Press for Welthy
Honsinger, *Behind the Moon Gate*; Jonathan Cape Ltd. and the author for
Han Su-yin, *A Mortal Flower*; William B. Eerdmans, Publishers, for
R. Pierce Beaver, *All Loves Excelling: American Protestant Women in
World Mission*; Harper & Row, Publishers, Inc. for Pearl Buck, *The Exile*
and *Of Men and Women*; Moody Press, Moody Bible Institute of Chicago,
for Christiana Tsai [Tsai Ling-fang], *Queen of the Dark Chamber*; Harold
Ober Associates for Pearl Buck, *The Fighting Angel*.

The staffs at Houghton Library, the University of Oregon Special
Collections, the Library of the United Methodist Church, and especially
Martha Smalley of the China Records Project have patiently assisted this
project over years of visits and queries. Karen Bourassa and Mary Getchell
typed and retyped this manuscript on a bug-ridden word processor, and
Kathleen Gillespie helped in the final stages of manuscript preparation.
The American-East Asian Relations Committee of the American Historical Association funded two years of language study, and the American
Association of University Women provided a crucial year of research
assistance. The Dean of Faculty at Colby College generously subsidized the
illustrations. At Yale University Press, Barbara Folsom has strengthened
my prose and Chuck Grench has been patient, straightforward, persistent—
the ideal editor.

I am particularly grateful to friends who have read and commented
astutely on this manuscript over the years: Eddie Ayers, Gerry Burns,
John Endean, Elliot Gorn, Phyllis Mannocchi, Ruth Nelson, Anne Rose,
and Michael Smith. They and others—Jacqui Bernard, Harriet Chess-
man, Bryan Wolf, Wai-chee Dimock, Peter Dimock, Donna Greenberg,
Anita Harris—have cared for the author and her project in more ways than
one. Karen Halttunen has listened carefully and offered the unparalleled
advice of a wise and true friend over many years.

I have been as fortunate in mentors as in friends. John Morton Blum,
Nancy Cott, Michael Hunt, and Jonathan Spence have offered generous
readings and crucial encouragement at various stages along the way.
Marilyn Young gave this book a sensitive and helpful evaluation for Yale
University Press. I am especially grateful to David Brion Davis, who first
allowed me to take American cultural history to the far corners of Asia and

then offered brilliant observations about what I found there. The Hunter-Morrison family gave me peace and confidence through long years of research and writing, and my brother, Bill Hunter, offered creative rephrasings and a poet's touch in the final stages.

My greatest debt is to my husband, Joel Bernard, who has all along managed to combine serious evaluation with steady support, who has been both my best critic and my most enthusiastic advocate. This is a better book because of his faith and wit.

❧ 1 ❧

CHINESE REFORM, AMERICAN MISSION,
AND "WOMAN'S WORK"

To missionaries arriving from turn-of-the-century America, China seemed mired in the timeless dirt, death, and degradation of the ages. The authority of the dead was apparent everywhere. When one missionary first arrived in the city of Kucheng in 1913, she wrote that there were more dead in coffins above ground than there were people alive. "I thought I was living in a city of the dead," she remembered. Another arrived in Foochow in 1900 in a flooding rain and spent her first night weeping, as she listened to the haunting sounds of China—men crying out for rescue and birds calling lugubriously. The keening of mourners was a constant sound in Chinese cities. ("You simply cannot imagine the Chinese wailing until you hear it," one woman wrote back.) The respect paid the dead, the public pathos of the dying, and the ritual wailing of the bereaved left witnesses from the American new world steeped in melancholy, confusion, and distress. As one of them put it, most missionaries found "the first impression of China a *de*-pression."[1]

When missionaries tried to place China in history, they looked back to past centuries. "Were the Syrians as untaught, as primitive, as animal-like as the Chinese?" Elsie Clark wondered. "Jesus knew such people as these." Lucile Jones, too, thought of the early days of Christianity, when lepers, "some of them without fingers, some of them without eyes," shoved their begging baskets at her. "Well, I knew there were lepers in the Bible, but I thought they were still there," she remembered thinking. After her sedan-chair ride through rice paddies and "the street, the pits, the filth" of a large town, she could not eat the Chinese food she was served at the home of a church member. "I was nearly a nervous wreck," she remembered. These

I

were only the first experiences of the strain of living with "one foot in the twentieth century and one in the ages B.C.," as one woman put it.[2]

The sense of disorientation that missionaries experienced could seem to be surreal dream as well as historical nightmare. Ruth White early visited a Buddhist temple where she watched the incense smoke swirling before the "idols." When we "really sensed that we were in the midst of people who believed in it all, it seemed too strange to be true," she wrote home. Emma Martin described Japan, the first mission stop in Asia, as a phantasm: "We had seen so many unexpected things that I would not have been surprised at anything—even to have seen Ma and Pa. Sometimes I could hardly remember who I was and how I came there. I have had the same feeling several times since." The dissonance of Asian experience sent missionaries looking for touchstones of continuity. "There are four things that sound just like home," Mildred Rowland wrote, and listed "the rain, the caw of the crow, the singing of the cricket and the crying of the babies"; the sounds of the functions of nature were the only bridges across a great chasm of culture.[3]

While Western missionaries found the entire Chinese environment strange and unnerving, Chinese focused their fear and wonder on the physical person of the Westerner, with his pale skin, long nose, deep-set eyes, and furry hair. Like the Westerners regarding them, Chinese were reminded of the animal kingdom and of the supernatural. The urbane Chinese hero of the Opium War, Lin Tse-hsu, noted that the bodies of foreign men were so "tightly encased from head to toe by short serge jackets and long close-fitting trousers," "that they look like actors playing the parts of foxes, hares, and other such animals on the stage." "The first time I had seen the tall man with the black beard," one Chinese woman remembered, "I had thought he was a devil and had squatted in the road and hid my head in my arms." Lin Tse-hsu had to agree that "they do really look like devils; and when the people of these parts call them 'devils' it is no mere empty turn of phrase." The Chinese epithet for Westerner, "foreign devil," transmitted this initial fear to common parlance.[4]

The startled responses of Westerner and Chinese to each other's person, dress, and habits, particularly in the vast Chinese hinterland, have a timeless pattern to them, still occasionally repeated today when Western guests visit provincial China. Yet the missionaries who arrived in China at the turn of the century were participants in a specific historical drama as well as a timeless antipathy. While peasants and missionaries regarded each other with mutual disbelief, official China was beginning to modify its resistance to the West and, following the Boxer Rebellion, to extend greater protection to missionary representatives. In response, missionaries hailed the awakening of China and moved new recruits to the field. For this they received the newly enthusiastic backing of their country's leaders, who now regarded them as useful allies in a competition for world influence. Even as missionaries and Chinese repeated rituals of estrangement around the empire, "China faced West," as one historian has put it, and confronted a new American campaign to export its culture. Playing a major role in this campaign were the women of the newly feminized mission force. As early as 1890, women constituted 60 percent of missionary volunteers and proved to be particularly persuasive voices in the crusade for American influence in China.

The radical reversal of Chinese policy toward the West during the first twenty years of the century enabled the flourishing of mission activity in China. One historian has argued that the year 1900 was the pivot in the evolution of China from a traditional dynasty looking backward to a reforming nation looking outward. With the cataclysmic defeat of the court-supported Boxers, the balance of power in China began to shift from the conservative officials of the Chinese hinterland to the reformers of the Chinese seaboard. In the nineteenth century the Ch'ing court had attempted to incorporate the Western nations into its own network of vassal states. By the twentieth century it had learned that, if it wanted to survive, it would have to counter Western nations with Western notions. Following the Boxer aftermath, China moved to control the West by learning from it and extended a new if still grudging toleration to its missionaries.[5]

The court's decision to support the Righteous and Harmonious Fist Society, or the Boxers, in their campaign against the foreign presence was the victory of official impulse over calculated self-interest. The Boxers believed themselves protected from Western bullets by magic and conducted a campaign of extermination in the north which left 250 foreigners and nearly 2,000 Chinese Christians dead. The invasion by an allied expeditionary force to rescue besieged survivors put Chinese autonomy temporarily in jeopardy. This near brush with imperial subdivision seemed to chasten the exiled court. When they returned to Peking, it was with a new spirit of respect for the West. Reformer Chang Chih-tung's aphorism "Chinese learning for the essential principles; Western learning for the practical applications" expressed China's hopes for both autonomy and strength.[6]

Chinese leaders were all along more interested in Western science and technology than they were in Christian religion. The "essential principles" of Christianity were just what China wanted to avoid. Nevertheless, missionaries represented the largest contingent of foreigners in China, a force that could not be expelled (as the Boxer disaster indicated) and thus might as well be utilized. China aimed to control the Christian influence, but it also aimed to exploit it. The question became who would exploit whom. As John R. Mott, a missionary spokesman, wrote in 1911: "It is Western education that the Chinese are clamoring for, and will have. If the church can give it to them, plus Christianity, they will take it; otherwise they will get it elsewhere."[7] Increasingly, after the Boxer uprising, reformers and officials turned to missionaries for advice and example as they moved toward modernization. With the revolution of 1911, interest in the West further enhanced the stature of Western missionaries in China.

Both adversaries in the republican revolution, which overthrew the Manchu dynasty, were scrupulously careful of foreign property. Both sides agreed that foreign intercession would likely result in the partition of China. The establishment of the republic brought more Western-educated Chinese, some of them Christian, into power. Until 1911, graduates from Christian schools had been ineligible for government jobs, nor could they run for the new provincial assemblies. "Do you all realize that we really have freedom of religion now, and what a wonderful change there is in the feeling toward Christianity and toward us?" Luella Miner wrote thereafter. The interest of the overthrown Manchus in the church was a particular source of gratification to missionaries who had endured the disdain of China's ruling race for many years. More importantly, the republican government asked for a day of Christian prayer for their new nation. The revolution seemed to confirm China's movement into modernity. During the eleven years following it, the Protestant forces counted 200,000 new converts, a figure nearly equal to the total number of converts of the hundred preceding years.[8]

The famous nationalist uprisings of 4 May 1919 did not directly threaten the missionary presence. In fact, many missionaries themselves were fearful of Japanese designs on China and gave their ardent support to this outbreak of student nationalism. Missionaries had all along been hoping to inculcate their students with Western notions of patriotism, and came to see the May 4 movement as further proof of their influence. But the nationalist ferment had other lasting consequences for Christianity in China. The accompanying New Culture movement, centered at Peking University, addressed directly the interrelation of politics and culture. In repudiating the antiscientific Confucian tradition, it provided a new basis for old attacks on the Christian presence in China.

The new Christian influence in China received its first serious challenge in 1922 with the founding of an Anti-Christian Student Federation, which included both former mission school students and supporters of the newly emergent Chinese Communist Party. The meeting of the World Student Christian Federation near Peking in 1922 provided the occasion for long-brewing anti-Christian sentiment to coalesce. As representatives of Christian organizations from around the world gathered in Tsing Hua, the Anti-Christian Student Federation issued a manifesto denouncing an imperial alliance of Christianity and capitalism under American leadership.[9] American missionaries rejected the accusation, but the increasingly heated nationalist climate of the 1920s impelled them to new self-scrutiny. During the years between the antiforeignism of the Boxer uprising and the nationalist anti-Christian movement, though, the focal years of this study, missionaries enjoyed a dominion which seemed to them a natural consequence of their faith. They felt honored and respected in China, and had reason to believe that with the 1911 revolution God's Kingdom was nearer than ever.

✳✳✳

As China became more receptive to the lessons of the West, the American missionary force in China increased rapidly; it more than doubled between 1890 and 1905, and by 1919 had more than doubled again, to thirty-three hundred workers. This rapid growth in the American force reflected a resurgent interest in missions accompanying late-nineteenth-century American expansion, and a particular enthusiasm for the development of the "New China" rising from the ashes of the Boxer debacle. By the early twentieth century, American missionaries seeking a hearing from the Chinese had replaced their reliance on military force with a reliance on the broad appeals of their culture. American national leaders supported this shift in strategy, and with missionaries, sought cultural rather than political empire in China.[10]

American missionaries who first arrived in South China in the 1830s were inspired by the emotional certitudes of the Second Great Awakening and welcomed the use of Western force to gain their ends. Imprisoned in the foreign factories of Canton, which served as the Chinese land base for the tea, silks, and opium trade, they construed the Anglo-Chinese Opium War as a providential measure, a gift of God. At the first sign of trouble, for instance, Henrietta Shuck, an American Baptist, wrote of her hopes from Macao: "How these difficulties do rejoice my heart because I think the English may be enraged, and God, in His power, may break down the barriers which prevent the gospel of Christ from entering China." To Shuck, Christian faith was its own justification; even military force was righteous when it was on the side of God.[11]

The treaty accompanying the end of the Opium War granted missionaries and Chinese converts the right to practice Christianity in five coastal cities. But missionaries were largely unsuccessful in converting the heathen of the treaty ports. Their struggles to acquire land within the walls of such cities as Foochow excited antipathies, and popular association of them with the sailors and merchants of the opium trade did not enhance their stature. One Canton native described the Westerner as one who "loved to beat people and to rob and murder" and often "could be seen reeling drunk." Missionaries succeeded in winning their first convert in Foochow only after a decade of proselytizing in the crowded streets. By the end of 1860, four years later, the fifty missionaries from several denominations could still count only sixty-six converts.[12]

The Treaty of Tientsin (1858) extended rights to proselytize to the countryside, and there missionaries discovered more fruitful territory. Using Chinese workers, hired and trained as they went, missionaries poured more energy into opening outstations, shifting their focus from the major ports. By 1880, for example, the Congregational missionaries at Foochow had opened ninety-six new outstations in the countryside with Chinese help, and claimed three thousand new adherents. Outstations were the scenes of some of the greatest victories; perhaps not surprisingly, they were also the scenes of frequent antiforeign disturbances. The less sophisticated peoples of the interior were both more susceptible to the heterodox appeals of Christian ritual and more suspicious of its magical powers.[13]

When missionaries were threatened, they unambivalently called for protection. "Missionary incidents" of the 1860s, 1870s, and 1880s, in which outraged Chinese attacked foreign intruders, involved far more French Catholics and British than Americans, but property disputes and

popular outbreaks occasionally sent American missionaries to their legation demanding that their rights be defended or avenged. At the time of
the Boxer uprising in 1900, of course, voices from the field were particularly loud. They demanded full American participation in any allied
European military solution and vigorously protested the early withdrawal
of American troops. The retaliatory raids of American board missionaries
William Ament and Gardner Tewksbury received immediate coverage,
first by *The New York Sun* and then by Mark Twain, in his famous essay,
"To the Person Sitting in Darkness."[4]

Until the 1890s, however, the American State Department was reluctant to defend aggressively either missionary rights to hold property in the
interior, never officially deeded by the Chinese, or the provocative actions
of American evangelicals, who attacked Chinese folk religion and challenged gentry sovereignty. Forced to face Chinese protests over the American maltreatment of Chinese laborers in the United States, the State
Department did not have the temerity to press demands for protection
abroad that it could not honor at home.[15]

By the time of the Boxer uprising, though, the gulf between the forces of
church and state had narrowed. President Benjamin Harrison's 1893 order
for the construction of gunboats for use in Chinese waters foreshadowed a
newly aggressive China policy. From that point, his administration began
to follow up missionary claims with threats and personnel. With the
Spanish-American War and the occupation of the Philippines, Washington briefly considered whether its presence in China might be extended to
limited empire.[16]

But church and state found other common ground during the early
decades of the twentieth century. Wary political leaders and missionary
supporters of the social gospel converged in a campaign for American
influence rather than empire in China. The attendance at a 1900 Conference on Missions in New York suggested what would be a new compromise
coalition of American leaders supporting informal empire in China. In
addition to noted imperialists Admiral George Dewey and Alfred Mahan,
many opponents of empire also attended. Former President Benjamin
Harrison, the honorary president of the conference, had refused to endorse
McKinley that year because of his expansionist policies. And Grover
Cleveland, also in attendance, like most Democrats opposed territorial
aggrandizement. Supporters of American empire considered Christian
religion a necessary accompaniment to American expansionism, and in
some cases the very justification for it. (In fact, the patriotic and militarist

enthusiasms of the Spanish-American War were responsible for a needed outpouring of contributions to the mission cause.) But when the costs of imperialism became apparent, American leaders withdrew their support for political expansion and used mission organizations as a partial strategy to retain the exhilaration of empire without paying its bills or taking on its corrupting responsibilities.[17]

Theodore Roosevelt was one of those whose attitudes toward empire changed between the 1890s and the early twentieth century, leaving him with a new program for China. By the time he acceded to the presidency, Roosevelt had lost his earlier infatuation for formal empire. In an article in *The Outlook* in 1908, he argued instead that missionaries in China could contribute substantially to American interests there. All Americans, including those outside of "the so-called mission circles," should donate to the mission cause for moral and practical reasons, he wrote. "The work of the missionary tends to avert revolutionary disturbance in China, and to lead her into a position for peace and righteousness." Roosevelt's conclusion revealed that he had another practical goal in mind: challenging growing Japanese influence in China and defeating a united Asia under Japanese control. He concluded: "*Now* is the time for the West to implant its ideals in the Orient, in such fashion as to minimize the chance of a dreadful future clash between two radically different and hostile civilizations; if we wait until tomorrow, we may find that we have waited too long." The best defense against the "yellow peril" ("whatever that may be") he wrote, "is not the repression of life but the cultivation and direction of life."[18] Roosevelt's assertion of the Progressive ambition to achieve political and social ends through "cultivation" revealed that, along with many statesmen of his time, Roosevelt had replaced a youthful enthusiasm for the "repression" of political empire with a more mature and uplifting conception of cultural empire. His tribute to the missions was based on his appreciation of their usefulness to this new campaign.

William Howard Taft and Woodrow Wilson both shared Roosevelt's regard for the potential of the missionary presence in China. For Taft, the study of modern history led inevitably to the realization that "Christianity and the spread of Christianity, are the only basis for the hope of modern civilization." Wilson's support for mission work in China dated from well before he became president. A particularly earnest supporter of the YMCA and its work in China, Wilson credited it with "transforming the face of great kingdoms" and argued that probably "the YMCA has had a great deal to do with the political revolution there, because nothing is so revolutionary as the light." (Roosevelt only four years earlier had argued the counter-revolutionary influence of missions.) Nine months before being elected president of the United States, Wilson celebrated the ambition of the YMCA to order the world according to Christian principles:

> And so it is in foreign countries as well as in America. . . . We are not merely organizing our life; we are standardizing it; we are standardizing it by the only standards that are eternal, the only standards that have borne the test of long experience, the standards that underlie the very process of civilization and furnish the genius of human liberty. It is Christianity that has produced the political liberty of the world.[19]

In endorsing "our" impulse to "standardize" life in foreign countries as well as in America, Woodrow Wilson was allying national and mission interests in the cultural transformation of the world.

National leaders committed to a large international role for their country found natural allies in the mission movement. The social gospel provided the framework for the broadening of the missionary message. Devised in the 1880s and 1890s to meet the challenges of evangelism among the immigrants of American cities, the social gospel proclaimed the responsibility of the true Christian to address the needs of the whole man and woman for education, employment, good health, and adequate living conditions. Chinese interest in Western institutions encouraged the missionary practice of the social gospel, and increasingly missionaries supplemented their religious message with the practical lessons of a civilization.

In this they diverged from the earlier evangelical missionaries of the nineteenth century who had maintained that schools were secondary to preaching and had spurned the teaching of English, which they felt would distract their students from the worship of the Lord. An 1877 missionary conference still insisted that evangelical work came first, but admitted that it seemed to be most effectively done by Chinese helpers familiar with the dialect. The adage "Foreigners for teaching; natives for preaching" captured the principle which allowed for the expansion of educational work in China. At the fourth triennial missionary conference in 1902, the call went out "for persons especially qualified along educational lines." By 1907, the call for more teachers had become particularly urgent to meet new opportunities in post-Boxer China. But it was not until the republican revolution that the missionary forces threw their efforts unreservedly into secular work. The vice-president of Nanking University sounded the cry: "During this time of transition, when looking to the West for light and leading in all departments, the Chinese will be as plastic and as sensitive to influence as young men and young women when they first leave home to go away to college." The appeal for influence "in all departments" signaled the broadened mandate of missions in the twentieth century. By 1911, a full 50 percent of American missionaries in China were no longer engaged in direct evangelism. Most of them were teachers.[20]

As the social gospel extended the missionary mandate, it simultaneously deepened missionaries' sense of responsibility for their own civilization. As Walter Rauschenbucsh, both a leader of the social gospel and a militant nationalist, put it, "The social wrongs which we permit contradict our gospel abroad and debilitate our missionary enthusiasm at home." Missionaries in the field felt that the drinking and gambling of the ports compromised their message. So did the use of gratuitous military force. Increasingly, after the rancorous years surrounding the Boxer uprising, liberal Protestants in China resisted making demands for protection that might jeopardize their credibility with the Chinese. Americans had always felt they had a special moral relationship with China. After the Boxer uprising, as they extended their claims to influence and limited their claims to power, missionaries took this moral relationship more seriously than ever.[21]

American policy interests in the work of missionaries did not influence male or female missionaries to revise their program of education, conversion, and ministration to the sick. Mission work of its own accord had broadened from the mid-nineteenth century to include Western lessons more popular in China than strict gospel lessons. It is a meaningful coincidence, however, that these lessons were nearly identical to those favored by American policymakers eager to foster China as an American "junior partner" in the world of nations.

The closeness of American national and missionary interests in China unavoidably tainted the missionary enterprise. It also allowed Americans at home to remain blind to the moral implications of their ambitions to power there. Throughout the twentieth century, Americans regarded Christian missionaries as emblems of the purity of American motive. This was particularly apparent following the Communist victory in 1949. Of all missionaries, women, the majority in any case, seemed to represent the highest ideal of national selflessness. Women's traditional separation from politics had already guaranteed the disinterestedness of their commitment.

More than men, they served throughout the twentieth century to reassure Americans that their intentions in China were honorable.

Missionaries of the general boards early discovered the importance of women's work to their cause, but not until the arrival of single women after the Civil War did missionaries develop a sustained program for Chinese women. Gender taboos barred the female half of the population from the preaching of men, and all agreed that without reaching the women, who were the wives and mothers of converts, the entire work was in jeopardy. Christianity stood little chance of taking root in Asia without the aid of the Christian home. The earliest missionaries to Asia were accompanied by wives, who were designated assistant missionaries and were expected to see to this important task.

But missionary wives had other responsibilities that complicated their work. As Rufus Anderson, secretary of one mission board, put it, "Woman was made for man, and as a general thing man cannot long be placed where he can do without her assistance." For the male missionary, therefore, the boards agreed that marriage to a like-minded woman was "AN INDISPENS-ABLE DUTY." The woman might be expected "to exert much influence in the department of education," but "the center of her appropriate sphere is, indeed, within the domestic circle."[22]

When the responsibilities of missionary mothers to work and family conflicted (as they almost invariably did), board, husband, and wife all agreed that the family took priority. Particularly energetic women managed to make a beginning in evangelical and educational work, but their efforts were frequently thwarted by family demands. Missionary journals measured the accomplishments of missionary wives more in their travails than in the conversions they achieved. Married missionary women consequently were some of the early voices begging that single women be sent to the field.

Prior to the Civil War, the sending boards considered single service for women an impropriety, and single women who sought to serve met with scant encouragement. Despite this, a score of intrepid single women engineered their own service in the foreign field before 1860. Affiliating themselves with relatives or with married couples, such women as Eliza Agnew and Fidelia Fiske pioneered work in education and evangelism in Ceylon and Persia in the 1840s. These single women possessed an extraordinary ambition. Their careers were testimonies to extreme individual fortitude and ingenuity. By 1860, there were only eleven single women serving in foreign fields.[23]

Women's experience with organized work during the Civil War, most historians agree, brought them the confidence to found their own separate sending boards to do together what solitary women had struggled to do alone. As Helen Montgomery, a historian of the movement, put it:

> During the awful struggle the women both North and South received a baptism of power. They were driven to organize, forced to co-operate by their passion of pity and patriotism, and in the management of the great commission for raising and distributing aid to the soldiers they discovered powers of which they themselves and the nation had been quite unconscious. It is not accident that it was the decade following the close of the Civil War that saw the launching of scores of organizations, among them the Missionary Societies.

Women's missionary organizations, like other women's initiatives of the time, reflected the influence of the early generations of female college graduates, particularly those from evangelical colleges such as Oberlin, Carleton, and Mount Holyoke. Since the founding of Mount Holyoke in 1836, Mary Lyon's "protestant nunnery" had fostered ideals of Christian service for several generations of students and had guided them to consider mission work. But during the middle years of the nineteenth century most had gone as missionary wives. In the new postwar climate, women who had missionary ambitions eagerly followed the example of their founder and embarked upon "woman's work for woman" in the Lord's name. The Woman's Board of Missions (1869), affiliated with the Congregational church, was the first denominational board, to be followed the same year by the Methodist Woman's Foreign Missionary Society.[24]

Despite an increased need for women workers in the field, the general boards presented early obstacles to the formation and functioning of women's boards. The women of the women's boards, most of them matrons previously connected with mission auxiliaries, constantly struggled to assuage their fears. Most women's boards agreed to depend on a "second gift" for their work to insure that women's work would not deplete the coffers of the general boards. But despite this practice, which required that women supplement their normal donation with an extra gift, the general boards remained jealous of the women's fund-raising abilities. They preferred that the women continue to function as fund-raising auxiliaries, with the selection and support of women on the field remaining the responsibility of the general board.[25]

These tensions resulted in a wide variety of institutional relationships governing women's work. The Woman's Foreign Missionary Society of the Methodist Episcopal Church, founded in 1869, was one of the most independent boards. Its founders insisted that the WFMS function in a coordinate relation with the general board rather than as a traditional auxiliary, and that it retain complete control of its finances. Perhaps in retaliation for this independence, the general board prohibited the WFMS from collecting money in public meetings or recruiting through the Sunday schools.[26]

In the South, opposition to separate women's work was always greater than in the North. The Southern Methodist Woman's Board of Foreign Missions, like all southern boards smaller in scope and membership than the northern boards, ran into fierce opposition from general board officials when it proposed and raised the money for a separate missionary training school for women. The bitterness at the fund drive was so great, a board historian wrote, that "many of the women feared lest its phenomenal success would be the undoing of the work which was already being carried on in the mission fields"; general board officials brought up the question "as to the right to establish such a school under the constitution of the WBFM."[27]

By 1900, forty-one American women's boards of varying size had come into existence. A few of them increased their authority beyond that of prewar auxiliaries only to the extent of raising funds that were now specifically designated for the support of single women; even such boards, which allowed the general board final authority on selection and policy, retained a greater sense of responsibility for the work in the field than their predecessors. Many women's boards also published journals and newsletters to further home interest in the mission field. The largest women's boards published major periodicals on a monthly basis. The Congregationalist *Light and Life for Heathen Women*, the Methodist *Heathen Woman's Friend*, both founded in 1869, and the Presbyterian *Woman's Work for Woman* of 1871 all represented substantial business endeavors which both exploited and subsidized missionary work on the far side of the globe.[28]

The vitality of the women's missionary movement gradually came to pose a threat to the general boards that was not merely financial. The women in the field vastly outnumbered the men. By 1919, both northern and southern American Methodist boards had more than twice as many women as men in the China field, and the Congregational ABCFM could boast of nearly as many single women as married and single men together. The flocking of women into the field in the 1880s and 1890s led some general board officials to feel the need to remind women of their place. The secretary of the American Baptist Missionary Union, for instance, said at an 1888 conference:

> Woman's work in the foreign field must be careful to recognize the headship of man in ordering the affairs of the kingdom of God. We must not allow the major vote of the better sex, nor the ability and efficiency of so many of our female helpers, nor even the exceptional faculty for leadership and organization which some of them have displayed in their work, to discredit the natural and predestined headship of man in Missions, as well as in the Church of God: and "the head of woman is the man."[29]

Although many general boards were successful in limiting the scope of women's missionary activity to ministration to women, the numerical imbalance threatened to define the nature and reputation of the mission force. By 1888, the opposition to women's work had changed from concern about its impropriety to a beleaguered effort by men of the general boards to retain minority control over a majority of female workers.

As in other professions, the feminization of the mission force accompanied a decline in male interest in mission work during its dark days in the 1880s. The efforts of the general boards to restore the waning prestige of mission work in the early twentieth century not surprisingly focused on an effort to restore its reputation as a manly calling. The Laymen's Missionary Movement, an organization of businessmen founded in 1907, consciously projected an image of virility and pragmatism to counter the dominant image of the effete idealism of the mission field. Biographies of male missionaries in the twentieth century described them as "real boys" in their youth and "he-men" in their adult years.[30] Men retained control of the general missionary organizations and women often held only limited citizens' rights within them; nonetheless, the work of the women's boards guaranteed that the majority of those representing American Protestantism in the mission field would be representatives of a female culture.

In the United States, women's mission organizations were delicately engaged in defining their relationship to the men's boards—raising money from the same congregations and submitting plans, and sometimes candidates, to the general boards for approval. No longer auxiliaries, they were still constantly engaged in discovering their areas of overlap and independence from the general boards with whom they shared supporters, congregations, and general mission.

China was divided more distinctly along gender lines, and "woman's work" was clearly differentiated from man's. The prohibitions which barred male missionaries from converting Chinese women reserved them for Western women. "The peculiar barriers of the East," one mission historian wrote, made it easier to "point to what is distinctively the fruit of woman's work" there than it was at home.[31] Women who had performed auxiliary work in American parishes, raising money and doing promotional work for projects carried out by men, found that the gender stratification of Chinese society worked to their benefit; it allowed them to claim sole credit for the initiation and completion of their own work.

Women's formal missionary work fell into three categories, which paralleled men's work: medical work, the management of an extensive school system, and evangelical country work. Medical work was by far the smallest undertaking of the three, but the need for female doctors to attend to Chinese women illustrates the way in which Chinese sex segregation proved an opportunity for Western women. About 3 percent of American women missionaries were trained as medical doctors, most of them specifically for the mission field.[32] Particularly relative to their greater proportion in China, American women were still badly underrepresented in the medical profession. Even so, mission needs inspired the professional education of numbers of women who would probably have remained schoolteachers at home.

The standards for medical work varied according to the training and demands of its China practitioners. Undoubtedly care was often rudimentary. When Ruth Hemenway arrived to take up medical work in the Fukien countryside in 1924, for instance, she was appalled at the facilities which Dr. Mary Carleton had been using for many years. She found no laboratory, nor operating room, no rubber gloves to use with infected patients, nor any screens for the windows. A 1920 survey by a British missionary doctor suggests that Mary Carleton's hospital was far from atypical; his research indicated that 65 percent of missionary hospitals in China lacked an isolation block, and half of them seldom or never bathed their patients.[33] Despite such primitive conditions, missionary medical care seems to have been an improvement over Chinese practices and constituted an important recruiting device for the church.

In ever-increasing numbers, missionary women also devoted their energies to the development of an educational system for girls. Village primary schools, taught by Chinese converts, customarily sent students to a girls' boarding school located at the mission station. Missionary women might ride circuit inspecting day schools, or administer and teach in the station boarding or "middle" school. They also ran Bible training schools to teach the rudiments of Christian belief to the wives of Chinese pastors and the women, frequently widows, whom the church employed as assistants or "Bible women." The middle schools sent students on to three colleges for women founded in the first decades of the twentieth century, all of them under American direction. By 1916, women's boards were able to number some fifty thousand Chinese girls under their tuition.[34]

Aside from native and frequently male instructors of Chinese literature, the small staffs of middle schools tended to be foreign into the second decade of the century. Not until the nationalist anti-Christian campaigns of the late 1920s did Chinese administrators take over mission schools. As a result, the curricula and the teaching methods were imported from abroad. In the early twentieth century, mission middle schools instituted physical training and domestic science, according to current fashion in American education, as well as more traditional American subjects of study. Missionary women attempted to reduplicate familiar patterns in their middle schools as they did in their homes, within mission compound walls.

The village day schools of the extended mission dominion owed more to Chinese traditions. Luella Miner described a girls' school she visited in North China in 1888: "I should hear, as soon as I entered the court," she wrote,

> a perfect Babel of sounds. At first glimpse from within, before they saw me, I should see all of the girls sitting Turk style on their kang or raised platform which occupies half of the school room. They are sitting at all angles, some with their backs toward me. Each girl is reading or reciting from memory, independently of the others the louder the better. . . . As soon as they catch sight of the visitor, there is a general scramble. Each girl gets off the kang with as much agility as possible, clasps her hands together, and shakes them which is the Chinese mode of salutation. Each girl says, 'My gooniang, hao' (How do you do Miss Miner). . . . Our little girls begin with the 'Three Character Classic' which is made up of clauses of three words each, after the style of an old Chinese classic, and teaches Bible truths.

Girls' school, 1907: Students file into the Ing-hok Girls' School, Fukien.

Women's college: Luella Miner sits
at the desk as a student recites
at North China Union Women's
College, founded in 1905.

Bible women, 1901: Emily Hartwell stands at the Foochow mission
gate with women trained as assistants
or "Bible women."

When they can recite this book through from beginning to end they take up the catechism, then probably some part of the Bible. Arithmetic, Geography, etc. come at a more advanced stage and are a foreign invention.[35]

Missionaries inspecting day schools several decades later frequently tried to change the emphasis on *pei hsu*, or reciting from memory; their criticisms did not acknowledge the resemblance in substance, if not in style, to the memorization that took place in nineteenth-century American schoolrooms.

Although women's educational and medical work flourished in China, missionaries and missionary sponsors still agreed that the heart of the work was evangelism. Bringing the Word to Chinese women usually meant gaining access to their homes. Evangelists customarily traveled to the home of a local Christian, and within her courtyard began to speak to the curious women from the neighborhood. The multiplicity of village dialects made language a frequent obstacle; Bible women, who were local Christians trained by the church, were frequent intermediaries. Luella Miner had already gained a reputation in mission circles for her language facility when she went on her first village trip. Her problems were common to many others: "I have been in China more than a year and a half," she wrote,

and labored under the delusion hitherto that I both understood and could speak a little of the vernacular. But the jargon which these country women, speaking a slightly different dialect, poured into my ears fairly started the cold sweat, and it was equally appalling to see the vacant stare with which my supposedly choice Pekinese was received by many of the women. So I soon meekly told Ssu Mei (the Bible woman) that I thought it would be better for her to talk, and I crawled to the back of the kang and tried to cover up my big feet with my long Manchu garment that they might not attract the attention of the women from the sermon. I had, as I thought, eschewed all foreign articles of attire, going bare-headed and looking as much like a Chinese woman as big nose, big feet, and light hair would permit, but still my long robe of fine cotton cloth was quite different from their homespun short garments and my umbrella now and then proved more interesting than the difference between the true God and the temple idols.[36]

Village evangelism: Missionary women brought the Word to local villages by boat in Fukien. Here Emily Hartwell (*right*) and a friend (*left*) are on the mission's "gospel boat."

Missionary women found the novelty of their appearance to be an initial advantage in attracting attention but perpetually lamented that they could not direct attention away from their person to their message.

Female missionaries focused their own attention on Chinese girls and women, and during their sojourn in China saw both cultural attitudes and official policy toward women undergo a radical transformation. When they arrived in the mid-nineteenth century, respectable Chinese women were not seen outside their family courtyards. After fifty years of mission exertion, footbinding had been abolished, the government had established schools for girls, and Chinese reformers were equating China's national strength with the strength of its women. Missionaries liked to take credit for this progress.

But along with other changes missionaries observed in Chinese society at the turn of the century, the feeling of influence they reported was a symptom of deep changes taking place within Chinese society rather than a cause of those changes. For years, missionaries had advanced a consistent program for Chinese women with little to show for it. Only when Chinese nationalist reformers made the cause of female education their own did Chinese attitudes begin to change. The reformers sought the advice of Western female educators, and welcomed their aid, in their own efforts to bring China to self-sufficiency.

In the early years of female missionary work in China, antiforeignism and Chinese gender mores reinforced each other to make women's work with women and female education nearly impossible. Foreign women were at first excluded completely from the foreign factories of Canton. Missionary J. Lewis Shuck wrote in 1836 that his wife had not been allowed to accompany him from Macao to Canton, adding, "The Chinese say that foreign sailors, foreign firearms, and foreign females are the great exciters of all disturbances and therefore are forbidden to enter their confines." It is not surprising that when Chinese officials were seeking new measures to try to avert missionary incidents, which culminated in the 1870 murder of French nuns, they proposed that "foreign women should not be permitted to propagate the doctrine in China."[37]

The joint attendance of Chinese women and men at church, which followed the conversion of women, seemed to be at the root of Chinese resistance to female evangelists. Antimissionary polemicists exploited the fear of sexual co-mingling in their salacious tales of random fornication during Christian worship services. The 1870 proposal to control foreign incidents addressed this concern when it proposed that not only should foreign women be prohibited from preaching the doctrine, but "Chinese women should not be permitted to enter churches and chapels."[38] Powerful taboos on the social mingling of men and women insured that the number of female converts would never equal the number of male converts.

In the early days, therefore, missionaries customarily offered financial inducements to procure girl pupils for their schools. When Henrietta Shuck opened an elementary school for boys and girls in Macao, she required that each boy who enrolled be accompanied by one girl. Missionary historians report twelve Protestant mission schools for girls in 1860, and thirty-eight in 1877. Schools for girls represented a radical departure in Chinese female education, which previously had been carried on rarely, and only by indulgent and wealthy fathers within courtyards.[39]

Considering constraints on women's lives, missionaries reached a surprising proportion of women. Women had traditionally been followers of heterodox, non-Confucian Taoist and Buddhist sects, and they undoubtedly discovered similarities between such mystical religions and the "Christ doctrine," with its celebration of resurrection and triumph over death. The Protestant missions reported that roughly a third of their communicants were female from as early as 1890. Even this limited popularity of Christianity among Chinese women is highly significant, given the restrictions limiting women's movements outside of family courtyards.[40]

Besides education, missionaries advanced another social goal for women: the abolition of footbinding. Missionary publications in the United States graphically depicted the horrors of the practice, and missionaries frequently lamented its barbarity. Nonetheless, they were reluctant to add the requirement that feet be unbound to the already considerable barriers to a sympathetic hearing in Asia. Prior to the 1890s, and the growth of an indigenous anti-footbinding movement among Chinese reformers, most missionaries tolerated what they could not change. A description of a Swatow Bible Training School noted that between 1873 and 1904 its middle-aged pupils all had bound feet. Thereafter, the majority of its pupils had unbound their feet, encouraged by the exhortation of their missionary mentors, but also by a larger reform movement and an imperial decree.[41]

The nationalist reform movement following China's defeat by the Japanese in 1895 provided the context for the indigenous movement to

Anti-footbinding propaganda, 1905: After the turn of the century, missionaries intensified their campaign against footbinding, accompanying indigenous movements. This photograph in a missionary album was captioned "Chinese women never allowed the unshod bound feet to be seen. This is why Mrs. Tse looks so unhappy."

improve the status of Chinese women. Prior to that, the leading scholar of Chinese women's history concluded, only missionaries were interested in either education for women or an end to footbinding. In the late nineties, such male reform intellectuals as K'ang Yu-wei and Liang Ch'i-ch'ao argued for improvements in women's status as part of their program for national self-strengthening. At the worst, women's ignorance was undermining China from within; at the best, women represented a vast untapped resource which China could not afford to waste. Furthermore, China's maltreatment of women was exposing China to the ridicule and contempt of other nations.[42]

Chinese movements to abolish footbinding and to establish schools for girls in the 1890s predictably originated in the areas of China's treaty ports, among Chinese who had already been exposed to Western ideas. Shanghai's first anti-footbinding society was founded in 1894, by K'ang Yu-wei's brother K'ang Kuang-jen. K'ang Kuang-jen was also instrumental in founding an early Chinese school for girls in 1897, which was run by his wife Li Ruhn. Enrollments in mission schools for girls rose to nearly seven thousand students in 1896, and Chinese pioneers in female education looked to missionary women for aid and advice. Manchu viceroy Ch'ang Chih-tung was said to have consulted Chinese Christians Mary Stone and Ida Kahn and missionary Gertrude Howe about his plans to open a school for girls in Shanghai. And the papers of Luella Miner amply document the particular interest of female reformers in Peking a decade later in the work of the American Board. The interest of Chinese reformers in missionaries was limited, though. Missionaries privately railed with frustration at their inability to capitalize for Christ on reformers' interest in female education.[43]

The repression of 1898, which left K'ang Kuang-jen dead and K'ang Yu-wei and Liang Ch'i-ch'ao in exile, temporarily marked the end of Chinese efforts to modernize and westernize China. But the Boxer aftermath saw the court gradually move to incorporate the programs of reformers it had previously executed and banished, including programs to improve the status of women. The court first moved on the issue of footbinding. The women of the Manchu ruling caste had never bound their feet, nor in fact did Manchu women observe the same rigid seclusion that characterized women of the Chinese Han tradition. The Empress Dowager issued an anti-footbinding edict in 1902, "after sustained pressure from foreign women of various nationalities," according to one historian.[44]

The movement to educate women spread more gradually from reform circles to the Imperial Palace. Some female Manchu nobles joined upper-class reformers from Shanghai, Hangchow, and Canton to form private Chinese schools for girls, but the court itself was slow to authorize government schools for girls. The Education Commission declared in 1903 that it was too early to attempt schools for girls, and a 1904 memorial from the throne was even more definitive when it announced that "it is not appropriate to establish female education; the etiquette and customs of China and the West are not the same." Private pioneers in female education met frequent setbacks around the empire. A Hangchow widow called national attention to the plight of female education when she committed suicide in 1906 over her inability to raise money for the second year of her school. Memorial services were said to have been held for her all over China.[45]

Finally, that same year, a proclamation mandated the government establishment of schools for girls. Early schools for girls in China, like schools in nineteenth-century America, did not aim to challenge traditional ideas about female responsibilities, instead instructing students in the three Confucian obediences to father, husband, and son. But as in the United States, the consequences of collective education for women transcended the original intent. By 1908, the number of girls in government schools exceeded the number in missionary schools.[46]

Even after these years, though, government education continued to lag far behind mission education in its relative allocations for girls. In certain areas, such as the countryside, there were no schools of any kind for girls, leaving a 1922 publication to conclude that in that area "the Christian Church has a free field." The same report noted that mission schools consistently educated more girls in proportion to boys than did government schools: on the elementary level, eight times as many; on the secondary level, nine times as many; and ten times as many on the post-secondary level. Missionaries opened a college for women thirteen years before the major government university admitted its first female student.[47]

The preeminence of missionary institutions in the early education of Chinese women is claimed by friends of the mission enterprise and acknowledged by its critics. Luella Miner contended that missionaries were "largely responsible" for the awakening and the new ambition of Chinese women, and though few would go that far, even later nationalist critics of the missionary enterprise credited the positive contributions of female missionaries in introducing public school education for women. Nevertheless, the persistent antipathy to Christianity of late-nineteenth-century reformers limited and channeled missionary influence. Elite Chinese reformers responsible for the Chinese women's movement sought out missionaries, as one of them put it, "not because we are believers, but because foreign ladies have been leaders in establishing schools for girls." When all was said and done, it was frequently missionaries' own example, rather than their agenda, which constituted their most significant contribution. The key to the impact of missionary women on Chinese women's history lies less in their religious program than in the secular message transmitted by their lives.[48] The significance of these lives, defined by the intermingling of feminine subordination, Christian duty, and colonial authority, constitutes the focus of this study.

❧ 2 ❧

COMMITMENT

On 29 March 1900, Emma and Lizzie Martin knelt with their family in an Otterbein, Indiana, farmhouse as their mother prayed "that God will bless and keep us a united family and bring us all together again." When they were done praying, their father and brothers packed their luggage into the family buggy and drove them to the train station. They were bound for Peking, China. "After the train pulled out, Lizzie and I were just about to yield to an irresistible inclination to 'bust out' [crying]," Emma wrote in her diary, "when in walked cousin George Taylor, smiling and as neat as you please. He asked where we were going and thought we were very foolish and would never get back alive." Emma and Elizabeth Martin, aged thirty and twenty-seven, had been away from home before. They were both graduates of DePauw University and of the Chicago Training School, a missionary preparatory school. Emma had spent four years at the Chicago Woman's Medical College and a year of internship in a hospital for women and children as well. But the sisters felt like "greenhorns" on the train ride across the country. When the conductor told them they were in the wrong car and would have to move, Emma wrote, "I soon felt that it was a good thing for we had made such a scene when we got on. . . . We found after we had traveled a day that we had had about as much advice we could not use as we had baggage that was useless. We could get a good meal for 40 cents; and we were ashamed to be seen eating the Grape Nuts and condensed milk we had brought along with us for we had no way of serving it." Six days later, "after the shadows began to fall," Emma wrote, "we quietly opened the car window and bidding our can of peach butter goodbye I pitched it out the window and after it the dry buns and butter."[1] Overcome with feelings of ignorance and self-consciousness on the trains that daily sped through their native Indiana farmland, Emma and Lizzie set out trustingly for the perils and possibilities that would face them on the other side of the globe.

Even as the Martin sisters pitched the symbols of their American provincialism out the train window, secret society warriors in northern China were threatening the foreign population. They would arrive just in time for the Boxer siege. They only barely made it back to America alive, nearly proving their cousin right in his prediction. But in March they knew nothing of the Boxers; nor did they know much of China. Their calling came from other forces in their religious background and adult experience. Domestic American currents propelled the Martin sisters in their avowed crusade to save the world in their own generation.

Although the American missionary movement was born in New England, by the twentieth century it owed the majority of its volunteers to the rural Midwest. Headquartered in Boston, the American Board of Commissioners for Foreign Missions (the ABCFM) appealed to the once-established Congregational church in New England, but only 18 percent of its female missionaries in China in the first two decades of the century were born in New England. Forty percent came from the Midwest, another 11 percent from the Atlantic states, and a sprinkling from other parts of the country and the mission field. The Methodist women's board for this same period numbered only 8 percent from New England, half coming from the Midwest. This generation of midwestern missionaries were the children of westward migrants, not migrants themselves, and they identified strongly with their native heartland.[2]

Missionary recruits tended to be from towns or rural areas rather than from major cities. Of the twenty female American Board volunteers from Ohio in China, for instance, two were born in Cleveland, one in Cincinnati, and the rest in towns like Rootstown, Lorain, Degraff, and Shelby. The American Board volunteers from Massachusetts had been born in Plymouth, Brookline, Sturbridge, and Salem, but not Boston, Lowell, or Worcester. The population of Massachusetts was 69 percent urban in 1890, according to that year's census, but only 40 percent of the missionary force were born in towns of over eight thousand. Missionary backgrounds contrasted with the origins of another group of women active in service work at the turn of the century. Settlement workers, like missionary women, tended to be Protestant, native-born, and college-educated. But unlike missionaries, they were likely to have come from the city. The difference in community origins of these two groups might help to explain the important differences in the nature of their callings.[3]

The occupations of the fathers of missionary volunteers reflected their backgrounds. Over a quarter of the fathers of female missionaries of the American Board were farmers; aside from the large combined category of home missionaries and clergymen, this was the single largest occupational category. In explaining their missionary motivation, women frequently mentioned the sense of freedom they had experienced as girls growing up on farms. Lida Ashmore and Jennie Campbell both described themselves as tomboys, Campbell noting that she liked to help in the fields. Emily Hartwell was born of missionary parents in China but raised by an uncle in Minnesota. She pointed to the latter experience to explain "the courage and determination" of her life work: "How much it meant to her to grow up at the west in a thriving town where everything was new and must be started a first time. It was in surroundings where new things were the every day occurrence, where everyone considered all things possible, and courage and determination reigned." Mature women did not enjoy equality in the American West, as several recent studies have demonstrated, but until puberty, farm girls ran freer than city girls. Perhaps their readiness for the adventures of the missionary field did incorporate some of the "pioneer spirit" they liked to invoke.[4]

Missionary workers differed from settlement workers in class as well as community origin. Settlement workers had to be able to support themselves in city work without earning a salary and were thus moderately well-to-do; missionary women came from humble backgrounds and expected to go out to work before marriage. Women who left their parents on farms to go to China frequently sent money back from their modest salaries and worried that it was too little. Ultimately, they looked to their families to accept the loss of their earning power as a sacrifice in God's name. Emma Martin dedicated her diary "to my Dear Brothers and Sister, who are helping to bear the home burdens, thus making it possible for two of us to Evangelize the World in this generation."[5]

Though from families without many cash resources, missionary women were seldom of working-class origins. Among nearly one hundred fathers of American Board volunteers, only one was a wage laborer. Small businessmen and self-employed tradesmen made up 14 percent of the paternal pool. The parental families of missionary volunteers were of a consistent type, "poor, but in good standing and ambitious, Mainly Christian," as

Blanche Search described her family. With this description Search distinguished her proud, native-born family from the immigrant and laboring
families of the American cities.[6]

Missionaries revealed their homogeneous class origins in their reactions
to those few among them from the monied and working classes. Jessie
Ankeny, daughter of an Iowa farmer, wrote home her curiosity about a
self-supporting missionary of means: "She is a women of 35 I should think
and is independent of any Missionary board—She was one of those rich
women at home who have fine houses and wonderful dogs. She had no
special aim in life until she met one of the FooChow missionaries at
home—She is now out here supporting 400 women." Later that year she
testified to her continuing amusement: "Say, Jean Adams had the most
peculiar suit—on the lapelles were things which looked like gunney
sacks—I went out driving with her in a swell rig all over the city and came
back to the hotel—Jean gave the driver two Shillings etc etc, Oh but she *is*
funny." Those of genuinely impoverished background excited equal interest. "Just think, Family, until she was seventeen she was working as a
weaver in a mill and learned to spell from the newspaper!", Frederica Mead
wrote of Florence Warner. Rural middle-class women who would later
volunteer learned to spell in country schools, which they attended until
they were seventeen or eighteen years old. At that time they too went out
to work, but frequently as teachers in the schools they had recently
attended.[7]

Missionary candidates were likely to have had a long association with
the institutional church as well as country schools. They frequently cited
the experiences of both attending and teaching Sunday school, and also
noted participation in Christian Endeavor, an evangelical youth movement that trained young people in the activities of Christian life. Religious
commitment provided turn-of-the-century rural women with a focal point
for social activity of all kinds—from church suppers to charitable aid.
Missionary work represented a logical continuation of an early reliance on
church organizations as a locus of group experience.

Evangelical religion was far more than an institution, however; it was
also a burning emotional responsibility. Missionary candidates frequently
dated their missionary ambition from a dramatic conversion experience
that had convinced them of God's sovereignty and their own debt of
servitude. A conversion experience was nearly obligatory, and in the
retelling often took on a formulaic tone. Clara Collier's conversion followed her brother's attendance at a revival meeting; his recounting of the

message of sin and salvation brought her to her knees beside her four-poster bed. "When I got up," she wrote, "'It seems as though the world is all turned over.' And it was for me." Conversion experiences most frequently took place during adolescence, but they might occur earlier. Phoebe Wells, orphaned in early childhood, became a Christian at the age of seven, she wrote.[8] For those affected by a transcendent religious experience at whatever age, later missionary work might seem a way of prolonging a moment of remembered glory.

Not all of those embroiled in an evangelical culture experienced conversion by the expected hour of adolescence. For women and men of religious training, this failure could generate a prolonged state of religious anxiety. According to Pearl Buck, Caroline Sydenstricker's missionary motivation arose from such a sense of guilt and failure. Unconvinced of God's glory, she watched her own mother's death in horror; on the spot she made a missionary pledge. She became a missionary, not because she had received a sign from God, but because she had *not* and felt herself a hopeless sinner because of it.[9] Missionary service could not offer escape from the arbitrary doctrine of salvation by grace, but it did provide some solace to penitents, who could thereby serve the Lord even if they could not know Him.

The missionary cause offered the satisfactions of a collective crusade and a chance for personal testimony to the Lord, but it also offered human gratification. The missionary was a heroic figure within the home church and enjoyed the fruits of that status on furlough visits to the United States. Pulpits customarily closed to women sometimes opened for visitors from the field, and missionary periodicals found that female heroes were sometimes even more affecting than male. The popular press in particular explored the appeal of the exotic adventures of missionary women. The dramatic story of Ann Judson, who braved the cruelty of Turkish jailers to save her husband from certain death, was included in at least six nineteenth-century collections of American heroines. Girls censured for reading romantic fiction, which was considered dangerously provocative, could feel elevated by their reading of similarly sensational true stores about missionaries.[10]

Given the limited number of adventurous options presented to late-nineteenth-century girls in their younger years, it is no wonder that some of them seized on a missionary vocation as a route to glory. Missionary work struck a chord so early that some spoke of their missionary service as a nearly preordained destiny. Carrie Jewell did not receive an explicit call until just before her enlistment at the age of twenty-six, she wrote, but at that time she could not remember "when I did not want and expect to be a missionary." Anna Gloss ascribed her missionary destiny to Higher Powers, citing her "constant feeling that such was God's plan for my life." Ruth Stahl pledged her life to missionary work at the age of nine. Such childhood commitments should not be freighted with too much meaning. One volunteer captured the exotic associations of missionary work for late-nineteenth-century children when she recalled her three childhood ambitions: "One was to be in a circus, one was to be a missionary and the third was to be a Santa Claus." More sober Carolyn Sewell, who was ten in 1899, remembered that at that time she had wanted to be either a missionary or a natural scientist.[11] Considering the exigencies of their professional alternatives, it is perhaps no wonder that both women ended up on the missionary rolls.

❧❧❧❧❧

Many women who chose to do missionary work had strong family precedent for their choice. Over 40 percent of the American Board's female volunteers had fathers and mothers who did church work. (A full quarter were from home or foreign missionary parentage and another 18 percent from ministers' families). Both missionary service and the responsibilities of a pastorate involved wives as well as husbands in community life; in choosing to do missionary work, women were to some degree emulating both parents. But the sense of vocation which inspired women to solitary missionary service frequently resulted from identification with fathers. Missionary and ministers' wives, and farm mothers too, provided religious and emotional support for their daughters more often than models they were conscious of following.

A considerable number of missionary candidates were eldest daughters, many of them from families of girls only. Over 30 percent of the American Board women for whom sibling order is known, for instance, were eldest daughters, half of them being from families of girls only. (Fifty-four percent were middle children, and 15 percent, youngest children.)[12] Given the large sizes of the rural families which tended to produce missionary offspring, these statistics are particularly significant.

Especially when there were no male children, eldest daughters often received the paternal attention that was the normal prerogative of sons. Susan Skinner, the eldest of four children in the family of a Methodist home missionary, attributed her decision to enter medical work and to volunteer for the China field to her father, "my teacher and comrade." Though she married during her medical training, she lived out the plans she had made under her father's influence. Luella Miner was also the eldest daughter of home missionaries and particularly close to her father. After she completed the Kansas public schools, she studied at home with him. "She and Father were both much interested in both botany and geology and I can still see them with their heads together studying some new specimen," her younger sister wrote. The paternal influence of missionaries and ministers clearly led to daughters' religious vocation. But evidence indicates that a strong relationship with a father of any calling might encourage in a daughter the kind of ambition and assertiveness that could lead to service overseas. Welthy Honsinger, for instance, identified with her blacksmith father, whom she apparently resembled, and went on to lead an extraordinary life of international service in a realm quite different from his. [13]

Mothers active in the organized religious work of the nineteenth-century benevolent empire might also inspire their daughters' service. A referee for a candidate in 1867, for example, recalled the influence of her mother's work during the Civil War. The mother was "one of the first to go and one of the last to return," the referee wrote. "Always at the front. Alike at home presiding over the soup kettle, the hospital, or the distribution of religious reading. . . . The daughter is like minded, almost prematurely so. She does not seem to have had a proper girlhood." On candidate papers thirty-five years later, Bertha Reed noted that as a child she had been involved in her mother's temperance and missionary work "in children's ways" and acknowledged the example of her mother, "a woman of aspiration, one who always, no matter what the discouragements and difficulties held to the best and highest in life, and refused to be quenched by everyday cares."[14]

Everyday cares were frequently women's lot, though, and many who could not take their mother as vocational models did receive their most articulate and watchful encouragement from them. Not only young girls but mature matrons and ministers' wives thrilled to the stories of female heroism in distant corners of the world; and women whose own lives were already set could plan adventures no longer open to them for their daughters. Marjorie Rankin Steurt ascribed her vocation completely to her mother: "Mother always wanted me to be a missionary. She had wanted to be a missionary, so I was to take her place. She completely dominated my life. It never entered my head to disagree." Perhaps even more effective than maternal directives were the unexpressed wishes that women only later made public. When Edna Terry died in China, only then did her mother confide that her daughter's missionary vocation had been the fulfillment of her lifetime dream; on the day of Grace Rowley's enlistment, her mother reportedly wrote, "the happiest day of my life." Wishes from death's door may have been the most coercive of all. Alice Powell's mother, dying in her daughter's early childhood, expressed the desire that her daughter be a missionary—a wish nearly tantamount to an invisible hand.[15]

Mothers who did not harbor a specific missionary ambition for their daughters frequently were sources of a more diffuse climate of inspirational piety and tactical support. Midwestern women were more likely than men to have provided the religious environment in which many missionary women grew up. Mary Ledyard explained the influence on her of "a sainted Mother." From her, she wrote, "I learned all that I know of a religion that *lives* a religion of mind and heart and deed." Sarah DeHaan's mother "created the missionary interest" in her by reading from the Congregational periodical *Light and Life*, and Mabel Daniels noted the influence of "the high regard Mother showed for all missionaries." The Bement sisters received more than encouragement from their mother, who worked to supplement a small inheritance to send them to college, when it was thought "to say the least, foolish, for us to be spending money in attaining any farther education."[16] The example of fathers might have predisposed daughters to consider a vocation, but the encouragement of mothers facilitated that decision and suggested the form which that vocation might take. Missionary work offered young women the opportunity to transfer any burden of paternal identification to a field of endeavor honored by women. In choosing missionary service work instead of the ministerial vocation theoretically open to Congregational women, female candidates were demonstrating the strength of their bonds to mothers as well as fathers.

Missionary women seem to have sensed the possibilities their lives might offer to redeem their mothers' investments in their children. Ethel Wallace, whose aunt preceded her in mission service, recalled the sense of futility her mother had felt, particularly in contrast with the accomplishments of her sister. She "thought her sister Lydia had done great things in God's work, but that her own life spent in 'the daily round, the common task,' had not counted for much." Wallace recalled this fact as she was writing to her brothers of how their mother "had given her life for us."

Wallace, meanwhile, had followed her aunt's example to make good on her mother's sacrifice.

Jeanie Graham, too, hoped that her life might offer an opportunity for her mother, but her correspondence reveals the complexity of her inspiration. In her junior year of college she wrote ingenuously of her possibilities:

> Here's what you're going to be, Mother. All that you couldn't do because you didn't have a college education, or a chance, or years enough to accomplish goes on in me. Weren't there things you dreamed of doing when you were my age that can't be done because girls didn't count enough when you were my age? Haven't you wished that you might come nearer the fulfillment of your dreams? Then here is your chance in me. I've inherited some of the good in you, I've listened to your teachings thru the years, soon I'll have had a whole college course, an earlier start, a larger opportunity. What can't be accomplished? And how much honor will accrue to you. I mustn't be foolish any longer. It will make Dad wish that some of us were boys. [17]

In the last line Graham suggested that although she planned to make her life a gift to her mother, it would be a gift based on emulation of her father, a gift based on his approval of her sense of vocation. Jeanie Graham's offer at the age of twenty-one hinted at her mother's disappointment in her own life. Four years later, in her candidate papers, Graham sketched another portrait. There she noted that her mother had always done a great deal of church work, despite her eight daughters, and had preached when her father was away. She concluded: "Our mother is a wonder woman." For Graham, and probably for other women who were the eldest in families of daughters, missionary work harmoniously blended several imperatives—a responsibility to her father to be as accomplished and responsible as a son, an equally pressing obligation to her mother to uphold and celebrate the lessons of womanly service learned as a child, and perhaps also a competitive desire to outdo her mother in the religious work which mother and daughter shared.

In addition to satisfying diverse family expectations, missionary work could also blend the somewhat conflicting vocational and professional needs female volunteers brought to it. Missionary service demanded a life commitment and paid for that commitment with a guarantee of modest economic security, opportunity for achievement abroad, and renown at home. It offered a project that all might agree was grand, with a chance for small personal victories along the way. Mission service offered women many of the gratifications of purpose, status, and permanence associated with the developing professions, without requiring the bold assault on female conventions demanded of the new "professional" woman.

The vast majority of missionary women led lives closely monitored by economic and family need prior to their enlistments. Few women pursued an uninterrupted course of study; most attended normal school, business college, or liberal arts college intermittently, ceasing their studies when ailing relations or depleted coffers required their attention. Between years of schooling they worked at a variety of occupations. Some worked as stenographers or typists. Nearly a fifth of the Methodist women had had some such "business" experience. By far the largest group, however, had spent some years teaching, frequently in country schools. Over 70 percent of the American and Methodist board women fell into this category.[18] Their decisions to quit teaching for foreign service reflected the limitations of that vocation.

During the mid-nineteenth century, teaching had become a common occupation for young women looking to support themselves temporarily, presumably prior to marriage. Salaries were low, conditions erratic, and there were few possibilities for advancement. Teaching under these conditions was a "way station," as one historian has termed it. By the turn of the century, it is true, the forces were already at work that would result in the systematization and professionalization of the occupation of teaching. (The teaching profession would follow the medical and legal professions in this direction by a decade.) This erratic movement had not caught up with the majority of the women teaching, however, and it was from this population that missionary candidates emerged. Women who would later volunteer might have taught to earn money for a sister's education, as in the case of Carrie Bartlett, or to pay debts, as in the case of Agnes Edwards, but they did not consider teaching a sacred calling or a fulfilling vocation. Such women might well seize upon mission work, as did Ellen Lyon, as an "answer to prayer for guidance for the future of the eight years of teaching"; teaching in itself contained few promises for the future at all.[19]

Women expressed their motivation for the China field as a desire to increase their influence for good rather than as a desire for higher status or greater security. Mabel Craig's first reason for her application was "a desire to put myself in the way of making the most of my life"; Mathilde Goertz wanted "to serve Jesus Christ in the place where the need is greatest"; Evelyn Worthley believed China service "will be putting my life where it will count for most." The premillennialism of the turn-of-the-century mission movement helps to explain the conviction of American evangelicals that their lives would count for more in China. Premillennialists believed that Christ could not come for the second time until all of the world's peoples had heard his message.[20]

The consistently expressed desire to make their lives worth more than at home, however, reveals a kind of frustrated ambition as well as Christian zeal. Women seemed to appreciate the favorable exchange rates for their influence in China and sought to invest their lives there rather than spend them as debased currency at home. Certainly schoolteaching at home was of crucial importance to the future of the American democracy. When women sought a place where "one's work counts for more," as did Adelaide Thomas, they could not have been holding their nation's future in the balance. Instead they were simply reflecting the prevailing American allocations of social worth. "I want to teach where Christian education is more needed than anything," Eunice Thomas wrote, and stated her demand that her work receive adequate social tribute as well as conspiring to serve the Lord.[21]

In their candidate papers some women actually articulated their desires for more opportunity for personal authority. The YWCA, in particular, attracted and nourished women who enjoyed leadership. Katherine Crane had been a leader in Christian Endeavor during her youth, and confessed that when she finished college she found herself wishing for some such work "rather than a routine job of general teaching." "I knew of no such opportunity," she wrote. She finally found it though, first in the YWCA and then in China. Her college YWCA had given Elizabeth Perkins gratifying opportunities to exercise "initiative" which she also hoped to discover in China. Mary Ledyard, who had organized kindergartens in Los Angeles, also sought new arenas for her efforts in China. "I am by experience and training an organizer," she wrote, "and I feel sure that I am making the most of my powers only when placed where such work is to be accomplished." Whether explicit or not, women who applied to go to China invariably offered some evidence that to them it represented "a wonderful opportunity for achievement," as Alice Huggins put it.[22]

Women sought recognition and scope in China, but they needed vocational security. At the turn of the century, there were few professions open to women which offered viable life alternatives to marriage. Library work, in common with teaching, could provide respectable females with means to self support, but, also in common with teaching, the pay was low and the opportunities for advancement few. Women in such service professions frequently continued to live at home and felt suspended indefinitely in a vocational and personal limbo. A study of female librarians of this period argues that the typical librarian, like the schoolteacher, was a "woman who most likely lacked scholarly ambitions or preparation; who had no lifelong vocational commitment; and whose attitudes toward feminine sex roles led her to accept, and expect, administrative controls, low autonomy and subordination to clerical, routine tasks." Such a woman was likely to be eager to marry, the study asserts.[23]

Missionary work, however, was a lifetime commitment and lifetime support away from home, beyond marital pressures. Welthy Honsinger and Elsie Clark enlisted in part to evade insistent suitors, Honsinger concluding that she was willing to seem "queer" in return for her independence. Escape from marital pressures could be equally appealing to those women who felt that matrimony had passed them by. Alice Reed agreed to leave her parents' home to go to the field partly because she had concluded that at twenty-six, the minimum age required by most mission boards, her chances of marrying were "nil." Like Alice Reed, many women may have decided to volunteer to make something out of a life that was not fulfilling social and personal expectations.[24]

Missionary work offered the independence, status, and opportunity for achievement associated with a profession, but it was not a profession. As a calling it was characterized by a rhetoric of self-denial rather than of personal ambition. Unlike the "professional woman," who in popular turn-of-the-century parlance had cast off her feminine nature to adopt the hard competitiveness of the world of men, the missionary woman placed feminine qualities of empathy at the center of her lifework. Rather than withdrawing into herself, she identified with all humanity. Missionary women, like participants in other sororities of charitable Christian work, shared many of the needs that led women into the professions; but they had one unique need—to clothe their ambition in a garb which did no violence to their sense of feminine Christian virtue.

The depth of the stereotype of the professional woman, and perhaps the truth which lay behind it as well, emerges in an exchange Elsie Clark reported in her diary. Clark was a feminist and a woman's suffragist, with the education and prosperous urban background that might well have led her to entertain professional ambitions. She had long concluded that she was not suited to domesticity and had dismissed early marriage as an impossibility for her. Her YWCA work and religious background instead led her to divinity school and onto the mission field. During her divinity school days she noted in her diary an encounter on the shores of Lake Michigan which may have helped to firm her missionary resolve: "Walk to lake. An encounter with a lonely, pathetic professional woman, a lawyer. She told me of her business and much more of her philosophy of life. She was hungry for the idea of doing a deed of kindness."[25] Clark's description captures the essence of an image, perhaps shared as a self-image by the hapless professional woman. To be a professional woman meant the severing of ties with humanity, the surrender of the opportunities for kindness with which a woman earned her identity. When Clark chose to be a missionary rather than a lawyer or even a writer, a possibility she considered, she declared her unwillingness to go that far in her search for fulfillment and opportunity.

Rural, evangelical background, family tradition, and professional need, in differing combinations, could predispose women to consider missionary service. A few women were so steeped in the traditions of service that these factors of background were in themselves sufficient motivation. Sarah Luella Miner, born in Oberlin, Ohio, the daughter of home missionaries, was one for whom missionary service was "a natural development."[26]

Luella was the eldest in a family of four daughters in which missionary tradition ran strong on both sides. Her grandmother Miner had dedicated each of her children to the missionary cause, and her mother's sisters as well as both parents were home missionaries. As her father's eldest child, Luella received his particular attention and remained closer to him than to her mother, with whom she frequently clashed. After four years at Oberlin, Luella confessed to a reasoned missionary resolve. "I have always felt as if no other work could satisfy me so completely," she wrote, but added, "I don't feel at all as if I had had a 'call,' and would not be in the least disappointed if you should not think it best." Three years later, she wrote to her parents of her continuing ambition to serve on the foreign field: "The greatest drawback is that I fear a time might come when you would need me at home, and when financial help especially might be needed. I had quite set my heart on fully educating one of the children, and I am by no means fully persuaded that my duty does not lie here at home." Her parents reassured her on this count, however, and Luella continued with her plans to enlist for the China field. Like other missionary women, she expressed her ambition as a desire to enhance the influence of her life beyond what it could be at home—even among needy freedmen in the American South where she had been teaching. "I read lately that there are two ways of hiding your light," she wrote, "one by putting it under a bushel, the other by keeping it where there is such a blaze of light that its shining has no effect."[27] Only the vast darkness of the foreign field would satisfy Luella Miner's needs for radiant influence.

When Miner sailed for China in 1887, her enlistment represented the coincidence of many levels of motivation—the pioneer spirit of the American West, the strong Miner tradition of missionary service, the example of an attentive father, the influence of evangelical Oberlin College, the expanding ambition of an American schoolteacher. For Miner, missionary service was overdetermined. Few women could rely on so many layers of appropriateness when they forsook family and friends for the far side of the globe. Most women needed a distinct adult experience—whether a call, a family tragedy, a persuasive recruiter, or a collegiate compact—to set their missionary resolve. Most women needed a push of home circumstance or a powerful personal pull to get them to China.

⁂

A family death and the subsequent breakup of a home sometimes forced decisions on religious young women. Those who had not been able to reconcile China service with their responsibilities to parents of course were free to serve when parents died. Mary Thomas, the daughter of a Methodist preacher and a mother active in the support of the women's mission board, had always planned to volunteer, she wrote, but only after her father's death in 1898 and her mother's in 1903 did she finally enlist; by then she was thirty-six years old. Of those in the American Board whose family circumstances at the time of departure are known, 17 percent were without both parents and 51 percent without one. Over one-half went to China leaving a troubled or disrupted family behind. Dormant missionary interest became active commitment in the context of the insecurity suddenly afflicting women at the loss of families. When the beloved aunt whom Katherine Crane had nursed for seven years finally died—after a time "often disturbed by loneliness and bewilderment as to what life could hold for me," she wrote—Crane considered a number of alternatives. She finally chose mission service as, at thirty-seven, she "faced life anew."[28]

Women orphaned in their younger years also, perhaps, saw in the mission field a possibility for a "fresh start in life." The lack of home family did not present the same disadvantage in China that it did in the United States. Mabel Craig and her sister, the children of "poor working people" in Canada, moved to Maine to work as nursemaids after their father's death and mother's remarriage. There they joined the local Baptist church and sang in the choir. "Our friends were of the class of people better educated than ourselves and we became interested in bettering," she wrote. "I was interested in becoming a nurse and missionary even at that early date." Maria Davis was born of Irish Catholic parents on an immigrant boat, then orphaned, and early adopted by Methodist parents.[29] Her decision for service, like Craig's, may have been encouraged by a desire to assert membership in a respectable middle-class Protestant society denied her by birthright. For neither Davis nor Craig did parental death provide a catalyst to service, but rather the kind of lifelong need which made missionary service a practical decision.

At times of family disruption the decision to volunteer was more than a reasoned response to dislocation and uncertainty. Both during family sickness and following death in the family, women pledged their lives to the field as a kind of penance. When a parent was sick, this penance might take the form of a bribe to the Lord in return for recovery. Thus, when May Bel Thompson's sickly father lost his voice during a mountain expedition, his daughter purportedly offered her life as a missionary in exchange for his. After tragic family death, commonly the death of a husband, women sought service in a spirit of renunciation similar to the retreat of Catholic widows into the nunnery. Charlotte Jewell had considered foreign missionary service prior to her marriage. When she got word of her husband's death, she wrote, "That day I knew I was to be a foreign missionary." When Susan Tippett lost both children and her clergyman husband, she "realized God's call very forcibly." Behind these calls, perhaps, was a survivor's self-castigation at being the one spared from family disaster. Clara Pearl Dyer wrote:

> My childhood memories are built mostly around sickness, death, and funerals, because from the time I was four till I was eleven the six members of my family (parents, grandparents, and two sisters) all died. . . . From my earliest years I had the feeling that the Lord must have some special work He wanted me to do, or he would not have saved me the only one of my family.[30]

Such selection to live brought a burden of guilt which the mission field was well equipped to relieve. Many of the women moved by family rupture into the field already possessed the predispositions of background, family tradition, and personal zeal to suit them for mission work. For them, however, it would take the dramatic freedom and disorientation caused by family death, or the burden of their own survival, to bring them to candidacy.

❦❦❦❦

Family disruption pushed some women onto the field; recruitment pulled others to China. Despite a desire for a vocation and an abiding purpose, many women needed reassurance or an experience of collective enthusiasm to seal their commitment. Women who expressed a desire to be useful, and to make their lives a service to others, sometimes felt even that ambition was presumptuous when it involved the elevated moral posture of a foreign missionary.

Women expressed their tentativeness in many ways. Vera Holmes offered her energies "such as they are" to the service of the Lord, and Grace McConnaughey explained that she was offering herself as a "chinker," someone who was good at tailoring her services to the big projects of others. "My talents, if I have any, are for everyday use," Myra Sawyer wrote, and Katie Myers asked for assignment only "if you think there is a corner for me anywhere in the vineyard."[31]

Some of the most vigorous recruiting for China service was performed by single male missionaries in need of wives. A full two-thirds of the married women of the American Board who went to China with their husbands were married in the same year they sailed and entered marriage prepared to serve. Many of these women were already enrolled in missionary training schools when they met their prospective husbands; for them, the decision to go to the field with a husband represented little compromise with their original plan. Others, however, lacked the conviction or the confidence to enlist on their own. Their candidate papers convey the important effect of matrimonial recruiting on their determination. Marion Wells, the youngest of seven children, wrote that "until I met Mr. Belcher [I] had no idea of going into missionary work," and gave her reason, "I never felt anywhere near good enough." Margaret Gillette explained the reason for her application succinctly: "In general—my interest in missionary endeavor. In particular—my interest in Charles Gillette."[32] For those like Wells and Gillette who had not considered missionary work on their own, a proposal for the field opened a novel alternative. Women already inclined toward missionary service but reluctant to enlist on their own, however, regarded a husband bound for the field as divine intervention.

Jennie Wortman Campbell felt that Providence had arranged her marriage to allow her to realize her fitful missionary purpose. Her original sense of calling came from her revered sister Callie, who read missionary magazines voraciously but was not well enough to volunteer on her own. In an autobiography, Jennie Campbell later recalled the way the torch was passed:

> With her heart stirred to its depth she told of her yearning to answer the urgent calls and go forth as a missionary. But she used to say that she did not have the health or education to go. Long before I knew I was accepted of God she urged me to go as her proxy and go in her stead. And looking back I know that it was from that time it seemed settled in my mind that I should be a missionary, not a purpose on my part, rather something planned by another and accepted without question. Nothing has been plainer than this influence and power, this almost unrecognized conviction during my early years. It led me to serious introspection which revealed the fact of unfitness— and that without the one thing needful—such a calling would be impossible.

Jennie Wortman's diary gives further evidence of her sister's influence and her own sense of unworthiness. An 1881 entry reads that "Callie thinks Jesus wants me to be one of ministers to heathen lands! How unable I am to *think* of so great a work." Home from seminary several months later, she wrote: "I taught Callie's class yesterday, and enjoyed *very* much. Oh! I want to *do* something." Though she had recorded once before her desire "to *do* something for Jesus" she constantly had trouble concentrating on Sunday's devotions. "Conscious that I did not qualify for teacher or evangelistic worker (felt 'too wicked and frivolous'!)," she wrote later, "I thought of medical work as a gateway to missionary service."[33] But Wortman would soon lose her pension from her father's death in the Civil War and lacked the money to attend medical school.

She had also considered and dismissed another route to the mission field. "Missionary-minded young men were few those days, and none had ever crossed my path," she wrote in her autobiography, "so my route to the mission field via marriage was quite definitely out of the possibility." Jennie Wortman's feelings about marriage were less calculating and more complex than she later let on, however. The same month that she confessed that she wanted to do something for Jesus, she wondered to her diary "if I will ever have a sweet little home of my own, or if I will ever be worthy of performing a woman's greatest mission, make one dear life happy, and bring into existence new souls! Oh! how grand it must be. . . . I have such a high ideal of married life, and supreme unselfish *love*, that I am afraid I shall never be permitted to taste its harmonizing joys."[34] Within the year, Jennie Wortman's problems appeared to be solved. The brother of her best friend at Mount Caroll Seminary was planning to be a home missionary; the board had been urging him to take a wife. The introductions were made, and after a brief courtship, largely through the mails, the two were married.

During the courtship, however, Jennie Wortman found herself afflicted by "a gloom, which I am entirely unable to understand." Provoked in part by her fiancé's frustration over her emotional reserve, this gloom seems to have made her temporarily doubt the union. "God is leading me through mysterious paths," she wrote. "The thing in the future which is most inspiring to me is my hopes of being a missionary." For Jennie Wortman, missionary service and marriage moderated and thereby reinforced each other. In contemplating her future vocation, Wortman could forget her anxieties about sex and surrender; in attaining the field through marriage rather than self-promotion, she could rest easier over her manifest sense of unworthiness.[35] For Jennie Wortman and other volunteers like her, recruitment through marriage served to facilitate a tentative commitment to self and to service made long before.

Of course, some women who accompanied their husbands to China were never recruited and won to the work but simply led to it. Seventeen percent of the American Board women who were married when they went to the field indicated that it was for their husbands alone that they were in China. Women married long before they set sail were more likely to be in this category. When asked if she had been involved in the China decision of her husband, Agnes Scott answered, "Well, yes, but I think my husband just felt that of course I would go along with his life work." Women from an evangelical background who did not want to go to China had difficulty in honoring their reluctance and refusing to go. Both evangelical and wifely duty lay in denying self and making the sacrifice. Lida Ashmore made this sacrifice not once but twice. When Albert Lyon proposed marriage and the life of a missionary in Burma, she later wrote: "I did not want to go. But the lesson I learned during my teens when I could not do the things I wanted to do helped me over this hard place."[36] Lida Ashmore crossed

Seminary classmates, ca. 1880: Jennie Wortman (*marked with an* x) realized her fitful missionary calling through marriage to the brother of one of her classmates at Mount Carroll Seminary in Illinois.

over this hard place again when, after Lyon's early death, she married another missionary and set off for China. Never reconciled to China service, Ashmore did indeed make a major sacrifice, for her life was embittered by her alienation.

Marital recruitments exercised extraordinary pressures and did bring a significant minority of reluctant female volunteers to the field. Recruitments of other kinds depended even more on a prior sense of calling, however wavering. Recruitments by missionaries on furlough ranged from direct exhortation to remote inspiration. Joseph Walker visited the Washington mountain valley where Martha Wiley lived and spoke some Chinese. Wiley "got kind of a bug about it," she wrote in her autobiography, and when China missionary Caroline Chittenden paid a personal visit, Wiley volunteered. Like Wiley, Chittenden herself had also been inspired by Joseph Walker, who had been her neighbor in Oberlin during his furlough year. Although the missionary call in theory came from God, women remembered more particular calls, sometimes even pleas published in mission periodicals; they cherished the bonds established through print as if they were intimate and personal. Thus Mabel Allen was "awakened to her missionary purpose by Lydia Trimble." Mary Porter "answered the call" of Eliza Jane Bridgman. Mary Porter, in turn, inspired Sarah Goodrich and Ada Haven to service. (Goodrich was hurt thirty-one years after her enlistment at Porter's apparent unawareness of their special bond.) Grace Wyckoff, meanwhile, read the appeal of Ada Haven in the Congregational mission magazine *Light and Life* and took her as her missionary progenitor.[37]

The indirectness of many of these "recruitments" suggests that missionary fervor frequently lay dormant, only waiting for the remotest kind of focus. That the focus frequently took the form of a person—a heroine or a model—suggests the need which women felt to share the responsibility and the daring of their vocation. Personalizing the missionary call was a way of displacing their ambition and transforming it into selflessness. The reluctance of women who had chosen their vocation to take full and individual responsibility for their desires reflects not only feminine scruples but the sensibility of a culture in which self-fulfillment was considered less laudable than Christian charity.

Perhaps the single most influential catalyst to mission service in the lives of both young women and men was the evangelical, premillennialist

Student Volunteer Movement. An offshoot of the YMCA, the Student Volunteer Movement was responsible for as many as half of the missionary volunteers of the early twentieth century.[38] The SVM appealed both to the sense of responsibility and to the enthusiasms of young collegians. Its slogan—The Evangelization of the World in This Generation—proclaimed a bracing message of generational idealism which drew on turn-of-the-century nationalism.

The early generations of college women already felt themselves a privileged band. Their new status as educated women brought with it a particular responsibility to amount to a force in the world, they thought. Undoubtedly this sense of social responsibility helps to account for the high percentage of college women in these generations who did not risk the compromises of marriage. (A mission publication acknowledged this trend when it announced a married volunteer from Boston University: "Another young woman to demonstrate the fact that a diploma from Boston University C.L.A. [College of Liberal Arts] does not necessarily imply a vow of maidenhood.") Women tried to explain what their college education had meant to them when it came time for their families to educate sisters. Lucy Mead wrote home that "Normal or University may be O.K. as far as lessons are concerned but there are so many other things to be gotten out of real education." Jessie Ankeny was bolder in pinpointing the intangibles of a college education: "Nothing is equal to it and it will give you more prestige and better standing than money. . . . Not that one is any better especially . . . but it does make a difference in ones standing and ability to do things and you get a certain self-confidence that you never have without it." Self-confidence was an important addition to the lives of provincial farm girls. One of the abilities "to do things" it gave them was, of course, the courage to move beyond conventional expectations of marriage and family to contemplate a more public social contribution. "The college education has meant so much to me," Luella Miner wrote her father in 1899. "I am trying to pay my debt to you by making it count for as much as I can in the world."[39] Women agreed that the social experience of college was more important than the academic benefits. Their sense of privilege translated into a greater sense of their own worth, capacity, and responsibility.

The YMCA, YWCA, and the SVM capitalized on the social energy unleashed by collegiate experience, but the vehicle for this appropriation was the revival. The SVM was founded following the first summer Bible conference for students held by evangelist Dwight Moody in 1886. Inspired by the fervor of those sessions, a group of classmates, "the Mount Hermon

Hundred," pledged themselves to mission work. Their subsequent travels to some two hundred campuses by 1888 enlisted some twenty-two hundred pledges and led to the formation of a movement that was to remain influential for the next thirty-five years.[40]

The mission meeting offered a powerful experience which resembled a conversion. For some it was the most compelling religious event of their lives. Myra Jaquet wrote that she had been reared in the church, attended services regularly, had always thought herself a Christian, but "did not realize the meaning of the term until after a conference at Lake Geneva in 1905." Welthy Fisher's story of her enlistment emphasizes even more the influence of one inspirational meeting. An aspiring singer, she went to Carnegie Hall expecting to purchase an inexpensive ticket for the opera. Instead she found a mission meeting in progress and stayed to listen to spellbinders John R. Mott and Robert Speer. She found herself among the many candidates recruited that evening.[41]

The recruitment of volunteer pledges at mission conferences was only part of the Student Volunteer program, which also consisted of the ongoing activities of campus "Bands" of recruits. Unlike Honsinger, most of those who signed pledges at missionary conferences had traveled some distance to attend and were in some way looking to be called. The missionary conversion contained a strong element of rational discovery. Minnie Wilson received her "first impression that she should be a missionary" while at college, and though she resisted this impression, she did attend a lecture by a missionary bishop which "strengthened her conviction, and all peace for her soul departed until her decision was made." Rose Lombard also resisted the call, she wrote, but "at Lake Geneva, the summer of 1902, I decided to volunteer or give up the office of president of the YWCA to which I had been elected the spring before."[42] The appeals of campus leadership supplemented the enthusiasm of mission meetings to bring volunteers to the field.

On certain campuses Student Volunteer Bands were especially vital. The small coeducational denominational colleges of the Midwest were among those with the strongest traditions of service and the strongest bands. Oberlin College alone sent 20 percent of the total American Board female delegation to China in the early twentieth century. Grinnell and Carleton also had strong bands, which not only worked together on campus but carried their energies together into the field. Their inspiration undoubtedly was similar to that of the nondenominational Yale-in-China band, which was founded from the desire of Student Volunteers to mount "some sort of unified endeavor on the mission field so they would not have to break up after leaving college."[43] Evangelical enthusiasm and school spirit combined in volunteer bands to form a romantic student movement that capitalized on a sense of generational solidarity.

The limited term of the college course itself could catalyze a sense of mission vocation. As a student at the University of Michigan at the turn of the century, Lucia Lyons had held off signing a student volunteer pledge because of her parents' objections. But as she moved toward graduation in 1902, she began to put more pressure on her parents. "I haven't many more weeks in college to be taking a new point of view, and I want to begin," she wrote home. "I want to gain the good of being one of the volunteer band and being with people of the same purpose. Some of them are such fine people, too, and I shall want to tell them that I am to be one of them." To the mission board she explained that "it was at the University and thru contact with other men and women of Christian character that I received the greatest inspiration and quickening of my spiritual life."[44] Missionary life might well appear to be a continuation of the collective enthusiasms of college life to those who had known the elite comradeship of Student Volunteer bands.

The collegiate connection sometimes overshadowed all other considerations in missionary candidacy, as the efforts to recruit Alice Reed for the newly forming Grinnell-in-China band revealed. During Reed's college years she had had no intention of becoming a missionary and was not a member of the Student Volunteers. ("I wasn't interested," her record reported.) Following her graduation Phi Beta Kappa in 1913, she returned home and taught school. In the spring of 1916, however, she was contacted by a fellow Grinnell graduate to solicit her enlistment for China. Alice Reed responded that she doubted whether she was religious enough, since she lacked "intense fervor" and was rather "a practical, unemotional person." Reverend Arie DeHaan responded:

We do not want "religious" people in the sense of which you speak. We want women and men who are deeply consecrated to the spirit of service and are willing to sacrifice. I know what you mean. You are a college woman with absolutely no use for sham in religion, but you do have the Grinnell spirit of wanting to serve your fellow man. I feel that we college men and women are on the whole, "practical, unemotional persons," which is not a sign of lack of religion but rather a sign of self control and strength. The persons with "intense fervor" in the sense that you mean it are not the strongest workers oftentimes.

Persuaded by DeHaan's argument, by the knowledge that her debts were paid, her marital prospects few, and her feeling "that I was not accomplishing as much as I would like to here," Alice Reed agreed to go to China. She was encouraged by her parents' acquiescence.[45]

For other candidates, parents presented more major obstacles. Some parents with children in the YWCA or the Student Volunteers resisted and resented the influence of a peer youth movement which threatened to take away their children. Lucia Lyons's correspondence with her parents reveals the tension she felt between the allure of the volunteer band and her filial responsibilities to her parents. Ruth White, a YWCA secretary and volunteer, also brooked disapproval from her family. Her brother protested to their parents: "Those YW Secretaries have probably been at her again. . . . Carolyn March hasn't any Father and Mother so she can go better. . . . Ruth is so ready to do as told. And some are always ready to tell." Ruth herself wrote that she wished her parents could hear missionaries on furlough speak at conference: "It seems so entirely different—so much more sensible and natural when you hear about it from these people who have been there."[46] The correspondence of Ruth White and Lucia Lyons with their parents seems to indicate that both women were dealing with parents fundamentally unsympathetic to and ignorant of the mission cause.

In fact, White and Lyons were both following established family precedent in their interest in mission service. Their parents may have resisted losing them, but parents had nevertheless prepared the way for childrens' recruitment. White's mother had been an enthusiastic supporter of the Methodist women's board; when White finally arrived in China, she wrote back about her excitement at finally meeting the mission personalities her mother had talked of throughout her childhood. Lyons's parents and grandparents themselves had been missionaries in the Pacific. Even Alice Reed, who had had no college interest in service, came from a midwestern minister's family and was prepared for the idea of mission life.[47] Generational pressures through the Student Volunteers indeed catalyzed the missionary enlistments of a large proportion of the front-line troops of the early twentieth-century mission force. But these volunteers were invariably prepared to be responsive to the new contours of mission vocation by their religious and familial background.

The most conducive background and the most active campus volunteer band did not inevitably make a woman into a missionary, however.

Supplementing factors of parental occupation, familial orientation, and work experience was the less tangible matter of personal energy. Women who subscribed for mission service were those who wanted more for themselves than they saw in conventional alternatives. Some of them wanted more opportunities for achievement; some, more renown; others, satisfaction, independence, adventure, status. But they all wanted to participate in a project whose dimensions both enhanced and diminished their own—a project that offered them, in Simone de Beauvoir's terminology, transcendence.[48]

The paradox, of course, is that these women expressed their desire for self-liberation in the language of self-sacrifice. Only occasionally did the ambition for glory and adventure escape these rhetorical conventions. Jeanie Graham was unusually frank in her acknowledgment of the lure of the foreign field. In 1912, while an undergraduate at Bates College, she decorated her room with a fishnet filled with pictures and postcards, and designated one portion "my conflicting interests corner."

> There I've hung a 19 x 11 inch map of the world with Foochow on a level with my nose and New England on the farthest corner. Just above I've placed Doc's and Frederic's [two beaux] pictures side by side. That's the conflicting interests part of it: supreme unselfishness and supreme selfishness; and beneath, the map, in contemplation of which I can easily forget the two of them.

Jeanie Graham's conflicting interest in marriage in fact seemed to dissolve before the magnetic attractions of China. "It's great to be a hero," she had crowed when she was elected to YWCA office the year before, thereby declaring her delight in independent achievement.[49] Graham was almost unique in her unabashed claims for self. For hundreds of other women less forthright than she the wispy rhetoric of feminine self-sacrifice masked a zeal which the freedoms of the China field would one day fan into activity.

~3~

SINGLE WOMEN
AND MISSION COMMUNITY

By 1919 the American missionary force in China consisted of nearly equal numbers of single women, married women, and married men. All mission boards encouraged their male missionaries to marry, so single men were uncommon, with single women six times more densely represented. Not only were single women represented in the mission community well beyond their numerical proportion in the United States, but their work appeared to be central to a mission organization in need of new strategies and additional personnel. Because of the scarcity of Chinese schools to accommodate the post-Boxer interest in education for women, the general boards looked to Christian girls' schools, run by single women, as a God-given opportunity to enhance the influence of the church in China. Single women did not need the medical attention which constrained the assignments of married men with families and could also staff some of the most remote stations in China. In 1919, 13 percent of all missionary centers in China were entirely staffed by single women.[1]

Despite the centrality of their work to mission purposes, the standing of single women within the mission community was low. The terms *spinster* and *old maid*, which indicated the marginal position of unmarried women in nineteenth-century America, circulated freely in China. Indeed, "old maids" joined "Chinamen" and "niggers" as humorous caricatures in missionary theatricals, appearing in one performance wearing black bonnets and mitts. Single women missionaries to some degree feared and shared popular assumptions of their marginality. But their collective service and joint community provided the means to convert a negative social identity into a source of personal legitimacy.[2]

❧❧❧❧

In some ways, missionary service ideally suited what were assumed to be women's attributes. Based on self-abnegation and service, mission work demanded in dramatic macrocosm the gifts of self-denial which each woman who married and subordinated her wishes to those of husband and family offered in microcosm. Echoing many nineteenth-century female spokesmen, Sarah Goodrich commented on this awesome coincidence between feminine and Christian ideals. "Sometimes I feel as if a woman could comprehend the Christ, this utter sacrifice of self as no man can," she wrote.[3] If self-denial was feminine, single women ought to have been the most feminine, for in their love of the heathen they had foresworn not only family, country, and friends, but also the domestic joys of married homelife. In denying entitlement to this last blessing, one might conclude that single women had achieved exemplary status.

In fact, in popular stereotype in the late nineteenth century the single woman missionary was characterized by her lack of feminine qualities. Missionary life isolated men and women equally from home civilization, but this isolation was particularly threatening to women who were customarily defined by their relationships to others. Men could point to an American tradition of independent, frontier adventure away from village and hearth. No such tradition could console American missionary women, who, like other women, gained their sense of worth from their connections to home culture and family members. A woman's isolation threatened to unsex her. When Sarah Goodrich described a single woman missionary, her admonition to home audiences not to picture "a mannish woman" demonstrated the common expectation.[4]

The stereotype seemed to threaten to shape actuality. Jane Addams wrote that being of a "serious not to say priggish tendency," she experienced "concerted pressure" to become a missionary while at Rockford Seminary. A seminary professor recommending Mabel Daniels for service considered her failure in fashion a unique qualification for the isolation of the mission field. He concluded that she was "one of the most unstylish young women I ever knew in the matter of dress," which helped to make her the "best fitted young person" he had ever known for missionary service. If lack of style qualified someone for missionary service, the enlistment of an attrac-

"Old maid missionary," ca. 1904: As a single woman, Flora Heebner (*middle*) was peripheral to missionary family life, but her work was central to the Taiku station in Shansi.

Not the missionary type, 1909: The enlistment of Agnes Meebold, who had "a dainty, slender figure, rosy cheeks, wavy black hair and a gracious smile," caused even chance acquaintances to grieve.

tive young woman such as Agnes Meebold, who had "a dainty, slender figure, rosy cheeks, wavy black hair and a gracious smile," caused even chance acquaintances to grieve.[5] Some women felt sufficiently threatened by such imputations to attempt to dissociate themselves not only from the spinster image but from the popular connotations of their own missionary identity.

Lida Ashmore, for example, wrote in her autobiography that she was always told that she did not look like a missionary. She described what we can take to be the image she feared in an account of a group of missionaries she met in Shanghai:

> I must say they are a queer looking lot, take them altogether. One Miss, a doctor, well along in years, 35 or 40 . . . had a big piece of bread, chewing on one end, the other stuck out to the corner of her mouth on the outside of her teeth and the end just *wiggled*. I could think of nothing but a worm that was protesting in its death throes as his head was being chewed off farther back in her mouth.

The absence of refinement in table manners and in dress signaled a defeminization which one married woman associated with the inability to attract a man. Counseling a single friend not to close a dress with pins, she warned, " 'No man when he puts his arm around you, will ever come back again.' " She insisted that she herself was not a missionary but just a missionary's wife. Sarah Clapp Goodrich kept up her appearance as a result of a commitment made to her horrified sisters at the time of her enlistment. Appalled by the recollection of missionary women they had seen in their father's parish, her sisters elicited a promise from her that she would curl her hair every night, their reasoning being, her granddaughter wrote, "that if a good deal of effort went into her topknot, Sarah would see that her whole person was well-groomed."[6] Though not all were as exacting as Goodrich in their tactics for evading the "missionary look," they all worried about the effects of isolation from civilized society on their feminine grace.

Isolation from genteel company was of course more dangerous than the separation from recent fashion, and for this reason missionary women emphasized their social life in their letters home. Elsie Clark described summer parties to her family to allay any fears that she might be "drying up," and Monona Cheney's claim that her coworkers were not "sticks" but had the "kind of personalities that win people everywhere" was primarily a reassurance about their sociability. Like women at home whose identity depended on relationships to others, female missionaries considered their social life as evidence of their health. When Elizabeth Perkins confessed fatigue at holiday frivolity and her preference for the peace of her isolated station, she wrote that she had to endure the disapproval of her colleagues. They insisted upon the importance of society for everyone, but especially for people like her. Perkins cautioned her family lightly, but perhaps a little nervously, not to become anxious too soon: "I don't think I'm queer yet!!!"[7] Single women who had already done an uncommon thing by enlisting for foreign service were constantly haunted by the possibility that they might complete a process already begun and become genuinely odd or eccentric.

⁂

Single women relied on membership in their paternal family as proof of their normalcy. Communications with families at home provided some insurance against oddity, and those who lacked this bond were at greatest risk. Jessie Ankeny, for instance, mentioned an unpopular woman who scarcely replied to a question about her home folks. "They say they never write her. . . . I think she has a queer disposition to overcome and a queer family too." Women without a letter-writing family clearly found it harder to resist the attacks of nerves which threatened missionary women far from home. Lida Ashmore described a woman for whom "nervousness" and lack of home mail were one and the same: a Miss Solman was "so jealous of Miss Weld because she has more letters than she (Miss S) does that she goes off in a pet and cries and sulks for hours after the mail comes and Miss Weld has to try to cheer her up by petting her."[8] Not only did family signify legitimacy, it contributed to sanity itself.

A single woman's family also proved to be her most sensitive barometer to changes in herself. When Elsie Clark sent home a photograph of the Foochow community, she accompanied it with an urgent request for reassurance: "*Do* look at it carefully and tell me what you think of our community. *Do* we look like freaks, sticks or scarecrows? I believe not. But tell me true." Only the confident dared to send photographs. When Luella Miner had a photograph taken after she had been in China for five years, she told her family that "not for love or money would I send the thing home to impress itself upon your memory." She could, she thought, "have sent it to you as the likeness of a pious, confiding, lantern-jawed, elderly member of the North China Mission, and you could have innocently introduced it to your friends as 'one of Luella's associates'—'a typical old-maid missionary.' " She added that her mother "would just weep tears if she thought I looked like that."⁹ Miner's decision to spare her mother also protected herself from the possibility that her family, looking at nearly a stranger, might be tempted even for an instant to withdraw its validation from her.

On the face of it, many families offered little enthusiasm for the single lives of their offspring and disapproved of their spinsterhood. They were quick to construct romances when provided with the scantiest information. "Don't, please, build any air castles," Elizabeth Perkins requested after mentioning a man by name, and Monona Cheney moved to "relieve the mind" of her family about matrimonial prospects in the vicinity. Despite teasing and goading toward matrimony, however, familial faithfulness enabled single women's continued freedom. When Jessie Ankeny's family decided to move from Iowa to Nebraska, she protested their departure from the home she had known, and when she had to have a bladder operation in 1911, she propped the family picture up at the foot of the bed. The fate of an older single woman whose family had died prompted Ankeny to write to hers: "If I ever tho't that you folks would all die off and leave me I'd get married I think."¹⁰ For Jessie Ankeny, single missionary service was a luxury sustained by the social connectedness provided by her folks at home.

The need for a family was not the need for a male connection. Missionary Ruth White found from an informal poll among her friends that the missionary's principal home correspondent was her mother. Mothers had inherited responsibility for the family affections in the nineteenth century, and well into the twentieth they made good on their reponsibilities to wandering sons as well as daughters. Maternal loyalty probably made women away from home depend especially on their mothers' letters. Elsie Clark wrote that "nothing satisfied me but word from her," and Monona Cheney, in soliciting letters from other members of the family, warned her mother not to stop *her* weekly letters: "I just have to have them," she wrote.¹¹ For women who had chosen to remain single, a sense of womanly identity required the constant reassurance of mothers.

But women did not willingly dispense with letters from fathers. Cheney told her family that if her father had not written, he had "better," because she did not want "any proxy work on my family correspondence," and Jessie Ankeny scolded her father, saying "he sure is a bad one never to write." When letters from fathers came they were occasions for celebration. Jeanie McClure had been a married missionary in China for two years when she first delightedly heard from her father; and when Ankeny's father finally wrote, she announced herself nearly overcome. "I had to labor over it some," she wrote, "but I was glad to do it." Letter writing, with its attendant skills of penmanship and conversation, had been allocated to the female side of the family. Fathers tended to write with greater difficulty because they were less accustomed to it. William Brown's letter to his married daughter Florence in 1895 was written only under protest. He began, "Florence why did you go so far away from us half way around this Globe of ours that we cannot here [sic] from you for two or three Months," and then went on:

> This is the third letter that I have written since I came to Iowa I must say I do not like the job of writing. I would rather chop wood or anything I can do as write. Mother has put off writing so as to get me to see that I must try. But I find it hard to get ideas out of nothing and to put them into a letter and think is still harder, but excuse I see mistakes but I wont alter them.[12]

The separation of male and female spheres not only allocated cultured skills to women but the cultivation of emotion itself.

Daughters' comments addressed to their fathers often dealt with state and national politics, perhaps reflecting the content of fathers' letters to them. Jessie Ankeny followed her expressions of gratitude for her father's letter with the comment, "I imagine there will be great things doing next year in the political world." This resort to public issues signified both the infrequency of communication and the estrangement between male and female worlds which caused it. Like William Brown, fathers often seemed puzzled by their daughters' vocation; they were less likely than mothers to be church members themselves, and perhaps were less able to understand even this most conservative expression of female ambition.[13] Fathers who were ministers and who supported their daughters' vocation, though presumably more comfortable with "getting ideas out of nothing," were no better correspondents than their less literary brethren. Even strong relationships between fathers and daughters did not generally produce articulated intimacies.

Missionary papers testify that even the sustained efforts of mothers, with occasional aid from fathers, sisters, and brothers, often proved inadequate to respond to the needs of women in the field. Isolated China correspondents exhorted their weary families on to higher endeavors. Elsie Clark told her family that if they knew the extent that "letters are the breath of life out here" they would never miss a week, and Jessie Ankeny urged her family to "write! write! write! oftener!" and the next month, "Write oftener than possible." The absence of mail caused hurt, depression, anger; a good foreign mail temporarily suspended all social life. Though letter writers who left extensive collections are a skewed sample, their letters demonstrated the impact of the mail on others besides themselves. Jeanie McClure repeated a single friend's comment: "Do you know, I'm not fit to live with after six o'clock at night," and when queried as to why, "Because then I know that I can't expect a foreign mail any longer that day."[14] The possibility of a good mail from home seemed to be the meaning of hope itself.

For many single women, homesickness was a chronic condition that abated only occasionally throughout lifetimes of separation. Emma Martin, who had been in China for seventeen years and was temporarily involved in relief for Tientsin flood victims, was so busy she did not think of home "for hours at a time—perhaps all day." Monona Cheney could write: "I think folks and things at home are more real to me than those here; certain it is that you don't seem very far away, and I fairly live with you a good deal of the time." Correspondence both fed on and fueled a sense of the vividness of home. Luella Miner wrote and received weekly letters for thirty-five years, and through that conduit, which involved a delay of over two months between writing and hearing, as she put it, she "lived." On her twenty-eighth birthday, after three years away from home, she stole away from her missionary family (whom she had not informed of her birthday), to commune instead with those at home:

> When I came to China I thought that perhaps as the years passed by I would become so used to the separation that without really loving you any less I should become in a way less a part of your life and I would lose the sense of being transplanted. I am glad that it hasn't been so. I would far rather feel the pain of loneliness sometimes than to grow away from those who are nearest and dearest to me. . . . How I miss you one can never know who is not situated as I am.[15]

Miner's relationship with her home family, separated from her by months and oceanic distances, allowed her to freeze time; even successions of birthdays could not destroy the idealized family relations of childhood when they were celebrated on the other side of the world. Missionary service in China allowed Miner, and perhaps also other women, to

preserve her place as a daughter in her home family without confronting
the inevitable stresses of age and changing needs. In China, Miner could
achieve her own independence without ever challenging the domestic
sanctity of her parental home.

Letter writing absorbed enormous amounts of energy and trained missionary correspondents in discipline and fluidity of style as they prepared
letters for mission societies, home boards, and newspaper columns, as well
as home families. Luella Miner explained the secret of her technique in an
opening resolution written home: "I mean to be very regular in my writing
to you, and very minute, and I shall expect the same at the other end of the
line. The danger is that we shall gradually drop out the little details which
will make life seem real because they seem so unimportant." The majority
of missionary correspondents were at least semiprofessional writers in the
investment of time, cultivation of imagination, and refinement of skills
that their epistolary exertions entailed. Through this writing, missionaries
asserted their reality and, as Elsie Clark joined Monona Cheney and Luella
Miner in affirming, sometimes did their "most intensive living."[16]

Despite the distance separating them from home, missionaries continued to participate in the events of home family life. When her sister was to
be married, Elsie Clark arranged to provide the bridal lace, and when the
Martin family engaged in a family dispute, Emma weighed in on the side of
her mother. Luella Miner contributed financial aid for her sister's education, and Jessie Ankeny expressed her disapproval when her younger
sisters started going out with men. Emily Hobart, a married woman, once
sent her mother a dozen threaded needles to make up for her inability to
perform that daily service. Generally, though, China missionaries contributed in foreign adventures what they could not offer in daily attentions.
Elsie Clark, who arranged for a former student to attend college in her
home city, pointed out that for her family, "life would have been more
humdrum" were it not for her life in China.[17] Through the colorful stories
of mission correspondents, families incorporated the Orient into the
family circle.

More major family obligations were attenuated but not annulled by
China service. Particularly on the occasions of sickness or death at home,
single women often returned to provide the care that would have been
their natural responsibility had they lived in the United States. Harriet
Osborne, for instance, received and ultimately obeyed a summons from her
family to care for an invalid sister who needed constant attention. "Poor
girl," Elizabeth Perkins wrote, "it is so hard for her to know what to do. She

Home continuities, 1921: When she wrote her long weekly letters home, Jeanie McClure sat near the portraits of her seven sisters and her parents.

really feels that she ought to go home, yet the situation here is most critical."[18] Though it was hard to leave the field, single women would go when called. Caring for ailing members of the family was the responsibility of single women in particular and of women in general. When William Ament's mother was dying, for instance, his wife, like him a full-time worker, returned home to attend her through her last months.

Rarely, women could fulfill this responsibility by bringing a needy family member to China rather than returning home themselves. When Luella Miner's mother died, Miner had just taken charge of a developing Peking woman's college. She allowed her aunt and two married sisters to care for her newly widowed father temporarily, but was prepared to return home to fulfill her prior filial responsibility as an unmarried daughter. She ultimately arranged to meet clear and welcome obligation by arranging for her father to live with her in Peking for the first year of his bereavement.[19]

But family obligations could seldom be dealt with so imaginatively. When family needs dictated, most single women abandoned careers, converts, and coworkers. Despite the distance and the years which separated missionary from family, for single women the home ties remained time-consuming, emotionally compelling, and finally binding. Whatever independence they displayed in forsaking home and family for a life of exile and service was only conditional, to be revoked voluntarily in case of family need. For the legitimacy offered by their families through the years, single women paid in this commitment.

☙❧☙❧

In their relationships with their home families, single women relied on bonds formed in childhood that in some form were common to most men and women. True, they stretched these bonds across the Pacific and demonstrated their strength and flexibility, but the authority and deference communicated through correspondence remained familial. The affirming of continuity with home could provide an ideal prototype for the social acceptance single women desired, but it could not provide that acceptance itself. At the root of the relationship with their families was an illusion— the illusion that their extraordinary missionary experiences need not change single women, who in the hearts of their families far away could remain the conventional daughter or sister for whom all was still possible. As crucial as this illusion was, had home families remained the only source of single women's social identity, the story of their lives in China would have been one of denial, of failure to confront and transcend their marginality.

As the density of the single women's population increased, however, a community evolved which began to provide a strong and alternative source of identity. The construction of joint "ladies' houses," as they were called, allowed for the development of self-sufficient homes, with characteristic rituals, patterns of relationship, and rules of governance. By means of this common society, single women converted individual eccentricity into a group pride in institutionalized spinsterhood.

Prior to the construction or conversion of ladies' houses, however, the living situations of single women in China were unstable. Until the formation of separate women's boards after the Civil War, single women were sent to mission fields only to accompany married couples. Based on common nineteenth-century practice, this custom of lodging single women with families continued well into the early years of the women's boards and sporadically thereafter. The assumption that women needed the protection either of marriage or of a married man was only exaggerated by the real and imagined threats of the foreign field. Living with a family did provide a convenient and comfortable initial arrangement for single women away from their homes. The mission boards had not anticipated, however, that the presence of two women in one household would cause confusion among local Chinese, who assumed that one of them was a secondary wife. Nor had they considered the problems that secondary status would cause single women.

Boarding made single women dependent on households they had by no means chosen and subject to the constraints of daily family schedules that were not their own. Tensions could be resolved easily only by the single woman retreating to her own chamber and her acceptance of an isolated existance. Bessie Ewing, observing with the pity of a married woman, was probably correct in her sense that under these conditions single missionary service provided a forlorn existence.[20]

Beyond the daily surrender of autonomy and the possibility of personal friction in which the single woman would most likely be the loser, boarding meant constant domestic impermanence for single women. Mission boards frequently shuffled personnel from station to station. Furloughs and breakdowns, both physical and nervous, also kept missionary households and boarding possibilities in a state of flux. Particularly when a boarding arrangement had been harmonious, the disruption of both family and home was devastating. When Lucy Beach had a nervous breakdown and departed for America, Luella Miner also had a temporary breakdown at the thought of losing a woman she loved like a sister who had "made such a lovely home for me." After the Beaches left, she wrote that she nearly made herself sick: "In fact, I collapsed onto my lounge Tuesday night, sending my English pupils away and skipping prayer meeting, and the next two days I spent either in bed or on the lounge. Pretty proceedings, weren't they? The ladies petted me up, copied poetry for me and sent me things to eat just as if I had been disappointed in love!" Miner never reacted so strongly to a departure again, partly because in her early years in China she grew accustomed to them. The need for a secure home affected all mission-aries in an alien society, but for single women, whose needs were the greatest, the chances of finding such stability were slim.[21] In their boarding arrangements with different families in China, single women enjoyed a marginal state of insecurity even more severe than would have been their probable lot as American spinsters at home. Having traveled halfway around the world in response to a personal call, but perhaps also to escape dependency in someone else's household, they rediscovered some aspects of the same situation in China.[22]

The increased density of the single women's population and the growing wealth and independence of the women's boards allowed for the gradual construction of homes for single women around the turn of the century.[23] This development transformed single women's missionary experience. Residence in collective women's houses allowed women relative equality in settling the domestic details which governed their lives and also accorded them full membership in a family life that supplied stability of domicile, if not always of family members. Within ladies' houses, women developed and maintained an actual woman's sphere, divorced in fact as well as in theory from masculine domestic prerogatives.

The move to a women's house was welcome, as the case of Luella Miner reveals. Although she moved four times in her China tenure, Miner was devoted to all the families with whom she boarded, and in 1891 she wrote home that she had only one serious friction in the entire mission com-munity: she clashed with her fellow women's-board worker Jane Evans, with whom she got along no better than "scarlet and crimson." Yet five years later she talked about the house she and Jane Evans were designing together; their differences had obviously been transcended. She looked forward to living in "a place which I could really call my own," where she could plant trees and shrubs.[24]

The home life supplied by single women's houses was often assertively familial. The entire house turned out to welcome newcomers such as Monona Cheney, who wrote on her arrival at the women's residence in Peking that her own family "couldn't *act* any gladder to see me," and added on her part that "it was a real home-coming." Though all missionary houses provided lodging and hospitality for traveling missionaries, the constantly shifting populations of the single women's house made it necessary to elevate the sense of family to an ideology there. Cheney recognized the necessity for extra energy to make a family out of strangers. When she worried that she spent too much time "visiting" with other household members, she reminded herself that "if we don't make our family count for something, it will be hard on everybody, since this is our only home this side of the States, and you must have a *home*." In fact when she was later transferred to Tientsin, she pronounced herself lucky to have two "real homey families" on the mission field. Her new Tientsin family celebrated her thirtieth birthday with "Happy Birthday" sung, as new people joined the breakfast table, three times in all, followed by a fourth chorus sung by 150 schoolgirls at daily prayers. The single women's houses, particularly the larger ones, managed temporarily to blot out the long distances from home in the comprehensiveness of their collective life. Though she and her friends often thought of their families back home, Ruth White felt so cared for in her YWCA house that she could write home, "we really never get homesick."[25]

Within the women's houses, of course, several generations coexisted, and inevitably disagreements broke out between women who had grown up in the morally conservative 1870s and 1880s, and those who were coming of age in the era of the "New Woman" in the 1890s and thereafter. Seniority counted for a great deal within the mission organization, and generational deference marked relations within the women's quarters. The earlier Victorian generation determined forms of address and of social intercourse. Welthy Honsinger judged that she had seriously breached decorum when she hugged all the single women she met on arriving in Nanchang in 1906, since "Some of them, I understand, had lived together for five years and still call each other Miss W——, Miss P—— etc."[26] Members of Honsinger's generation distinguished between their own contemporaries, whom they referred to by first name, and their seniors. Formality between generations characterized all Victorian families, however, and did not necessarily qualify the familial assumptions of the women's residences.

Missionary morality, too, tended to catch by surprise recent arrivals from an America of changing mores. Monona Cheney wrote with chagrin in 1919 about the supervision her social life was receiving: "I find that Mrs. Jewell thinks it is hardly proper for a girl to have the same gentleman caller two or three times, unless he is courting her; and then she must have a chaperone, even in her own parlor! Shades of the freedom of American youth! And I'm nearly thirty!" The compromise worked out by the community represented more of a capitulation on Cheney's part than a mutual surrender of generational principles.[27]

Despite such conflicts and capitulations, however, Cheney made sure to rescue the reputation of her housemother from the taint of missionary eccentricity and to reassure her family at home that it might sound "as if Mrs. Jewell were a crank, but she really is a dear." Reciprocal good feeling born of mutual need repaired most generational rifts, and familial vocabulary provided the rhetoric of this harmony. Luella Miner, who had decided in 1915 that the family was "too big and hilarious to quite suit this old lady," in 1917 seemed reconciled to feeling "quite like a grandmother" among the seven women she described as a "pleasant family." Lucy Mead wrote that one of the older ladies mothered her and almost always came in to kiss her goodnight, and another missionary referred to a group of young women who had recently attended a slumber party as "we 'kids.' " "People who couldn't and wouldn't live in the same block at home harmonize beautifully in the same house in China," a new worker on the field reported. In her home, she wrote, four people "dramatically opposed, absolutely different in temperament, viewpoint, methods, training, etc." were "living, working and sharing together and loving each other" in a way that made her wonder.[28] Just as tensions in real families could be accommodated under the family roles of rebellious child and reproving mother, so the women's houses used these expectations to maintain social harmony among women from different backgrounds, temperaments, and generations.

Without actual responsibilities for child rearing or automatic lines of familial authority, however, women's residences occasionally resembled college dormitories more than hierarchical families. The high spirits of the younger missionaries could overwhelm the reserve of the older women and reverse generational supremacy. Lucy Mead, for instance, described a pillow fight with the rest of the house massed against her and one of the older members of the household, forty-six-year-old Grace Wyckoff: "Someone occasionally mentions 'the serious melancholy, lonely, dull life of missionaries in China' which words bring peals of laughter. Not even in

Generational harmony, 1905: Ladies' residences drew together single women of different ages and backgrounds in families formed by mutual need. Here Emily Hartwell (*standing*) is shown with Edna Drake (*left*) and Martha Wiley (*right*).

the most hilarious of college days have I had more fun than right here in this bunch of 'old maid missionaries.' "[29] The women's residences made out of spinsterhood a sphere of spontaneity and stability.

But they did not foster either privacy or individual freedom. The communal organizations of "ladies' houses" meant that all rooms, sometimes including bedrooms, were shared, as were property and habits. Alice Reed commented on the custom of her house "to loan any good garment you have to anyone going on a visit," and when Lucy Mead was asked about how she was sleeping and eating, "the family unanimously voted" for her to answer that neither could be improved upon. Lacking automatic hierarchical controls, the women's residences exerted majoritarian ones to insure the nourishment of group life. In 1915, for instance, Mead's family "passed a vote" that no one could go away for Christmas, as so many were away for Thanksgiving.[30] The precedence which communal life took over individual prerogative characterized most missionary institutions. Evidence indicates, however, that the willingness of single women to surrender individual preferences for membership in a vital family household granted ladies' houses an extra source of communal energy.

Elsie Clark had trouble making the compromise. An ideological liberal and a worker for women's suffrage, she was a "New Woman" of a Progressive cast. After a year at Chicago Divinity School, she enlisted with the Methodist women's board to join the faculty of Hwa Nan, the newly emerging Foochow women's college. She was rare among missionary women in her ambition and her sense of solitary self-worth. Her reactions to the women's communities in which she lived in Foochow, in the Chinese interior, and at summer resorts offer a valuable critique of these institutions.

Clark found the social pressures of the women's residences a constant infringement on her private projects and pursuits. After sharing her room with a visitor for two weeks, she reclaimed it for her own as "my little home, my little kingdom, my little treasury" and announced herself ready to shut herself up in it alone for a week. When theology and psychology books she had requested finally arrived, she spent all her time with them, noting in her letters that "sometimes I get secretly annoyed when people come in just to chitchat and make me lose a whole good hour's time." She saw her annoyance as a personal defect, however, and announced herself trying to be "more human."[31]

Elsie Clark sometimes even tried to convert her strength into the self-denial and sensitivity which she felt marked the true Christian temperament. She frequently chided herself for her lack of sympathy with the needs of fellow missionaries and remained fascinated by the examples of pure missionary self-denial she saw among women working in the interior. For a woman working almost alone on a barren, offshore island she expressed her awe: "I am hushed at the thought of the way Miss G. gives herself to the work. I could not do it. I think too much of self-cultivation, self-realization. I could not pour myself out so." Clark did not undervalue the psychic cost of such self-sacrifice, but, adopting the perspective of William James, she found such extreme behavior heroic. In the remote station of Yenping, for example, she stayed with two women who seemed to her "overwrought, nervous, hurried at their meals." They "seemed more like *real* missionaries," she wrote, than those like herself who were living and working in the coastal city of Foochow. Elsie Clark focused on the Chinese interior as the area of greatest female self-sacrifice, but her observations also point to an important truth about the women's community that she belonged to in Foochow: it did not promote the individual growth or female accomplishment which she still aspired to but encouraged instead denial of self in furthering the harmony of the group.[32]

Limitations on female activity were apparent in the relations of Elsie Clark's Foochow community to politics, to social organization, and even to her fondness for oratory. When Clark made a triumphant speech in 1912, her colleagues congratulated her but were surprised that she "displayed no agitation or embarrassment at all, which was unnatural." The reaction of her friends caused Clark to feel as though she must be "a strange creature." Two years later, she once again confessed to the "oddity" of enjoying public speaking and wrote that "so many people dread it so, or pretend to, that one feels like a person with an infirmity to take delight in it."[33] This designation of female oratory as "unnatural," "strange," "odd," and "infirm" represented a logical extension of nineteenth-century definitions of women, which emphasized their social relatedness. Solitary achievement, such as oratory, demanded some compromise with social dependency. It only stood to reason that the sense of women's community which combatted single women's isolation would also impose a check on their exceptionalism.

Clark's relationship to the women's community provides a useful device for evaluating its successes and failures. Certainly her group associations did not contribute substantially to her success. For her and the rare women like her, the women's community might well have represented an unnecessary retreat from Chinese reality and from the sources of influence within the greater mission organization. The most prominent women missionary leaders, Luella Miner and Ida Lewis among them, seem to have been less involved than others in women's residences, undoubtedly for reasons similar to Clark's. For the bulk of the women who came to China as single women, however, the women's residences provided a means of converting a negative social stereotype into a positive source of identity. Lulu Golisch, for instance, who weighed over two hundred pounds and required an extra bearer when she traveled by sedan chair, wrote somewhat poignantly about the new life she had found in Chungking, deep in the interior: "We have a fine piano from America and [I] was a wallflower before I came but I keep it going quite lively now Sundays and out of study hour other days. . . . We have some fine times together." She preceded this by announcing, "I am getting to be a first class old maid,"[34] a fact she could accept with equanimity when it brought with it the joys of collective life in a house that unequivocally declared itself her home.

The centrality of female friendships in China was as natural to missionary women as their closer familial relations with mothers and sisters. Descriptions of intense female friendships, some lasting a lifetime, appeared routinely in letters home and were an accepted part of missionary life, as they were of American girls' school and female collegiate life at the time. Such friendships, like associations with home families and ladies' houses, were considered evidence of social and emotional health which might help to ward off the "oddity" or "queerness" of missionary isolation.

The prototypes for female friendships were relationships between natural sisters. Among the one hundred single women of the Congregational board in China between 1900 and 1920, there were eight pairs of sisters, five of which enlisted, worked, and lived together as constant companions during their mission stay. A difference in age characteristically allocated authority unevenly between sisters and fed a tendency present in most female friendships to exaggerate differences rather than to affirm similarities. Emma and Lizzie Martin, for instance, were born three years apart, the daughters of a farmer in Otterbein, Indiana. The elder and more clever Emma took a Student Volunteer pledge at DePauw University in the early 1890s and attended medical school. Meanwhile her younger sister was going to college and missionary training school. They arrived on the mission field in Peking just in time for the Boxer siege and counseled each other through its traumas. Their relationship was complementary. Emma wished she could be a man so she might participate more fully in the legation's defense. Lizzie attended to cooking and sewing, and after the siege did evangelical work with women and children. When the sisters were temporarily separated in Japan in the aftermath of the Boxer rebellion, Lizzie wrote that it was the first time they had been apart for as long as twelve hours since leaving home. "I almost feel like an orphan," she wrote. Another pair of sisters who divided the field of work along conventional sexual boundaries were the Woodhulls. Kate Woodhull did medical work, while her sister, two years younger, did evangelical work in the home she kept. One pair of sisters broke this pattern. The Wyckoffs, Gertrude and Grace, emphasized their similarities throughout a lifetime of shared service, even to the extent of dressing alike. But the Wyckoff sisters could not determine preeminence by age, because they were identical twins.[35]

The congeniality based on long acquaintance which existed between sisters also characterized some special friendships between unrelated women. Evelyn Worthley and Harriet Osborne were schoolteachers in Poughkeepsie, New York, before they went to China. When they applied to the Congregational board, they requested that they might be assigned together, for, as Worthley put it, "Our work together has been so delightful during the past year, and we can both accomplish so much more,—at least I can when working with her, that I very much hope we can secure work in the same station." Harriet Osborne was initially reluctant to let the board know her age, which at forty-two was beyond the official limit, but the board accepted both Osborne and the twenty-eight-year-old Worthley and posted them to a new station in Fukien to open a school. When Worthley married a missionary widower in 1907, the two women remained friends, although Osborne had to continue their formerly joint upcountry work alone. Often she would join the married couple for some of the summer months, but through her China years she remained bereft.[36]

Many missionary relationships, marriages among them, were based less on common prior experience than on common interest in missionary work. For many of the same reasons that women committed to missionary service might enter wedlock, they might also seek a female companion. Althea Todd, a Boston woman returning to China after the Boxer siege, advertised in a mission paper for someone to accompany her back to the Fukien uplands. Jessie Marriott, who had been associated with evangelist Dwight Moody in Chicago, answered the ad and the two embarked on a joint life of service. Todd nursed Marriott through smallpox; their itinerate evangeliz-

Twin Sisters, ca. 1885: Gertrude and Grace Wyckoff of Elmwood, Illinois, lived and worked together—and appear to have dressed identically—for their entire lives in the China mission field.

Special friends, ca. 1905: Evelyn Worthley and Harriet Osborne had requested to be posted together and are shown here in their Diongloh station.

ing service was said to take them a thousand miles a year on foot. They returned to the United States together in 1936 and later died within one hundred days of each other in the same missionary nursing home.[37]

The most notable special friendship on the mission field involved a Chinese woman, Shih Mei-Yu, popularly known in the United States as Mary Stone, who had received medical training under Methodist auspices at the University of Michigan. A talented, spirited woman, she became perhaps the most widely known symbol of the goals and successes of the Methodist women's work in China. As her own sister lay dying in 1906, she had met Jennie Hughes, a recently arrived Methodist missionary, and they remained inseparable for the rest of their lives. Correspondence in board files suggests a common assumption of Hughes's ability "to dominate Dr. Stone"; at any rate, when Hughes had a doctrinal dispute with the Methodist hierarchy in 1920 and her departure was announced, Hughes rather than Stone received the pleas of the board that Stone retain her Methodist affiliation.[38] Board efforts were unsuccessful, however, and the two women left to form their own mission to orphans in Shanghai.

Evidence as to the exact nature of this cross-cultural relationship is slim. Sarah Goodrich, who visited them in 1914, added slight substance to the board's supposition of Hughes's dominant role. She described her as "a slender body, intense and full of push," and Stone "as like a breeze" exuding "efficiency and good cheer." She noted that Stone managed their house, an interesting observation in view of the leadership role and extensive medical work that Methodist literature attributed to the "little Doctor." Mary Stone's own memorial tribute to her friend, circulated in 1952 by their Bethel Mission of China (by then in Hong Kong), celebrated a balanced friendship: "God gave me the most loving and wonderful companion for forty-five years. Friends said 'David and Jonathan were not in it.' They added, 'Jennie tones Mary up and Mary tones Jennie down—a good combination.' We called each other Gemini—'The Heavenly Twins.' She was the Occidental Gemini and I was the Oriental one."[39] Jennie Hughes and Mary Stone seem to have adopted a version of their friendship which, like relations between older and younger sisters, stressed complementarity. But instead of using sexual analogues to describe the balance between their active and acquiescent personalities, it is significant that they freely adopted the cultural analogues of Occidental and Oriental.

What can be made of this friendship and others like it? How should relationships of such duration and intimacy be interpreted? (Sarah Goodrich's letter to her son noted that Mary Stone managed the home, "Miss Hughes and she occupying one room and bed.") Like many aspects of female missionary life in the early twentieth century, special friendships between women manifested what have been considered nineteenth-century patterns. The separation of single women in women's residences made geographic the functional separation of male and female spheres which characterized American Victorian society. It was common for American women to develop deep friendships with those with whom they shared work and social rituals in America; the circumstances of China service made such friendships almost inevitable.[40]

The rhetoric of intense female friendships did not disappear in the United States in the twentieth century. The college letters of Jeanie Graham, who later went to China with her husband, recounted dormitory playfulness at Bates College, a coeducational institution, in 1912. Referring to sleeping in a friend's room, she explained to her parents that "Mary Smith is the Freshman that I got engaged to last term. She calls me her 'fancy.' As I am Bessie's husband, she threatens to get a divorce quite often."[41] Within four months, Graham confessed to having a "crush" on a boy in her class, and her female flirtations dropped out of her correspondence. In many ways, single women's missionary residences captured and preserved the spontaneous, innocent air of college dormitories.

As in dormitories, an atmosphere of emotional and physical intimacy existed in many of the women's houses. Lucy Mead, the best reporter of this atmosphere, mentioned sleeping with many different friends as a way of exchanging conversation and confidences; the communal circumstances of the women's houses rendered the nighttime and the bedroom the only time and place for private communication. Mead wrote that she slept with one friend "for fun of it. . . . We don't talk much after we get to bed till we wake up and don't go to breakfast."[42] If anything, this dormitory spirit seems more ingenuous than Jeanie Graham's sometimes coy tales of her college days.

But Lucy Mead was involved in a more serious relationship when she first arrived in China. This semimaternal association, in which an older woman intimately instructed a younger one in the spiritual life, seemed to be a particularly common form of special friendship within missionary communities. Such friendships promoted intergenerational harmonies as well as easing the transition into missionary service. Mead was twenty-five years old when she met Grace Wyckoff on shipboard. Wyckoff was a twin who, with her sister, had been in China for twenty-two years; they were returning together from furlough. In her letter home, Lucy Mead described "Miss Grace" as her "special":

> We were together so much she won the name of "chaperon." You may judge from the picture what a severe one she was. . . . They've been out 22 years, but Miss Grace and I were chums—so much alike in thots, interest and ideals. It was beautiful to be together. Neither of us love rough weather but we made the best of it by being side by side, either in chairs on deck or in the stateroom—often in one narrow berth.

The relationship continued to be of sufficient significance that after their arrival Mead felt the need for circumspection at a group function and deliberately settled herself away from either twin "lest comments might be made." Apparently she was being more careful than circumstances warranted, for she "was delighted" to have a message from Miss Gertrude asking her to come help serve her.[43]

The instructional nature of the friendship emerged in nighttime heart-to-heart talks, and most evocatively in a summertime Sunday ritual involving the twin sisters, Mead, and a fellow novice: "Sundays we do have such lovely times. Misses Grace and Gertrude go off together for an hour or so alone, then Gertrude Chaney and I hunt them up wherever they are in the shade of the rocks by the sea. We four then sing hymns, read addresses or sermons from [the] convention book, talk, have a prayer and sing some more." Following the group service, the couples recombined and Mead and "Miss Grace" went off for a private talk on the rocks, as presumably did Chaney and "Miss Gertrude." To Mead the drama of that particular service was sacred. "It is beautiful," she wrote, "the tie that binds our hearts is Christian love."[44] Certainly, though, as in much of the richest liturgy, the sacred drama derived from the symbolic reading of tangible human emotion.

Physical and emotional intimacy were one in the Mead-Wyckoff relationship. Mead's description of a shared night on a winter visit to the Wyckoffs' distant station suggests a kind of uncomplicated physical warmth which might have seemed a reasonable alternative to mysterious marital sexuality:

> When we reached Pangkiachuang about 8:30 we had supper and visit. I had nice hot bath and when returned to my room found Miss Grace

in bed. My we did cuddle up and love each other! "Two are better far than one For labor or for fight—For how can one keep warm alone— Or serve his cause aright? beats hot water bags out of sight." . . . We slept that night and early morning Miss Grace got up to crawl in with Miss Gertrude—we exchanged hugs and I went to sleep and next I knew 'twas 8 o'clock.

The language of this description, written in 1911 to Mead's home family, suggests a diffuse sexuality; the issue of genitality, so important to a modern age, did not seem to arise for those writing or reading about special friendships at the time. Indeed, Mead's light description, written to her parents, implies that such friendships were accepted as routine, and even healthy, for women into the twentieth century. Havelock Ellis, the British medical writer, had censured intimate female friendships of all kinds in his *Sexual Inversion* published fifteen years earlier (1895), formalizing a view which the culture would come to share. Well beyond the date when other historians see such sanctions as gaining acceptance, though, women on the mission field adhered without apology to the traditions of the female world of love and ritual.[45]

The passions in such relationships could be powerful and possessive. Rather than contributing cohesion to the women's community, rivalry over flirtations sometimes caused serious rifts. The unhappy correspondence of Anna Hartwell, an aging single woman in Shantung, is evidence of the lonely desperation which attended the wooing of new recruits at the loss of old friends. Following the death of her longtime companion Jane Thompson, whom she knew as "Tommie," Hartwell welcomed a young coworker with whom she immediately struck up an intimate, protective relationship. She copied adoring letters to Leila Watson, who was away at language school, into her own copybook, addressing her by the pet name "Dorothea" and signing her name "Evangeline." When Watson mentioned in a response that she felt herself spoiled, Hartwell wrote back maternally:

As I read I wanted to take you in my arms and say "No childie, I never want to "un-spoil" you,—neither gradually nor suddenly nor in any other way." If the way you were, when in H. H. with me those few happy days was you as you are in a spoiled condition then I want you spoiled always! . . . I sit here in my warm sunny sitting-room these chilly fall days, and think how cozy and dear it will be when you come and share my nest with me.[46]

Ultimately Watson and Jane Lide, another new recruit who was involved in a similar relationship with Anna's sister-in-law Bessie, did come to live with her in a single women's house. At the end of the year the house broke up, with some criticism that Anna was providing inadequate fare for her housemates. Anna was sent away by the mission doctor for recovery from what all described as a nervous breakdown.

Evidence from Anna's copybooks indicates that the main problem was rivalry between Anna and her married sister-in-law, Bessie Hartwell, over their relationships to the two younger women. This rivalry echoed earlier mutual jealousies over Bessie's husband and Anna's beloved brother, Charles Hartwell. But Bessie's letters indicate that now she, as much as Anna, was in a state of nervous collapse over her uncertain hold on her younger female friend. She claimed total possession of Jane to ward off the threat she perceived from Anna:

> I am sure that you are mistaking the sympathy which Jane is giving you for the sort of "love" which you always seem to demand of those whom you desire to hold, in life. . . . *You* must never expect to take *my* place with *her*, for you never can or will—it is impossible. The tie between Jane Lide and myself is rather unique, in a way, and is made of the stuff which holds, and is not easily broken. Our demand, one of the other, is loyalty—anything else is not to be tolerated at all. To my mind it is the one and only ground for faithful friendship between women. There can be no room for suspicion or jealousy, and no unhealthy weed should be able to grow in this soil.[47]

The desperation of Bessie and Anna Hartwell contrasts radically with the generous sharing of affections described by Lucy Mead. The differing ages of Mead and the Hartwells, among other reasons, surely contributed to their different experiences. Anna Hartwell's crisis, which occurred, she wrote, at menopause, pointed to problems which even the densest women's community did not seem able to solve: the problems of dying friends, of loneliness, and aging.

In a more controlled moment, Bessie Hartwell observed that she and her sister-in-law might have been caught by changing social mores as well as by their own increasing age. Writing in 1921 a few weeks after her tempestuous outburst, she judged that perhaps the nature of women's friendships was changing from those she and Anna were accustomed to. Her analysis heralded a new age:

> I cannot see why we should not all be friends without being lovers or confessors or any of the many relations which *must* be unhealthy, and

are dreadfully so. Life is changing much and women do not have these fearful crushes which once seemed frequently to happen. Everybody now is careful to assert his own personality, and I for one am most thankful that it is so.[48]

No longer did the need for social affiliation completely eclipse female individuality. Changing mores ultimately did cast a shadow on the crushes and romances of women such as Bessie and Anna Hartwell. It should be added, though, that both Watson and Lide appear to have been willing participants in the intrigue which undid the Hartwells. The mission field perhaps attracted women whose orientation, even in the 1920s, was toward an earlier, interdependent woman's world, rather than toward the sexually integrated world of the future, in which women as well as men were careful to assert their "own personality."

❦❦❦❦

The single women's community offered women missionaries an alternative to a marital family. Women's residences provided stable domicile, rituals of home, and opportunities for intimacy to those who lived there. They perfectly incorporated the domestic culture by which women defined themselves. Though women's households invariably required the surrender of privacy, no contract bound missionaries to any household, and to that extent single women were free. Women's communities did not encourage exceptional female achievement, but they did provide single women with the means to do the Lord's work, which was also their own. The single women's community offered a viable alternative to marriage, but it remains to be determined whether and for whom the institution of spinsterhood was a preferred or a radical alternative.

Married women in particular assumed that single women who joined missionary service had done so in desperation and were still in search of a husband. Contemporary folklore supported this supposition, as can be seen from the wide publicity granted four single women in central China named Hunt, Search, Seek, and Rob, "none of whom ever got a husband." To what extent was marriage an object for women serving single in the field? When provided with marriage options, did they take them? Certainly some of them did. Jessie Ankeny wrote about a woman in her conference who was to be married and concluded that "she was one who wanted a man badly and we all rejoice that she has one"; several commented at the marriage of a Foochow domestic science teacher that she was the "married type."[49]

There was, however, a distinct "unmarried type," and many women consigned themselves willingly to that category, looking with dismay upon the unwise matches made by less serene friends. Elsie Clark, who had strenuously rejected a suitor before her departure for China, expressed herself "shockt and a little saddened" upon hearing news of the engagement of her college friend Jessie Wilson, daughter of the newly sworn-in twenty-eighth president. "I've always thought of Jessie as a Diana," she wrote, and indeed the analogy to the protector of female autonomy could well have been applied to her own proud self. Luella Miner felt that life would have been easier on the mission field if she had been married, but confessed to her sisters that despite several proposals of marriage through the years, she had been unwilling to surrender her freedom. "She decided that she wouldn't get married unless the other was the 'better half,' " she wrote lightly of herself, "and she is so conceited that it isn't easy to find anyone whom she will accept as her superior in all respects." Even Ida Lewis, who was sensitive about her unwedded state, noted upon the marriage of both her brother and her sister that "then it will be for me to hunt a wife—I couldn't manage a husband."[50] Lewis, Miner, and Clark all had in common education, ambition, and positions of authority in China. For all of them, marriage would have meant a surrendering of professional autonomy and the necessity to perform uncongenial domestic tasks. All three felt that their strong personalities unsuited them for marriage's compromises. Their commitment remained to their mission, however, rather than to the single women's community itself.

Such devotion to mission did not permanently preclude marriage. Ida Lewis and Elsie Clark maintained active lives of service for a number of years, marrying rather suddenly within the context of full professional lives. Missionary widowers and young men, encouraged by the scarcity of Western women in China to look beyond conventional ages, were one source of unexpected proposals for some women. Jessie Ankeny married a persistent suitor she had been calling "the Kid" only after he had returned from the United States more mature, and Miss Heath was said to be "*years*" older than her intended. Ada Haven, "the last person in the world . . . that we would ever think of doing such a thing," was married for the first time at the age of fifty, after twenty-five years in single service.[51]

One woman admitted conscious intent in her life pattern of early work and late marriage. Like Elsie Clark, Welthy Honsinger said goodbye to a demanding suitor when she first set sail for China. Her later marriage at the age of forty-four, she felt, had allowed her to have it both ways. "The gamble was whether I could eat and have my cake," she wrote in her life story. "I wanted to do the work I did, and I found in the end the man who loved me for this and also for me." Welthy Honsinger and Elsie Clark used single service both as a retreat from conventional marriage pressures and as an opportunity to pursue a complex calling. Mission service, like school-teaching, bought women time; unlike schoolteaching, it also bought them space—away from blandishments, pressures, temptations. Mission service for such women was not a permanent Catholic commitment to a women's order, but rather a Protestant commitment to follow individual con-science, whether it led a woman away from home to China, or whether it led her, in the same spirit of experimentation, to enter wedlock.[52] Mis-sionary calling for such women was in part a commitment to self-determi-nation.

For a significant number of single women, however, mission service held appeal less for its freedom than for the nature of its community. Lucy Mead was a sociable, nonintellectual woman whose disinterest in marriage took a different form than Clark's and Honsinger's. She lacked the ambition which contributed to their service and did not share their distaste for the mundane duties of housekeeping, instead filling her letters with accounts of her garden and her sewing. In her domesticity, she was undoubtedly a more typical single woman missionary than such women as Luella Miner. (Mead once wrote that the sight of Miner sewing "dumbfounded the ladies," none of whom had ever seen her sew before.) When Mead had her "bumps" read by an amateur phrenologist, she concluded that the interpre-tation was correct: "love of home and children great," but "not care for men as men." She rebelled at the matchmaking efforts of a Peking matron and passed up the opportunity arranged by a Seattle hostess to take an auto ride around the city with " 'a nice young lawyer.' "[53] For such women as Lucy Mead, the single women's residence represented the fulfillment of domestic and of temperamental needs. For them, the single women's community was one of the few alternatives which could have satisfied their requirements for homelife and female society.

Whether women participated in the single women's community as a preferred alternative, or whether they used it as a refuge where they could live and work in peace, women's residences provided single women with a collective base for social autonomy. Unlike American spinsters, who were likely to be domestically as well as economically dependent, single women missionaries could participate within the greater mission community from a position that was dignified by their joint self-sufficiency. Women's houses supplied single missionaries with an identity that subverted ascriptions of oddness by institutionalizing them.

Their need for substitute families in China already supplied, single women paradoxically found the mission community more hospitable than when they were forced to live as members of surrogate families. The custom of incorporating new missionaries as family members conveyed warmth without incurring obligation to those already suitably accommodated. Corda Gracey, a former missionary married to a consul, wrote to Elizabeth Perkins's parents of her "adoption" in 1907. "Indeed, without her parents consent, I have quite adopted her into my heart, and our home will always be as open to her as her father's house. We shall hope she will come to us as to her parents and it will be our pleasure to receive her as a daughter." When Mary Gamewell wrote to Jessie Ankeny's parents of her selection as "our niece," Ankeny herself had to write to reassure her parents that they were not thus being replaced.[54]

These adoptions, which had few repercussions, were perhaps the only way of conferring particular intimacy in an entire overseas society which considered itself "a great big family affair." Mission service appealed to a pool of like-minded church people in the United States, and often single women encountered earlier acquaintances in a common small world in China. In the cities as well as the remote interior, however, women discovered hospitality and extended it equally to complete strangers. Since nationality itself proved a sufficient claim to friendship, members of the same board, whether the women's or general board, considered each other next of kin, "as it were one immense family."[55]

Relationships between single women and the men of the general boards partook of the intimacy of their joint endeavor in an alien land. Single women who had previously been part of such largely female professions as schoolteaching found that circumstances in China encouraged camaraderie which extended across sexual lines. Alice Reed put it most directly when she wrote home about the wealth of new friends she had made her first year in China, "especially among the young married people":

> I really have very few friends at home of that sort for I knew none of the husbands of my girl friends, but here are the MacEachrons, Mileses, Cadys, Robinsons, Childs and Arnolds, all of whom are personal friends of the finest kind, and I feel that they would do almost anything for me that my own family would. . . . I am enjoying getting acquainted with the husbands as well as the wives, for I lived through the years of my life in America without making very many men friends.

Married men tended to take a friendly, proprietary, and often chivalrous interest in the well-being of unattended women far away from home. Without fear of compromise, these relationships were often downright playful. Jessie Ankeny wrote of the impending visit of Mr. Caldwell that he "always brings fun with him and he would cheer any old maid." On his previous visit he had complimented her on how good she was looking and said, "Mrs. Lewis was letting out skirt bands but she was not so fat as I." For particular women, proprietary concern led to frank admiration. Edward Bliss wrote about Grace Funk that she "has an unusually fine mind, is warm-hearted, dresses well and is popular socially." He concluded that he hoped his brother would have a chance to meet a woman the likes of her. Ida Lewis expressed her appreciation for missionary men and attributed their exemplary conduct to the constraints of their estate: "Our missionary men are *mighty decent*—tho they're mostly married or engaged. Maybe that's the reason they're so nice." Prior commitment forced men to be "decent" to other women, as Lewis recorded; the conditions of joint missionary service allowed them to go beyond decency to be actually "nice."[56]

Such relationships were often patronizing. Male missionaries could not take seriously the young women and "old maids" whom they teased and flattered. At the same time, though, their good humor might well have reminded women of fathers and brothers at home, from whom they received a similar paternalistic acceptance. Freed from the indignities of private dependency by women's houses, single women could appreciate the family feeling which incorporated men, women, and children into one greater mission community.

The social acceptance that single women found in missionary community life in China did not bring with it political power. The separate sphere of single women's endeavor isolated their influence within the missionary society and limited their official voice to questions pertaining to women's work. In this, women's missionary work resembled such sex-segregated service professions as teaching or nursing in the United States. Historians have argued that missionary service represented a field for female achievement in which women had relative equality with men.[57] But women's inequality in voting rights, salary, and marital rights suggests that it is in other terms that missionary accomplishments must be evaluated.

The policies toward voting at station meetings held by the different denominations differed substantially but were consistent in curtailing the rights of women. Methodist women maintained a separate women's conference until at least 1927, and except in a consulting capacity did not participate in the governance of the general community, which was restricted to ordained ministers. The Congregationalist board in 1888 granted women neither the right to vote nor the right to speak at their station meetings. (Luella Miner wrote that she and the other women brought their crocheting.) By 1894, the American Board had decided that women in the field should have a voice, but only "in consideration of questions touching their own work," a policy which remained in effect until the 1920s. Female membership on important policy committees was limited to token representatives of women's work. The China Continuation Committee, for instance, an important 1913 interdenominational body which numbered fifty members in all, included twenty-nine missionary men, sixteen Chinese men, and five women, of whom one was Chinese. Chinese female church membership was substantially lower than Chinese male membership, though not in a proportion of one to sixteen, but missionary women constituted well over half the total mission body.[58]

Of course, a major source of inequities in the field lay within the structure of the home church. The Presbyterian denominations, as late as 1927, denied women lay privileges at home, a restriction that also limited the participation of women in the church polity in China. The Methodist conferences barred those who were not ordained and automatically barred women who were ineligible for ordination.[59] The reconstitution in China of the male domination of Protestant churches in the United States should not be surprising.

Women's subordinate status in the mission church was not solely a result of domestic church regulation, however. For though the policy of the home church and the parent boards determined ordination requirements in the United States and voting qualifications in the field, the women's boards themselves regulated the salary, the terms, and the admissions to service. Though the Congregational church had long ordained small numbers of women, its women's board at first turned down a woman minister applicant on the grounds of an "over insistent" personality. When the board later reconsidered her candidacy in 1909, she became its only ordained woman missionary in the China field in the period of this study. The women's board itself, whose 1869 constitution provided only for the appointment of "assistant missionaries and teachers," did not conceive of its mandate as the direct promotion of women's equality within the church hierarchy.[60]

The matter of salary was indicative of the women's boards' stance toward equality. The major historian of women's mission organizations concludes that "all missionaries were supposed to serve sacrificially, but women missionaries generally existed on mere subsistence salaries." As in church work at home, women's organizations paid women less than general organizations paid men.[61] Meaningful salary comparisons are difficult, because general board missionaries also had to support families, but the standard of living maintained by the single women in some cases did seem to fall below that of missionaries of the parent board. Anna Hartwell, who was also influenced by other concerns, compared her situation with her married sister-in-law's in these terms: "Bessie has the piano, and the music. . . . She has money—plenty of it, and no financial worries; she has a comfortable home, beautifully furnished—beautiful pictures,—her *den* with its outlook unobstructed. . . . She has an attractive home there; she sets a good table." Anna's breakdown, from severe personal tensions, seems to have been exacerabated by her financial problems, of which she was deeply ashamed. Luella Miner, perhaps a more objective viewer, protested the comfort of housing, furniture, and clothing enjoyed by some missionaries, but at the same time noted her feeling that "we single women economize too much on our food." Her protest that one meal did not last her until the next gains added validity in the context of the lifetime of self-denial her service represented, culminating in her decision in the 1920s to remit to the board a salary increase which she felt she did not need.[62]

The terms of service for both general and women's boards were austere. The minimum uninterrupted term of service for any board was five years, and the Congregational women's board only reduced their seven-year term to five years in 1919. The additional dependency of single women on home families made these conditions an especial burden for them. The most controversial condition of single women's service involved an implicit expectation that they would remain unmarried. When women chose to break this understanding, they were frequently subjected to the censure of the women's boards. Jessie Ankeny, for instance, received a "curt letter" from the Methodist women's board telling her she must stay, and the letter to Anna Kauffman expressed the Congregational women's board's "strong disapproval" of her plans. The boards could not ultimately prohibit marriage, but they did require the repayment of travel and outfit expenses if marriage, even to a fellow missionary, took place in the first term of service. On the occasion of the women's board's response to Kauffman, complaints were registered with the board by single Luella Miner, married Sarah Goodrich, and general board secretary James Barton. All three protested the policy which allowed a Protestant insititution to try to stand between a woman's conscience and her God on such a sacred, personal matter as matrimony.[63]

The success of the women's boards, however, rested exactly on an institutional appropriation of Christian feminine self-sacrifice. By paying low salaries to single women and asking for reimbursement, the women's boards made their money go further than the monies of the parent boards, which expected to support dependents as well. Perhaps the matrons who administered the women's boards were exploiting single women in their use of inadequately compensated labor, but single women were being willingly exploited. Service through self-sacrifice was an integral part of women's self-justification and conveniently took advantage of their social resources. The Peking residence that skimped on food and Luella Miner who remitted her salary slighted themselves instinctively. They demonstrated the automatic self-denial which allowed Emma Martin to write of her pity for a missionary man whose family was far away: "Its no easy job to be a missionary in this dreary land if a man (women don't count) has no home of his own to go to. I am awful sorry for the men."[64] Women's boards tapped the resources in which women were rich and used those available pools of labor and self-denial to aggrandize their collective reputation and moral stature.

For if women occupied subordinate positions in the mission field, if their salaries were lower and their houses less comfortable, their boards tended to be more solvent. Luella Miner wrote in 1894 that the general board appropriations, but not the women's board appropriations, had been cut 23 percent, and again in 1905 that the general appropriations were less than half of what had been asked. "Our brave women's boards granted in full all that we asked, even to new appropriations for building," she wrote. "What is the trouble with the men in our home churches? Do they give all of their spare money to their wives to take to woman's mission meeting?" The truth was not that the women's boards were wealthier than the men's, but only that they allocated funds more economically. Undoubtedly also, women workers in the field made more modest requests than did male missionaries. Emma Martin, working with the Methodist board in North China, urged her father on two separate occasions to give to the parent board rather than the women's board, for "there is a law that our ladies cannot go anywhere except where there is a parent family lives."

The money-raising apparatus of the women's boards in the United States and the working power represented by the field staff appeared attractive to the beleaguered general organizations; since the inception of women's work, the parent boards continuously struggled to reintegrate the women's work under their control.[65]

Historians of the mission movement as a whole, however, suggest an additional reason for the interest of the general boards: "the wide-spread masculine fear that this missionary effort primarily masked the woman's suffrage and Woman's Rights movement." Other historians conclude that men eventually came to favor women's work overseas because it deflected rather than incorporated the feminist energies likely to be more upsetting at home.[66] Were churchmen correct to fear the women's missionary movement for its feminist potential? Or did women's uplift overseas successfully divert women's enthusiasms in conservative directions? To what extent were the single women in the early twentieth-century China field feminists?

Increasingly in the twenty-year period preceding the 1920 passage of the woman's suffrage amendment, a few single women came to China with a suffragist position which they were willing to defend aggressively. Women with these views tended to be graduates of eastern women's colleges such as Mount Holyoke and Goucher, rather than graduates of the conservative, midwestern, coeducational colleges that supplied much of the missionary body. Their advocacy of American women's rights sparked their original interest in missionary service. But China service did not nourish their commitment nor foster an American feminist consciousness among other single women. Women who maintained their feminist perspective did so without influencing or receiving the support of the older, entrenched single women's community. Thus, at the same time that Elsie Clark was answering the query "Is Miss Clark a suffragist?" with the response, "Surely I am. . . . Don't I look intelligent?" Luella Miner was decrying the outrage of the Chinese women's suffrage movement and advocating in its stead the significant innovations of women's education and moral reform.[67]

Perhaps those churchmen who anticipated the deflecting effect of mission work on Christian initiatives for women's rights were correct in the short run. Advocacy of the rights of Chinese women to education and to freedom from footbinding allowed American women safely to displace and diffuse any personal frustrations onto a woman's crusade with which no American man could take issue. Challenging Chinese boundaries provided the satisfaction of an actual, righteous women's struggle without the internal conflicts that would inevitably arise from a more direct, self-referential feminism. For feminism to have gained a foothold among the women's missionary community would have entailed the replacement of the underlying premise of women's mission work, self-denial, with its opposite, self-advocacy.[68]

More basic, even, than feminine taboos against self-advocacy was the nature of the women's mission enterprise itself. Women who volunteered as missionaries did so for spiritual reasons that impelled them to personal service. They aimed to convert through Christian love rather than administrative skills, and their backgrounds had rarely equipped them to be sensitive to inequities of power. Elsie Clark's distress at the procedural incompetence of her associates, confessed only to her diary, undoubtedly could have applied to other conferences besides her own. She wrote:

> I was greatly sickened by the haphazard inefficient way in which our women's conference proceeds to business, in the electing of a president who entering upon the positions suddenly is entirely unfamiliar with what is to be done. The proceedings were really insulting to the intelligence of the Chinese women. I felt dispirited enough to cry; felt like severing all connection with such an organization. I reproacht myself too with being as bad as the rest for not protesting and making a stand for other methods. Ah, I was tired.[69]

Missionary women often had had no experience in leadership, having been chosen primarily for their religious sincerity. They were rarely politically sophisticated.

At the same time, however, their collective service furthered a pride in the "honor of the Women's board" which was perhaps a necessary precursor to political consciousness. Despite customary chivalry from the men in peaceful times, in times of real danger the single women were prepared to fend for themselves and did not expect the same protection afforded wives and children. And though parent board policy preferred the stationing of single women only where there were representatives of the parent board, in numerous instances where families could not or would not go, the single women went on alone. The circumstances of women's missionary service allowed for the cultivation of "esprit de corps," in Elsie Clark's language, in an arena of sufficient colonial liberties that such constraints as were imported from home simply ceased to feel like constraints and perhaps even to *be* genuinely restrictive of Western women's movements.[70]

Greater restrictions at home produced more conscious feminist orienta-tion among the administrators and secretaries of the women's boards in the United States than among missionaries in the field. Though not advocates of individual rights, the women's board secretaries were loyal defenders of the economic and administrative autonomy of their organization. Unlike missionaries, who took as their adversaries a wide range of "heathen" practices, the women's board administrators had as their genuine adversar-ies the aggrandizing male parent boards. Women's work in the United States in supporting missions, according to a 1927 report, proved the "largest expression of women's organized work within the church" and could be credited with gains which eventually extended well beyond their mission concerns. If women's actual mission work in foreign countries did not involve confrontation with male authorities, women's domestic sup-port for that work sometimes did. When women missionaries diverted essentially feminist energies into self-denying service to other women, these energies circulated back into the women's boards at home in the boards' defense of women's right to control their own self-sacrifice.[71]

As for the women in the field, they found in mission service a rare opportunity to synthesize limited aspiration with broad accomplishment. They discovered scope for their capacities but at the same time embodied high feminine ideals of personal service. Inequalities in salary or voting rights verified the feminine credentials of the service rather than constrain-ing its possibilities. Mission service thus offered both the opportunity for self-fulfillment and the ideology for self-denial. Somewhat paradoxically, though, it was just this individual self-sacrifice in the field which led to the strength of the women's boards in the United States. What had started as feminine submission of self provided the basis for the self-advocacy of home-board feminism.

But it would be a mistake to overemphasize the distinctions between the field and the home office, or to overstress the contrast between feminine abnegation and feminist self-advocacy. The opportunities for achievement under the guise of submission were in many ways equal to those available under more overtly ambitious pretexts. The women's missionary endeavor provided ample scope for female temperaments that were simultaneously self-effacing and imperious.

4

MARRIED WOMEN

AND MISSIONARY VOCATION

Over half the women missionaries who went to the field as wives were married in the year of their departure for China, and many of them spent their honeymoons cramped by seasickness and bad weather in cabins below deck. Some married only for love and found themselves thrust bemusedly into mission service by the zeal of the men they wanted to marry. But for most women, marriage to a missionary confirmed a vocational and religious decision along with a romantic one. Those who met their husbands in missionary training school or at a Student Volunteer convention had made a prior commitment to service which matrimony only reinforced.

To women reluctant to set off around the world alone, marriage to a missionary often seemed God's vehicle for the fulfillment of their calling. Jennie Wortman's story has been elaborated in chapter 2. Carie Sydenstricker, mother of Pearl Sydenstricker Buck, resolved to become a missionary at her mother's deathbed, but, like Wortman, she was aided by a man in her efforts to see her way to the mission field. She married for her soul rather than her heart, according to her daughter, and saw in her union the possibility to know God and do His will. Jeanie Graham, as a Bates College student many years later, broke off several romances because her suitors did not share her commitment to mission service. Graham's requirement of the men who paid her court was also a requirement she made of her own life: she would live a vital, consecrated, public life in far-off lands, and if she could have company, so much the better. If not, Graham was prepared to go by herself. Few were quite as strong-minded as she, but most shared her sense of missionary marriage as a partnership in service. [1]

Women setting out for China as missionary wives generally brought with them ambitions to carry out missionary work and the personal resources to carry through on their resolve. Wife and husband shared an assumption that together they would do the Lord's work. The sex segregation of "heathen" societies furthered this joint understanding: the husband would see to the men and his wife to the women. Certainly missionary husband and wife were not entirely equal, but then, neither were the men and women of the host society. This inequality was less significant, in the eyes of new missionaries, than their shared purpose. Husband and wife expected to bear the same relationship to "their people." Both would be shepherd, apostle, sibling, and solace. Both would have a compelling vocation.[2]

There was much that was both naive and courageous about these women as they set out with their husbands to meet their fate. With only the mythic, romanticized wives of missionary propaganda as their models, they were bolstered by faith and their own sense of mission. They knew the cost of their commitment, and they could only imagine that God would honor it by allowing them to do the work He so obviously wanted done. In many ways, however, these married women were mistaken in their estimate of God's plan for them. Unanticipated children brought down-to-earth responsibilities which could compromise the most divine female ambition.

In these early days, the likelihood that they would have children did not seem to enter the minds of many missionary women. They rarely mentioned children in their hopes for missionary service and they seem to have been unprepared when children materialized in the mission field. When Carie Sydenstricker was first pregnant, her daughter wrote, she could not imagine what was ailing her. "Somehow she had taken it for granted that she would not have children since she had dedicated herself to a cause." Jennie Wortman Campbell, who already had three children when she went to China, wrote to her sister that she had always thought that a small family would be best for her, and "coming to China thought that would excuse me from raising more children." This evidence suggests that some married women missionaries subscribed to the nineteenth-century notion that a vigorous public or professional life was incompatible with a woman's procreative function. Commonly used as an argument against higher education or public life for women, this logic could perhaps serve equally

well to allow women to contemplate public work and marriage simultaneously. For missionary women, such thinking might even have amounted
to a theory of vocational birth control.[3]

Those few who confronted the issue directly seem to have acknowledged
the difficulties children would present to a woman engaged in the missionary cause. At the same time, they recognized only the most limited forms of
control over conception. Florence Brown wrote her fiancé in China in
1893 about their plans, couching her rumination in delicate prose: "It has
been a great question in my mind whether such desires should be wholly
subdued after marriage; in other words, whether people should marry
unless they are satisfied that they are ready to undertake any responsibilities such a relationship would naturally bring." She concluded that perhaps
they should not marry were they to practice abstinence thereafter, as
they seem to have been planning. Postponing their marriage was clearly
unacceptable to both, however, and they were married upon Brown's
arrival in China, remaining childless for three years. Restraint as a form of
birth control seemed to be expected by some mission communities, which
considered excessive family size to be in bad taste.[4] Children and China
service presented complex problems for each other, and perhaps for this
reason married women who had received a missionary call often did not
stop to consider the possible inconsistencies in their plans.

Anna Seward, who arrived as a single woman, found herself married and
pregnant before three months had elapsed. Carie Sydenstricker also became pregnant within her first three months in China. Gertrude Kellogg
became pregnant on the voyage over. The arrival of missionary couples in
China, where everything was strange, often coincided with their first
domestic acquaintance with each other, the launching of their careers, and
the arrival of their first children. Both husbands and wives found China
alien and threatening, and both at first participated eagerly in the domestic
chores attendant upon their status as new arrivals, newlyweds, and new
parents. In their joint private existence, women and men found, at least
temporarily, a companionship in missionary endeavor.

The disorientation which missionaries felt at first led to a natural desire
to reestablish familiar rituals in a familiar setting. For American missionaries living in China, the only such setting was the home, and the rituals
available there were traditionally female ones. Thus, when Jeanie Graham
McClure made fondant candy, her husband was glad to beat it for nearly
forty minutes, and when Grace Smith was making a dress she got her
husband to help her. "You girls would have had convulsions, I guess," she

wrote to her sisters, "if you had seen Ned trying to drape a waist and get the one-sided artistic effect I had in mind."[5] The involvement of men in women's domestic work, which would have been rare in the United States of that time, seemed patterned instead on the participation of American boys in household chores.

What was a natural temporary regression, however, could eventually become a sign of maladjustment. Lida Ashmore described several recently arrived male missionaries and noted that one, who had no confidence in their Chinese help, "mixes the milk and gets diapers and watches (or did) during the bath." Six years later she observed the same response in another missionary, who "does not do much of anything but play with his baby. . . . He spends hours with it and then complains that he will ask to be sent some place else if he is not given more equipment."[6] Both husband and wife relied on homelife as a refuge in a strange land, but because the home was a female preserve, the wife frequently directed the activities. In their early days in China, women's prior experience in the home granted them the dominant role.

Practical reasons also dictated the participation of men in household work. The care of new infants temporarily marshaled young husbands in female routines which extended well beyond the realm of diversion, recreation, or comfortable home ritual. At times of childbirth, prior to the engagement of Chinese nurses, husbands were the linchpins of the domestic work unit. Jeanie McClure reassured her family that in their village station, husbands did not go itinerating beyond easy recall for two months preceding and following a birth. In these early days of married and China life, women frequently mentioned their husbands' handiness with their children and their willingness to assist in cooking. Before their acquisition of fluent language skills and substantial station responsibilities, young men, like the single women who drew the job of housekeeper, provided labor sufficiently dispensable that it was easily surrendered to domestic imperatives. Most often men were expected to pitch in at their own homes only, but occasionally, as in the case of Edward Manly who drew frequent babysitting stints prior to his own marriage, they helped out in other homes as well.[7] In the first days in China, husband and wife did seem to be participants in a partnership, but it was a partnership of domestic mainte-nance rather than Christian service.

The assistance of men at times of childbirth led to a gradual reversal of authority. Emily Hobart valued her husband's advice above her doctor's, "as he will have all the bother if I get sick," and stayed at home long after the birth of her child. "I feel sorry for the poor women at home who have to have a hired nurse to take care of them when they are sick instead of their husbands," she wrote. "There are many compensations in life out here after all."[8] Men erred on the side of caution in their unaccustomed responsibility for their wives' health, and began to formalize an attitude which seriously circumscribed the work that women could do. The interdependence of missionary couples, which proved to be the grounds for initial comradeship, quickly became converted into a protective chivalry which undermined the basis for equality in work.

Jessie Ankeny, for instance, had been an intrepid member of the women's board who delighted in the adventures of solitary itinerating when she married Henry Lacy. Her husband, at the instruction of his missionary father, insisted that she take two-hour naps every day after their marriage, and "wouldn't hear" of a twelve-mile walking trip she proposed; "so I suppose I won't get even to do it," she wrote. A Chinese friend, who could not pronounce the English s sound, had told her before her marriage "how nice Jessie Lazy would sound!" Lacy went on, "I did not appreciate the joke then as I do now for surely no one could be much lazier. I sleep a lot and Henry only encourages me in my easy life so I don't know what will become of me if I don't get busy soon." Jeanie McClure's husband was carrying her up and down stairs a month after the birth of her son, a precautionary measure that she explained to her family as "going thru what we foreigners all have to because we come to China."[9] Even strong-minded missionary mothers were reluctant to take risks with what they perceived as a biological responsibility to present and future children. They generally complied with restrictions on their physical activity, and thereby set the stage for acquiescence in other activities as well.

The limited expectations of others combined with women's own fears to lead women voluntarily to restrict their study of the Chinese language. Language study in some form was imperative for everyone. Without a good command of the language, day-to-day functioning in China was difficult, the preaching or teaching of the Christian word impossible. Often at first, particularly after the establishment of union language schools, husband and wife would receive equal tuition, devote comparable amounts of time to the arduous acquisition of strange tones and stranger written characters, and become classmates—with all the rough equality thus implied. Without children or the imminent arrival of children, missionary couples who lacked access to a language school could still establish their own egalitarian routine, which closely approximated the original ideal of joint service. After Florence Brown had arrived and married Edward Manly, he described their life to his family in balanced terms: "We are enjoying our work. Florence studies and takes care of the house. I study and take care of the school. We both have to talk Chinese a great deal. Florence has women visitors and I must talk to the school."[10] Though the wife's location in the home and her husband's in the school ostensibly represented separate female and male spheres, wife and husband shared immediate goals, similar techniques, and a common global purpose.

This initial equality in language training, however, often broke down over important inequalities in expectations of husband and wife on the part of the mission board. Acknowledging the primacy of language skills to mission work, in the late nineteenth century mission boards had instituted language examinations which young missionaries must pass as a condition of their continuing service. Wives were sometimes exempt, however, or required to meet substantially lower language standards than their husbands. Bessie Ewing wrote home that she intended to take examinations anyway in September of 1896; but by the beginning of the following year, due perhaps to lack of encouragement as well as family responsibilities, she had relinquished that hope. Netta Allen, who was studying at the Peking language school when she was pregnant with her second son, wrote that the school head "was very tender with me for some reason. He ruled some with an iron rod, but he never came down on me. In fact, he would never let me do all that I wanted to. I was not allowed to read or write; all I could do was talk."[11] The chivalry which led missionary boards and husbands to protect women from physical strain could sometimes extend to discouragement of their mental exertions.

Other subtle factors sometimes influenced women's decisions to curtail language study. Many missionary wives found the spoken language easier to learn than did their husbands. Esther Lewis's daughter thought that her mother's music training allowed her to grasp the tonal principle of Chinese more easily, but recent studies on second-language learning indicate that perhaps cultural conditioning might have accounted for the difference in language facility. These studies suggest that those with "empathetic personalities" find language learning easier than those with strong needs for mastery.[12] Turn-of-the-century American women still defined themselves according to their powers of the heart and cultivated their abilities to identify and sympathize with others. This capacity undoubtedly served them well when facing an earnest Chinese teacher begging in pantomime for their efforts and good will.

The Chinese language consistently thwarted those who tried too hard. "If our main job out here were to master the Chinese language," one missionary woman wrote home, "we might as well all take bookings for home before we begin, for it just can't be mastered." More dependent on command of their environment for their self-esteem, men, perhaps, were more likely than women to be overwhelmed with shame at their manifest inadequacy. If speaking another language was like "wearing fancy dress," as another theory proposes, this too might explain women's greater facility. The strange sounds of Chinese might have struck turn-of-the-century American women as an embellishment or an amusement, but American men as an affectation.[13]

In any case, the skill of a wife in the acquisition of language, which was the precondition for all other professional success, often caused both husband and wife dismay. Martha Crawford's nineteenth-century diary finds her repeating and suffering over the shame her husband expressed at his inadequacy in speaking Chinese: "The contrast would be observed always unfavorably to him. It would be bitter that he [be] in any respect inferior to his wife. It would be a continual trial. This was unexpected to me. I had prayed long and earnestly that God would make me willing to see my husband daily outstripping me. . . . But O I was not prepared for this." Martha's prayers for stoicism in her submission of self suggest that, for her, submerging the competitive instinct may not have been easy—leaving her with guilt over the success she prayed she would not want. Like T. P. Crawford, Pearl Buck's father found his wife's skill "a little trying . . . reared as he had been in the doctrine of male superiority," his daughter wrote. In common with Esther Lewis's husband and many other missionary men, Andrew Sydenstricker exerted himself in the mastery of written characters, rarely considered necessary for women to acquire, thus making him a "real scholar" and reestablishing his linguistic preeminence in this marriage.[14]

Jeanie Graham McClure solved the problem of her language superiority herself. As an undergraduate at Bates College she had had a brilliant record, which included high achievement in Greek and in mathematics (where she was one of the few women in the class) and leadership of a host of activities ranging from women's basketball to the YWCA. It was Jeanie Graham who had dismissed several suitors because they had not taken the

Student Volunteer pledge. Her early life suggested that she would be a dynamic, spirited missionary wife, unafraid of competition and eager to participate in all spheres open to her. For their first year in China in 1916, Jeanie and the husband she adored were stationed in Nanking for language study. As her early record predicted, Jeanie did well, but her husband, his difficulties aggravated by the diminished aptitude of greater age, found the language fearfully difficult. Jeanie confided in her family a year later that his troubles were great enough that only her confidence that he would eventually be "a splendid missionary" kept her from getting discouraged about him. Her account of a skit presented at the end of the language-school year in April 1917 undoubtedly had some relevance to the problems the Chinese language had created for the McClures:

> One scene was supposed to be between a Language School wife and husband. He says he got 77 and she says she got another 100. Then he says not to rub it in and that if she spent as much time over him as she does over characters he wouldn't be wearing such holey socks. She's getting nervous and will probably get sick and exchange is only $1.62. Then she says he thinks more of the money than of her and begins to cry—then he comforts her, of course. She forgives him and then reminds him that they still have a half hour before supper in which to practice characters. It was very funny and came so perilously near the truth in some instances that we students could well appreciate it.

The light humor perhaps temporarily diffused tensions between Jeanie and Bob McClure, but the problem remained. Since qualification for the vote in mission meetings after 1914 was linked to language proficiency, Jeanie won the privilege before her husband. When she wrote home to tell her family, however, she added, "I don't intend to avail myself of the privilege until Bob gets it too."[5] Jeanie McClure was for a while unique among the wives of her station in her language ability and in the voting privilege it bestowed upon her. Her public career, however, had peaked at this point. Thereafter, she set herself to raising a family and maintaining an ideal home for her itinerating husband to return to. Her missionary work was limited to occasional assistance in the boys' school. Her daughter remembered later that neither of her parents had ever achieved particular facility with the local dialect.

Jeanie McClure's voluntary limitation of her language achievement represented the surfacing of conservative feminine values, perhaps observed as a child, which had lain dormant during her high-spirited adolescence. A letter to her parents a month after she had declined the vote informed them that they would probably find her more pleasant to have around than she used to be. "Three years of wedded life have noticeably softened my sharp corners," she wrote, "and developed hitherto unguessed powers of self-control and self-denial."[16] For Jeanie McClure, growing up meant taking her place within a tradition of women who surrendered ambition to the emotional imperatives of marital harmony. And Jeanie McClure's was not an isolated case. Despite women's early skill in learning Chinese, the implicit priority of men's careers insured that husbands would ultimately surpass wives in language facility as well as in other measures of missionary success in China.

❦❦❦❦❦

The problems married women encountered in continuing their work were partly a result of their own upbringing. Their ambiguous institutional status contributed to their difficulties. Technically under the salary and support of the parent men's boards, their work often fell into areas controlled and administered by the separate women's boards. Missionary wives who had been the original pioneers in women's work increasingly found their position unsure, their authority under question, and their efforts unremunerative. The women's boards, interested in a high return on their investments, were rarely willing to support mothers with children at home. Sarah Goodrich, once a single woman worker who as a young mother had resigned from the women's board to preempt her dismissal, in later years led the crusade to gain more support for married women.

Goodrich maintained that it was the responsibility of the women's board to provide a schoolteacher for women's children, freeing them for service, "as we ladies . . . would all do woman's work"; but at the same time she acknowledged the habitual attitude of the women's board "never other than in words to enter into the life of missionary wives and mothers." When the girls' school she had founded ran into funding problems in 1905, she fired off an angry letter of complaint to the women's board, the contents of which she summarized for her husband: "Someone must tell the *truth*. . . . The money for our little School could be raised if it was Miss Brown's work. . . . I don't believe one little [?] bit if after all I have spoken in New England and for that Board but money could be raised for my school too."[17] The women's boards, although not antagonistic to the work of wives in the field, did not support the work of married women or lend their

Marital realignments, ca. 1919: Jeanie McClure, shown here with her husband Robert, wrote that "three years of wedded life have noticeably softened my sharp corners." Earlier, a mission skit had teased, "if she spent as much time over him as she does over characters he wouldn't be wearing such holey socks."

extensive auxiliaries to its aid. They considered missionary wives and their work the responsibility and financial liability of the men's boards.

The women's board's censure of a single woman worker's decision to marry provided an occasion for Sarah Goodrich to express her resentment at the board's discrimination against married women and families. In refusing to support married women, the women's boards, themselves consisting largely of married women, she wrote, were abdicating responsibility for the influence of the American family on Chinese society; without the influence of American homes, the Protestant endeavor would be no different from the sterile efforts of Catholicism: "Women like bargains, and so married women at home prefer to support the work of single women, so as to get full time, and their money's worth. All married women, and the children with their lives that are doing more than all the preaching to change the child life of China must be supported by men. *God bless the men of our churches!*" To the engaged woman herself her advice was more moderate. She summarized it for her husband:

> I could only place before her, as I would before my own daughter, the need of single women, and the much more in quantity they can contribute to the work. I could portray the life of a single woman. . . . a life rich in rewards, a life too of great peril, lest there be crushed out what God meant to be its most beautiful development. I could also portray before her the life of a missionary wife, for a goodly number of years disappearing, as it were, so as to reappear in the children; a life little valued by the mission women at home, a life of real sacrifice, but if met rightly, a life rich in love.[18]

Goodrich's language reveals her own ambivalence. Ultimately, for her as for others, the truly feminine was validated by its sacrifices rather than by its rewards.

Married missionary women, caught between their original mission ambition and their limited possibilities, found the lack of sympathy of the women's board at home particularly painful. Women who justified their sacrifices for family and motherhood on the basis of their female natures were chagrined to observe that American womanhood, at least as represented by the women's board, was extending the greater honor and monetary reward to single women. Goodrich again was eloquent on this point:

> Somehow this question of matrimony for our single ladies must be settled, so that God's appointed plan for united lives must not be made to seem a stepping down from some high plan to a lower

one. . . . With woman's entrance into new fields and new occupations, marriage becomes an interruption to a career; hence it has come to be thought by many to be a lowering of ideals. . . . Let us get back to fundamentals. Is marriage of his ordaining?[19]

The matrons of the women's board had followed the logic of economy to an endorsement of spinsterhood which seemed to challenge the domestic ideal that lay at the heart of their enterprise.

It is understandable that women who had been thus deserted would occasionally express resentment toward the single women who were receiving the special support of American women, and that they would focus their attacks squarely on the issue of the femininity of those who chose the single life. Lida Ashmore maintained a particular antipathy to many of the single women in the Swatow station. "For pure hard-heartedness and unsympathy give me an old maid Dr.," she wrote home. Sarah Goodrich, who truly championed many single women, in her letter of complaint about the treatment of Anna Kauffman, lost momentary control: "I honor beyond words many bachelor women, but I have my scorn for the selfish lives of hundreds of them, who crush their woman's nature, so as to live lives of greater ease and independence."[20]

Perhaps this sense of inequity at some level encouraged missionary matrons in their sport of matchmaking. Lucy Mead wrote home about one married woman who had said "she was going to do her level best to marry off all the single ladies." In view of the total dependence of the women's board on the single woman's work, this merry plan betrayed a lack of sympathy for the difficulties of the women's boards. The marriage of workers was a constant problem for such women as North China Union Women's College president Luella Miner. Though she too complained of the censure of Anna Kauffman at the time of her engagement, she protested the romantic scheming of married women and dared to voice her wish "that some of our married ladies felt more strongly the obligations of unmarried women to the boards which support them."[21]

Missionary wives initially affiliated with a parent board at their time of enlistment and, lacking encouragement from the women's boards, remained dependent on the general boards for their needs as mothers and as field-workers. Sarah Goodrich's plea for a teacher was abject: "Some way you *fathers* have always been the ones to whom we turn. You had mothers once. You can guess how our mother hearts long that in the lifting up of the world we may not be asked to pay a price above that which is necessary."[22] Goodrich's shameless appeal reflected the powerlessness of her situation.

As a married woman she lacked a true institutional advocate. Her success with the parent board was to be based largely on the pathos of her pleas rather than her importance to the work.

For in point of fact, though women of the American Board at this time had limited voting privileges, like married women of other boards, they were considered by the parent board to be extensions of their husbands. The Episcopal Protestant policy of requiring widows to return to the United States, for example—a policy which denied them livelihood and uprooted them from their homes—reflected this perception. The Presbyterian station meetings which Pearl Buck remembered from her youth dramatized the status of missionary wives in the work. Women were not even allowed to speak in this conservative denomination into the 1920s, but instead sat by their husbands knitting: "They all knitted those women while their men gave reports and passed laws of the church and made prayers. Their strong hard fingers flew while they had to remain mute. Into these stitches went what curbed desires and stubborn wills and plans! They would have burst without that vent." Pearl Buck's deep feminism had its origins in her outrage at the treatment of her missionary mother by both her father and the Presbyterian church, which followed Saint Paul in discrediting the contributions of the Christian woman.[23]

In matters of the work, projects undertaken by married women remained subordinate to men's projects. Lida Ashmore, who briefly ran a girls' school, tried to negotiate with her husband for the use of a larger space at his disposal, but as in decisions within the family, his word prevailed. "Of course the girls will have to be crowded and the boys have their 6 or 7 empty rooms. It is the same old story enacted over again here." This flash of rebellion was uncharacteristic, for Lida Ashmore customarily deferred to her husband. When she worked at all, she did so with his encouragement and under his auspices. Elected editor of the woman's department for a mission publication, for instance, she wrote, "Dad wants me to do it. I tell him I am not smart enough, that I do not know enough, but he seems to have unlimited confidence in me, so I may try it." The "unlimited confidence" of a husband could prove an unexpected burden for a dutiful wife. In 1912, Lida's husband William took on two jobs against her advice, as Superintendent of Sunday Schools and manager of the station bookstore; "and now he wants me to do the work," she complained.[24] As assistant missionaries to their husbands and to the parent boards as a whole, married women remained caught within domestic and male hierarchies.

Married women sometimes became involved in conflicts between their husbands and women's board workers. Lida Ashmore ended up as an unwilling pawn in one of many such misunderstandings. When Ashmore sensed a conflict with a single woman about who would supervise the local day schools, she backed off from her claim immediately. When she told William Ashmore that she had withdrawn, however, "he did not approve because he said then I would have nothing to do in missionary work and for one he was not willing to admit that married women had no place or work to do." For men who felt threatened by the independence of the women's boards, the work of their wives represented a source of information and a potential avenue of influence. Power struggles between parent and women's boards were not infrequent, and married women often ended up, perhaps partly because of women's board exclusivity, allied with their husbands against their own sex.[25]

Their work sporadic and inadequately supported, married women were often insecure about their capabilities in relation to those of single women. Though married women in earlier days had less educational background, by 1900 the preparation of wives and single women was remarkably similar. Nonetheless, married women constantly deferred to single women in matters of work. Mildred Rowland turned over the organ playing in the church to a Miss B., "as she can play better than I," but also because "I think it would suit Miss Glover better." Three months later she announced that she was temporarily supervising some industrial work only until the arrival of a single woman, a Miss Week. "I am going to try to work her into it, show her the stitches and then let her boss the women for she is a better boss than I am," she wrote.[26] The full-time, unhampered commitment to mission work made by single women impressed married women as itself an indication of ability. Married women experienced their own divided mandate as diminished competence.

Whether deferential or antagonistic, married women seemed to maintain an abiding respect for the accomplishments and the efficiency of the women's boards. Mildred Rowland compared the men's boards unfavorably with the women's, reflecting that "maybe in the next eight or nine years they will have things on as sound a basis as the ladies are running their missionary work."[27] The overwhelming success of the women's boards in running a sustained, solvent, varied program inspired vicarious excitement as well as distanced admiration in married women, who had rarely been able to sustain their individual work. Women whose work was circumscribed by their husbands' ideas, as well as their own domestic obligations, could grow wistful at the freedom and autonomy of women's board workers.

Jennie Campbell's jealousy of one single woman worker was palpable. Her second year in China, Campbell found herself alone in a Swatow foreign community caring for her children, while her husband made preparations in the new country station they were to open. Jennie wrote him repeatedly that she was longing to begin the work, was forgetting the Hakka language she had learned, and was prepared to join him at any time with their children in whatever accommodations he could arrange. The consensus of the foreign community judged their station in 1890 an unsafe location for Western children, however, so Jennie reverted to patient waiting, feeling, as she wrote her family, that "I have not yet crossed the threshold of missionary life." But arrangements had already been made for George Campbell's sister, who was also Jennie Campbell's best friend, to join them as a worker for the women's board. Her husband's lively interest in the aid of his sister, a free agent who could bring energy and talent uncomplicated by family responsibilities, inspired Jennie with envy: "George wants to take you with him up to Ka-yin-chu for a while. This I am sure you will find *very* pleasant. I wish I could look forward to being with you. George seemed set last year on having you outdo the natives in getting up the language."[28] Women chafing to work found it painful that they should be valued less rather than more by the husbands for whom they had sacrificed their possibilities. Certainly part of the problem experienced by married women was the lack of institutional support for the work they had come to do. The women's boards offered them no tangible encouragement, and the men's boards, like the men themselves, subordinated the work of wives to the needs of husbands. Though both claimed that wives were mission workers, neither honored that claim by distinguishing possibilities for their mission work from their service to husband and family.

❧❦❧❦❧

The mission boards were no different from the married women themselves in granting priority to women's family responsibilities. Indeed, the reluctance of women's boards to support married women not only fed but also reflected their substantially lower productivity. The complex task of raising children in China consumed both the time and the imaginations of missionary mothers. In the United States the home was only one of a number of institutions charged with forming the child. In China it was the only such institution. If missionary mothers wanted their children to be

American, they had to see to it that they recreated America around them. The immensity of the task threatened to overwhelm mothers, who lived in fear that their children might fall short of "the standard of life and thought in their own country" and slip into Oriental languor. As missionaries they were concerned that their children be virtuous, but as middle-class Americans they were concerned that, on that inevitable day in early adolescence when their children returned alone to "their own country, to American schools and colleges and to the life of their own generation,"[29] they would fit in.

With responsibility for imparting an entire world to their children, women turned to home families and American experts for advice on subjects from children's hairstyles to child-care theory. Bertha Allen, a single woman trained in kindergarten work, wrote about a 1917 audience of mothers she addressed: "I've never seen such a student group of mothers. Every one of them has read all the latest books on child life and psychology and they are always alert for anything that will help them in their problems." Their responsibility for providing their children's elementary education caused particular anxiety among missionary mothers, who were intimidated by the increasingly professionalized American elementary school. Emily Hobart dreaded for years the time when she knew she must begin teaching her children, and Jessie Ankeny Lacy maintained a lifetime gratitude to a friend who told her about the Calvert correspondence course, which sent lesson plans to parents around the world.[30] Though every mission compound conducted a mission school for Chinese children, missionary parents never enrolled their own children, whose education was to be the means to their Americanization.

Contemporary theory of infant care provided mothers with one of their few reprieves from the responsibility that threatened to imprison them. In the early twentieth century, proper technique mandated a regular, three-hour feeding schedule for an infant and minimal stimulation between feedings. Missionary mothers particularly emphasized this theory because it represented such a contrast with Chinese custom, in which a baby was constantly handled and fed on demand. Lucile Jones remembered that it also allowed her freedom: "The baby was fed every three hours but between that time, I could go away and leave the baby, you see. I very often just left the baby in bed."[31]

A child is not an infant for long, however, and thereafter missionary mothers labored to provide their children with all the features of a "very close family life" to make up in intensity what their children lacked in the

The family circle, 1913: Missionaries like Rose and Harry Martin worked to create a "very close family life" in China to make up in intensity what their children lacked in the breadth of American experience.

breadth of American life. Picnics, parlor dramatics, family readings—all these contributed to the halcyon China childhoods of missionary offspring. Dorothy Jones remembered her family's courtyard with its roses and the treehouse in the dragon-eye fruit tree as a "fairyland." She was, as her mother said, "very much protected."[32] The walls that encircled mission compounds not only kept nurturing family life in, but also kept the harsh sights and rank smells, the disease and the crowds, out. American mothers could not help fearing corruption from without as they tried to encourage wholesome growth within.

Their children gave them cause to worry, for despite the best efforts of American parents, children born in China, cared for by Chinese servants and surrounded by Chinese faces, were bound to adopt certain disconcerting Chinese habits. The McClures, anxiously awaiting the first word of their infant son, reported hearing "something which certainly sounded like the Chinese word for bread," and added, "We think the Amah [the nurse] must have taught him." Missionary parents themselves remained fussy about most Chinese cuisine but found that their "degenerate offspring," fed by merciful servants, universally preferred it. Parents tolerated their children's facility with the Chinese language but rarely supplemented it with instruction in characters. Sarah Goodrich went to the heart of missionary concerns when she described her daughter's reaction to two of her dolls—one a Japanese doll dressed in Chinese clothes:

Now *your* child would think the dolly curious and like it, but she would clasp to her heart the flaxen curled dolly. . . . Not so *my* girl. She scarcely notices her lovely American child but day and night she holds this really Chinese doll clasped to her heart glorying in the cut of the clothes, the color everything, calling it "precious one" and naming it "Dragon's Blessing."

Goodrich ended her lament with a sigh, "Ah me!"[33] Parents labored to save their children for themselves and worried about the outside influences which they could not control.

They controlled those they could. Though missionary children remembered occasional Chinese playmates, few had constant companions or youthful friendships that endured. One reason was that Chinese children of compound personnel went off to the station school at school age, where they studied long hours memorizing characters and the Chinese classics. Missionary children studied with their mothers at home. Ultimately, though, the reason missionary children did not play with Chinese children was because their parents did not encourage it. Emily Hobart wrote that, unlike their previous home in a crowded city, their new home "is a lonly [sic] place here for children. I am glad for that every day. They have such a large place to range in and no boys from across the street to teach them slang or disobedience." Jennie Campbell considered it "very demoralizing" for her children to play with Chinese children, "even the Christians," and therefore worked to prevent it. Even Florence Manly, an unusually courageous missionary mother in many regards, did not like her daughter to play with Chinese children, despite her concern that she learn the "pleasure and discipline" of group play. The "enriched and controlled environment" which one missionary contrasted with the child-rearing environment in the United States was the creation of protective mothers. [34]

Almost all missionary mothers hired a Chinese nurse (or *amah*) at some point in their careers, but they all did so reluctantly, with deep ambivalence and much rhetorical disavowal. Some went so far as to discourage their amah from touching their children, but even those who turned over their children to her for much of the time expressed their regret at this necessity. [35] Missionary mothers valued Chinese nurse-companions for the useful insights they could offer into Chinese society and often became personally dependent on women who worked as their amahs. But they remained uncomfortable about the nature of an amah's influence over their children. In their eyes, their very qualification as cultural interpreters seemed to disqualify Chinese women from the nurturing of American infants.

Mothers worried particularly about two influences in their children's contacts with Chinese playmates and nurses. They feared that their children would learn deceit and that they would become imperious and spoiled. Missionaries constantly railed at Chinese etiquette, which demanded that unpleasant truths be communicated indirectly. Their inability to look beyond literal Christian standards of truth and falsehood to comprehend Chinese practices remained one of their more persistent cultural blindnesses. The practical problems were more acute for missionary parents than for their children. Although parents frequently could not distinguish courtesy from truth, their children, who were learning Chinese etiquette and morality as an integrated system, were not so readily deceived. When queried about her understanding as a child, Ida Pruitt remembered that she had learned early the difference between politeness and fact. She made sure to distinguish fact from truth, however, because in Chinese thinking "politeness is a kind of truth." [36]

Chinese class distinctions, reflected in servant child rearing, contributed to American fears that their children would grow up undisciplined. Chinese servants were deferential to the children they supervised, and they could not understand the American theory according to which children of wealth and position were forced to do the manual work of laborers. When Esther Lewis insisted that her two children should "make our own beds, dust and tidy our room, and (this was what we hated), even empty the slop pails," her servants reinforced her children's resistance. "Although this experiment in the principles of democracy was supposed to teach the servants as well as ourselves that no kind of work was menial, it seemed to them absurd and out of keeping. The snickers of Lao Quang and Chang . . . seared my soul and made me feel rebellious,"[37] her daughter remembered.

Sons in particular received special favor from servants, both Ida Pruitt and Pearl Buck observed, and Buck recalled her mother's fear that the entire environment conspired to give her brother "a false and exalted opinion of himself." Bessie Ewing, who cut back on one of her servants in an effort to instruct her children in household chores, lamented that in the Chinese environment, "it is hard for them to feel any responsibility and they have to be reminded every day."[38] Whatever the social position a missionary family occupied in China, the work ethic remained a crucial part of child-rearing theory. Sober, middle-class missionaries, whose status was artificially inflated by the political circumstances of their China tenure, worried about the problems of cultivating a Christian character of modesty and independence in an atmosphere of Chinese subservience and flattery.

Class practices contributed only partly to the indulgence of missionary children by Chinese servants. Part also was the result of standard Chinese child-rearing theory. For, unlike American infants, who were subject to parental discipline almost from birth, Chinese infants customarily received an extended period of grace in which they enjoyed almost perfect freedom. During this time, which corresponded in theory to a prerational state, children were indulged, coddled, and carried. Only at the age of six or seven, when a child became a rational being, was he required to exercise self-discipline.[39] Missionary mothers, observing their own willful infants, however, saw no end to such behavior. None tried to understand the process by which "spoiled, pampered" Chinese infants turned into the courteous models of Chinese childhood who so demurely filled their mission schools.

Imperious children, 1899: Parents often feared that the Chinese environment would give their sons "a false and exalted opinion of themselves." Clarence and Frank Foster sitting with their amah and their sister Grace in their South China garden.

The status of missionary children as foreigners reinforced the tendencies of class and local custom to allow them excessive privilege. Dorothy Campbell, a missionary child who later adopted a psychoanalytic view of her experiences, attributed what she termed her "abnormal egocentrism" to her experiences as a missionary child. "The Chinese are apt to give foreign children too much praise and attention partly out of courtesy," she wrote, "and partly because they do compare favorably with underprivileged children who started to work as soon as they were able to hold buffalo ropes." Bessie Ewing worried that her daughter would be spoiled by the Chinese, who "all think a foreign child so wonderful because it has some life and ideas of its own." Undoubtedly, American practices, which threw children on their own early, produced more precociously independent children than did Chinese practices of early indulgence.[40]

But the high-handedness of growing children rested primarily on assumptions they were exposed to within the missionary community. Children's actions often crudely reflected more mediated parental attitudes. Edmund Lee's suggestion as a boy that he and his father destroy the heathen idols in a village temple, though carefully resisted by his father, nevertheless was based on a correct understanding of Christian attitudes toward indigenous religion. The same misapprehensions which flawed more adult undertakings influenced at least one abortive childhood missionary endeavor. Gertrude Wilder founded a school with a fellow nine-year-old "for the benefit of the cook's children" because she felt that she should "be doing some good":

> We started with six pupils and our course of study was to memorize the Lord's Prayer and to learn to read the three character catachism. Our school lasted for only two weeks for much to our confusion, we always got muddled when about half way through the prayer and we found that our pupils could outstrip us when it came to learning new characters. We were poor teachers whose small charges gradually melted away.

More adult missionary institutions suffered from similar liabilities. Ultimately, although they wanted their children to be polite, missionaries believed that their children were superior to Chinese children. In her 1904 essay on "The Relationship of Foreign Children to the Chinese," Sarah Goodrich admitted that it was easy, but asked, "Is is necessary for our children to lord it over the children of the East?" She concluded that Western children ought to become leaders, not tyrants. When she explained what she had in mind, she described a relationship between

Westerner and Chinese based on the noblesse oblige of polite princes and princesses.[41]

Parents unwittingly reinforced the willfulness and imperiousness they regretted in their children. Though they tried strenuously to compensate for what they took to be the corrupting effects of the environment, they could not conceal the underlying message of cultural preeminence which their very enterprise communicated. Mothers lamented the isolation of their children but tried to reenforce it, and even as they lamented their arrogance, they contributed to it. Responsibility for child rearing induced missionary mothers, as it has induced mothers in many climates and circumstances, to take a defensive position toward other worlds and other possibilities. Even personally adventurous women were unwilling to inflict adventures on their children. Instead, women worked hard to recreate an American home environment, to educate their children according to American standards, and to keep them as free as possible from the opportunities, as well as the corruptions, of their Chinese surroundings.

The cultural conservatism fostered by child-rearing responsibilities limited the relationships of American mothers with China and with their work. Most women found it difficult simultaneously to sustain a secure American homelife for children within compound walls and to embrace the innovation and experiment of a working life outside the home. Women who had confidently envisioned their work as a female contribution to the global expansion of Christian influence found that, instead, their responsibilities led to their participation in a defensive domesticity at home.

Sometimes even after the birth of first children, it is true, intrepid women tried to keep up the work that had brought them to China. In the early days after the birth of her daughter, Florence Manly described an evangelizing trip she made with a member of the women's board in a small, reed-covered boat. After enumerating all those present, she added, "I quite forgot Marian who makes the twelfth one." Her casual inclusion of her daughter in her work constrasted with her later protective attitude. Clara Foster also mentioned in 1890 that she and her husband took their one-year-old daughter with them on a river evangelizing trip. During the day an amah would care for the baby on the boat while husband and wife went out to preach to their respective sexes. "To come back to the boat and

Learning noblesse oblige, ca. 1903: Helen Smith being carried by compound children Robert Wang and Ling I-sa, who, in their childhood play, are imitating adults.

find her sweet little smiles welcoming us back, it is very precious," her mother wrote of her daughter's apparent acquiescence in her work. By the time she had two children, though, two years later, she told of her longing to accompany her husband on a similar excursion to tell the "Old Old Story," and her conclusion that "my mission, at present, seems to be to raise a family." Early efforts to subordinate family to work almost always gave way, leaving only a token responsibility in their wake.[42]

Women phrased their involvement in work as a commitment to themselves rather than to the elevation of Chinese society. Jeanie McClure, for instance, wrote, "I am glad to be teaching because it makes me feel as tho' I were accomplishing something." By measuring accomplishment primarily in terms of her own feelings, McClure betrayed fears that her teaching was helping no one else. Sarah Goodrich, who had severely curtailed her mission work because of home obligations, wrote that she was grateful to be able to do even her meager counseling, for "so many married ladies in Peking do almost no work."[43] Married women clung to one obligation almost as a talisman of their earlier commitment; their token work often served only to reveal their distance from their original vocation.

The problem seemed to be only in part the lack of available time in which to do mission work. Emily Hobart, a missionary mother, wrote home of the busyness of two single women houseguests, and commented, "only I seem to be idle." Only married women were knitting and sewing for the First World War effort, Elsie Clark noted, for they "have much more leisure than the unmarried." The presence of servants meant that homemaking responsibilities were often abstract and managerial rather than concrete and immediate. Jessie Lacy decided to continue with her teaching in the early years of her marriage because "there really isn't anything to do at home so I'd feel like a hypocrite to sit with folded hands doing nothing. I told you I think that it offended the cook to have me go to the kitchen to cook and we have a *fine* washerman and he does most all the house work besides." When children added duties to the household, emotional and psychological burdens tended to outweigh physical ones. Jeanie McClure compared her actual work schedule after the birth of her first child to that of her sister:

> I haven't any brilliant record like yours to report—sewing and travelling and cooking and so many other things. I think I could do it if I were at home but this climate certainly gets under one's skin. All I do is bathe John, feed him five times, study one hour, eat three meals, make a call or spend an hour at the tennis courts. It sounds incredible,

doesn't it? And you're not to infer that I'm sickly because I do as much as many other missionary wives do.

Although the hot and humid climate did impose hardships on North Americans, it also could serve as a metaphor for an entire environment. Jeanie McClure went to China expecting to be more active than she had been at home. With what appeared to be time on her hands, why did she, and other missionary wives, do so little missionary work?[44]

The answer seems to lie in the awesome responsibility of maintaining a family in China, which overshadowed the time required by actual tasks. The ideology of home, by 1900 long since reified in American society, came to assume an exaggerated significance in China, where there were fewer actual jobs for the housewife but a much greater need for her sustaining core. If the home was to be available for socializing children, women must create it by domesticating some corner of an alien world. Missionary women received special tributes for their skill in rearranging heathen surroundings to claim them for the American home. A memorial for Annette W. Atwood celebrated her in these terms: "If it were only a bare room in a Chinese inn, in a few moments she could bring about an atmosphere of cheer and homelikeness, as if the whole were part of a picnic. In her own home guests were surrounded by welcome and comfort produced magically out of most unpromising materials."[45] Domestic ideology emerged in China partly as a defensive mechanism to ensure that American home values would be preserved and recreated amidst the chaos of barbarism.

American domesticity in China was theoretically evangelical as well as defensive, however. Missionary periodicals and board publicity frequently emphasized the power of the missionary home to transform China. Margaret Burton's *Women Workers of the Orient*, a 1918 study manual for mission auxiliaries, repeated the litany: "No missionary agency has done more to change the home life of the orient than the missionary's home. What the social settlement house is to the crowded slum districts of a great city, this, and even more than this, is the Christian home set in the midst of people to whom home life, in any true sense of the word, has been unknown."[46] However zealously mission spokesmen advanced evangelical domesticity as a justification for the upkeep of missionary homes, married women often found its satisfactions illusory.

To begin with, the theory of evangelical domesticity depended upon the Chinese recognizing the merit of American home arrangements. It did not occur to most missionaries, "in the goodness of their saintly hearts," as

Pearl Buck put it, "to ask themselves whether or not the Chinese had a sort of home life which was perhaps as valuable in its way as ours, or at least better suited to China than ours was." But when troops of curious Chinese visited missionary homes, they seemed impervious to the opportunities for inspiration there and instead marveled at the oddness of foreign contrivances. Ideology became lost in bric-a-brac. Chinese visitors were more likely to judge than to learn from the foreigners' example. "'Ah, you are like the people of the South, you also keep your night pot in your room,'" Ida Pruitt quoted one country woman inspecting her family home. Pruitt went on: "There was the scorn of the Northerner, the people of Han, from the Han dynasty, for the Southerner and his ways. . . . They themselves always went outdoors, whatever the weather or time of day or night, to the latrine in the corner of the courtyard behind the house."[47] The American home did not work as a missionary force in China because the subtle emanations of domesticity could not cross the vast cultural chasm between East and West.

In practice, missionary women themselves found evangelical domesticity trying. The American home in China was the final repository of familiar values and served for many missionaries as a refuge from China. Missionary women had worked hard to make their homes into oases of civilization in the deserts of heathendom, and welcomed with ambivalence inquisitive visitors who smelled of garlic, opened drawers, and banged on precious pianos. Like the Chinese, American mothers valued the walls around them for the protection they provided. But walls blocked the outflow of influence from the Christian home and symbolized a domesticity too defensive to be inspirational.

Because of these inherent contradictions, missionary women did not find the running of American homes in China satisfying work. Women who had traveled to China in search of a more public sphere found little gratification in providing "an object lesson" for the Chinese. The missionary returns from evangelical domesticity were so tenuous that Jeanie McClure wondered "if the influence which radiates from our Christian home is worth the money it takes to keep us here."[48]

Missionary wives, however, rarely perceived their problems as the result of fundamental contradictions in their mission or in the expectations of mission boards for them. Nor did women who went to China to do public service for God anticipate the centripetal force of a growing family. They had not imagined that traditional chivalry would be doubly compelling in a land of unknown dangers, nor did they understand that it might limit even the most sincere of female callings. Missionary women had not anticipated the vast array of forces that would interfere with their plans for work, nor did they for the most part ever confront those forces. Rather, they experienced their problems as punishments for personal failings.

Women who aspired to Christian service within an expanded women's sphere, which included such areas of public life as schools, hospitals, and churches, found the isolation of their child-rearing years after their husbands' work had begun particularly difficult. Clara Foster wrote in 1891 that her husband was often away for so long that their daughter did not know him. When *her* husband was away for long stretches, Emily Hobart found it hard, but even when he was at home, she wrote, he "is very busy with the Chinese all the time. I don't see very much of him except at meal times." Her own home responsibilities cut her off even from the religious community which should have been her consolation. "I am not able to go to meeting when Will does," she wrote. "I have only been to two services in over four months."[49] Carie Sydenstricker's story was even bleaker. Following her husband to ever more remote stations of the interior, she repeatedly had to set up housekeeping in the grim accommodations available to unpopular Westerners; even then, her husband was frequently away itinerating. She bore four children in her first ten years in China and lost three of them—the bearing and losing endured almost entirely alone.

The social deprivation suffered by missionary wives recalls American pioneer women, who were also isolated from the centers of civilization and the artifacts of domesticity which defined them. The need to see another woman of her kind, which prompted Carie Sydenstricker finally to rebel against her isolation, was a constant need expressed by women who settled the American West. A valuable study of Overland Trail diaries concludes that women, whose work consisted of the repetitive, cyclical chores of cooking and making camp, found the journey more traumatic and trying than did men, who were responsible for more strategic decisions.[50] Unlike pioneer women, who often protested the westward move, missionary wives had embarked voluntarily on their perilous adventure and sailed with a sense of vocation in the service of their God. The discrepancy between the mission work they aspired to and the routine work they ended up doing thus brought them particular anxiety. For women whose initial decision to enter missionary service indicated a need to control the course of their lives, the daily tasks of housekeeping seemed doubly futile.

Thus, isolated missionary women doing routine chores rather than totting up students educated or souls converted often experienced severe depression. When Sarah Goodrich was forced to reorient her energies from the mission work which she enjoyed to the rearing of her delicate children, she suffered the intense and morbid pains of frustration and ennui. "I was married," she wrote later, "and then went away down in the valley for so many long years." At the time, she explained her vexation to her mother:

> I think life here without doing Mission work is harder than life crowded full. It is so tiresome to walk up and down the walk that one doesn't do it very often. Shut up in the house day in and day out is very tiresome too. You know here when full of work we live on happy and unconscious of the life at home, but just shut one up in one's house six weeks with nothing but the daily task—the common round—and the body grows tired and the mind preys on itself.

The letters a missionary was expected to write home, she wrote, haunted her "like a nightmare."[51] The depression she lived in undoubtedly made it impossible to achieve the formulaic uplifting tone which such letters demanded.

Like all missionary mothers who had foregone their mission work, Sarah Goodrich faced occasional bouts of uncertainty about exactly where God's will lay. Before she decided to set aside her work, she submitted the decision to God and concluded that "God wants me to tend to my babies this winter." She added, "I have not without a struggle put my study of Chinese away, put away my ambitions in a sense." Like other missionary mothers, she was caught in a bind of guilt. Maternal ideology made her feel guilty for neglecting her children if she was working; but if she remained at home, her missionary calling, through which she expressed her own ambition, caused her to feel guilt as well. "I shall still put my babies first but I must not make idols of them," she wrote the next year. Bessie Ewing expressed the anguish of missionary mothers most directly:

> Last winter when I was doing so much outside work I felt contented in a way but only half so for I neglected home duties, which ought to have come first, and so some how felt my work was not amounting to much. Now I am trying to go by the word in Is[aiah] 28, 26 and it may lead me into staying at home altogether this winter, that is not going out to schools, meetings, etc. I hope not, but if so I hope I shall be contented. If there were only some one who could do this work in Peking then I would not feel so badly but I will be the only one. . . . I

am the only one to help the women or the children but as Charles put it the other evening, "There isn't you either." Well! I am bound to see to my home first and then if I haven't any more time or strength the work must get along without me. You will pray for me won't you that I may do what is right and that the work may go on.[52]

For women who volunteered as missionaries in the first place the need to "do what was right" was a powerful motivation: it caused them endless suffering when the responsibility brought by children presented them with two contrary "rights."

The burden was particularly heavy for women who in America had hit upon their vocations as a solution to spiritual crises of their youth. Such women, Carie Sydenstricker and Jennie Campbell among them, hoped that their extreme sacrifice would enable them to feel God's presence as they had not before. Instead, women raising families in isolation found that God was often more elusive in heathendom than at home. Cut off, sometimes even from regular worship as well as from redeeming work, they experienced both spiritual and social solitude. Jennie Campbell wrote in 1890: "My time is so much taken up in my home cares and in teaching children's lessons, that I do a very small amount of real missionary work. I find more and more what a poor sinful Christian I am. I do long to grow more like the Savior, and have him in my life." Three months later she wrote that her "spiritual life seems just as dead as possible and yet be called life."[53] Rather than finding food for their starving souls in the mission field, women who did their service as wives and mothers often found themselves struggling to maintain the uncertain faith they had brought with them.

The death of their children occasionally pushed missionary mothers over the edge into guilty despair. Prior to 1900, when the establishment of cool summer resorts spared missionaries from the ravages of summer diseases, adults and children alike frequently suffered and died from malaria, diphtheria, cholera, and dysentery. When children died, parents, as always, wondered sorrowfully why they had been so cursed. Unlike her stoic husband, Carie Sydenstricker, who eventually lost four of her seven children, could not accept the deaths of those she had so labored for and loved. After she lost her fourth child, her daughter wrote, "She went back to her old morbid fear lest it was through some sinfulness of her own that she had lost her children, some sinfulness and inner rebellion." The death of Emily Hobart's child made her consider whether the sin for which God had judged her might be more specific—the neglect of her mission work.

She wrote home of her plans to do more work with the Chinese: "I seem to be so idle these days and I don't want to compel the Lord to take away all my children but my stupidity in understanding if He means that I ought to do something and on the other hand I am so afraid of neglecting the children if I get other things on my hands [sic]."[54] The death of children, which the good Christian was supposed to accept with equanimity, became for all missionary mothers a challenge to their faith. For some it seemed more a judgment on their faith—a judgment on the inadequacy of their daily home toil either to seem or to be the fulfillment of the calling which had first induced them to set sail.

Those who did successfully resolve the conflict between their own ambitions to do the Lord's work and the lowly needs of their families did so by using the logic of self-sacrifice employed by generations of Christian women. Sarah Goodrich in later life pondered again the options she had faced earlier between her missionary cause, which came to be temperance work, and her family responsibility: "What is my supreme duty to my Lord and my husband. Can I put the Temperance cause first. . . . God's Kingdom must be first. In giving up the Temperance work I do not give up God's Kingdom. First to keep bright and cheerful I help Chauncey. . . . This *is* sacrificing for a cause. God's Kingdom wherein they serve." Because their ambition had initially been couched in the vocabulary of self-sacrifice, most missionary wives were vulnerable to rationalizations which appealed to them on that basis. Jennie Campbell, in despair over her isolation from her husband and their joint work, finally concluded, "Perhaps this waiting is my service for the present."[55]

When Bessie Ewing experienced conflict between her family and her work, Emma Dickinson Smith, the wife of missionary publicist Arthur Smith, proffered counsel. Emma Smith based her argument for family not on the duty to self-sacrifice but on her perception of the old Arminian error in Ewing's thought. We "think we must *do* something to receive the blessing when all that is necessary is to *believe* that we have it and act accordingly."[56] Though the doctrine of grace was appropriate for missionary wives who lacked the circumstances to perform good works, it neglected the important truth for many of them that without the opportunity to work for the Lord it was hard to feel His existence. Missionary women thus depended less on this doctrinal logic than on feminine ideology. They tried to see their responsibility for maintenance rather than innovation, for daily chores rather than progressive accomplishments, as the biggest and most noble sacrifice of all, the sacrifice of the opportunity to keep self-denial itself from becoming ordinary and mundane.

※ॐॐ※

The only other sacrifice missionary mothers considered a comparable deprivation was the final one of their maternal years: the relinquishing of their children. Mothers commonly educated their children themselves through the elementary grades, but they acquiesced in community opinion that at the age of twelve or thirteen children needed home-country influences and the more structured education of American secondary schools. To women who had set aside missionary work for the duty of motherhood, the trauma of having to surrender their sacred charges to relatives and homes for missionary children in the United States was a cruel reversal of expectation. "We missionaries face this time of separation for years," Minnie Bliss wrote when it came time to send another daughter home. "Missionary sacrifice—*this* is our sacrifice." Lida Ashmore remembered that the separation was so traumatic she experienced a psychosomatic reaction:

> It seemed to stop the orderly functioning of the organs of the body. On the train I hurt my finger, trying to raise a window. Instead of healing quickly it made a sore that healed with difficulty. I did not leave the children until they were willing, in one sense of the word to let me go. I felt numb, and appeared and felt dazed. It was the supreme sacrifice I had made up to that time in my life.

Mothers frequently resisted the grim necessity of parting with children, and many of them repressed until the onset of children's puberty this further evidence that missionary work and the raising of American families were incompatible. Only when the family of a Chungking magistrate inquired about the marriage plans of their thirteen-year-old daughter did Spencer and Esther Lewis make plans to send her home.[57]

Like other sacrifices, the decision to send children back to the United States brought its own uncertainty and guilt. Sarah Goodrich's request for a teacher for missionary children in China gained its force from her anticipated parting with her fourteen-year-old daughter. She based her request on her own anguish, but also on the social disapproval she felt for this surrender of maternal responsibilities. Only a teacher for American children in China, she felt, would spare mothers like herself from the "taunt," "Missionary work makes women unnatural mothers!" Lida Ashmore decided to leave her children in a missionary home, where they would be supervised along with others by an elderly church couple, rather than entrust them to unsympathetic relatives. "Aggie don't much believe in leaving children behind for other people to care for and coming out here, so I don't want to ask her to help take care of them," she wrote.[58] Missionary mothers undoubtedly experienced some disapproval, but whether they were universally condemned for their neglect is almost irrelevant; women who had set aside their own calling for a greater maternal responsibility could not then set aside this greater responsibility without judging themselves harshly.

The adjustment from being primarily mother to being primarily missionary was not easy. Women who had previously felt isolated from work often felt the absence of their children so acutely that they were incapacitated. Lida Ashmore's letters to her children expressed her disorientation: "Where are you now," one went. "I don't know. And I can't think of you as anywhere. I am so lonesome for you." Jeanie McClure anticipated the return of Minnie Bliss with apprehension:

> I dread to think what it will be like when she comes back . . . now that she will have sent both daughters away. For months after they got back here after leaving Ruth at home she simply could not even mention her name without bursting into tears, and people say that she hesitated a long time before she decided to come back to China with her husband instead of staying at home with her children.[59]

Both Bliss and Ashmore remained ambivalent over their decision to stay with their husbands and work rather than with the children who had been their clear priority in the face of severe challenges during their adult years.

Given this priority, why did so many women make the decision to return to their busy husbands and occasional work rather than to see through their urgent maternal responsibilities in the United States? Christine Pickett, herself a missionary daughter, wrote that she never did understand it and knew that her older siblings who had grown up alone were bitter about being "abandoned" as their parents' "living sacrifices." The boards encouraged married couples to remain together, which undoubtedly contributed to some women's decision. The Baptists even made a ruling that husband and wife should not part. Reasons for encouraging marriage for male missionaries in the first place presumably applied in even more force after the union; if local attachments were dangerous for unmarried men, they were doubly so for married men whose wives were overseas. More significant than board policy in bringing married women back to the field, however, was the dominant myth, pertaining among those at home as well as those in the field, that married women *were* missionaries, however limited their possibilities for work. For women whose missionary work had almost always been defined by sacrifices—of home, of work, even of children to death—relinquishing children to institutions or relations seemed like only one in a series of God's trials. When Clara Foster finally left three of her children in the United States and returned with her two youngest to her limited China work, she found it *"very hard,"* concluding, "Only for the Master's Sake will it be possible."[60]

The separation from children, however, was generally the last big sacrifice. Women who could transcend their sense of loss and guilt after parting from children, often found in their later years, as Pearl Buck wrote about her mother, "the years for which she really left her own country"— the opportunity finally to embark on the Lord's work.[61] Women like Carie Sydenstricker, Sarah Goodrich, and Emily Hobart, whose strength had been successively worn away by anxieties over children, guilt over work undone, distress at solitude, and finally anguish over their loss of children, again and again managed to regroup and recover a long dormant missionary purpose.

Sarah Goodrich's transformation in later life was most dramatic. With her children away at school, she emerged from her morbid inactivity to become a major figure in a kind of social mission work. A prominent lecturer who spoke on a variety of subjects from temperance to interior decoration, she impressed people with her elegance, her expansiveness, and her aggressive, worldly spirit. At her death, a younger missionary who had grown up in Peking remembered her as someone who proved to him the equality of men and women, "a splendid example to prove that marriage by no means ends a woman's career." Her later years certainly bore this out; but her misery during her child-rearing years suggests that Goodrich might have been correct when, before her enlistment, she judged herself temperamentally unsuited for the compromises demanded by a family. She would continue to need public life to erase private insecurities well after the departure of her children. Within the context of their fond, genteel union, she and her husband led nearly independent lives of professional initiative and individual travel which well answered this need.[62]

Clara Foster's early years resembled Sarah Goodrich's. She, too, had come to China as a single woman in the 1880s and then embarked on a stimulating career in which she invested three years. Following her marriage and the birth of her first child, like Sarah Goodrich, she tried to continue her instruction of Bible women. "I enjoy the work very much," she wrote to her husband's parents about one day's long hours, "and found it difficult to tear myself away, there is so much to be done. But daughter Anna protested most vigorously both times when I came back today that I had been gone too long."[63] Gradually her work tapered off, and except for an occasional class, she did no more mission work for twenty-two years, nineteen of which she spent in the United States raising her six children.

In 1915, at the age of fifty-six, Foster returned to China, to her husband, to her work with Bible women and to village itinerating. She frequently worked with the single women of the women's board, and rediscovered associations cut off years before. One friend had first arrived in China a month after her, and then "we saw considerable of each other, and had good times visiting back and forth staying over night, were friends. Then when I married she turned a cold shoulder on me, and we saw little of each other. Now since I've come back alone she has been her own delightful self of 28 years ago, always calls me 'Clara' and is as cordial and friendly as is possible." The rift in intervening years resulted from Foster's marriage and her sense of growing inadequacy to the work. Many years before, as domestic pressures were mounting, she explained, "I would like to go on, but the two ladies are now able to do more." The single women's community rarely accommodated mothers, whose loyalties to the work were only secondary. But it often included women like Clara Foster or Mary Ament in their later lives when they could bring their full energies and, in the words of one single woman, could "give as much time to the work as an 'unencumbered woman.'"[64]

The segregation of men's and women's work meant that Clara Foster rarely worked with her husband. "I do hate to leave father here so much," she wrote, "but it seems almost destined that we two must go separate paths." Nevertheless, she discovered with him a youthful comradeship which she recorded in a journal for her children. On one of their rare country trips she described an hour of rest on a village hillside, wife stretched out on her coat, husband reading aloud from "Billy Sunday's

Late-life harmony, 1901: Charles and Hannah Hartwell traveling in the Foochow mission's "gospel boat."

Life," and later in the year she mentioned a swimming lesson: "Father and I were in the ocean together for the first time in many years. . . . The water is great! You children would enjoy it so! If father keeps on being here a few nights and helps me as he did tonight—held my two hands while I kicked and tried to swim, I really have hopes of learning to swim yet." In her later years, Clara Foster held in equilibrium service to others and devotion to her own. With her long-time husband she shared a home, children, and a greater purpose, but within that greater purpose she found personal scope for the travels and teaching she had always enjoyed. Sometimes work and family even merged: she carried pictures of her children when she went itinerating and found that "having six children in America is a great honor." Her conclusion, after years of difficulty and isolation: "I'm finding China is a good place to be growing old in."[65]

Such late-life harmonies were common between couples who were both dedicated to a common mission and endowed with the energy to pursue their commitment. Rare missionary couples achieved this balance in earlier years. Elsie Clark, a single woman who had gone to China convinced that traditional marriage could not offer the breadth of challenges she demanded, experienced a change of perspective from observing missionary marriages in the field. In 1917 she wrote home that "the happiest husbands and the happiest wives I have ever seen are those on the mission field," and recently remembered in particular John and Elizabeth Gowdy as an "ideal couple." Both young husband and young wife led full teaching careers, freed by servants from domestic drudgery. A similar sense of partnership emerges in a recent study of Calvin and Julia Mateer, who ran a boys' school together; Julia drew out the students and tended to the needs of the elementary school, and Calvin imposed discipline and standards upon the upper school.[66] But the Masters and the Gowdys were united by one uncommon circumstance: neither couple had any children.

For although China could be a gratifying place for American women to work, it was a difficult place for them to raise children. Missionary mothers shared board expectations that they would both nurture their own children and convert the Chinese, which added to their difficulties. Certainly there were severe restrictions on the time which women responsible for educating and grooming their own children could devote to station work, but absolute time restrictions were less significant than the problems of integrating the two imaginative enterprises. Raising an American family and participating in the Christian reform of Chinese society were goals at fundamental cross-purposes. A woman who was preoccupied with isolating her children from the effects of moral contamination was invariably compromising her ability to decontaminate. A woman who was steeling herself against Chinese influences was shutting off possibilities for Christian conversion. The work of missionary mothers was therefore characterized by its partialness, its superficiality, and its subordination to the work and plans of husbands.

Women who went to China young, then married and had families there, did earn a reprieve in later life, a chance to develop a work in their own right. This work brought them possibilities for discovering meaning in life at a time when mothers in the United States were often finding themselves stripped of their primary purpose. The abiding sense of alternative responsibility and prior vocation which plagued women during their youth and their child-rearing years proved to be their salvation in their maturity. It brought missionary wives out into the world at just the moment when loss of family, as children left home, was driving women in the United States back in on themselves.

The sense of family which Clara Foster carried with her in the tangible form of photographs, furthermore, provided a sense of rootedness and continuity unavailable to her single counterparts as they grew older. It was in these later years that married women missionaries realized their comparative advantage in stature and in self-content over both single women and middle-class American matrons who had raised their children in more congenial American surroundings. The often painful tension of the middle years between family loyalty and personal ambition paid off in an accumulation of resolve that propelled missionary wives and mothers into energetic, expansive, and fulfilling old ages. This was the unanticipated exchange: isolation shouldered and endured in youth in order to be spared the generational isolation of the childless or the inactive domestic isolation of homes organized around children no longer there. In the end, missionary mothers who later took up their work had the worst and the best of it. Maternal responsibilities demanded more from them than from most women of their class, but their public work brought some of the highest rewards. At the conventional time of retirement, the sacrifices of missionary mothers finally brought them a long-awaited blessing in a fresh sense of relevance and even a first discovery of vocation.

❧ 5 ❧

DOMESTIC EMPIRE

Responsibilities for the missionary home structured and limited the work of women missionaries in China. Particularly married women with children, but single and childless women as well, fretted and toiled to insure that the essence of the American home would be maintained in the far-off corners of China. Missionary women brought with them the material goods of their homes—the utensils, the pictures, and the bedsprings. But they came to adopt the social arrangements of an overseas colonial community. In receiving guests and supervising servants, they enhanced their investment in civilized refinement and participated in the transformation of a democratic domestic sphere into a form of domestic empire. Their points of stubbornness and compromise reveal the contours of American domestic ideology at the turn of the century.

❧❧❧❧❧

In 1907 Elizabeth Perkins answered her family's urgent request for information about the American Board mission compound outside Foochow where she had just arrived: "You say tell you all about things, people, house, room, etc. Everything is so like America that there isn't much to tell."[1] She went on to describe the jobs of the large household's three servants and to outline the household diet—beef roasts, fine butter, cream and milk from the cook's cow, bread, cake, and puddings. Perkins' observations could have applied to any of the established mission stations in China. In furnishings, food, bric-a-brac, and styles of dress, they made little compromise with the Chinese environment. Instead, at great cost in Chinese labor, they transported beds, stoves, pianos, and endless cartons from Montgomery Ward's up tortuous rivers and across mountain ranges to reproduce American homelife in China. The important question to ask is why missionaries of this period were so faithful to the artifacts of home that they transported them around the world. The answer to this question lies in the association of the idea of civilization, which was at the heart of the missionary enterprise, with the stuff of the late Victorian woman's sphere.

Chinese cities were dominated by walls. High walls surrounded low buildings and courtyards to delineate a family compound. American missionaries had grown up in houses surrounded by fields or opening onto village greens and often found the walls of Chinese cities oppressive. They enjoyed their summer travels to the mountains or the shore "where it is *open*, without walls to obstruct your view or transit" and often looked forward to expanding mission operations outside the city wall, where they could have houses with glass windows and views.[2]

But Americans came to welcome compound walls within cities for the very reasons that the Chinese had built them, as security against the physical and sensory assaults of an impoverished urban populace. Descriptions of arriving again within the protection of the compound suggest this accommodation of American village expectations to Chinese urban practice. Several accounts describe mission settlements as like a paradise regained after the horrors of the street, and Lizzie Martin spoke for many China missionaries when she wrote, "there is so much that is depressing outside, that it is a real rest and change to come in and find this beauty all around."[3] Long idealized as a moral preserve, under China circumstances the American home easily evolved into a physical preserve as well.

Missionary women worked to create beauty within courtyards. Through a garden, women deprived of a view could still preserve some of the colors and seasonal changes of a pastoral ideal. Nearly a universal female avocation, gardens provided a focus for married women who were largely confined to their homes. In 1918 Lida Ashmore took the time to count 249 rose blossoms in her garden, which also included calla lilies, daisies, hydrangeas, hyacinths, wisteria, iris, hollyhocks, dahlias, and peach and plum blossoms. Alice Linam's garden in isolated Yenping contained eighty-nine rosebushes alone. Flower seeds often came from family gardens at home and became a way of asserting living continuities. In the darkness of Chinese cities, women allied their spirits, and perhaps

Mission compound, 1915: Mission buildings such as these at Ingtai, Fukien, were commonly surrounded by a wall for protection against intruders. Missionaries came to appreciate walled compounds as a retreat from the threats of an alien population.

their mission as well, to the growth of blossoms remembered from child-hood. Lida Ashmore wrote of her roses: "They are so pure and beautiful. And they grow and bloom in this land and even in dark gloomy days try their best to look cheerful and scent the air with their perfume."[4]

Gardens in Chinese courtyards remained dwarfed by alien walls; within houses, particularly under lamplight, the correct arrangement of home objects could accomplish more convincing transformations. "If you were to look in on us as we are seated at the dining room table, with my nickel lamp between us, you would think us in a New England home," Elizabeth Perkins wrote from her remote Fukien station. Elsie Clark wrote of her admiration for the Hollister household in Sienyu: "It would do your heart good, as it does mine, to think that a young bride and groom could have such pretty things so far removed, as you would say, from civilization. Silver, cutglass, Haviland china, and silk candle shades made the table as pretty as most that you could find in Roland Park." Home furnishings more frequently reflected the familiar than the elegant, though, and were especially valued for their "homey" quality. Ida Pruitt remembered a copy of Millet's *Angelus* on her family's wall, and Harriet Osborne and Evelyn Worthley put a reproduction of the Venus de Milo on their mantel. Jessie Ankeny, of a later generation, hung a "pretty Coca-Cola" girl over her desk, and Lucy Mead decorated with college banners and magazine pictures which she had framed, using passe-partout.[5]

Missionary homes imitated late Victorian American homes in the density as well as the quality of goods they contained. The preparations made for short trips within China hinted at what overseas preparations were. A day boat-trip to conference, for instance, required plates, knives, cups, steamer rugs, pillows, and narrow mattresses. When Luella Miner went to stay in a mission camp in the hills outside Peking, she wrote, "every piece of furniture, dishes, and most of our provisions must be taken, wash tubs, hooks for hanging clothes, everything imaginable is on our lists." No wonder Elsie Clark noted in a letter home how useful had been the fruit knives and orange spoons which she had thought to bring to China.[6] Why were home objects treasured and transported in such density?

China served to exaggerate an association between women and material homelife which had been developing throughout the nineteenth century. Marketers of endless bric-a-brac had successfully cultivated women's identi-fication with the artifacts of the home. Furnishing a home in China was more of a challenge than in America, but it also brought more gratification.

"We live so much in our little home life here in China," Grace Smith suggested in 1902, "we derive great pleasure from things you at home might think trivial." Material goods were sometimes pleasures, but they were often "needs." When Sarah Goodrich and her husband were contemplating a trip to the hills around Peking, for which Luella Miner had packed up her entire house, Goodrich wrote: "It is a hard trip and very expensive if I go. We have to carry such a troop. Food, bedding, servants, etc. Chauncey just goes and lives anyhow. I'd like to but can't seem to manage it." Later in the year, as she was settling into her summer house, she quoted a male missionary: "'Oh these ladies have wants. We gentlemen would never need all these things.'" Women's needs were nearly always associated with greater variety and higher quality of furniture, china, silver, and linens. "We were in need," Grace Smith wrote in thanks for table linens she had just received. "Ned tries to tease me often says 'Grace, we'll have to resort to oil cloth.'"[7] Women's dependence on the goods of their home culture, and on linen rather than oilcloth as the means to insure their family's proper training, became, if anything, more urgent because they were in China.

The earlier generations rarely used Chinese objects in their homes. Although summer resort areas were frequented by "curio men" who sold Chinese statuary, lace, lacquers, drawn work, and embroidery, women purchased Chinese objects as curiosities to be sent home rather than as furnishings for their own houses in China. They perceived American objects as a way to subscribe to American norms and took fewer liberties, rather than more, as a result of their distance from Grand Rapids and Des Moines.

Only with new standards of fashion, which required that the home express unique personality rather than conventional taste, did missionaries exploit the decorative possibilities of Chinese handiwork. Arriving in China in 1912, Elsie Clark contrasted the rooms of four American YWCA secretaries with the interiors of missionary homes. The YWCA secretaries, she wrote:

> had the prettiest rooms imaginable, furnisht with beautiful pieces of Chinese work . . . . The rooms were bright with brass and china and well-selected articles of furniture, and were just such as cultured women would enjoy living in. They were an object lesson to me of the value of a discriminating taste; some of the other missionary homes lookt shoddy because they were furnisht with miscellaneous odds and ends brought from America: the owners had not had individuality or

Citadel of Victorianism, 1907: With the exception of the Chinese banner ("To serve God with all one's might"), the decor of the J. Boardman Hartwell home in Shantung might have come from any upper-middle-class home in England or America. (Anna Hartwell and her special friend Jane Thompson—"my precious Tommie"—are also pictured.)

enterprise enuf to look around them, discover the products that China excels in and utilize them in their houses.

The contrast between the tastes of "cultured college women" and old-fashioned missionaries represented a contrast between two eras in American consumerism. The mass production of American "quality" goods, such as were cherished by missionaries, eventually inspired a new emphasis on individuality in decorating. Clark herself tapped the 1920s consumer interest in novelty items in her postmissionary career as an importer.[8]

Under greater difficulties, missionaries at the turn of the century demonstrated the same loyalty to how and what they ate that they did to home furnishings. When Elizabeth Perkins and Harriet Osborne neglected to pack silver on an excursion to Sharpe Peak, they were nearly "driven to chopsticks," before being rescued by neighboring Europeans. "Oh, no, thank you," Mildred Rowland said to the suggestion that she use chopsticks. "The way they shove it in with their chopsticks is certainly a sight." Missionaries clearly agreed with Sarah Goodrich that "civilization is shown so clearly in the way one eats."[9]

Missionaries seemed to appreciate Chinese food more than Chinese table manners, but despite problems in procuring fresh meat, they replicated home menus within their families. When Bertha Allen was trying to reassure her parents that she was eating well, she reproduced a day's menu to prove it. Her 12:30 dinner included chicken, meat, or fish, two kinds of potato, rice, creamed onions or bamboo sprouts, pudding, and fruit. Supper began with soup, followed with a baked dish with sauce, cake, and cocoa. Elizabeth Perkins's dinner one night included consommé with rice, cold roast beef, sweet potatoes, rice with cream and sugar, biscuit, and sponge cake. Missionaries ordered many of their staples from Montgomery Ward, including canned goods of all kinds and a variety of grains and sugar. Not until World War I brought food conservation measures to the United States did they begin to rely on China for their basic food needs. The patriotic impulse behind this decision drew on the same cultural chauvinism which allowed missionaries to maintain home eating habits, despite difficulties, in remote corners of Cathay.[10]

Missionaries felt that home food, like other home customs, was the best defense against the threats of an alien environment. In 1889, for instance, Clara Foster wrote to her husband's family that all missionaries made an effort to eat a lot of meat due to "the wearing enervating effects of this climate." Like the Chinese themselves, missionaries did not eat raw vegetables, which were often grown in fields fertilized with human manure. But locally grown vegetables, which cooked with rice were the staple of Chinese cuisine, seldom entered into the missionary diet and then only as substitutes for home varieties. Nor did missionaries adopt the Chinese custom of drinking tea as their major beverage, but instead mixed lemonade and postum made with boiled water. Like the contents of their homes, the missionary diet was heavy in substance and rich within a narrow range of variety. It is not surprising that many women wrote home that they were getting fat.[11]

The preservation of the American diet, usually implemented by Chinese servants under the direction of a housewife, may not have been a victory in nutrition and health over the cooking of Chinese gentry, but it represented a substantial triumph for American missionary women, who ordered provisions six months in advance, taught Chinese cooks how to make American sauces and puddings, and presided over the serving of multicourse meals. Late Victorian cooking, so different from Chinese cuisine in preparation and ingredients, did share its social origins; the variety and abundance of both cuisines had originally been an indication of the host's social standing. In the United States, though, agricultural abundance had removed the threat of famine ever-present in China and modified the class meaning of food. Many courses, followed by finger bowls and served on a linen tablecloth, did not require extraordinary wealth; missionaries themselves were decidedly middle-class. Rather, such eating, with the proper etiquette for each course, had moral connotations as an indication of a refined and improving home atmosphere. The serving of multicourse American cooking, like the collection of American bric-a-brac, fulfilled the American woman's self-conscious responsibility to promote culture through a multiplicity of home goods.

Providing a proper environment through the home arts of cooking and decorating was a woman's responsibility to her family. Her own style in dress was a responsibility to herself and to her sex. Women far away from the dictates of home fashion found the distance temporarily liberating. Luella Miner wrote somewhat paradoxically that her blue sateen dress was old-fashioned, "but as I am in blissful ignorance of what is stylish that doesn't effect my happiness at all. It is one of the privileges of missionaries to be old-fashioned and not to know it." The relief women expressed at their freedom from fashion is some indication of the extent of its tyranny at home. Jessie Ankeny wrote that, on the basis of this freedom, her mother would find China a peaceful place to live:

> I'm just sure, Mama, you would like the restfulness of our life out in China. I don't mean by that we work less than at home for we don't but then there isn't *any* worry about styles or hats or anything until the last thread of it is gone and must be replaced. Sometimes I wish for our rag barrel if I had it I think one could get a lot out of it for the way the Chinese patch and darn and turn and clean is marvellous. My skirts out here wear almost twice as long as at home.[12]

Most middle- and lower-middle class Americans could feed their families full on carbohydrates and farm produce without financial hardship, but keeping up with changing urban fashions presented women with economic as well as emotional problems.

In practice, women had difficulty making the break from American fashion which they felt their China circumstances should have allowed. Residual investments in the precepts of female fashion caused missionary women to write earnestly for recent fashion news, and to remodel old clothing according to its specifications. Women who preserved their homes to inspire elevated sentiments could not ignore the responsibility of insuring that their own person would make the correct improving impression on family and visitors. If their femininity was somehow involved in the goods of homes and tables, it was even more involved in the style of their dress.

Sometimes it almost seemed as if style and feminine worth were the same. Frederica Mead's comment on a Chinese woman with whom she had dined left the emphasis on her criticisms. "She is a splendid girl in lots of ways," she wrote, "but I wish she were a bit more up to date." Elsie Clark's diary entry about a dinner with the Minors was similarly phrased: "Dinner with the Minors, old fashioned missionaries who never could be in style if they wanted to be. I should have preferred writing letters." Though perhaps both Mead and Clark meant to refer to other qualities besides habits of dress, their decision to cast their criticism in the language of style rather than more universal language indicates their lingering involvement with standards of fashion. Jessie Ankeny's description of missionary Florence Plumb indicates the place that style could occupy in mutual evaluation. "She is fine," she wrote, "She wears such pretty clothes. She is just out from home and she is so nice."[13]

Women who wrote home that dress did not matter in China seem to have been trying to convince themselves. Their disclaimers perhaps were also directed to a home audience which did not expect a missionary to confess even to her family to a frivolous interest in clothes. Luella Miner, who over the years wrote continuously sober and thoughtful letters both to her family and to her supporters, asked her mother offhandedly for "any stray fashion sheets that come into your possession" so she would not get "too antiquated." From a furlough visit to London, however, she wrote a different kind of letter to a fellow missionary in Peking:

> Perhaps I would have liked Paris better had my money bag been full enough to buy an elegant, simple black silk gown which set me reciting the Tenth Commandment to myself. . . . [In London] I had my gray Chinese silk made up. You will groan, for London isn't considered a stylish place, but really it isn't half bad. Perhaps I'll have my picture taken in it when I get home and send you one, since you helped me select it. . . . If you want a "swell" party gown, get Chinese gauze, white or black, for a half length skirt, some chiffon to mix in with the waist, and the rest white or delicate colored plain silk or satin. Brocades in big figures are stylish too. Skirts are longer and slightly fuller—the latest have a box pleat in the back, stitched nearly to the bottom.[14]

Miner's interest in the specifics of contemporary fashion indicated a positive investment in the mandates of the fashion industry rather than the passive acquiescence she confessed to her mother.

Feminine and material values did occasionally conflict with the self-sacrifice of women's missionary expectations. To her diary Elsie Clark synthesized her worries into "One thought that has tormented: my very imperfect achievement in practising the presence of God; my excessive interest in clothes, and furniture and goods; my disinclination to discomfort."[15] For women who had grown up during the late nineteenth century—years that had given women's domestic influence a material, Victorian component—an interest in clothes, furniture, and goods was hard to avoid. It had become not a failing but an important female responsibility.

Women adopted Chinese dress rarely and with reluctance. In 1881, Lottie Moon, a single woman with the Southern Baptist board, addressed an essay to men on the "Advantages and Disadvantages of Wearing the Native Dress in Missionary Work," because she thought it did not pertain to women. "No woman of her own free will and accord would give up her own becoming attire to don the less pleasing garments of her Chinese sisters," she wrote. To her male audience she warned "a man begins by wearing Chinese clothes, eating Chinese food, and adopting other Chinese customs; is there no danger that he may lose, by the constant habit of conformity, the power of prompt, manly protest against evil?" Moon advanced another caution that might have explained women's loyalty to home fashions. The danger that missionary children would be seduced or corrupted by China were "increased a thousand-fold to those children whose parents adopted the native dress," she wrote.[16] If native dress could corrupt children, probably the "becoming attire" of home could redeem them. Despite her own adventurous and solitary career, which drew her closer to Chinese villagers than perhaps any other missionary of her generation, Lottie Moon remained convinced of the intimate connection between home fashions and home values.

Particularly in the 1890s, many male missionaries did not heed Lottie Moon's advice to persist in wearing Western clothes. Men writing to the Presbyterian board from Wei Hsien, Hainan, Nanking, and Canton announced their decision to adopt native dress. One wrote that he wore "Chinese dress complete—shaved head, pigtail, shoes, fan, umbrella, pocket on belt." Another correspondent reported that five out of six male missionaries from Wei Hsien had decided to wear native attire. He was more equivocal in describing women's dress, however. "All the ladies have their Chinese garments and bonnets for use in travelling or out of door exercises,"[17] he wrote. Even in the earlier period, women seem to have been less likely than men to accept Chinese dress as a daily necessity.

After the Boxer uprising, and the fresh strength of the foreign presence in China, such compromises as these were rare, particularly in the coastal provinces. (In the interior provinces of Hunan and Szechwan missionaries retained for a longer time the custom of adopting Chinese costume.) When Grace Smith's husband "tho't it would be nice to adopt the Chinese costume," in Fukien she resisted. "From this point of view it is not feasible or at all desireable," she explained. "Our Christians wouldn't approve I feel quite sure." "Not for little me," Mildred Rowland responded to a similar suggestion in 1911. Elsie Garretson's letters of advice to Elizabeth Perkins before she sailed in 1907 told her that she would "live and dress about the same as you do here in America," and suggested that she bring several suits. "The jacket hides your form when you travel, but in the house you can remove it and enjoy your cool thin blouse." Western female dress, tailored to the body, could be offensive to a Chinese society whose women dressed in loose garments. Indeed, one account of a 1900 anti-Western riot in Nanchang attributed its origins to the presence of a Western woman missionary who was conspicuous because of her Western dress.[18]

Native dress, 1904: In the interior city of Chungking, some missionaries wear Chinese garb for a missionary wedding. After 1900 it was rare for Westerners on the coast to adopt native attire. (Edward and Florence Manly are fourth and fifth from the right in the last row.)

"The same as in America," ca. 1910: As she had been advised, Elizabeth Perkins dressed in Western clothes in Fukien, wearing a suit jacket to hide her form when she traveled.

Although women engaged in village itinerating occasionally adopted Chinese garments both before and after the turn of the century, the majority of women resisted this step even for practical reasons. Elsie Clark described a 1914 journey to a country village when she was wearing a green silk waist with crystal buttons. "The women who gathered to look at the foreigner did nothing but examine my clothes and comment on how rich I must be, because I wore pearls so lavishly." Clark's experience led her to conclude that perhaps Chinese Bible women should conduct village meetings, not that she should adopt Chinese attire.[19] After 1900 and a new sense of American power and righteousness, American women rarely "went native," even to the extent of adopting the convenient Chinese garb for women.

When women made concessions to China, they tended to make them to the climate rather than to social practice. They accepted the necessity of protecting themselves from the midday sun with the ungainly pith helmet. Elsie Clark wrote that "it looks very heavy and clumsy, but in reality is very light and cool; at any rate we must put looks aside and wear it." She added that even this functional item had been touched by feminine artistry, however, for "we greatly improve the appearance of the hat by having embroidered covers made to wear over it." Sometimes Chinese practice contradicted practicality. Jeanie McClure wrote of her difficulties in getting tailors to make dresses as short as she would like. "When I consider all the vermin on these streets which seem to be waiting for a chance to fly onto my skirts and crawl up farther I decided to have them as short as the law will allow." Three years later she followed home fashion rather than Chinese practice when she considered bobbing her hair as a means to control its humidity-induced shedding.[20] Although missionary women who lived in China adjusted their habits to its geography, they less frequently acknowledged the stringent demands of its social climate.

The reproduction of home fashions in China, similar to that of other manufactured products, required labor and ingenuity. The work that increasingly would have been done by American machines or specialized craftsmen, in China was done by amateur hands. Elsie Clark arranged an elaborate wedding for a fellow missionary for which she molded eggs in the shape of a flower and mashed potatoes in the shape of a basket for creamed chicken. Afterwards she concluded that "one can have just as beautiful a wedding here as at home if one is willing to think out for oneself what persons in America ordinarily hire a caterer to think out for them. No one could reasonably desire a prettier bouquet than Miss Hall carried made by

Mrs. McLachlin."[21] American needs, which had been created by an increasingly specialized, versatile economy, exacted extraordinary energies from home seamstresses and caterers in China. But when missionary women successfully reproduced a home commodity, they experienced the glee of individuals outwitting a complex economic system. By making themselves what would have been mass-produced at home, missionary women reclaimed refinement as a female accomplishment rather than simply a female purchase.

The grueling ordeal of the 1900 Boxer siege was the ultimate challenge offered late-Victorian missionary women's feminine resources. Entrapped within the British legation, nearly five hundred Westerners lived for sixty days under fire and in the constant likelihood that they would be overrun and massacred by the Imperial and Boxer troops outside. Their journals indicate that they survived on horse meat and slept in their clothes on vermin-infested floors. Water was low and severely rationed during the first month. Despite the other demands on their time, including the endless stitching of all available fabric into defensive sandbags and the nursing of the sick and wounded, American women attempted to keep up standards. Emma Martin wrote that she and her sister were able to keep clean and neat and that "Lizzie has even kept her hair curled most of the time." The besieged ladies greeted the "half dead, bedraggled relief army clad in fresh summer suits," American newspapers reported. Luella Miner protested the implicit criticism of female insensitivity conveyed by journalists:

> The American woman who will not try to make herself look presentable under the most adverse circumstances is considered a disgrace to the sisterhood. Then every woman who had a decent shirt waist had been saving it for weeks 'to wear when we welcome the relief army.' It is sad that our efforts to honor the occasion led to such miserable misapprehension. . . . I wonder whether I shall subject missionaries to further criticism because of the hat which I constructed, frame and all, from pasteboard, wire, brown cotton velveteen, pink satin, and a slide from an old belt.

American journalists' disapproval of female gentility represented a clash between two overlapping currents in American culture as the century turned. Journalists were early voices for a masculine, experiential revolt against the feminized overcivilization of late-nineteenth-century American life. The journalists' contempt for refinement on the field of battle signaled a new valuing of direct and strenuous experience which did not catch up with the female mission movement in China until the second decade of the century.[22] Until then, women maintained standards of dress and decorum that guided them through the most arduous and disconcerting adventures.

Within the culture of gentility, of course, women allocated significance differently. Thus Lucy Mead wrote disparagingly of her housemates:

> I never was in a place where they talked so much about clothes and styles as *some* do here. If they'd pay as much attention to the way servants don't clean the radiators, the floors under them, the rugs, pictures, etc. as they do to the number of times a person wears a certain hat or dress, or the style book it is taken from, some of the rest of us would be much happier and the house would make a better appearance to callers.[23]

Mead's distinction between the meaning of fashionable dress and conscientious housekeeping, even as a managerial responsibility, should not be minimized; fine dress enabled the exercise of personal influence, while a clean house communicated a more diffuse, environmental influence. Ideally, though, a woman's home and her person should be mutually reinforcing.

They were for Ursula Stanley. Her daughter remembered that she loved flowers and had a sumptuous garden. Other missionaries frequently came to her for aid in remodeling clothes and trimming hats, her daughter wrote. "When the editor of the Missionary Herald asked for suggestions that would add value to the magazine, Mother thought of suggesting a fashion supplement." The combination of these feminine accomplishments made Ursula Stanley especially successful in a certain kind of mission work among Westerners in China. After her death, a British admiral, who had been a footloose midshipman as a youth in Tientsin, was reported to have said that he owed his rank to the home and influence of Ursula Stanley.[24] Whether or not the report was correct, its preservation in family lore paid tribute to a feminine ideal in which material goods were shaped by womanly influence to effect moral transformation.

❦

Concern with refinement gained a new, social dimension for American missionary women in China within the context of cosmopolitan European society. The personal and moral significance missionary women accorded to perfect propriety made them sensitive to comparison with the more polished Europeans. Missionaries in the Chinese interior strove to duplicate the material aspects of American homelife, but when they journeyed into the semicolonial world of major cities or summer resorts, both married and single missionaries tried to exceed home standards, to be more cultivated and more refined than they were at home, in the name of national pride.

In many ways, colonial practices structured American life in China. The port cities where Pacific ocean-liners docked had major European concessions, in which Western merchants lived under the protection of extraterritorial legal rights. The spacious concessions of Foochow, Shanghai, or Tientsin had much more in common with the capitals of Europe than with the crowded Chinese districts or the impoverished Chinese interior. Originally confined to designated neighborhoods by Chinese mandate, European merchants gained privileges throughout the nineteenth century, so that, by 1900, the segregation of European and Chinese communities was Western rather than Chinese practice. American missionaries first experienced China from mission quarters adjacent to or within these foreign sectors, and for the large numbers of missionaries who worked in such cities as Shanghai, Foochow, or Peking, the foreign sector was an ever-present influence. Even those who worked in the interior, however, came into cities several times a year for conferences or to visit, and experienced the novel demands of cosmopolitan society.

Emma Martin wrote to her family for some baby-green velvet braid and belt to match, explaining "I fear the folks at home think we are extravagant sometimes but you just can't understand the way folks have to live in the east unless you have been here." Monona Cheney described the cape she was having made in 1919 and anticipated home reactions: "I suspect you think this sounds rather foxy for a missionary don't you? But I'll just tell you right now that from the clothes standpoint, living in Peking is no joke. . . . It's not just a matter of wanting to be in fashion; it's necessary if we and our work are to be respected." Cheney's concern with winning the respect of colonial Peking society pervaded the experience of American missionary women in China. Lida Ashmore made clear that it was a national as well as an individual concern. She wrote that one missionary compatriot's white tablecloth was "dirty enough to almost make me sick," and added tellingly that she "could only hope none of the foreign [European] women saw it."[25] Given that missionary women were in China to convert, elevate, and transform the Chinese, their concern with European opinion deserves serious attention.

Expecting to find China completely alien, Americans were at once reassured and enchanted by the familiarity of treaty port surroundings. Sarah Goodrich found Tientsin "most delightful here when home ways [and] home surroundings make one almost forget they are in a foreign land," and Ruth White wrote of a concert she attended in Peking's legation quarter: "The queerest thing about it all was that I couldn't believe I was in China. It seemed like New York or Syracuse. . . . The whole place—seats, stage, scenery (trees and a river) looked exactly like America. . . . It was significant that the 'No Smoking' signs were in English."[26] The parallel Americans drew between British colonial architecture and their own home cities prefigured a more important identification between American missionary and European colonial practices.

Missionaries living in major cities found well-established practices governing their social responsibilities. Though the custom of calling consumed the energies of many upper-middle-class American women in the late nineteenth century, missionary women from rural areas found it a novel obligation. From Tientsin in 1894 Bessie Ewing described the complex sequence of calls she was expected to make as a newcomer. In return, she wrote, she would remain at home on Thursdays to receive calls. Twenty-three years later, Monona Cheney wrote that her Peking Methodist ladies' house had chosen the second and third Fridays of the month as their receiving days.[27] American women missionaries lacked the time for such social obligations, which had arisen within a leisured women's society, but they nonetheless accepted and scrupulously fulfilled community expectations.

Calling hardly exhausted the demands of treaty-port society. During Chinese New Year, Jessie Ankeny wrote from Foochow that she had gone out every day, and Elsie Clark described an equally frantic social life in November. During one week, she went to an afternoon tea and two formal dinners, one at the consulate and one at a fellow missionary's house, for which she wore a "black satin gown with a Queen Elizabeth riff at the back of the neck" and a red poinsettia at her waist. The next week she went to a reception at the Japanese consulate in honor of the Mikado's coronation, and that Thursday to a literary society meeting.[28]

The proliferation of clubs and societies among expatriates far away from other home institutions intensified social obligations. Ruth White belonged to the Friday Club, which was made up of "foreigners both from the missions and the business people" in Peking, and Myra Jaquet belonged to a literary club of foreigners in Tientsin, of which she was the only one who could read Chinese. The Past-time Club, "the name of the body of foreigners gathered for a good time," sponsored a Halloween Party in

Missionary musicale, ca. 1895: Such amateur orchestras as this one in Pangchuang, Chihli, drew residents of foreign communities together in home rituals. (Grace and Gertrude Wyckoff are at the organ.)

"With our own kind": Presbyterian missionaries in Kwangtung on an excursion to a scenic spot for tea.

1913, and in honor of a recently married couple, all who had them wore their wedding dresses, although as it turned out four had been lost in the siege. The Nanking Association included missionaries, the consular staffs, and business people and, like many other such clubs, divided its time between musical evenings, lectures, and parlor games. "There are so many things in the way of clubs and societies, that everybody has her hands full," Monona Cheney wrote her father when he asked in 1920 if she had yet located the Oriental Branch of the DAR.[29] Foreign societies and clubs in China were formed in order to preserve ties with a real or imagined homeland and had only defensive relevance to their Chinese surroundings.

Few missionaries confined their work to treaty-port society, and those who were stationed in Tientsin or Shanghai often chafed at the social responsibilities the foreign sector imposed upon them. Missionary summer resorts, however, ended up institutionalizing the habits of life of the European concessions. Originally established as sanitariums, resorts in mountains or on the sea served the missionaries stationed in the surrounding countryside and fulfilled a desperate health need. The summer months particularly devastated Westerners with outbreaks of malaria, cholera, and other fevers. When the mission boards in the United States protested the need for summer retreats, missionaries in the field responded that the "church at home must choose between paying such expenses, or paying funeral expenses." Particularly after 1900, the home boards capitulated, and the summer retreat to one of six or seven gradually growing bungalow communities became part of the missionary year.[30]

Once filled, however, the health need tended to drop out of missionary correspondence, and missionaries used other reasons to explain the significance of Pei-tai-ho, a beach near Tientsin, and Kuliang, a mountain in central Fukien, where missionaries of all denominations gathered. Chinese were not allowed to purchase land in central China's Kuling Valley, and Jeanie McClure noted that the small Chinese population of Kuliang, probably mostly support personnel, was not much in evidence. Particularly for missionaries who were isolated in small country stations during the year, the summer resort provided primarily an opportunity to recharge national and racial identities through association "with our own kind."[31]

Summer resort social life was less formal because it was more comprehensive than missionary social life even in the foreign concessions. A day frequently consisted of study in the morning, with a teacher brought along for the purpose, and occasional mission meetings in the afternoon. Rehearsals for musicales, reciprocal teas, thematic parties (an immigrant party at Ellis Island, for instance), and moonlight picnics competed with "the strenuous life of the Western world," as Welthy Honsinger described the long hikes and tennis matches, to occupy the rest of the missionary day.[32] Missionary women caught in the material complexity of Victorian culture also embraced its social complexity. If anything, China only added a sense of urgency to their celebrations of racial and national communities.

Because the Christian community itself was involved in so much foreign life, missionary women found it difficult to retain their sense of mission priorities. Both at summer resorts and in major cities, the missionaries adopted and to some degree lived by the largely segregated practices of colonial society. Alice Reed reported when she came back from a "County Fair" given at the American legation that "almost everything that I have gone to this winter has been a benefit for one sort of charity or another; otherwise the missionaries wouldn't feel they could afford to go." When Monona Cheney returned at midnight from a "Plantation Night" of "old darkey songs" given at the Union Church Literary Guild for the British, she wrote, "if we went to all there is doing, we should never get time for the work we came to do. . . . It's no small problem for most of us here, to know how much to go to, and where to draw the line." The antics of the Anti-Cobweb Society, a self-improvement society of missionary women, drove Elsie Clark to despair. "Oh may I break down from overwork or wear out my soul on problems, rather than degenerate into a mercenary who forgets the great passion that led her to the fight,"[33] she pleaded to her diary.

Missionaries involved in the social life of either major cities or summer resorts tried to draw lines, but they rarely ventured to challenge the set of assumptions which lay behind social obligations. When Lucy Mead had prayer meeting to lead and saw callers coming, she skipped to her room rather than excuse herself, and she so despaired of being able to keep her social life in bounds that she wished she were in the country where there were not so many foreigners. The enormous danger that "the side show would swallow up the circus," as one missionary cautioned Cheney, requires some consideration of American feminine and national identity at the turn of the century.[34] The British colonial sideshow was irresistible to Americans in part because it dramatized issues of international status at the forefront of middle-class consciousness.

The American missionary enterprise had not originally identified itself with a specifically national purpose. In the early nineteenth century, traveling to India or China represented a radical withdrawal from the political concerns of one's generation; it was perhaps the purest demonstration a religious man could make of the disinterestedness of his benevolence. (Only later could women enlist as missionaries in their own right.) Missionaries who volunteered in the late nineteenth and early twentieth centuries, however, often subscribed to a social gospel which stressed the importance of human institutions in preparing the way for the Lord. Though missionaries were not universally political imperialists, they were staunch cultural chauvinists who took pride in the vigor of their young nation.

China service enhanced this nationalism, and missionaries frequently wrote home of the new appreciation of their nationhood that China had given them. Monona Cheney wrote in 1918 that "you have to come to the Orient to find out how much 'spread-eagleism' some of us Americans have"; and Sarah Goodrich wrote that the "dear colors bring tears to the eyes of us banished ones, as they never did when we lived under the folds of the Stars and Stripes." The flag itself was the focal point for American patriotism, and like the Bible constituted a key item in missionary iconography. When the Epworth League, a mission support group, sent Elsie Clark to China, it presented her with a Bible and a large flag, and when Lucy Mead heard that a church group was sending her a flag, she wrote, "The dimensions sound as tho it would be big enough to cover the whole church." When Leonard Christian married Agnes Meebold on Washington's Birthday, as he reported it, "the large flag was hung so as to form a canopy over the place on which we stood, so that literally we can say we were married under the Old Flag." Edna Terry, who was "intensely patriotic," according to a friend, wished that at her death she might be buried in the Chinese quarter, but wrapped in the "dear stars and stripes."[35]

Missionary nationalism had a strong clannish component to it. Americans sought each other out and discovered common bonds which transformed nationhood into collegiality. The American cavalry practice of selling horses only to Americans "just to insure that the horse has a good home," demonstrated the way in which national affiliation could translate into bonds of trust. Fourth of July celebrations at summer resorts were charged with particular enthusiasm and zeal. On one Fourth, Elsie Clark got up early to raise a flag to the top of a pine tree and, with another woman missionary, shot off five revolver charges to salute the flag. Missionaries felt that their love of country was sacred and remained naive about the consequences of such chauvinism. Clark's account of a 1916 fireworks

"Spread-eagleism," 1903: Grace Roberts teaches Bible women under the Stars and Stripes in her Kalgan, Manchuria, outpost.

celebration revealed this naiveté: "Large numbers of Chinese gathered outside the club grounds to watch us," she wrote, "and I couldn't but wonder what effect the sight of our united love of country would have on them."[36] Generally a sensitive observer, Clark in this case seems to have been unaware that the real effect of such celebrations may have emerged from their segregated structure rather than their exemplary, patriotic content.

Perhaps national affiliations were particularly robust in order to cement an expatriate community that was still conscious of American regional differences. A significant affiliation for most Americans in the late nineteenth century, region of origin elicited occasional suspicion, discomfort, and misunderstanding among China missionaries. When Luella Miner, the midwestern president of a missionary college, had to deal with the officials of Wellesley College, she wrote, "I wished my grandparents had never left Connecticut. Then perhaps I'd naturally know what was coming and how to act!" Lucy Mead, like Luella Miner a graduate of a small midwestern college, was also sensitive to regional and educational differences between Midwest and East. She wrote of Bertha Reed, a Phi Beta Kappa graduate of Cornell University, that though she was "so lovely," "I don't feel as well acquainted with her because its hard for me to get acquainted with people from Mass. etc." When two women, one a Smith graduate and the other from Mount Holyoke, broke down over their studies, it reassured Mead about her own slow progress: "It doesn't pay to be so strong and smart and do more work and learn more Chinese than anybody else when it brings such results," she concluded. New England women could be as vulnerable as midwesterners. Lora Dyer and Jeanie McClure considered apologizing for their bashfulness on the grounds that they were brought up in New England, and Elizabeth Perkins reacted with hurt to a fellow missionary who "said some very tactless things about New England people one evening to me when she knew I was N.E."[37] The China arena made regional distinctions personal and immediate, and even when such distinctions were subsumed in public nationalism they remained sources of private uncertainty.

Foreign community life threw all American classes, as well as diverse American regions, into a novel proximity. Most missionaries, who came from farm families in the Midwest or New England, were at first acutely conscious of their humble origins when they found themselves among diplomats and world travelers. But they wrote home from China in surprise at the intimacies they were being shown. Lucy Mead found the wife of

minister Paul Reinsch to be "perfectly lovely, so natural and friendly," and
Elizabeth Perkins described Corda Gracey, the wife of the Foochow consul,
as "very good looking, tall, fine figure, very good talker and not a bit
patronizing." Monona Cheney was more open about the consequences of
her experiences in Peking society: "I am outgrowing my fear of rich
people, since we have had several of them here in our home."[38] Regional
sensitivities remained, but American missionaries found their sense of
American class differences eroding with their cosmopolitan experience.

For one thing, the low cost of living meant that in many regards
missionaries themselves were becoming "rich." Anyone who had enough
to eat and a staff of servants was wealthy by Chinese standards, but by
American home standards, too, missionaries felt that they were leading
privileged lives. Partly a result of fluctuating exchange rates, which sometimes made missionary salaries particularly ample, American life-styles
were also conditioned by colonial standards of reference. "We live a little
better than we do at home here in Nanking," Jeanie McClure wrote, and
Elsie Clark thought they were "better provided with the things of the flesh
than many and many a teacher in America." Christine Pickett, whose
family lived in a handsome house in Foochow furnished by a previous
German harbor master, suggested that considerations of living standards
might have entered into her parents' decision to return to China after their
Boxer uprising furlough. She wrote that on furlough

> my mother, who had never been interested in domestic skills, had to
> take care of a family of nine with none of the several servants she had
> had in China. . . . Certainly my mother was not fitted to be the wife
> of a country parson. . . . Although she charmed the audiences of
> church ladies to whom she gave missionary talks, she would have had
> trouble coping with poor little parsonages. A family of nine in that
> little house in West Haven!

A historian of the Congregational board has claimed that the "humblest
missionary considered himself an aristocrat" based on his or her *moral*
superiority. But the sense of aristocracy which missionaries felt was also
based on the real material advantages they were sometimes able to enjoy.[39]

For Jessie Ankeny, residing in China provided an exhilarating experience of freedom and plenty which she wanted to share with her family. She
dreamt that they came to visit her:

> I went to your house and found Mama scrubbing in the heat and ready
> to get supper in an old Chinese stove—When I went over I took a

woman along put her to scrubbing, hired a cook and a woman to take care of the kids and then we all went out on the hill to see Foochow. I can remember how beautiful papa that it was and how glad you were you came.

In comparing her mother's hardships to those of a Chinese working woman, Ankeny revealed her guilt about the hardships she no longer endured. Her dream of dismay turned to delight, however, when she could share with her parents her discovery that colonial hierarchies entitled the humblest American farm folk to live well. Other women besides Ankeny dreamed of supplying their families with Chinese servants who would enable them to "sit down and take your ease."[40] The class advantages of living in China brought glee, if occasional guilt, to American missionary women and raised their expectations of their social due as well as their sensitivity to social slights.

New national pride and social confidence influenced the relations of American missionaries to Europeans in China. The British in particular represented a constant source of reference and a perpetual challenge to Americans of all regions and both sexes who in the early twentieth century were struggling to acquire a sense of international stature. Troubled by feelings of social inadequacy in their dealings with the Old World, Americans built their case for their national culture on the superiority of American democratic political instincts. Their critique of the British emphasized English authoritarianism, rigidity, and arrogance—all results of the British class system which Americans found so threatening.

Americans commented on the authoritarianism of the British in their relations with consular superiors and Chinese subordinates. In 1894, when British officials ordered their nationals to go south to escape the effect of the Sino-Japanese War, Luella Miner wrote that "they, poor things, having never breathed the free air of America, obeyed." Sarah Goodrich noted that "the English have profound respect for Authority as vested in the Government, their Legation their Bishop; but a company of English can't do team work as we understand it." If British missionaries were overly obedient to those above them, they shocked Americans by their treatment of those below them. Ruth White wondered if the English people were "less democratic, as a whole, and more 'bossy' around servants" than Americans. She noted that one British couple was "very nice to talk with, but they make us feel so badly in the way they act toward the China boys." During the Boxer siege, when dysentery struck the daughters of a Chinese doctor, Emma Martin treated them with calomel and zinc sulpho carbonate after the English doctor had refused to do so. "The drugs the English have are too precious to waste on the Chinese," Martin wrote.[41]

Americans considered that the instinctual British adherence to hierarchies of authority led to inflexibility in times of stress. During the Boxer siege, American women constantly remarked to their journals on the superior ingenuity of their countrymen. "If they want a thing done they put Americans on it," Emma Martin wrote. "The English are so queer. It takes so long to get an idea into their heads." Sarah Goodrich added, "the work of the British on their fortifications seems slow to American hustlers." British expectations made the resourcefulness of American women during the siege especially impressive. Emma Martin told of a British soldier's response: "We were such a marvel to him I think, because of our adaptability and willingness to do any kind of work."[42] In their own view, Americans' flexibility in the work they would do was only one indication that they belonged to a freer, more open society.

For American missionaries the most significant feature of the English personality was the sense of nation and class which made Americans feel inferior. British snobbishness irked, outraged, and also challenged Americans. It invariably most offended those particularly attracted by the British sense of caste, who were frequently women. The American male identity had evolved through the nineteenth century in opposition to a notion of European refinement. Based on the frontiersman of American legend, the ideal American male was more direct, rugged, and democratic than his European counterpart. As the masculine ideal moved away from the model of European refinement, however, the American feminine ideal came to embrace qualities of delicacy and gentility that were increasingly associated with an upper class, or with British standards. Domestic ideology originally celebrated women's power to counter social divisions, but by the turn of the century it had acquired unmistakable hierarchical connotations. This hierarchical meaning of American domestic ideology was acted out in American experience in China's foreign community.

Matilda Thurston demonstrated gender, class, and national sensitivities in her comparison of British and American mission communities. Thurston particularly appreciated the inland city of Changsha in China because of the British influence there. When she moved to Nanking she found the quality of the servants lower: "I imagine the fact that American middle-west standards prevail in Nanking has something to do with this. English standards prevail up river in housekeeping and the English know how to

use servants. But in missionary work the case seems to be the same. The
Bible women are coarse and of a lower class than they ought to be———"[43]
By associating high standards in servant management with good missionary
work, Thurston touched on a complex of insecurities particularly significant for American women.

American women agreed that refinement was best cultivated by those of
pure, uncontaminated, upper-class background. Those American missionary women who could point to highborn British antecedents did so, and
those who could not defended themselves proudly. Esther Lewis, "whose
parents came of well-born families in England" according to her daughter,
was annoyed at a British missionary woman whose condescension suggested that "all Americans were a cross between Red Indian and the
questionable characters who settled Virginia." Emma Martin's ancestry
was more vulnerable to condescension, however. She wrote:

> Nothing makes me so indignant at the Britons as when they show
> their conceit and think their manners and customs—language and
> institutions are superior to the Americans because they are oldest. I
> feel like flaring up and saying—though my father may be only a
> descendent of the fierce and warlike tribes of Northern Europe and
> tho' (on the other side of the house) my grandfather was a coachman
> and my grandmother a lady's maid who fell in love with each other
> and ran off to get married and afterward came to America—and tho' I
> have no ancestors to boast of—my folks were always honest—and I
> was born in the land of the free and the home of the brave and I am
> proud to be an American and a lot more I would like to tell them.[44]

Emma Martin lacked highborn ancestors, but she made sure to establish
her descent from the Nordic peoples deemed by American nativists to be
the founders of American democratic traditions. When Martin announced
her birth in the "land of the free" she aimed to assert her independence
from European aristocratic traditions, but she also distinguished herself
from the sluggish immigrant masses.

This concern with family and class origins preoccupied native-born
Americans at the turn of the century and made them palpably sensitive to
the condescension of British of whatever class. Sarah Goodrich, who was
proud of her New England ancestry, found that "the snobbishness of
England was quite as offensive as anything in the world." But she greatly
admired "the cultured manners of really cultivated English people," and,
like other American women of her time, she felt acutely her own lacks in

this area. She was ashamed of her ill-trained handwriting, for instance, which she liked "no better than a frowsy head, a carelessly dressed woman, or an ill-set table," and felt—perhaps without basis—that an English education would have provided "neatly penned, well-exercised letters" and other evidences of good breeding. She and Lida Ashmore both insisted on instruction in music and spoken French for their children in the United States in their efforts to create refinement among their offspring.[45]

American men were not immune to concerns about the American reputation for good breeding either. Colonel Charles Denby, minister to China in the 1890s, despaired of his countrymen, who in "the society of quiet and elegant men and women of the world" always seemed to "get up an argument." Denby himself, however, came from a genteel Richmond, Virginia, background, and there had acquired the upper-class standards of refinement which middle-class women acquired as part of their feminine education. Middle-class missionary men were less sensitive to British standards of gentility. When a British woman criticized the propriety of Esther Lewis's ornamented wedding band, for instance, Lewis was prepared to replace it. Only her husband's strenuous objection prevented her from capitulating to the superior pretensions of her British middle-class colleague. Children remembered the particular fascinations with the British of their mothers rather than their fathers. Lottie Hartwell recalled the exaggerated respect of her mother for the chauvinistic British principal of the British school she was attending. Jeanie McClure's daughter wrote that her mother, in particular, had "loved anything English," and had gone out of her way to be friends with "a Victorian English businessman who lived a 'Kipling in India' kind of life."[46] American women conscious of English condescension resented it but in some sense believed in it—believed that the British were superior to Americans in matters of breeding and culture important to women.

Understandably, they took British society as a challenge as well as a model. Elsie Clark had originally shared with many Eastern women an Anglophilic predisposition. She arrived in China, however, and found many of the English women unfriendly and stiff. "I hate to admit it," she wrote, "because it contradicts an ideal of mine." She courted the British community, and through her wit and perhaps her experience in Baltimore society, she was uncommonly successful in penetrating it. A year later she wrote in her diary: "Nothing has warmed my heart more this summer than the cordiality and spontaneity of the said-to-be formal Britons who seem to have taken me into their circle. Last year I did think them cold. Have they changed or have I." Needless to say, neither Clark nor the British community had changed; rather, their relations to each other had adjusted as Clark won admission to a closed society. Clark came to play on British club field-hockey teams, to attend British parties, to understand, if not fully appreciate, British wit. When a Bible group was proposed for the wives of the largely British business community in Foochow, Clark wrote home: "It's been whispered that if there should be a class, I would probably be the leader chosen, which means well, since the group would contain nine British women to one American, that I have managed to reach a sympathetic footing and get along well with our English cousins." [47]

Elsie Clark's flirtation with and adoption by the Foochow British community did not betoken a weak character or a Tory temperament. As a supporter of woman's suffrage, she found herself in constant conflict with much British opinion, and as an advocate of simplified spelling, she threatened to violate the sacred vessel of English culture itself. At the same time, she could not resist the national challenge felt by all Americans at the turn of the century, but particularly by women, to prove themselves as capable of discernment, refinement, and sensibility as the most cultivated Englishwoman. Inevitably this contest had consequences for American missionaries' definition of their work and relations with the Chinese.

At some level, American women were conscious of the consequences. Sarah Goodrich wrote that although her English friends were "naturally much more cultured than American missionaries . . . who know almost nothing of polish," Americans likely made better missionaries, "for they know better how to get the hearts of the poor and lowly." But Americans, she wrote "almost none have ease of manner and smooth speech until they have mingled with those who have. . . . The English always carry about a sense of superiority because they are *English* and may in the long run be more disagreeable, but they never make you smile with their bragadocha [*sic*]." Goodrich distinguished between virtue and refinement and accepted the special merit of American democratic values. At the same time, she felt a national pique at being considered "second rate," reinforced by a feminine offense at being considered vulgar. This double sense of inferiority contributed to American participation within a hierarchical system epitomized in Dorothy Campbell's experience as a missionary daughter in a British missionary school. "I developed quite a feeling of inferiority because of the attitude of a snobbish clique who looked upon the few Americans as uncouth and peculiar," she wrote later. "I made up for this by pride in dominating a few girls who seemed pleased to be my 'fags.'" [48] This form of graduated domination had indoctrinated generations of English children to the idea of class. But perhaps the particularly national form it took for Dorothy Campbell suggests a consequence of American social insecurity in China. The experience of British colonial attitudes, like Campbell's British public school experience, integrated American missionaries into a social system whose political premises they consciously repudiated.

※※※※※

Overseas society in China rested on an extensive system of domestic servants. The relations between American missionaries and Chinese retainers influenced missionary attitudes, work, and reputation. The home was the only arena of mission service for some women, and their servants were thus their only converts. But domestic experience conditioned much of the interracial experience of women who worked outside the home as well. The employ and supervision of Chinese servants in missionary compounds limited and directed the associations that missionaries would have with these same servants, their children, or Chinese from similar backgrounds in churches or schoolrooms.

American missionaries arriving in China found well-established traditions for hiring servants. Lida Ashmore wrote in her autobiography that the regulation number was three—a cook, houseboy, and coolie—but if a family had children, a nurse could be hired as well. Chinese society was labor-intensive, and to some degree the use of manpower was an inevitable adaptation to existing conditions. In justifying the large staff of her household, Elsie Clark wrote that "each individual family has to do for itself things that the community does in a well ordered city. We have to supply our own sewer and garbage system, be our own health department, and arrange for our transportation whenever we want it." Lacking telephones, missionaries adopted the British colonial practice of using "chits," messages carried by coolies, to communicate with each other. Traveling required even more labor. Clark wrote of an eight-person missionary picnic to a Buddhist monastery which required the assistance of thirty-three Chinese: three for each missionary to carry the chairs, six men to run the boat, and three more to carry the food and steamer rugs.[49]

Women from farm backgrounds who had dedicated their lives to service in China found their dependence on servants absurd. Even women from urban families which had employed a cook or a maid found the abundance

Human transportation: In all parts of China, missionaries relied on the traditional means of transportation, which was often local manpower. The familiar sedan chair was used primarily in the south and is here shown carrying Elsie Clark. Emma Martin (*opposite, above*) and a friend are riding in Shantung mountain chairs, which Martin termed "our aeroplanes." Other Methodist women use "back chairs" at Mount Omei in Szechwan (*opposite, bottom*).

of servants discomfiting. Mildred Rowland considered it "ridiculous" that she and her husband had three servants to care for them and their three rooms, and even Lida Ashmore, who liked having servants, could see the absurdity in excessive numbers. "I don't know what I shall do," she wrote, "for I have only 5 servants to wait on lone me——." For women not accustomed to sharing home duties and home intimacy with strangers, the presence of servants could be a burden. Monona Cheney particularly enjoyed trips to Western Hills, where "we were just by ourselves, to do exactly as we pleased, with no servants to get in our way." Later she wrote that "ordinarily picnics here lose half of their fun because those ever-present servants do all the preparing." Mildred Rowland finally told their houseboy to leave them alone at dinnertime: "Its all right when there is company but I don't like to feel the presence of his company standing rigidly behind my back." She concluded sourly, "Oh I tell you there is style in China."[50]

Missionary women spoke in an aggrieved tone which suggested that they lacked control over the hiring of servants. Particularly when they conclud-ed, as Elizabeth Perkins did, that "it is almost more work to keep after them than to do the things one's self," or, as Sarah Goodrich did, that "if one's muscles get more weary one's nerves get less weary," why did these women continue to keep house with a retinue of Chinese servants? Mildred Rowland and her husband found themselves financially pressed one year and decided to do without servants. When they broached their plan to the longtime mission residents, however, the community objected. "Let your servants go—NO, and then they began to say what they thought and when they got thru Henry had made up his mind to write to M. K. [the Board secretary] and tell him about [financial] matters." Unfortunately, Mildred Rowland did not detail the mission community's objections. But her account documents the fact that missionaries had servants in part because everyone had servants, because it was accepted practice.[51]

Rowland did indicate that one objection raised against the discharge of her servants pertained to her own mission work: "Miss Glover is inter-ested in not letting the servants go for that would mean that I would have to give up the kindergarten or the industrial work and that is 'boo shing,' won't do." Like turn-of-the-century women reformers, women missionar-ies were able to maintain active public lives only through the assistance of servants at home. Some women thus found justification for their servants in the freedom it gave them to do their own mission work. Marjorie Steurt said that she had had three servants to do her housework, "but I had a terrific load of teaching." Servants' wages were so low in China that financial calculations always encouraged their employ. Edward Manly wrote that his wife's time for the work was worth more than the "price we expect to pay a cook," and Elsie Clark noted:

> Since we have to pay each one of our employees only $2.50 a month, the four of them costing less than one servant in America . . . we think it useless to make things hard on ourselves just for the sake of making our life "sound martyrlike" to the people at home. We live comfortably and well, believing that we can do our best work when we are free from unnecessary household duties.

The result, as Elsie Clark wrote, was that their household routine was not just functional but "indeed very easy and soft."[52] American women feared that reports of their domestic servants would compromise their reputation for self-sacrifice at home. They seldom considered that institutionalizing racial hierarchies in their homes might compromise their missionary work in China.

Of course, at the turn of the century, all Americans subscribed to some variety of racial thinking. Missionaries, too, assumed the superiority of their own Caucasian, Anglo-Saxon stock to the other racial blendings of the world, and they sometimes arrived on the mission field expecting to be greeted by an alien form of humanity. Consequently, when they discovered the familiarity of basic Chinese responses, they wrote home in amazement. Shortly after Lizzie Martin arrived in Peking, she met some Chinese students who had been in America: "I have been surprised that they have as much personality or individuality as any Americans I ever met," she wrote. "They can talk and think just as well as other young men." Elizabeth Perkins had expected heathen people to be ugly and unhappy, she wrote home, but had been impressed with the women and children. "Some mothers with their babies have almost Madonna faces," she wrote. When Jessie Ankeny found that an old Bible woman reminded her of her aunt, she commented bemusedly to her family, "Isn't it strange tho'."[53]

Perhaps in compensation for their low expectations, American missionaries strenuously protested that race was not an issue in their lives. Monona Cheney expressed a common sentiment when she wrote, "I love the Chinese folks, as I love Americans, as individual people. Except for the language . . . one very soon forgets to be conscious of race distinction at

The omnipresent servant, 1910: The Methodist foreign community in Tzechow, Szechwan, sits down to dinner.

all." When Jessie Ankeny thrilled at seeing some Caucasians in her country station, she corrected her language—"rather some folks who talked English I'd better put it. We are not superior to the yellow man." Racial pieties filled letters home, and most of them denied the significance of racial categories.[54]

But at the same time, Darwinian thinking conditioned missionary attitudes. Missionaries were proud of their racial backgrounds and sometimes explained that their idealistic sense of mission was a result of superior natural selection within their own race. Sarah Goodrich reminded her son Carrington of "the drive of the heredity heeding of the call of Higher Powers [sic]" when he contemplated a worldly pursuit, and Luella Miner cautioned fellow missionaries not to make unfair comparisons:

> It is well to remind ourselves with all humility, that we are not average Westerners; we are the result of selection, probably far more than one generation. We may have the start of some of our Chinese colleagues, but given our heredity and environment, they may have outraced us.

Like many of her countrymen, Miner did not have a coherent racial theory. At the same time that she denied "supposed superiority," she measured Chinese achievements as victories of Chinese spirit over a less promising initial inheritance. Her reminders, "with all humility, that we are not average Westerners," may have referred to the Anglo-Saxon racial origins of most missionaries, but more likely it referred to the missionaries' own sense of their higher call and purer motive as compared to most of their countrymen.[55] A system which distinguished missionaries from Chinese on the basis of an unequal distribution of hereditary gifts, on whatever basis, provided the groundwork on which colonial practices could build.

The physical intimacy of servants and master living in one house encouraged the maintenance of racial boundaries. Missionaries who arrived in China expecting to encounter a degenerate race found their grossest expectations overturned. But different standards and facilities for personal cleanliness confirmed more subtle distinctions. Lizzie Martin wrote that her sewing woman was convenient: "she has to sit in our bedrom all the time and we don't like that very well though. She has the peculiar strong odor about her that most of them have. When we are out we fear she will use our combs and toothbrushes, we tried for a while to keep them hid, but just cant all the time." China experience fed rather than diminished personal racial paranoias. Elsie Clark came to China well informed and eager to explore ancient Chinese culture. She did not find any examples of the venerable civilization she had expected in Foochow, however, and instead found herself becoming increasingly fastidious about her contact with Chinese people. She wrote, "Perhaps we're over squeamish but seeing too much has the effect of making one not want to touch or be toucht. I feel the same way in regard to the food, which I don't enjoy as much as when I first came." [56] Missionaries dealt with the threatening environment servants brought into their households by maintaining strict hierarchical and racial distinctions.

Because of their inexperience, most American women needed coaching in dealing with servants, and certain missionary women gained reputations as authorities on the subject. Eleanor Sheffield and Mary Ament, for instance, were said to be "inspiring" in their expertise in servant management. American women quickly discovered that household administration required firmness and indirection rather than the benevolent love associated with missionary work. Ellen Suffern learned that she must raise her voice at her servants: "At home, people would think I was angry, but I am not." The Chinese custom of "squeeze," which entitled servants to levy an informal surcharge on all household transactions, struck missionaries as dishonest and corrupt, but for practical reasons most learned to tolerate it. "Of course they don't get more than a few dollars a month out of you," Jeanie McClure wrote, "and if you want peace you have to close your eyes to some things." Considering the difficulties involved in running a smoothly functioning house, it is no wonder that women took pride in just that limited aspect of mission work. Grace Rowley's tribute to Elizabeth Root Luce, mother of the founder of the *Time-Life* empire, emphasized this particular achievement: "She never got the language very well, couldn't talk to the Chinese too much, but she was a great house-keeper. . . . I know her servants always looked better than any of the rest. She had them keep their garments so clean, and no wrinkles." Jeanie McClure ran a more modest establishment, but she too found that household management in China had its satisfactions. "It's rather fun, after all, to be running my own house and bossing my own servants," she wrote. [57]

The business of bossing servants was essentially an adversarial relationship, missionary women found. Servants challenged Western women with Chinese squeeze and missionary women struggled to retain their freedom and authority in the face of servant expectations. Jessie Ankeny noted that when one of their coolies came in and saw her washing her clothes, "he nearly had a fit to see me doing such coolie work," and when Mildred

Rowland first arrived in China she waited until her servants had gone to bed to sneak into the kitchen to put up tomatoes. When salary cutbacks necessitated economy in mission households, Sarah Goodrich's servants thwarted her efforts: "This servant or that, is determined your scale of living shall be kept up and they are like vultures sucking your life blood. They won't let you save on anything." Sometimes relations came to an impasse, and missionaries learned that servants must be replaced. In 1916, Clara Foster wrote that they were giving her husband's helper of the past seven years to another family. "He is so mighty independent and seldom deigns to accept my suggestions," she wrote. Elizabeth Perkins's washerman left "because he wanted to control us instead of our controlling him."[58] The issue of control governed the relations of missionary managers with their Chinese employees.

The same issue spread beyond domestic management to influence relations between missionary women and Chinese people in general. Women overcoming fears and gaining confidence in their ability to boss Chinese servants had a vested interest in depicting the Chinese as a naturally compliant and servile race. Despite much evidence of Chinese stubbornness, missionaries concluded that the Chinese were well suited to be domestic retainers. Florence Manly found them "ideal servants," Luella Miner considered them "such efficient servants," and Ruth White noted that her household's staff were "a good set of people—so good-natured and knowing their place so well." In her dealings with "the Chinese," Sarah Goodrich wrote, she would put up with no nonsense; the context revealed she was referring to her servants, but her generalization revealed how servant relations could structure an entire social perspective.[59]

If the Chinese made good servants, however, it was clear that the best servants were not only Chinese but Christian as well. Christian and servant communities overlapped substantially, since obliging servants often became Christians and needy Christians, servants. Certainly missionaries exerted some of their most strenuous efforts at conversion on their servants. Bessie Ewing was unwilling on Christian grounds to accept the popular wisdom that no Chinese cook was completely honest, and though she did not want to be stingy, she wrote "we want to help them up to higher standards." Higher standards usually made better servants, and it almost seemed as if that were the point. In an article on "Our Duties to Our Servants," Emma Smith reminded her readers that "we are no better Christians than we are masters and mistresses." She included guidelines for mistress behavior and scriptural passages designed to inspire improved service. "Is the servant Lazy?" she wrote. "Let us try, 'Not slothful in business.' Rom. xii." Smith included lessons for the saucy, tardy, untidy, wasteful, quarrelsome, and unsystematic servant and a special lesson "for the one who was Unwilling to Entertain." Although occasionally Christian affiliation destroyed a good servant—as in the case of Lida Ashmore's cook A Ngi, who after he became a deacon "has got the big head and really does not have time to do our cooking"—more commonly the Christian faith bound mistress and servant in a sustained and mutually profitable relationship.[60]

As a result, services within missionary households sometimes seemed designed to promote the social harmony of the establishment more than the salvation of individual souls. Ruth White described returning home from a walk at the beach resort of Peitaiho in time for a Chinese worship service. As she and her companion drew near their new house, they could see the Chinese servants coming over the hill from their quarters on the outskirts of the community. White reported her companion's comment: "Isn't that a wonderful sight—see them coming! I feel as if these Sunday services were a sort of consecration of our house."[61] Christian mission work within households reinforced institutional order rather than equalizing missionary and convert in a shared community of sinners before God.

In the management of servants in China, as in certain other domains at the turn of the century, American women followed the implications of a domestic ideology which accepted the inequality of men and women. When women rested their claims to authority on their particular moral refinement and gentility rather than their inalienable rights, they set the terms for their power—but also for their insecurity.[62] American women already concerned with promoting civilized values to establish their social worth at home were unable to resist the additional challenges British standards posed to them in China.

A source close to the mission community made the most striking indictment of American household management in turn-of-the-century China. Prevented herself from missionary service by a spinal disease, Alice Tisdale Hobart was the sister of a respected member of the Presbyterian women's board. She spent many years in China with her sister, married a Standard Oil Company representative, and wrote successful novels about her China experiences. For her, the correct analogy for American domestic life in China was the Southern plantation. In her By the City of the Long Sand, Hobart created a romantic image of the American home in China which formalized attitudes only suggested in missionary correspondence.

She described her home as a personal fiefdom surrounded by walls to keep out the evil spirits of heathendom. "Our homes like the Southern planta-tions," she wrote, "were little kingdoms where we were supposed to rule supreme." She broached openly a concern which many missionaries shared—"the problem of the discipline of that race who served us." Hobart's frank comparison between domestic life in China and plantation life in the United Stated conveyed an ease with the concept of aristocratic paternalism which missionaries did not quite share. Nor did missionaries think to ask, as she did: "How had Martha Washington and other women of the South handled their black people?"[63]

At the same time, Hobart's bold language did point to a truth about the experience of American women who were managing households in China. Within their compound walls they were engaged in a form of domestic empire based on paternalistic premises and racial distinctions. In their relations with retainers in China, as in the South, women experienced limited, direct authority, which supplemented the indirect authority they exercised through feminine influence. These two modes of authority did not conflict but reinforced each other. When Catharine Beecher first expounded a domestic ideology earlier in the nineteenth century, it is true, she hoped that a separate woman's sphere would counter other societal distinctions and provide a unifying force for all regions and classes. But affiliation with the simple virtues of the middle class turned out to be inadequate compensation for women's lack of political and economic authority. While some women expanded their notion of woman's sphere to gain access to limited public authority, others remained caught within a narrow definition of woman's domestic sphere. Such women increasingly sought outward social evidence of the higher moral authority they laid claim to. Rather than encouraging egalitarianism, they became advocates of social hierarchies. Constance Fenimore Woolson, a contemporary ob-server, articulated the extreme view: "If our government were delivered wholly into the hands of women of fashion and society, we should have a monarchy and hereditary order of nobility established within a twelve-month." Missionary women were not women of fashion and society, but they shared with them some aspects of a common feminine culture. They too valued the feminine refinement which a properly appointed home could display. They too could appreciate the contributions made by staffs of servants to the elegant emanations of domestic influence. Missionary women could not resist the opportunity to embellish the American home into a Chinese fiefdom. They found the domestic ideology originally meant to compensate for their lack of economic power fully adequate to sustain their new managerial duties.[64]

The distinctions between the Southern and Chinese cases are as instructive as the similarities, however. Christianity at most served only as a secondary support for a slave system which found its major justification in economic and racial thinking. The confusion which missionaries allowed to exist between Chinese Christian and Chinese domestic service represented a graver ambiguity. Originally the justification for missionary authority, the exercise of Christian influence within the home, emerged as the *means* to missionary authority, and with it the goal of missionary work changed from the salvation of souls to the maintenance of the missionary presence. American middle-class women missionaries found new authority in Chinese households less in preparing God's kingdom than in managing a domestic empire which exploited it.

✥❦✥❦✥

The female rulers of this domestic empire did not necessarily support commercial or political empire. Women who managed households of Chinese servants justified their authority on the basis of mutual bonds of the heart between servant and mistress and on high standards of personal rectitude. They validated their dominion by arguing for the improving power of woman's moral influence rather than the superior force of the Western world.

Women helped to justify their position on the basis of sentiment. When Sarah Goodrich left for the summer and realized that a dying woman would not be there in the fall, she wrote of her sorrow, and said that "our people become like our dearly beloved children." Mutual need bound missionary women and servants in shared dependency. Jessie Ankeny wrote, upon an old servant's death: "She was the best servant I ever knew and we were great friends. When she heard I was sick she cried and when she heard I could not go to Haitang she not only cried but did not want to go back again." Goodrich expressed her gratitude for "our faithful servants and their love for us," and wrote, "I think the real secret of the faithfulness of our servants is the sense that we like them and belief in our interest in them."[65]

The illusion of missionary moral superiority to Chinese heathen was even more basic to missionary claims for authority than their love. Missionaries consciously worked to protect their own stature before their servants. The older missionaries of the Shaowu station refused to play games even with novelty cards "for fear the servants would think we were gambling," and at Peitaiho, Lucy Mead's household avoided dominoes because of the game's resemblance to the Chinese gambling game mahjong. One missionary mother's play theatricals created a stir in her Baptist station, as missionaries frequently criticized Chinese pageantry connected with Buddhist and Taoist rituals. Matilda Thurston expressed a common missionary attitude when she explained her diligence in reviewing the Chinese for her morning prayers: "I should hate to lose face with the cook."[66]

The practices of the overseas commercial community, however, threatened to undermine the carefully cultivated impression of the superiority of Western institutions. "We missionaries tell them that America is the vestibule to Heaven," Jeanie McClure quipped, only slightly exaggerating common missionary mythology. Although missionaries adopted some of the habits of the commercial community, the drinking of the foreign community in Foochow and the smoking, drinking, and dancing at the American legation in Peking proved embarrassing to them. When a group of Germans who had been aiding in the construction of a railroad became drunk at a public celebration, Emma Martin wrote home, "We are so sorry the Chinese knew the Germans got drunk but we can't help it." Missionaries tried to create and maintain Chinese belief in the superiority of the West, and thereby made the fatal error of allying their claims to higher religious authority with the dubious moral claims of a civilization.[67]

Missionaries remained ambivalent about commercial efforts to introduce the products of the West into China. Women favored the importation of some goods, such as oil and sewing machines, but like women reformers at home, they fought a vigorous battle against efforts to disseminate Western vices. The introduction of such products as alcohol and cigarettes discredited the moral claims of the West, as had opium imports before, but it also threatened to draw souls already benighted by heathendom further from the missionary grasp. Missionary women felt that China itself was at contest in their competition with Western vice industries. Sarah Goodrich, an early representative of the China chapter of the Women's Christian Temperance Union, launched a concerted attack on the British American Tobacco Company and its goal to put "a cigarette in the mouth of every man, woman and child in China." Imported liquor never became a major problem in China except with the foreign community, but Goodrich's participation in the WCTU suggests that at some level and for some women, the missionary battles of China were the same as those of women reformers in the United States. "A warning has been sounded that we ought not to come in conflict with vested interests," Sarah Goodrich wrote in relation to her anticigarette campaign. "Have we as missionaries no vested interests in China?"[68] Goodrich's mission program, like the programs of female Christian reformers in the United States, combatted a range of moral impurities which frequently had masculine associations and were promoted by Western commerce.

Missionary women were far less unanimous on the subject of another traditional masculine vice: the use of physical or military force for territorial gain. During times of trouble in China, female voices joined male voices in demanding protection from home governments. When French nuns were murdered in Tientsin in 1870, Harriet Noyes signed a letter drafted by male missionaries heralding the incident as an opportunity for an Anglo-Saxon invasion of China. At the time of the Boxer uprising, Helen Nevius joined the chorus of male voices which protested the American decision to withdraw troops early from Peking.[69] When the Chinese rose up against the foreign presence, women joined men in demanding a military response.

Lacking overt Chinese threat, however, missionary women frequently extended their sentimental identification with Chinese servants and converts to a protective, proprietary stance toward China itself. Ellen La-Motte, a woman traveler visiting Peking in the second decade of the twentieth century, expressed the maternal feelings displayed earlier by missionary women: "This is what makes Peking so absorbing—the peculiar protective feeling it gives one. In a way it seems to belong to us; its interests are our interests; its well-being is particularly *our* concern. You wish the best to happen to China, you wish Chinese interests to have the right of way." Throughout the turbulent late nineteenth and early twentieth centuries, women imaginatively moved into the power vacuum they perceived and spoke out on behalf of "poor China" to those back home. Harriet Noyes, who in 1870 had called for an invasion, in 1895 disagreed with Albert Fulton about the right of foreigners to be protected by gunboats. "More Chinese were killed in the U.S. in the riots than were foreigners killed in China," she pointed out. A year earlier Luella Miner wrote back her outrage at "those who are amusing themselves with cutting up the map of China with their little pen knives," and was joined by Sarah Goodrich. Like other missionaries, Jeanie McClure vigorously protested Japanese threats to Chinese integrity in 1916, declaring herself "press agent for China to all the ignoramuses at home." Edward Said has argued that generations of European Orientalists derived gratification from speaking on behalf of an Asia deemed powerless to speak for itself.[70] Missionary women shared the Western perception of Chinese muteness and took it as an invitation not extended by their own society to act as national representatives.

Missionary men as well as women sometimes spoke as self-appointed advocates for China. But women were more likely than men to express sympathy for China's powerlessness at the hands of the West. The reaction of American women in China to the Boxer uprising presents an opportunity to contrast male and female attitudes. After the Allied Expeditionary Force rescued Westerners from the legation, an international free-for-all of looting, rape, and murder ensued. Missionaries William Ament and E. G. Tewksbury led several armed parties of retaliation against supposed Boxer villages. These raiding parties received national publicity, provoked in part by reporting in the *New York Sun* and furthered by Mark Twain's biting essay "To the Person Sitting in Darkness," in 1901. Missionary women bridled at the censure which the missionary community received as a result of these incidents.[71]

At the same time, women who had been through the horrors of the siege were appalled at the conduct of the allied troops in China. Luella Miner remarked that for all the Boxer atrocities there had been no incidents of Chinese rape, and Emma Martin wrote, "It is just outrageous the way the allied powers especially the soldiers have behaved in China. If our indemnities have to come out of the poor people I don't feel as if I want any." Sarah Conger, whose husband was the American minister to Peking, wrote a letter of sympathy for the Chinese position shortly after her release: "Poor China! Why cannot foreigners let her alone with her own? China has been wronged, and in her desperation she has striven as best she could to stop the inroads, and to blot out those already made. My sympathy is with China. A very unpopular thing to say but it is an honest conviction, honestly uttered." Three and a half months later she wrote:

> China belongs to the Chinese, and she never wanted the foreigner upon her soil. The foreigner would come, force his life upon the Chinese, and here and there break a cog of the wheels that run their Government so systematically. . . . Could we, after taking these facts to ourselves, blame the Chinese for doing what they could to get rid of what they considered an obnoxious pest that was undermining the long-established customs of their entire country.

Sarah Conger reacted differently from her husband, who favored decisive reprisals. The previous year Edwin Conger had proposed that the United States seize the province of Chihli, which included the capital Peking, as a base in China.[72]

Women like Sarah Conger and Emma Martin responded to intrusions on Chinese sovereignty with sensibilities that they seldom used to defend their own autonomy as women. Lida Ashmore, for instance, who acquiesced in her husband's domination of her daily life, criticized him sharply for a constriction of Chinese rights. When he suggested that a Chinese missionary society consult with foreign representatives, Lida Ashmore wrote, "they did not like it. You could see how they would resent asking a foreigner if they could go into a field to work, where no work is done, when they are Chinese and this is China." Lucy Mead, with other American women not yet eligible for the vote in the United States, wrote possessively of China, "Why can't we decide what kind of a government we want, no matter what our neighbor advises?"[73] Like many other missionary women, Lucy Mead did not comment on public affairs in the United States, nor did she protest her lack of a voice in determining public policy. Yet Japanese threats to Chinese prerogative inspired her instinctive, proprietary ire. Of course, American missionary women never surrendered their own interests to China's, but at some level they identified the two. In defending China, they defended their own right to feel responsible, competent, empowered.

American women were also defending a female kind of authority when they defended China. According to the tenets of domestic ideology, authority was best applied indirectly, or, if in the relations between mistress and servant it was applied directly, it should be done according to rules of decorum. Luella Miner wrote that she was particularly offended by a medal imprinted as a memento for the survivors of the siege: "I do not at all approve of the design on one side, Europe, America and Japan trampling on the Dragon. . . . I object to this first because it isn't true to fact, as the dragon came out on the top side, and second because it isn't polite." Similar considerations of courtesy influenced Elsie Clark's reaction to a missionary party's decision to stop unannounced for the night with a Chinese pastor: "It was about 7 o'clock on Saturday evening, yet the whole troop of us, unannounced, descended upon the quiet household demanding quarters. I thought it very rude and imperious in us." Both Clark and Miner believed in themselves and in the superiority of mission institutions to Chinese ones. At the heart of this belief, however, was a conception of civilization which mandated civilized behavior. Although this ideal involved women in a never-ending struggle to achieve higher levels of gentility, it brought along its own rules to govern relations between unequals. [74]

The American male missionary was not only less sensitive to delicate, European-based social distinctions, he was also less conscious of the standards of conduct governing those distinctions. His identification with the figure of the American pioneer may have been more egalitarian in principle, but in fact it opened the way for a wide range of opportunistic abuses censured by rules of gentility. George Miller's practical counsel on how to build railroads for the Chinese perhaps reflected this opportunism. "Don't talk railroads to him—build them," Miller advised. Harry Caldwell's "he-man" missionary service also reflected the coercive directness of a frontier mentality. " 'You agree with me that this gun is better than yours,' " he was reported to have told villagers. " 'When you have listened to what I have to say about the Christ doctrine you will see that it too is better than the religions of your fathers.' " Civilized female culture was not simply a matter of style but of substance too when it limited such Western excesses in relations with China. [75]

Like the anti-imperialist Mugwumps, missionary women lacked a political base and tended to oppose the exercise of military, imperial, or commercial power in which they could have no part. Instead they mounted a moral crusade based on premises of social elitism which played up to their perceptions of themselves as guardians and founts of civilization. This women's crusade, for once in the early twentieth century, corresponded with the interests and policies of the American government in China. The American decision to preserve an open door and to work to maintain Chinese sovereignty enhanced the importance of missionary influence to American purposes and also encouraged a shared posture of national righteousness. Americans undermined their moral claims, however, by their maintenance of private fiefdoms scarcely less imperial for being domestic.

❧ 6 ❧

IMPERIAL EVANGELISM

Although some women missionaries in China lived most of their lives in their own homes and the semi-colonial society of summer resorts and foreign concessions, most of them knew a Chinese world—the world of the missionary school, the village church, the convert's home, and the rivers and paths between. Single women, who had more time for missionary work, were more likely to frequent this China. Like married women, they brought with them notions of woman's sphere which justified their adventures within a context of Victorian self-denial and Christian service. Like American housewives, they also found an added measure of authority in China.

But whereas some women found authority in the management of a household of servants, women in the field conducted an evangelism of intimacy. While women within households affirmed the centrality of woman's sphere, women who had already violated the constraints on Chinese women's lives found American constraints less binding. Women who had previously carried their sense of appropriate role as a constant if unconscious psychic burden allowed it to slip into the background as they grew comfortable with their new and unavoidable identity as "Western She-Tigers."[1] In China they found unexpected power and discovered that, even for women who had grown up docile daughters, power often led to fulfillment.

❧❧❧

Missionary women did not consciously work to enhance their own power in China or even to raise the status of women; rather, they aspired to bring Chinese women to the church in service both to God and to the Chinese Christian community. From the beginning, however, their efforts were severely limited by the restrictions on the movement of Chinese women. Missionary women were forced to fight for the freedom of women in order to gain the right to convert them. Like Chinese reformers promoting freedom for women to increase the strength of the Chinese nation, missionary attacks on the Chinese confinement of women were primarily tactical. When they opposed footbinding or arranged marriages, they were attacking the way the tyranny of heathen practices circumscribed missionary possibilities. They advocated dramatic changes in Chinese women's lot for religious ends considered conservative by American standards of the time.

Despite later claims, missionary women were alarmed at the radical changes in women's opportunities following the Boxer uprising and the 1911 revolution. Luella Miner quoted missionary publicist Arthur Smith in 1913: "The Chinese woman has 'come out' and you can't put her back. What will you do with her?" The China Continuation Committee, an interdenominational council, cautioned, "the walls which guarded the young girl are being demolished rapidly and the spiritual walls which can protect her purity and peace are rising only slowly." Luella Miner expressed her sense of the disparity between the liberty and the responsibility of Chinese girlhood in a more secular vocabulary:

> Some one has said, "Women of the West are constrained by a mass of conventions, of whose value they are perhaps unconscious. It is the existence of these conventions which makes their liberty possible." Unfortunately, liberty in its external aspect is more easy to introduce into China than conventions, which, unlike the old Chinese ceremonies do not always manifest their presence in outward form.

The need to create character, or to internalize conventions of control, at the heart of Christian training in the United States throughout the nineteenth century, gained an added immediacy from the dramatic and immediate changes in the status of Chinese women at the turn of the century. Looked at this way, the new freedom for women which so alarmed missionary mentors was really a great opportunity for building Christian character—now that women "had souls," as Sarah Goodrich put it.[2]

Missionaries especially worried about sexual challenges to the purity of adolescent girls. Sarah Goodrich felt the post-Boxer period to be "a very dangerous time, as the young men know no better than to try and rob the girls of their most precious heritage," and, she implied, the young women knew no better than to surrender it. Goodrich did not oppose the development of "womanly" sexuality; without temptation, how could there be the moral triumph of resistance? "I am trying very hard to impress upon these girls that it is fine to be perfectly healthy," she wrote, but "with all their powers under splendid control." Offended by the implications of the Chinese bridal color of red, missionaries supported the adoption of white by Christian brides to celebrate the inner triumph of purity retained. (Since white is the Chinese color for death, the compromise frequently was pink.) Christian self-control—which for Elsie Clark included the ability to keep secrets and to forbear from gossip—substituted moral restrictions for physical ones.[3]

Missionaries sought the purity of their converts for the good of their individual souls, but also for the reputation of missions and the health of the Christian community. For these reasons they promoted the same domestic ideology for Chinese women which structured their own service. They taught that women's nurturing responsibilities included education, culture, and public morality, but that the ultimate center of their lives should be the home, where they would act as a stabilizing force for the tides of change and the currents of history. Although they themselves had left the "shelter of our homes to do battle for God and Humanity," as Sarah Goodrich put it, "we missionaries are a conservative body."[4]

In specific terms, this meant that missionaries encouraged the marriage and domestic subordination of their students and converts. They aimed to dispel the illusion "that we do not want our girls to marry." "The 'emancipated woman' of China who has broken all the old conventions is both masculine and immoral," Luella Miner wrote. In fact, the students in Bible training schools were frequently already the wives of church members or Chinese pastors. Missionary women supported the higher claims of family responsibilities on the time and energies of these women even when they conflicted with schooling. Ella Glover wrote of a woman whose husband had needed her at home after only three months of school: "She wept and wept and said she would not go, but was finally convinced that a Christian wife might have duties at home. I heard my teachers exhorting her to show her husband how grateful she was for these months at school by being the best wife and daughter possible, and she promised to try." Althea Todd sent a woman off from school to journey forty-eight miles to a Methodist parsonage because her husband wanted to see her. "She did not want to walk two days to see her husband, but he had commanded it and we urged her to obey him." When Mamie Glassburner taught Bible verses, she interpreted them for her class of Bible women, as she put it, in a practical manner: "It was suggested that it might seem difficult to be patient when after a hard forenoon with a cross baby and possibly an aching head, the 'church brother' came home and complained because dinner was late. The woman nodded their heads emphatically; and one confided audibly to the others 'She *knows*.' " Glassburner clearly implied that God willed patience and forbearance with the demands of "church brothers." In times of stress, such as followed the 1911 revolution, missionaries agreed that Christian women might not only steady the domestic order but also the national order—intoxicated as it was "with the wine of independence, race consciousness, and patriotism."[5] In the lessons they taught Chinese women, missionaries advanced a conservative platform of physical cleanliness, moral self-control, and domestic and social compliance. By no means, however, did this conscious ideology of conservatism compose the total or even the dominant influence of missionary women in China. Working in counterpoint to their articulated messages were the less conscious messages conveyed by missionary strategies. While missionaries enjoined Chinese women to obey their husbands, their efforts to influence Chinese women often tended to enhance missionary authority instead.

The Protestant missionary effort was unsuccessful in achieving the wide-scale conversions in China hoped for by the American churches. In contrast to Africa, where entire tribes fell under Christian sway, Chinese conditions were not conducive to mass conversion. Official hostility and a strong state orthodoxy, combined with the thriving heterodox Taoist and Buddhist folk traditions, left little room for a demanding and exclusive Christian God. The precariousness of the Chinese economy, however, presented opportunities to missionaries which Christian ideology alone could not have done. The Taiping uprising and the colonial wars of the mid-nineteenth century added political unrest to the ongoing problems of population expansion, and the once stable Manchu court began to lose control. Family and clan organizations helped provide relief to those left helpless by the century's devastations, but many destitute remained for missionaries to approach with the possibilities they offered for employment, for schooling, and, many Chinese thought, for legal intercession. As one woman put it, "the unspeakable conditions of physical suffering constitute both our call and our opportunity to minister."[6]

Women in China, as in most societies, suffered disproportionately in hard times. Considered economic liabilities, they were less valued at time of birth and more subject to abandonment or sale in times of famine. At marriage, women were cut off from friends and family and transferred as property to husbands and families they knew little of. Though a woman's family, particularly her brothers, retained some responsibility for her well-being, only the most visible and well-substantiated abuse could free her from a disastrous match. Missionaries gained their early converts from a disadvantaged class; the significant numbers of women converts could be explained in part by the disadvantages of their sex.

Tales of abandoned children, daughters rescued from sale or death, and women saved from cruel mothers-in-law and brutal husbands filled missionary letters and propaganda. In the retelling, they assumed the proportions of melodrama. Jessie Ankeny wrote of a woman who overtook her in the road and "told me about her daughter who was about to commit suicide because of the cruelty of the mother in law 'Ah let me give her to you and you can do with her as you like—let her study or be your *slave*'!" Emma Martin, too, wrote of a woman attempting suicide to escape a "wretch" of a husband; she had been adopted by a Bible woman "till she can find new courage to live." Ella Glover provided care for a sick women whose mother-in-law, according to mission story, had instructed her to "never mind, let her die."[7] Although the numbers and the circumstances of needy women were exploited and perhaps exaggerated, they were not fabricated. Women missionaries working in China used their abilities to offer economic and institutional support to the needy as perhaps their most powerful means of recruiting loyal converts and Christian workers.

The dynamics of support varied from outright purchase to the acceptance of abandoned children; support or hire was sometimes a lure for potential converts, sometimes a reward for already professing church members. Missionary women offered economic support without cynicism, and sometimes even reluctantly, in conjunction with personal interest and institutional advocacy. Nevertheless, the ability of missionaries "to provide" remained central to the missionary appeal.

Those who fled to missions did so because missions had first taken initiatives in recruiting, supporting, and sometimes purchasing Chinese. When missionaries first moved into the interior after 1860, they often could not secure students for their schools. Missionaries aiming to demonstrate their good intentions by example would accept unwanted children, sometimes in return for cash favors, to begin their mission schools. As late as 1922, the Methodist mission interceded to save a worker from unwanted marriage to a non-Christian and settled a cash payment of $300 on the prospective bridegroom. "Didn't know we were in the girl buying business, did you?" quipped Monona Cheney.[8]

Missionaries who believed in the righteousness of their God were willing to compete for the souls of those they desired. Usually they competed with "cruel," non-Christian husbands or "tyrannical" mothers-in-law, but sometimes their adversaries were rival Catholic or Buddhist religious institutions. Louise Campbell wrote of a sixteen-year-old girl she had admitted to her school to "save her from the nunnery," and Martha Wiley described her daring "rescue" of a child from Buddhist priests: "I dashed out and there some Buddhist priests had bought one little chap and were bargaining for the brother and had their money out. I grabbed that boy and carried him into my gate and locked the gate. The Buddhist priests went off."[9] Missionaries condemned the stealing of children by rival religious organizations and private citizens, and certainly Martha Wiley's tactics were not those of most missionaries. Nonetheless, mission organizations did convince Chinese villagers that they wanted bodies as well as souls, and it is perhaps no wonder that during the xenophobic mid-nineteenth century Chinese imagined that missionaries used the bodies they were so eager for in perverse and diabolic rituals.

Women's mission organizations commonly argued in behalf of women students reluctantly betrothed or married to non-Christian men. They supported the domestic state for women married to Christians, but encouraged Christian women who were fighting the certain spiritual death of marriage into a pagan home. Missionaries' stress on the importance of maintaining Christian homes also reflected concerns that the Christian community perpetuate itself. The Swatow Baptists not only fought marriages of church-trained girls to heathens but to Christians of other denominations as well.[10] Generally, missionary women supported a woman's right to choose a husband or to remain single altogether when marriage meant that she would be pressured to leave the church.

This position drew women missionaries further into the Chinese struggle for women's rights than would have been their temperamental inclination. In a letter to Hu Shih, a prominent liberal Chinese educator, Sarah Goodrich justified her position:

Is there anyway to force a girl to marry against her will—any law to force her. . . . Perhaps you may deem me very one-sided but when a young man marries the young woman to whom his parents have betrothed him, even if she has not had his advantages intellectually, I feel he is doing right. The husband has it in his power to mold the life of his wife. He can have interests outside the home. I have seen wives wonderfully improve becoming real help meets under the loving patient guidance of a thoughtful husband. But a wife if wedded to an unlettered husband is often treated as if her education was a curse, a reason for making the husband seem inferior. . . .

She concluded, "personality grows through self-sacrifice, but there is a kind of self-sacrifice that kills every power of soul and body. It is from this we would save Miss Chang."[11] Goodrich's pleas for help for a teacher in a mission school demonstrated the cautiousness of the missionary argument. She did not mean to challenge parental authority, arranged marriages, or the virtue of feminine self-sacrifice. Only the combination of these factors, exacerbated by the proper and inevitable subordination of wife to husband, convinced her that Christian women could not marry heathen men.

This position frequently led missionaries to aid and protect the youthful rebellions of schoolgirls against their parents. Lydia Wilkinson and Evelyn Sites persuaded a student's father to allow her to remain single for church work rather than betroth her to a heathen, and Lucy Mead wrote home that the entire women's residence was encouraging another student's rebellion: "What do you think of missionaries trying to give all kinds of opportunities to a pupil to disobey her parents?! That is what a number have done, and just this minute I'm praying hard that the girl may have courage and strength to hold out and refuse to go home, altho her mother has now come for her."[12] The divinity of woman's higher sphere depended on male acknowledgment of its existence. In pagan homes, Christian women would be denied the moral and cultural ambience in which they could transform their subordination into elevation. The fragile flower of domestic refinement could not blossom in truly heathen soil.

When missionary women encouraged Chinese women's independence, they incurred responsibilities to provide them with support and protection. Missions offered a variety of occupations to uprooted Chinese women, including training as teachers and nurses for young women, training as Bible women to assist in the preaching of the gospel for older women, and assorted menial jobs as cooks, seamstresses, and amahs for women of all ages. These occupations were frequently temporary and did not guarantee security, but they did offer short-term relief. Christian women, as well as many Christian men, found that their religion cut them off from old sources of support. The gradually narrowing restriction of support to the mission community inevitably increased the personal dependence of Chinese Christians on foreign missionaries.[13]

Missionaries liked to exaggerate the extent to which unattached Chinese women depended on them for protection from angry fathers or husbands. Emily Hartwell, for instance, within three pages of her mission history wrote of three women whom she had saved from dangerous relatives. She had kept one from being sold as a child; another "ran away" to her "for protection" from a cruel mother-in-law; to rescue a third "lovely girl from the opium fiend father," she kept her virtually a prisoner until after his death. The physical protection provided by missionary women was occasionally overdramatized, but the protection of female reputation was always a real and serious responsibility. Lida Ashmore expressed "just a bit of fear" for the woman she had saved from marrying a pig butcher when she journeyed to Swatow "in with so many men and boys," and though Luella Miner swore she was not cut out to be a Female Seminary teacher, she did not mind supervising young girls in the streets in China because "there seems so much more reason for guarding Chinese girls." When Jessie Ankeny's Chinese teacher and friend Ding Miduang broke her engagement, she experienced ridicule from the local boys' school. Ankeny and her coworker Mamie Glassburner decided "not to let Miduang go outside the yard and not even downstairs only to teach her classes."[14] Having encouraged the breaking of sacred Chinese custom, missionary women had to be prepared to provide a moral haven as well as a physical one for Christian women. Beginning conservatively, they found themselves offering a radical social alternative to Chinese women. This alternative sometimes included a professional career, a single life, a rupture with family—and virtually complete economic dependency on the mission institution.

Women missionaries who bargained for the freedom of their converts frequently seemed surprised at their own audacity. American women did not customarily rely on their economic resources as their means to social authority, and they almost inadvertently discovered the power which their mission organizations possessed as employers and advocates. Their China circumstances had led them to adopt a new institutional strategy. But missionaries brought with them a more traditional female tactic in the struggle for souls. Economic support may have won a woman's body for Christ, but missionary women aimed to win her heart through personal influence and intimate evangelism.

The women's missionary enterprise had never departed far in theory from the domestic ideology which sanctioned it. Woman's extended responsibility for nurture allowed her to teach school and care for the sick, but the home remained her central province and sentiment her central strategy of conversion. Missionary women carried on a personal evangelism which aimed to gain access to women's houses and their hearts. Anna Kauffman explained her belief that the "greatest sphere for any woman is the sphere of the home," which influenced her plan to bring her "deepest and best vision of home and womanhood" to the homes that most needed it. "I have found no greater opportunity than to place my life in the rising homes of China," she wrote. Gaining access to those "rising homes" presented missionaries with major challenges. The missionary women of Peking, Luella Miner wrote in 1893, had had no success at all in securing admission to family courtyards. Nellie Russell of T'ungchow, however, with her more winning style, had succeeded in gaining access to over thirty homes "and is making the work boom."[15]

Even for those who taught Chinese girls in schools, entry to the Chinese home remained symbolically important. Miss R. J. Miller, who ran a Presbyterian girls' school in T'ungchow, frequently went on three-week trips through the countryside visiting the homes of her schoolgirls. Her reason for these trips, she explained, was that "it brings these girls nearer to me."[16] Entry to the home represented an important physical analogue for the entry to the heart which was the ultimate missionary goal.

Justifying their service on the basis of the uniqueness of their gifts, missionary women emphasized the power of Christian love to stimulate individual conversion. Of course, the evangelical tradition which spawned the mission movement had always placed a strong emphasis on the power of love and a faith founded on feeling. Whether the large female church memberships of the nineteenth century encouraged this emotional strategy or were recruited by it is unclear. But, as Ann Douglas has argued, as the century progressed, Protestant religion and female culture became sentimentalized in tandem. Distinctions between the evangelism of men and women were reinforced by the ordination requirements of the majority of the Protestant churches. Male preachers assembled congregations to hear the Word, while women were more likely to "look love."[17]

Evelyn Worthley Sites's description of an evangelizing meeting in a mountain village demonstrated the peculiarly personal nature of women's work. Clement Sites was conducting a service in the local church while Evelyn and a fellow woman missionary, a "live-wire California girl," were working the crowd outside. Sites's fellow worker encouraged a Taoist priest to enter the church by taking him gently by the coat and coaxing him inside. Once there, Sites wrote, "we divided the work, he prayed, with head bowed, and I watched! Watched to see if he really mastered the words! I slipped along beside him and quietly repeated them over and over two or three times until he knew the prayer." Such personal work had been the province of women all along. In revivals in Rochester, New York, in 1831, for instance, women engaged in house-to-house visitation to complement the preaching of such male spellbinders as Charles Grandison Finney. Personal work continued to be a woman's responsibility. In 1917 Ruth White could recollect with another YWCA worker "how our mothers used their opportunities for doing personal work" in talks with grocers and tradespeople; White identified her YWCA work in China in that tradition.[18]

Ideally, the missionary encounter consisted of an effusion of encouragement and love on the part of the missionary, manifested in soulful eye contact and frequently a held hand, to be met with an outpouring of guilt and remorse, leading to conversion, on the part of the potential convert. The intensity of the individual attention was the key. When YWCA evangelist Ruth Paxson came to China in 1918, she emphasized that souls could be conquered only one at a time. Missionaries customarily targeted particularly promising souls in advance. Congregationalist Sarah Goodrich hoped to "get hold of the heart of young Mrs. Wei," and added, "I covet her womanhood for Christ." When a Baptist woman's "special one" had become a believer, she selected another, a friend wrote. Anna Hartwell wanted every Christian to be a "soul-winner" and seemed to advocate totting up souls as if they were scalps, when she described a dying Chinese woman as "one of the trophies our Tommie [Jane Thompson] will lay at the Savior's feet."[19]

The love and encouragement the missionary poured out was sentimental rather than truly personal—what Sarah Goodrich referred to as the "releasing of power through personality through prayer." The successful evangelist aimed to inspire an outpouring on the part of the target soul rather than to give herself away. Irwin Hyatt's study of Julia Mateer noted that her strategy for "getting a hold" on her students entailed first an effort to learn personal information about each student, followed by a home visit, which showed results only when they started to talk more than she did. Ida Pruitt's Southern Baptist mother spent long hours doing handwork and conversing with Chinese women. Though she could not recall whether her

Intimate evangelism: Missionary women sometimes targeted individuals for special attention, as perhaps had Emma Smith, here tutoring a Bible woman.

mother herself told stories, Pruitt noted "she could get more out of people."[20]

The Christian conversion involved more than a surrender of secrets, however; it involved a surrender of will itself. With such high stakes missionaries ardently entered the fray. Luella Huelster described one conversion battle:

> Gwei Lan's whole body was in a tremor. Her teacher, sitting beside her, took her hands and held them firmly in her own as she prayed that the soul-struggle, so evidently going on, might cease. She hastily penned an informal little pledge and placed it in Gwei Lan's hands; but she, reading it, smiled and shook her head in negation; she was not ready to sign it. But the Father coveted her, and less than ten minutes had passed before the little pledge, which no other eyes were to see, was quietly signed and slipped into the teacher's hand, and Gwei Lan was on her feet.[21]

Gwei Lan's surrender was a victory not only for the Lord but also for his insistent aide, who in His name had presumed an awesome intimacy.

Not all missionary women in China endorsed the extreme intimacy of much of women's evangelical work. Particularly women associated with schools and higher education were dismayed at the emotionalism of women's evangelism. Luella Miner, president of Peking's North China Union Women's College, feared the "strong emotional element" which characterized revivals, and Matilda Thurston, patrician president of Ginling College in Nanking, wrote disapprovingly of Methodist Laura White, who was "full of sentiment" and was a supporter of "mother-craft" rather than higher education for women. Religious emotion did sometimes seem to have substituted completely for content. An old sick Chinese woman relayed a story of one missionary woman who had stayed overnight with her: "She pressed my hand and said Ah Sham, Ah Sham and I knew she was loving me and I have loved her ever since, but have never seen her again. I knew she must have been one of your people who tell of Jesus, though she could not talk to me of Him. She could not speak Chinese."[22] Given the less stringent language requirements for women, undoubtedly many women evangelists had marginal skills in speaking Chinese and relied on sentiment to make up for their inability to preach the Word. But intelligence or language competence by no means separated female evangelists from educators. Nor for that matter did a concern for personal

influence. Evangelists and teachers simply differed on the goals for intimate communion between missionary and convert.

For just as female religious work had transformed nineteenth-century
religion, so the feminization of the teaching profession brought with it a
new emphasis on Christian nurture, on the personal relationship between
student and teacher. Female missionary teachers, like female evangelists,
sought a moment of emotional recognition in which Chinese students
surrendered their reserve and their hearts. Lucy Mead hoped that she
might be allowed to "get close to the hearts of the people" rather than study
the thought of Confucius over one summer, and Ruth White wrote that
those teaching English classes who teach "with the real aim of getting in
close touch with the individual girls" were "in love with their job." Even
Alice Reed, who was persuaded to enlist despite her religious skepticism,
talked of the values of "making contacts" outside of the classroom. Alice
Frame, later dean of Yenching's women's college, was also concerned with
getting "in vital touch" with students.[23]

Missionary teachers sometimes approached the problem of getting to
know their students systematically. Lulu Golisch wrote to a friend of how
much she loved the schoolgirls "and how they each have won a place in my
heart." She was interested now, she wrote, "in writing up a little history of
each girl and making a special study of each girl's disposition." Frederica
Mead, who taught at Ginling College, wrote that she was getting "side
lights on the girls characters" from their compositions and that she planned
to keep a card cataglogue of the girls in her classes to record individual
difficulties.[24] Female missionary teachers, like missionary evangelists,
aimed to do more than communicate knowledge; they aimed to transform
character itself, and for them the best catalyst to this transformation was
the power of intimate, personal contact.

Missionaries did not find the Chinese easy to influence, and that
perhaps helps to explain their particular preoccupation with this problem.
Chinese propriety demanded polite toleration of a stranger's viewpoint.
Missionaries railed with frustration at the impenetrable "face" which
thwarted their efforts to get in "vital touch." They complained about
problems ranging from the lack of student responsiveness in class to the
formalism of the Chinese religious tradition, but their dissatisfactions
stemmed from a fundamental difference in the etiquette of emotion.

American evangelical traditions demanded that outward demeanor
reflect inner soul, and although consistence between inner and outer states

was hard to ascertain, at least a display of sincerity remained a strong cultural expectation. American evangelical and feminine traditions reinforced each other on this point. Evangelical thinking required that a pure countenance manifest a pure heart, while feminine values required that both heart and countenance communicate feeling.

American women faulted the Chinese for lack of feeling in their personal relations and their religion. At first Chinese students seemed "very unresponsive, like talking to a wall," Alice Reed remembered. In 1914 Matilda Thurston described the girls at Ming Deh as "too repressed and the most unresponsive girls I ever had to do with." Monona Cheney's description of visiting hours emphasized the lack of enthusiasm among students greeting relatives: "Some of them never can seem to find anything to say to their relatives, and the visits are short; others of them seem as glad as we would be—but these are all too few." American teachers constantly remarked upon the absence of emotional display among students and associates.[25]

Although missionaries admired Confucian ethics, they agreed that Chinese religion lacked feeling and "hasn't the life." They considered Chinese obeisance to Taoist and Buddhist deities to be empty ritual. "Keeping up appearances before the images seems to be the sole end of the religion, if one can judge from outward show," Elsie Clark wrote. Monona Cheney judged that she "had more comprehension of things spiritual at five years old" than most Chinese did at seventy-five, so "narrow and materialist" were their backgrounds. Even when Chinese did accept Christianity, missionaries worried that they did so in the wrong spirit. There is much evidence for Elsie Clark's impression that many times converts simply added Christian sacraments to Taoist and Buddhist practices. "Christian religion is made a fetish to many of these people. Prayer and the Holy Spirit are to them tools to be used, forces to have on one's side, magic to be evoked," Clark wrote. With probably less basis, Clara Foster saw Christian belief in China as a rational decision within a Confucian tradition and thought that such belief lacked "the sorrow for sin and the joy of knowing Christ as their Savior which are experienced in the homeland." She went on, "They are ready to talk glibly of all being great sinners and only by accepting Christ's righteousness can we be saved, but somehow it is difficult for them to make it a personal matter."[26]

Helping Chinese to make it "a personal matter" was at the heart of the missionary's self-appointed task in China. Professional, religious, and feminine traditions would have directed women toward personal work in any case, but the stubbornness of Chinese cultural resistance seemed to intensify missionary efforts. Their instructions in character became also lessons in culture. Alice Reed lamented that the Chinese lack entirely "what we call pep," and Agnes Scott, who had taught music at Fukien Christian College, felt that music offered an important emotional outlet to students and gave the school "college spirit." In 1894 Luella Miner delighted that "our Chinese associates are learning better every year how to be informal and 'folksey,' " but Frederica Mead in 1915 still lamented that "our girls have lots to learn in being at ease in entertaining and loosing themselves in the fun of it."[27] When missionaries stressed the personal nature of their work, they were in part stressing the fundamental changes they were seeking. Their lessons in Christian "character" frequently also fostered Western personality.

Missionaries' highest triumphs came when they could participate in a moment of personal transformation. Usually the moment involved a debate within an individual between "right" and "face." Florence Manly remembered some private talks with a Christian "in which my view of what he ought to do meant losing face and was at first intolerable to him, but I held firm and he finally gave in." When the potential convert had been recalcitrant, the victory was most gratifying. Lucy Mead described the resistance of one girl in her school to the conversion efforts of a YWCA evangelist:

> She came to the first meeting and sat thru it with a straight back, arms folded, and scorn on her face, even all thru the prayer. The next meeting was about the same attitude, an occasional expression in the following meetings betrayed a struggle in her soul, still she would not admit it, the girls still worked and all prayed. As she started to the last meeting she said with pride and scorn "She can't touch me, I'm not going to be effected by anything she says."

When by the end of the service she had confessed her sins and surrendered her pride, her missionary sponsors were euphoric.[28] Clearly, delight in conquering such a proud resister exceeded the delight in a less challenging conquest, though both alike totted up a soul for God.

In theory, however, God and not man brought about conversion. "There is no human agency that can cause a Chinaman to 'loose face,' " Jessie Ankeny wrote in describing the divine presence which inspired a Haitang revival. Her denial of the missionary's role was correct and orthodox. A month later, however, she noted that "People have confessed things in meetings that no official could possible make them confess."[29] Missionary tendencies to personalize religion meant that victories were often quite personal as well. Missionaries who wanted to feel the wonders of the Lord's work in bringing a chosen one into the fold could not help but feel a quite earthly gratification. When a Chinese disclosed confidences, or became "informal and folksey," furthermore, it was hard to know whether he had found Christ, was on the road to salvation, or more simply, as was often the case, was responding to human attention. When religion was so much more a matter of feeling rather than thinking, it was often difficult to tell religious transformation from cultural conquest.

Although good evangelical strategy demanded that a missionary elicit more than he or she reveal and enlist dependents rather than become dependent, the China reality for many missionary women, particularly those who were single, was a good deal different. Initially women who participated in "ladies' houses" found that the community of other single women provided a satisfactory alternative family life. Many women did not have access to such houses, however, and even for women who did, turnover and transfer through years of service meant that the women's residence was likely to remain less stable in membership than the population of Chinese Christians. The greater mission community extended good will to single women but did not entirely accommodate them, instead revolving around families.

As a result, single women frequently sought to make more of a life for themselves within the Chinese community than did either married women or single men. Luella Miner rebelled against the custom of racially exclusive summer resorts after her first years in China. In 1890, she wrote:

It seems strange to be so cut off from all of our Chinese friends. . . . To me their love and friendship means very much, taking a place which in some respects cannot be filled by intercourse with foreigners. Some missionaries seem to work with the Chinese at arms length as it were, and are a little inclined to criticize those of us who treat them fully as equals and let them see that we regard them as personal friends, but these are the exception. In a way I think that the Chinese feel that they have a special claim upon us unmarried missionaries. They realize that we have no cares or affections that can hinder us from entering fully into their joys and sorrows.

Two years later she had taken the bold step of remaining behind at her
regular station during the summer, for much of the time without other
missionaries. She explained to her family:

> Laying aside regular work is not rest for me—at least not in China.
> For those who have the diversions of family life, or who are very fond
> of society, going to the Hills for a long stay may be very restful and
> beneficial, but for me it is not. Such a life does not hold enough of
> interest to keep me from getting a little dejected and homesick.

Louise Campbell, herself a missionary daughter, spent most of her recre-
ational time with the women who were students in her Bible training
school. Her own sister, who arrived with her husband and children to join
Louise's station in 1917, wrote home that she did not see much of her.
"Louise is with Yau Tsi most of the time she isn't at work at the school. . . .
Well, as I started to say I'm thrown chiefly on the children for my social
needs."[30] Single women without children of their own likely found association with church members and Chinese children more pleasurable than
participating in the concerns of a married woman's society to which they
were marginal.

Women's gender enabled them to *be*, as well as *feel*, more "at home" in
Chinese society than foreign men. Male missionaries could not have the
same access to Chinese homes where the women were. Before Jessie
Ankeny married Henry Lacy and curtailed her itinerating, for instance,
she liked the travel of country work better than he. She wrote home to her
family:

> Henry is off for a three day Day School trip. He hates it so but I like to
> do them first rate. He doesn't like roughing it in old cold churches and
> eating any sort of food but I can get into some ones home and have rice
> and salt fish at least and relish it on a cold day and if it is cold get the
> Bible woman to take me in her room to sleep which makes lots of
> difference.[31]

If missionary women were right in their feeling that the home was the
heart of the society, clearly their brethren could never get as close to China
as they.

Single women demonstrated their loyalty to the Chinese community by
staying behind when others were evacuated and arranging, if at all possible,
to die and be buried in China. In 1894, during antiforeign riots in southern
China, Louise Johnston of the Presbyterian board refused to leave with two

missionary couples and remained behind by herself, unharmed. Over thirty years later, Martha Wiley, too, refused to be evacuated during the war with Japan and stayed on with the family of her adopted son. Lucy Hoag was "more at home in China" where she spent much of her life, and she wished to die there, as did both Louise Campbell and Luella Miner. Edna Terry even hoped, her memorialist wrote, "That her Heavenly mansion might be in the Chinese quarter." Even those who did not stay on and die in China sometimes retained China as their spiritual home. Spending her last years in Cincinnati in a missionary home for the aged, Martha Lebeus prepared for her death as if she were Chinese. The report in her biographical file explained that "Following the old Chinese custom, Miss Lebeus made all the arrangements for her funeral, even to the white dress that she was to wear, during the winter before her last illness. Her preparations completed, she spent her last days in her sunny room with its broad view of the valley and distant hills." As the record communicates, single women missionaries who had served into old age and no longer had family in the United States often felt their furloughs home for illness to be more like exile. For Lora Dyer, a friend wrote, it was "more like leaving home than returning."[32]

Single women were involved in the life of the Chinese community in several different ways. Nearly all missionaries had students, parishioners, or associates whom they counted as friends. Encouraged by the economic offerings and intimate approaches of female missionary strategies, these associations were based on reciprocal needs. The closest, and hence most significant relationships, were adoptions of Chinese children and "particular" friendships with Chinese coworkers. Incompletely documented, some of these relationships nevertheless deserve more careful scrutiny.

The domestic model for missionary service included all missionary work under the general rubric of "mothering." Teaching the young and caring for the sick in body and soul were feminine skills of nurturing which simply extended a woman's responsibilities from her own children to include maternal responsibilities for all God's creatures. Lacking children of her own, Mary Porter Gamewell used to say, "Chinese boys are my boys; Chinese girls are my girls!" and Alice Browne described herself as "mother to all my little schoolgirls." Such generalized mothering did not entirely satisfy the needs of missionary women for intimate connections and for a kind of posterity, however, nor perhaps did it satisfy the need for financial provisions for individual students. At any rate, missionary women fre-

quently went beyond mothering through their work by adopting abandoned or destitute Chinese children as their own. This practice was so
common, and perhaps such a challenge to the disinterested benevolence
the church aimed to offer, that many boards in the early twentieth century
ruled against official adoptions by missionaries.[33] Even before that time,
however, missionary adoptions were informal and unclearly defined, allowing for great variety in the degree and permanence of financial support.

The circumstances which allowed for missionary adoptions were as
varied as the poverty in China at the turn of the century. Families with
insufficient food were sometimes glad to turn children over to the steadier
diet offered by mission institutions, and occasionally, as mentioned before,
missionaries would contribute money in return. Jessie Ankeny wrote that
one day when she was tired she offered ten dollars to a destitute fisherman
who had been badgering her to buy his daughter. As the market price was
sixty or seventy dollars, she was surprised to find herself the titular owner
of a little girl. In this, as in many other cases, the purchase of a child was
primarily a financial transaction. Jessie Ankeny named the fisherman's
daughter Florence, after her sister, and arranged that the child should
continue living at home until she was further advanced in reading and
could attend school. Ankeny and Carrie Bartlett, a coworker, earlier that
year had bought another girl's "liberty," and when she came into the
school, Ankeny wrote, her father came to visit her twice a week. Whether
parents technically "sold" their children, gave missionaries a right to
educate them, or accepted monthly support payments, as in the case of a
mother whose child Florence Manly "adopted," the purpose seems to have
been the same—to provide for their children without having to resort to
selling them in less benevolent markets.[34]

Rarely did missionary women actually adopt children into their own
homes. When a child had been truly abandoned, a missionary would
usually place and support him or her in the home of a Bible woman or
Chinese Christian worker. Bessie Ewing explained that "Martha," a girl
she had adopted and placed with her Bible woman, "for her own good must
grow up a Chinese girl with the Chinese." Although Ewing worried and
wrote about Martha more than her own children until Martha's death
during the Peking siege, she held to that belief. During Martha's final
illness, Ewing saved rationed eggs, presumably depriving her own children
for whom they were intended, and prepared food which she carried to the
Chinese refugee section of the camp. Although Ewing never mentioned
such considerations, racial proscriptions undoubtedly influenced the living

arrangements of adopted children and missionary parents. Thirty years after the siege, Ruth Hemenway wrote that her adopted daughter had not been allowed to stay with her in mission quarters in Foochow.[35]

Clever, pretty, or beguiling children stood a much better chance of finding a missionary sponsor than did the dull, sickly, or sullen. When Emma Martin was in Japan after the Boxer siege, she described the winning tactics of one child whose mother was trying to acquire mission support for her:

> Tonight as we all sat there together the mother begged, and the oldest girl sat there and cried and the little girl is a beautiful child and was not afraid of me (which is unusual in such little children) she came and sat in my lap and was so content to let me put my arms around her and pet her. I begged Mrs. Seeds to keep her a while any way and I would see she was paid for. She is so cunning and bright.

Particularly when school fees were to be paid, achievement in school was a primary requirement for adoption. Mildred Rowland noted the accomplishments of the girl she was to support: "She can do anything that she sets her hand to and has a very sweet voice and stands at the head of the school in her lessons. Queer that I would want to help a girl that is so smart when I never knew enough to stand at the head of my class."[36] Rowland accurately observed that missionaries frequently adopted children in part for their own gratification.

Support offered on the basis of charm or intellect was conditional. Ida Lewis outlined the career options of a fourteen-year-old boy, the son of her recently dead cook of seventeen years, whom she had adopted conditionally: "He is a very bright fellow and seems anxious to study. If he is willing to do his best, will send him thru Peking, but he is on trial. Mr. St. John says he will try to make a preacher of him—but maybe he will decide to be a cook or a boy!" When Luella Miner went on leave in 1919 she left instructions for the several children she had been sponsoring. One was to be cut off. "I told Miss Mead I would not help my Academy girl any longer, and if she comes to you you can tell her the same," she wrote to Alice Frame. Understandably, such circumstances left children or youths uneasy about their futures. Myra Sawyer learned that the girl whom she had adopted in 1915 was troubled with the fear that she might be bereft of support in the event of Sawyer's death.[37] Legitimate fears that poor performance, transgressions, or a fall from favor would result in the loss of livelihood must have been even more common.

Despite these qualifications of the depth and permanence of missionary adoptions, adoptive ties seem both to have integrated many missionary women into Chinese families and brought Chinese students into prominence within the mission community. After Lulu Golisch's death, a memorialist wrote that she was an honored guest in many Chinese homes, that "Aunt Lulu was always the one chosen by each school bride to arrange the bridal veil, an act which made her part of the bride's family."[38] When Luella Miner died, her two adoptive sons were prominent figures at the funeral. The variety of social arrangements incorporated under the adoptive rubric in part reflected Chinese custom, which accorded familial address to a wide range of nonbiological relatives. These relationships nonetheless provided more than simply an occasional acknowledgment of family ties to many single women, who relied on them for their posterity.

Through private adoptions, missions gained some of their most successful and devoted Chinese workers. The story of Gertrude Howe, as preserved largely in mission legend, testifies to the value to the board of committed and unofficial missionary mothering. The daughter of an abolitionist who participated in the underground railway, Howe arrived in the inland Yangtze city of Kiukiang in 1871 with one other missionary woman. Charged with opening a girls' school at a time of anti-Christian hostility, Howe and her coworker Lucy Hoag remained for a long time without students until their language teacher agreed to try to arrange an adoption for them. The child's mother, Howe remembered later, "decided to risk us rather than the cruel treatment of a mother-in-law for her daughter." (Another version went that the horoscopes of the child and her intended betrothed had not been propitious, and that the child's mother turned her over to Howe, "all dressed in bright red even to her shoes and stockings, just as if she were being presented to a mother-in-law.")[39] This was the first of four children whom Howe adopted and, contrary to usual mission practice, reared herself.

The elegiac tone of the Methodist printed record, unaccompanied by manuscript material, makes it difficult to determine the exact details of Howe's upbringing of K'ang Cheng, known in mission literature as Ida Kahn, and her three other daughters. One publication reported that Howe was "frequently criticized for the methods of training used with these girls," and another publication recalled that Howe had lived in a native house with her four children. Probably subject to mission disapproval of her intimacy with her Chinese children, Howe moved her family upriver to

Adopted family: Missionaries were frequently absorbed into the families of Chinese Christians, as shown in this wedding picture of a kindergarten schoolteacher. Emily Hartwell is standing behind the bride.

Chungking for several years in 1886. Another prominent Chinese Methodist worker she had sponsored (though not adopted) wrote reverently:

> How many summers when the heated season came on and the other
> missionaries fled for much-needed rest to beautiful Kuling, the moun-
> tain resort for the foreign population, but where Chinese residents
> were not tolerated, Miss Howe would take her flock of "grand-
> children" and as many sick and needy babies as possible to the little
> hut-like home in the hot foothills, and there devote herself during
> vacations to the not easy task of mothering her very often trying brood
> of boys and girls.[40]

Even despite the mythmaking, the record seems to indicate that Howe
braved community censure in order to be a mother in fact as well as out of
pocket to her adopted children.

When Howe accompanied K'ang Cheng and Shih Mei-yu, known as
Mary Stone, to the United States and enrolled, coached, and cooked for
them through two years of medical school at the University of Michigan,
she assured their prominence in the mission church as examples of a new
kind of Chinese woman. K'ang Cheng and Shih Mei-yu were clearly
preeminent examples of Methodist missionary women's accomplishments
in the early twentieth century. In their own society, too, K'ang and Shih
achieved some notice. The prominent liberal and intellectual Liang Ch'i-
chao chose K'ang Cheng when he was seeking a model for Chinese women
to emulate. He concluded that she was of ordinary intelligence but extraordinary circumstance, and lamented that she alone, of all Chinese women,
had transcended ignorance, isolation, and passivity. On the basis of her
relation to K'ang Cheng, who ran a large dispensary in Nanchang, Gertrude Howe herself seems to have acquired a certain prominence in China.
Approximately fifteen hundred "friends and relatives" followed her funeral procession through the streets of Nanchang when she died in 1928,
the mission reported. In reputation within China, but perhaps even more
in appeals, profiles, and money-raising stories within the United States,
K'ang Cheng and Shih Mei-yu were invaluable to the Methodist organization.[41] They came to the church not as converts or students, but through
the leverage exercised by financial sustenance and personal adoption.

The cultural compromise which K'ang Cheng and Gertrude Howe ef-
fected through their filial and maternal relationship earned Howe a stature
in Nanchang and K'ang Cheng a Western career as a publicist and missionary doctor. Although K'ang Cheng achieved notable status within the
Methodist mission society, the balance remained with Western forms and

Western institutions, and she remained subordinate to an American hierarchy within her own country.[42]

Missionary commentators said that Chinese children should be brought up in Chinese homes for their own good. They said that missionary women should avoid particular Chinese friends for the good of the community. The frequency and the strength with which missionary women attacked such favoritism or "special" friendship suggested that it was perceived as a constant temptation. In her early years in China, Luella Miner wrote of her high regard for her Chinese friends and noted that her dearest friend was the wife of her Chinese teacher. In later years, she wrote an essay, "The Relationship of Chinese Workers and Missionaries," in which she counseled against such friendships:

> Among the mistakes of early years are exclusive friendships. . . . The heart of the lonely worker in the interior may long for the close companionship of the one or two Chinese associates or pupils who are most congenial, yet the life of service means just this, that we will bestow where they are most needed our gifts of love, sympathy, and time, regardless of returns. It will mean self-denial and giving sometimes to others out of a heart hungry to take in strengthening sympathy. It will mean not getting so close to the one or two as we long to do. But the sacrifice will pay in the wider range of influence and in the avoidance of the misunderstanding and jealousy which sooner or later rob every selfish joy of its flavor.

Luella Miner maintained her reserve as a source of pride, but other women also cautioned against too much caring, particularly favoritism. "It is so easy for those without the family life, all unconsciously to let the rivers of one's affection be smothered and lost in the desert sands of one's own heart," Sarah Goodrich wrote. She praised one who had avoided that pitfall and made her affectional rivers "a source of fructifying life to many."[43]

This fear of prejudicing the work through favoritism seems to have contributed to Chinese and Western segregation in housing as well as caution in friendships. In 1920 Anna Hartwell wrote to a younger friend Jane Lide about Lide's suggestion that a Chinese friend might share their residence:

> You know of course that frankly, I *personally* would never take one Chinese girl out of her Chinese environment and put her in with

foreigners to live in foreign style. It seems to me it would be bound to create jealousy in the hearts of others less favored and hurt her influence, etc. etc. etc. . . . but I am such a *strong* believer in the rights of missionaries to act on their own initiative, that, to me, the question of Yu Mei lies entirely with *you*. If you want to have her live with you here, you have a perfect right to do so, for this is your home as much as mine.[44]

Hartwell's response was surely conditioned by a number of factors, including both her desire not to alienate Lide and her jealousy of Yu Mei. Her response also suggests, though, that the mission community might have been accustomed to using its own vocabulary and its own explanations for a racial segregation which by the early twentieth century was so deeply established in treaty-port traditions as to be simply a way of life.

Traditions of segregation were strongest in cities where there was a substantial population of Westerners. On the island of Haitang, off the Fukien coast, Jessie Ankeny and Mamie Glassburner, unaccompanied by representatives from the parent board, directed a small Methodist girls' school. Ankeny brought her Chinese teacher with her to this hardship post, and for two years or so the two remained fast and inseparable companions. Without family of her own, Ding Miduang, or Eleanor, as she had been named by another missionary, worked as teacher, personal servant, and lively playfellow for Jessie Ankeny. Ankeny's frequent letters home documented the attentiveness, antics, and charm of her teacher, "a great little girl," and described a unique relationship that approximated the dynamics of a fond turn-of-the-century marriage.

The services Ding performed for Ankeny were perpetual and personal. "Maybe you get tired of hearing me tell of her but she is unusual," Ankeny wrote. "I never expect to find anyone so helpful." "She thinks she is wholly responsible for my well being," Ankeny wrote in 1909, "so when she sees a hole in my dress, a button off, she runs and gets a needle to mend and if I protest she seems to feel bad and of course I don't care." The next day Ankeny wrote, "She tells me where I spend my money and how and keeps everything in fine order." Ding anticipated Ankeny's chills, arriving with a shawl, and her need to write a note to herself by fetching a pencil from upstairs. Ankeny wrote her sister, "She runs here and there for me. Even worse, Louise, than you used to do." Ankeny seemed puzzled about how to explain their relationship. "I told Miduang she made a fine maid," she wrote. But she seemed uncomfortable with that description. "Of course this was a little ticklish but she said 'I would be willing to do anything for you.' I don't like to have her do so much for she isn't strong and of course according to their custom a scholar or teacher never does a coolie's work but she doesn't pay any attention when it concerns me." In a light mood, she tried another metaphor: "They say that old maids must have something for pet." I guess I have chosen her in preference to cat or dog or bird or teddy bear."[45]

But if Ding was a pet to Ankeny, she was far from a docile one. A constant tease as well as a constant aide, she was "full of the old 'nick,' " Ankeny wrote, "more like an American girl than any other person I have seen here." When Ankeny was writing a letter home she reported in mid-paragraph, "Eleanor came in with a plate of peanuts and tempted me into eating a lot and it is dinner time. She is now playing Home Sweet Home on the organ—She does it to try to tease me."[46]

Her missionary coworker left Haitang for a visit to Foochow shortly after Ankeny and Ding arrived, and Ankeny wrote to her family that Ding would be her only company, "but she's as good as I need." Ankeny was surprised to find that she could have such a friendship with a Chinese girl. "I am getting a case," she wrote. "I slept with her the other night. . . . The first time I have slept with a Chinese girl. I like 'em fine." The intimacy of Ankeny's and Ding's friendship did not mean that Ankeny could forget racial distinctions. A year later, when Ding Miduang returned from a visit, Ankeny reported, "I was just as glad to see her as could be; a foreign friend could not have made me happier."[47] Though she could not forget race, Ankeny demonstrated a rare capacity to look beyond it.

But she gradually became alarmed by her growing dependence on Ding. During a temporary separation Ankeny wrote, "I miss her so, but I was afraid of getting attached to her and depending on her too much and being with her too much." She was reassured by another missionary, however, and Ding joined her again on Haitang. Competition for Ding Miduang turned out to be high, however. "Simply everyone is after her," Ankeny wrote. "Everyone says she is so pretty." Other missionaries also admired Ding "because she does everything they want her to do and does it so willingly," Ankeny wrote later.[48]

The most troubling competition for Ding Miduang came from the man to whom she was engaged. Ding seemed determined to break the engagement, and Ankeny agreed that her betrothed was worthless; she did not mention whether or not he was a Christian. "She said she would leave the world before she would marry him and I am determined that he shall never have her," Ankeny wrote. Two years later, at the time of the 1911 revolution, Ankeny wrote: "Eleanor's young man has gone to war and I hope, since it is necessary for some to give their lives for their country, that his will be one. I don't mean to wish him bad luck but he is not much force and I hate to see her marry him." But that same year it was Jessie Ankeny's young man, who had courted her at the Fukien summer resort, and not Ding Miduang's, who broke up the women's relationship. Ding wrote a letter to the Ankeny family expressing her chagrin:

> Dear Mama, You know I was so glad Miss A. has come back [from Kuliang], but I am *so surprised* that she is so soon stolen away. Do you care? Well I like Mr. Lacy *but I don't like it one bit* he do that. This is something I had not thought of. . . . I know pretty soon Miss A. need not me to take care of her but *I would rather to do some hard thing better than give her up. Mr. L. is abominable when he comes over.*

Ding was losing a companion and a dear friend, but she had ample other opportunities for support. Sponsorship for kindergarten training in Soochow was arranged, and Ding Miduang left Fukien early the next year. Jessie Ankeny Lacy wrote several years later, saying that the Southern Methodists of Soochow had written wanting to "refund the money I have put into her and let them have her for keeps. They say she has made herself indispensable to their work. . . . They say they have fallen in love with her. I tell you it was a bit hard to turn her over to them but now that her love affairs are so bad she had better stay where she is. It sure did me good to hear such splendid things of her."[49]

Clearly the Ankeny-Ding friendship resists reduction. Ding's and Ankeny's shared needs were apparent, and their shared high spirits provided more than a sentimental bond between them. When Ankeny tried to pinpoint what was unusual about Ding, however—"I never expect to find anyone so helpful," she wrote—she was describing what was most historically significant about their relationship. Even more than a little sister, with whom Ankeny compared her, Ding had subordinated herself to Ankeny's needs. The quality of her concern was not that of a personal servant or a slave, who could hardly assume responsibility for anticipating wants and enforcing healthy habits. Nor was it the concern of a mother in its respectful subservience, although when Ankeny compared herself to "an eating-milk-baby," she made that analogy. Ding's relationship to Ankeny was rather that of a dutiful wife, helpful in work and playful in rest. Ankeny found it "unusual" for good reason. Customarily such harmonious relationships built on the complete and loving subordination of another person to one's own needs were only available to men in the United States. The competition among missionary women for Ding Miduang, who was pretty, helpful, and spirited too, suggests that American women who were slow to marry anyway could appreciate the opportunity, afforded by cultural circumstance, to reverse their expected role.

Ankeny regarded Ding Miduang with bemusement, dependency, and affection—but, as in most relations between unequals, with unwitting condescension. Her likening of Ding to a pet was a fair description of the part Ding played in Ankeny's life and in the lives of a number of other missionaries; but it was also naive racism. Racial and economic imbalances caused inequalities in their relationship; still, it is important to remember that rarely were inequalities combined with such lively and genuine regard.

Any indication of Ding's religious state was totally absent from Ankeny's descriptions, and indeed, religious scrutiny played a small role in Ankeny's life. Without an ordained male missionary to preach, Haitang's Methodist religious training was largely confined to Sunday school. Presumably, Mamie Glassburner handled that work, for Ankeny wrote to her "dear ones" at home, "I don't take in the church S.S. so when I want to lie abed on Sunday morning I do so. Last Sun. Miduang crawled in with me so we were gossiping."[50] Like many lay missionaries in China in the twentieth century, particularly female schoolteachers, Ankeny adopted her message to China circumstances and traded largely in personal currency.

The missionary work of Louise Campbell, a China-born missionary, demonstrated that personal evangelism could produce personal problems as well as victories. Because of her Chinese childhood, perhaps, Campbell particularly gravitated toward the community of Chinese women within her Baptist station in Swatow. To those women studying in the Bible training school, Campbell was a representative of the Western church that sustained them. The powerful combination of Campbell's institutional identification and her personal evangelism enlisted the extreme loyalties of many workers. But the combination was also highly volatile, as the story of Louise Campbell and Yau Ts'i demonstrates. This experience of personal friendship and social discord gives tangible meaning to the cautions of other missionaries about the divisiveness of particular friendship across racial lines.

Campbell's friendship with Yau Ts'i began in 1916 and lasted for at least four years of constant church warring. It started with a courtship:

April 16, 1916. Nice walk out with Yau Ts'i. she's a mighty dear girl, but I've got to be careful not to get too intimate.

April 20, 1916. After meeting, Yau Ts'i and I went to see the woodsy place across the river.

April 21, 1916. Gave my old Chinese jackets to Yau Ts'i.

April 22, 1916. Yau Ts'i up in afternoon and we had a lovely time looking at my cut out pictures. gave her some.

April 26, 1916. Yau Ts'i up after supper and we had a beautiful evening. she in hammock and I in chair. "Jonathan and David."

Even before their special relationship began, however, Yau Ts'i revealed the sensitivities that were to riddle the Chinese church with personal politics in subsequent years. On 12 March 1916, Yau Ts'i had told Campbell "about her tiff with Sin tsi over supposed insult—thinking chapel talk was aimed at her. Wish she lived on a higher plane—my fault." But if Yau Ts'i initially sought an alliance with Campbell as a means of acquiring influence within the church and an ally in her battles, the relationship survived for several years on other grounds as well. In 1920, Campbell wrote that on Yau Ts'i fortieth birthday she had given her a "mohair skirt." Campbell at that time still called her a "dear girl" even as she sympathetically commiserated with her over the disappointment she faced in her new daughter-in-law.[51]

Campbell paid for those years with distress and guilt over the rift in the church which her friendship fed. Her diary of the spring of 1916 alternates between bucolic scenes of budding friendship and distraught realizations of personal animosities:

May 15, 1916, Beautiful moonlight eve. Yau Ts'i over in eve and we told stories. I told her Jack and the Beanstalk, Little Red Riding Hood, etc.

May 23, 1916. Sam-pak-me led chapel and after a good talk—made a tirade against those who seized all the power and wouldn't share it and those who leaned on those in power—like their horse tender—meaning Yau Ts'i and I. Y. fearfully angry. had a great talk with her after school trying to calm her.

June 18, 1916. Walked out with Yau Ts'i and I felt about sick over the things she told me about the jealousy of the girls, thinking I was partial, they wanting to quit school, etc. Oh *dear!*

Although originally Yau Ts'i managed to deflect much of the blame from herself, Campbell gradually began to judge her for her participation in church bitterness. In November of 1916, for instance, Campbell wrote in her diary: "Yau Ts'i walked in with me and made me feel *terrible* by her expressions of hatred for Sam, Sin, and Yu Yin and her evidently thinking I was false to her by treating them fairly. It is *very* hard and embarrassing. Oh may God give me wisdom to do the *right* thing and may He give my dear girl a loving and forgiving *spirit*." As time went on, Yau Ts'i became more of a burden and a source of guilt. In May 1921, Campbell prayed "for greater consecration and relief from this oppression caused by Y.'s attitude." By October of that year, Campbell had assumed Yau Ts'i as a burden of sin which could not be set aside: "Discouraging time with Yau Ts'i again. how long Oh Lord! I've bro't it all on myself but the punishment seems almost more than I can bear sometimes."[52]

Cambell's relationship with Yau Ts'i continued within a mission and a greater European community which observed many racial distinctions in public matters. In the summer of 1916, when church rivalries were beginning to escalate and Campbell was showing signs of the stress that was to characterize subsequent years, the first of July arrived and she decamped from Swatow for Double Island with the rest of the missionary community, leaving Tau Ts'i behind. The community likely clung to the sanctity of the summer resort "with our own kind" for just such reasons. Campbell returned from her summer unreconstructed, however, to report, "My beloved was here to meet me." Early the next year Campbell's sister, who had joined the mission community in the fall with her family, wrote home that Louise spent most of her time with Yau Ts'i. "I do wish she'd rest more. She is so nervous," she added. The family had begun to worry about Yau Ts'i by then, although by 1920 the two women's friendship was such an established fact that Campbell mentioned a walk with her friend, her sister, and her brother-in-law. But segregationist instincts occasionally asserted themselves, not surprisingly in public places. Campell reported without comment a voyage with Yau Ts'i in November 1916: "Moved on to native boat before daylight. pretty crowded. Yau Ts'i and her brother and our servants in one part and we in the other."[53] Despite the crowding on the boat, it is significant that when a division was unavoidable, it occurred naturally on racial lines.

Louise Campbell was an earnest Christian who based much of her Christian influence on the personal nature of her evangelical work. Her relationship with Yau Ts'i was the logical outcome of this work. The background to the relationship, however, was the role of the church as an economic provider for the Bible women who worked and studied there. The resulting combination of economic assistance and personal attention was effective in recruiting Christians, but it was less likely to produce spiritual dependency on a Greater Being than practical reliance on His earthly representatives.

American women found unaccustomed authority in their economic resources and the emotional power which adhered to them, and were surprised to discover the personal satisfactions that relationships across cultural lines could yield. They found another source of gratification in a profound confusion of sexual stereotypes accompanying their status in China. Western women found Chinese men unmanly and Chinese men found Western women unwomanly. As a result, missionary women and Chinese men met on a basis of gender ambiguity which came closer to approaching gender equality than either had known before. Missionary women came to experience this confusion as freedom from the constant and subtle sense of unequal power that governed public relations between men and women in the United States.

This zone of freedom, of course, was based on cultural misunderstanding. Though they might have been accustomed to the rowdiness and abuse of American streets, missionary women in China did not recognize the subtle signs of sexual disrespect which were all that the more controlled Confucian order would allow. And the Chinese, for their part, judged the moderate, socially sanctioned initiatives of conventional missionary women by Chinese standards, which made out of every cautious missionary woman a bold rebel. This mutual misunderstanding, far from daunting missionary women with Chinese-induced fears for their femininity, instead delighted them. Without transgressing American sexual boundaries, they received the respect mixed with fear generally accorded only women who had fought for their freedom and paid for it with the opprobrium of their own society.

From the first, Americans frequently said they had difficulties in telling Asian men from women. Shortly after she came to Hankow, Lucy Mead "took a lesson in distinguishing between men with their queues done up on head and women with hair undressed. Unless the woman's feet are bound the hair is only distinguishing sure mark." Ruth White noted a similar difficulty in distinguishing sexes in Japan, where a woman's face "didn't seem to look different from a man's." In children, in particular, sex differences were muted. The similarity in appearance between boys and girls, missionaries felt, was exacerbated by their tendency to dress alike. Alice Browne wrote in 1905 that only the girls' earrings distinguished them from boys, since both sexes wore identical glossy black queues.[54]

American perceptions of Chinese men as similar in size and appearance to Chinese women drew on traditional Western stereotypes of the Asian man as less masculine than the Western man. Part of the stereotype was based on physical characteristics—smaller size and less facial hair—and reflected early Western contacts with the smaller southern peoples of Canton and Fukien. Elsie Clark wrote that "most of the men in this southern region are smaller than I am, and I feel as tho' I could be more than a match for any policeman I have seen." To her diary she was more open about her opinions of the Chinese men she could vanquish. In a tennis match, she and her American partner trounced the Chinese schoolboys with whom they were playing and Clark confessed: "I was more than a match for the Chinese lads, frail and slight as they are. I felt a bit of contempt for any young manhood that I could so easily beat; but I ought to be pitying them for the insufficient nutrition and other conditions that make them weak." Clark's candor revealed a pride that lay beneath many women's discoveries of their relatively greater strength in China. Monona Cheney wrote from Peking, where physical size differences were less pronounced than in the South, "I'd be willing to wager I could outwalk any Chinese man in this city—the gait of foreign women is a never-failing source of wonder to them."[55]

Racial differences in size contributed only part of the sense of power which American women felt in China; they were also members of a privileged class. Women expressed this power particularly in relation to male servants. When missionaries first arrived in China, they explained to those at home that male servants, like blacks at home, were customarily called "boys." "Our cabin boy, for instance," Ruth White wrote, "has some gray hair." Mildred Rowland explained that their "boy" was always bringing them flowers of some sort. "Nice lad even if he is thirty or more," she wrote. Women missionaries frequently exceeded even the use of the belittling "boy" to address or describe their cooks or household help. In one letter Sarah Goodrich wrote that the "pretty boy" had just brought her some tea, and Mary Carleton referred to a Chinese preacher and her assistant as "Handy Andy." Mildred Rowland, who at first used the term boy with irony, two years later had christened her male cook "Betty."

Elizabeth Perkins's teacher, a Mr. Pang, was "commonly known in the mission as Pansy," Perkins wrote. "He is authority on all subjects quite as much as the lady of that name in America,"[56] she added. The use of women's names or feminine adjectives to describe male household help was perhaps encouraged by the potentially dangerous intimacy of the servant relationship. Nevertheless, it reinforced a more generalized Western condescension to Chinese men.

Confucian precepts also influenced American perceptions of Chinese effeminacy. Contrary to Western standards of masculine virtue, which drew on a chivalric, military tradition, the Chinese man of virtue forswore violence and cultivated moderation and wisdom. Chinese teachers educated in this Confucian tradition received greater respect from missionaries than did servants. But missionaries honored their Chinese teachers for qualities of sensibility and refinement more often associated in the United States with women than with men. Ruth White described the teachers who instructed them over the summer as "fine"—"so clean, refined and gentlemanly." Jessie Ankeny used nearly identical terms when she described the Chinese administration of the Foochow church as "well educated refined men." "You would be amased [sic] at their fine faces," she wrote. Ruth Hemenway's young teacher was "quiet, refined and gentle," with "beautiful hands" and an aristocratic face. Women often grew deeply attached to their Chinese teachers, and Ida Lewis and Luella Miner both reported crying when their tutoring was over. But they explained their attachments as sentimental similarities rather than sexual oppositions. Thus Luella Miner wrote of her first teacher Meng Ch'ang Ch'un that she had "come to love him almost like a brother."[57]

Christian considerations led women to appreciate sensitivity and gentleness in men, but Western gender expectations sometimes qualified this respect. Luella Miner referred to a later teacher as "fastidious," and Elsie Clark remarked on her teacher, a college boy, who "says that if he were a soldier he couldn't fight, a feeling you wouldn't find many American boys expressing." On the basis of her observation of Chinese teachers, who frequently came from a scholarly class, Alice Reed concluded that "The Chinese seem to lack initiative, self-dependence and bravery." She continued with some incidents "from the Chinese teachers here":

Miss Tenney's teacher went with her to the shore last summer. She finally succeeded in getting him to try to go bathing in the ocean. He went in until the water was a little above his ankles, then said he was

Personal teacher, ca. 1910: Elizabeth Perkins studies Chinese with a Mr. Pang, "commonly known in the mission as Pansy."

"Chinese lads" and missionary women, ca. 1914: The young men standing at attention behind Martha Wiley and Caroline Chittenden are probably either students or Chinese teachers.

afraid and hastily withdrew. When he was ready to return to Peking, he asked her to find some one for him to come back with, saying he would be afraid to come back alone. He is nearly thirty years old. My teacher at Language School tried to put a rubber band around a bunch of small cards used in studying Chinese characters. He tried a while then said, "I can't" and handed it over to me; in fact, "I can't" is a very common expression.[58]

Manual labor and physical activity had been the customary route to independence and freedom in an America of expanding frontiers; in China, where land had long been unavailable, manual labor had connotations of servility with might have particularly inhibited the performance of small chores by a proud Chinese scholar before a Western woman.

When missionary women compared Chinese men with Western or American men, their meaning became clearest. A woman who arrived in China in 1914 remembered that Chinese men were more generous and "by and large less aggressive" than American men. She added, "they almost tend to be effeminate." Missionary women admired Chinese masculinity when it took forms comparable to Western masculine ideals. Florence Manly's tribute to the soldier sent to guard them during antiforeign rioting emphasized his strength. She wrote: "He is tall, well-built, muscular, conscious of strength and apparently courageous without effort, looking upon the street rabble as so far beneath him intellectually and physically that he can govern them by a quiet word or a look. He is always master of the situation. He commands the force of men and always has them under his eye." In her admiration for a Chinese soldier rather than a scholar or a member of the gentry, however, Manly was distinguishing Western standards from Chinese ones that considered soldiering inherently unworthy. American women could speak ironically about their "he-man compatriots" but still uphold such an ideal for Chinese men.[59] They considered Chinese masculine styles the product of culture rather than race and proposed ways of correcting the deenergizing effects of Chinese training.

Christian education was, of course, the first strategy. Sarah Goodrich acknowledged this in her 1894 letter to the Waumatosa Sunday School telling them that their gifts were "making *men* for China, Christian men." Alice Reed's 1917 recital of Chinese lacks in initiative and bravery came in the context of a more secular strategy—her bid for a kindergarten at her station in North China. The lack of resourcefulness among her Chinese teachers, she laid "not to racial characteristics, but to early training.

Children are taught to be afraid and are taken care of and waited on so that they have no chance to develop initiative." The basis for this cultural vision of masculinity emerged most dramatically in the case of returned students—Chinese who had studied in the United States and adopted American mannerisms and an American masculine style. In her description of three such students Ruth White added a significant new category to the usual portrait of Chinese men: "All of the men were so gentlemanly and polite," she wrote, "and had all the vim of American men. One of the Yale men was full back on the All Star football team when he was there," she added.[60] "Vim," with its connotation of sexual power, was an important defining characteristic of masculinity for Americans in the early twentieth century.

Chinese men might have failed to live up to the gender expectations of some missionary women, but in some ways they came closer than Western men to answering evangelical gender ideals. Temperamentally reserved, embarrassed by male or female sentiment, Luella Miner subscribed to an early evangelical model which promoted sensitivity rather than force in men. She considered the reserve maintained between the sexes in China to be a close approximation of genteel and evangelical proscriptions governing sexual morality. Ruth White reported hearing Miner lecture on Chinese customs. Westerners might regard the failure of Chinese men and women to shake hands as a weakness, Miner said, but "it is used as a safeguard and had been of the greatest benefit to the race." In another paper Miner wrote: "It will help us to be humble and loving to remember that in some things, for instance in relation to modest dress for women, and an innate sense of 'the eternal fitness of things' in relationships between men and women some of our Chinese friends consider that they stand on a higher plane than we do."[61] Miner clearly concurred, and found Chinese reserve a particular emotional advantage.

She also found it a practical advantage, however, because it made her feel safe when she moved around China. Twelve years before the Boxer uprising, she wrote her mother, "There is not half the danger that there is in America. A lady has never yet, I think, been assaulted in China." Several months later she added that there was less danger in traveling in China than in going from New York to San Francisco because "These Chinese are wonderfully law-abiding."[62] Even missionary women who did not share Miner's personal reserve or her admiration for Chinese standards of masculinity frequently did share her sense of the convenience and safety offered them by a functioning Confucian social order.

Particularly after the 1911 revolution, women wrote eloquently of their sense of security when by themselves in crowds of men. Alice Reed and a woman friend attended an opening of the President's Palace in 1917 and were the only women among hundreds of men and schoolboys. "I think we felt more comfortable than we would have among that many men at home," she wrote. "The Chinese policy of leaving people alone has some advantages." Jeanie McClure's walk in the country to meet her husband prompted a similar reverie:

> Why, I was thinking that day when I went to meet Bob and was out in the hills out of sight of any house and there were strange, unprepossessing men going and coming along the road of how free from any fear or even nervousness I felt, and yet on a strange lonely road in America with strange men around I would have felt at least a little nervous.

Another woman also made the explicit comparison between her sense of safety in China and the United States. Monona Cheney tired on a missionary expedition up a mountain and decided to drop out of the party and spend an afternoon by herself watching the scenery:

> A crowd of Chinese men were having a picnic on a ledge away beneath me, and along in the afternoon a couple of them came up to where I was, I suppose out of curiosity. . . . But after they had asked all the questions they wanted to, and satisfied their curiosity, they went back down the hill. I suspect this sounds sort of "skittish" to my mother, doesn't it? It would be in America, but it isn't here; I was as safe there on the mountain-side as I could be anywhere; I have no more fear of these Chinese men than of a child, and there is no reason to have. [63]

The perception of Chinese as children repeated an old cultural stereotype that served simultaneously to diminish and to unman them.

The safety American women felt in China in good times was connected to their foreign identity, just as was the danger they felt during the Boxer uprising. The customary fear of foreigners which added passion and violence to antiforeign outbreaks when they occurred, in peaceful times granted foreigners an extra measure of freedom. Luella Miner wrote in 1888 that the Chinese "stand in wholesome awe of foreigners, so we are safer here than the native." In 1894, soldiers who attacked a missionary woman were so severely punished that "foreigners never were reviled so little as now in Peking." After the suppression of the Boxer uprising,

Westerners enjoyed twenty-odd years of unprecedented security in China. Elsie Clark observed "that foreigners lead a charmed life in this land, and ever since the woeful lesson of Boxer times, have been scrupulously taken care of." "I have never felt afraid once here in China—not so much nearly as on the streets at home," Ruth White wrote. "Everybody feels the same I think—the foreigners I mean."[64] By the time the Boxer uprising had been so brutally suppressed, the Chinese at all levels of society had learned that Western lives would cost the Chinese in almost geometric proportion.

Protections granted foreigners explained the greater actual safety of American women in the post-Boxer period, but they did not explain the perpetually greater sense of safety which missionary women experienced even prior to the Boxer outbreak. Missionaries attributed this sense of safety to many things, but partly to the absence of drunks in China. In a land as crowded as China, Confucian order and family responsibility functioned to control tightly all aspects of interpersonal behavior. Perhaps there was a cultural logic to the prevalence of opium addiction, a vice that produced nodding withdrawal rather than boisterous alcoholism, in China. Though Western women appreciated the safety that such conditions produced, they were repelled by the physical intimacy which made such tight behavioral control necessary. Elsie Clark, for instance, wrote in horror of boat trips in Fukien which left her "huddled up with a company of Chinese men, the whole lot of us lying down, legs and arms and occasionally heads touching"; another time, she recalled, a friend found herself pillowing the head of a sleeping Chinese man with her knee.[65] Such crowded conditions demanded strict familial controls to discipline and diminish public expressions of desire or anger.

Such experiences as Clark's boat trip or the frequent sight of nude peasant torsos, which at first shocked missionary women, gradually inured them to close contact with Chinese men and left them feeling, not only safer in their company than they would be with crowds of their countrymen, but also more comfortable. Frequently missionary women traveled accompanied only by a male servant or a Chinese preacher, and they often remained alone at stations with male servants. Unequal status reinforced the shared sense that sexuality was not an issue between American women and Chinese men. But occasionally a voice of propriety would insist on maintaining some standards. When Sarah Goodrich allowed a Chinese teacher to remain talking with her alone until nearly midnight, her husband "reproved me as he should but I had never visited with Feng Hsien Sheng before and I felt I was learning a lot." Luella Miner felt that she had

Solitary itinerating, ca. 1910: Missionary women frequently traveled accompanied only by male Chinese bearers, although they were not allowed to be in the company of Western men unchaperoned. Here Alice Brethorst, above, and Lela Lybarger, below, of the Methodist board set out on a village trip.

to remind the "young woman from the West" who "sits for hours every day with a Chinese teacher" that when darkness comes she should get a light as soon as, or even sooner, than were he a foreign man; presumably it might not otherwise have occurred to her at all, so natural and unthreatening was the situation.[66]

Only in contrast to the relations of American missionary women with Western men does the extraordinary nature of their relationship with Chinese men come into focus. A shipboard vignette told by Ruth White highlights the difference missionary women perceived and undoubtedly influenced. Her story, she said, "shows how the China boys [the cabin boys] look after us." A sick woman in bed called the Chinese cabin boy to have a broken light replaced, and he in turn called a Western electrician, "but left him outside the door till he came in, put Hazel over in the other bed and saw that she was all in proper order with blankets, etc. spread over." Only then did he let in the Western electrician. "Someway, that is the way they all seem," White wrote. "They are so quiet and impersonal in all they do. You don't think of them as you would other folks."[67] By "other folks," of course, White meant other men. Racial and class differences had schooled the "boy" in a demeanor of sexlessness, which White came to reinforce by not thinking of him as she would "other folks."

The skittishness of American missionaries about male–female relations among themselves lasted at least until 1920. Despite the exigencies of the China field, which spread missionaries thinly over wide areas, the rules of chaperoning were strictly enforced. When Luella Miner was at the T'ung-chow station alone, for instance, and an ailing male missionary of another station arrived to visit, she would not let him stay. Although he did not feel well enough to ride a donkey, she "remorselessly sent him off on one," "scared for fear this good looking gentleman would be left on my hands for the night." Single women entertained male Chinese teachers alone, but Elizabeth Perkins stayed away from a dinner party with two Western bachelors in 1908 because the married woman who was to chaperone could not attend. And when a married couple went on furlough leaving an unmarried missionary man and woman alone in Fenchow, Luella Miner recommended that a missionary marriage be hastened to supply the station with a chaperone.[68] The extreme punctiliousness with which missionaries observed American visiting and chaperoning decorum proved that different rules applied to American and to Chinese men; these rules were based on the widely shared assumption that Chinese men did not pose a threat to American women.

Of course, despite the social and familial controls that restricted sexual or violent expression in China, a clear cultural vocabulary enabled communication among natives. Ida Pruitt, a missionary daughter raised largely by a Chinese amah, described the languorous promiscuity of the gentry youth when they rode into town:

> The men, young men, dashing young men, sat their high saddles in a fashionable slouch. Even the barbarian little girl could see that. Their knees were high and bent. Their long silk gowns, split up the back to fall on either side of the saddle, were blue or black with gay short sleveless overjackets of bronze or blue or red. . . . Sometimes the braid in their queues did not begin until well down on their shoulders, between the shoulder blades. The braids of respectable young men started against their shaved heads. Starting on the neck was smart and a daring act allowed even to the respectable. But halfway down their backs? Dissolute indeed![69]

The sexual nuance of a loosely braided queue largely escaped missionary women, who found the queue itself to be an unmasculine style of hair dressing.

If American women did not think of Chinese men as quite men, Chinese men more than returned the favor. For every missionary confusion over Chinese gender, there were many more episodes of village puzzlement over missionary gender. Clara Foster, by now an older woman, repeated the regular litany which greeted her in the country: "Is it a man or a woman? How old it must be!" Local people greeted Elsie Clark's party with the question "Whether we were men or women, and why we wore no earrings if women. Our feet were noticed too." Sometimes this confusion over the sex of missionary women caused complications. In 1910 Jessie Ankeny described a hostile outburst against itinerating missionaries: "One of the larger women was driven from another village because the people said she was a man with this Bible woman and they wouldn't tolerate such wickedness!" Such an outright assumption that female missionaries were men was less common, however, than a profound uncertainty among Chinese peasants about the identity of Western women, who had free ways, big feet, pale hair, and long noses. Even more than a Chinese woman with unbound feet, who had the head of a woman and the feet of a man, the saying went, a Western woman was "neither one nor the other."[70]

Chivalric traditions between Western men and women reinforced Chinese feelings that American women were somewhere between male and female. The curious trade-off in Western cultures which granted women signs of deference in return for a lack of privileges was unknown in China, and Chinese naturally enough misinterpreted chivalry toward women as an indication of their superior status. Edward Manly described a journey with women in sedan chairs and men on foot. "The Chinese can never understand how it is that the foreign women ride while the men walk. It is the other way with them. So they say that our men are inferior to the women." A probably apocryphal anecdote in the Methodist women's magazine pictured a missionary woman answering questions as to whether she could walk, run, ride, and swim as well as a man, whether she was as strong as a man, and whether she would let her husband beat her. Her answers prompted the conclusion: "Now I understand why the foreign devil never has more than one wife. He is afraid."[71] It is significant that missionary women relished, repeated, and even submitted these stories to mission publications. Anxious to remain within American gender expectations, they found their anomalous position in China a matter for delight, and gained vicarious excitement from an identity in China that they did not feel they had earned.

The physical size of Western women and the chivalric deference they received from Western men constituted only one part of their special status in China. The other part was functional. Missionary women consistently traveled distances, filled jobs, took liberties which were entirely out of the range of possibility for Chinese women. Until well into the twentieth century, many of the freedoms missionary women routinely enjoyed were so thoroughly barred to Chinese women that those partaking of such liberties could hardly *be* women in Chinese accounting. When Western women assumed a traditionally respected position, such as that of teacher, they also received the respect traditionally accorded the position. Luella Miner, for instance, taught a variety of subjects at a mission men's college in the late nineteenth century. She was continually amazed at the "close and natural" relationship she seemed to have with her students: "Occasionally it sweeps over me suddenly when I go to the college building alone at night what an anomaly my position would seem to some, in conservative China, of all countries in the world. But never by word or look in these twelve years has a student made me feel uncomfortable." Students would visit her rooms and seek her advice, sometimes staying, Miner regretted to say, until after ten: "They couldn't feel any less embarrassed with me if I were one of the patriarchs," Miner wrote, "And they want me to consider them as small boys, so I treat them accordingly, telling some of them of their faults so frankly that I should think they would get offended sometimes."[72] Miner's discomfort with student deference and her own role as "patriarch" at the age of twenty-nine reflected a natural initial transferral of her American expectations to a Chinese setting. Gradually she came to accept the unquestioning respect which a good Chinese student accorded to the pronouncements of a teacher and adopted the moralistic pedagogy of a Chinese sage.

With such experiences in China, the consciousness of gender identity which accompanied American women in all journeys through public life began to drop away. Fears of foreign retaliation helped to protect Westerners in China, and the extreme restraint of Chinese public life successfully masked other tensions from American awareness. Their own violations of Chinese expectations for women were so profound that, rather than eliciting criticism for their breaches, they were conferred a new status as "she-tigers" or "elephants," which granted them the refreshing opportunity to do as they pleased. Again and again missionary women explained that they felt "safe" in China.[73] It is true that these women maintained internalized American standards for their own behavior, but even these standards seemed to fade a little in the face of other privileges. The freedom they experienced was based on national, racial, and class inequalities and a radical misinterpretation of Chinese culture; nonetheless it was an extraordinary source of gratification for women whose public life had heretofore been measured by subconscious calculations of the limits and opportunities of a woman's sphere.

Women wrote home in delight and amazement at all they were doing in China. On nearly all sides they found honor and respect, and at the same time they felt a powerful self-esteem based on the discovery of the variety and multiplicity of their unsuspected talents. Their new margin of authority in China brought with it a missionary willingness to do anything, to try all manner of jobs and vocations. Once missionaries had broken the first Chinese sanction against female behavior, subsequent ones fell nearly effortlessly, creating a psychic space that accommodated a wide range of initiatives. Authority of one kind encouraged authority of another.

"Western she-tiger," ca. 1895: While they preserved the trappings of gentility, missionary women in China acquired a reputation for strength, which is captured in this portrait of Dr. Kate Woodhull with her class of medical graduates, Foochow.

Within the Christian community itself, as has been suggested before, inexperienced Chinese Christians relied on missionaries to form their impression of the Christian God. Nearly the sole interpreters of the Word, missionaries received deference as God's disciples. Monona Cheney explained that "one thing is sure, unless a person is used to thinking himself of considerable importance, he gets a good deal of a surprise in such a place, for important he certainly *is* in the eyes of the people. . . . It makes him realize that he, and in so many cases he alone, stands for all those people will know of Jesus Christ, and its a big contract." Although Cheney argued that such a responsibility was humbling, she also found it challenging and gratifying; the next year, when Christian villagers told her that her arrival was "like having Christ come to us," she said she felt deeply glad as well as deeply unworthy. Inez Marks reported that a student had told her, "I love God first and you next"; under these circumstances, it was not surprising that Marks reported that she loved China and her work and had never been happier. When Chinese considered female missionaries next to God, they never thought to question, one mission historian wrote, that women missionaries might not be "endowed with the same churchly powers as those enjoyed by their brother missionaries."[74]

The identification Chinese made between God and His missionary disciples was particularly dramatic in more secular mission work. Children whose only contact with Christianity occurred in the classroom associated the Christian message with school work and the divine being with their teachers. Elizabeth Perkins wrote home a story of a school child's confusion: "Miss Osborne was having her read, and coming to something about Jesus, she asked, 'What did Jesus come to earth to do.' 'To Examine books' was the reply." For another child, the prospect of Judgment Day called forth similar associations. As she was dying, the story went, she called to her grandfather, "Grandfather, give me my school books quick! And give me the ones I know best, grandfather, because when I get to Heaven and God asks me to stand up and recite my lessons to Him,—what if I shouldn't know them!"[75] In a society which awarded official merit through an examination system, it perhaps made sense that children would associate salvation with a recitation; surely, however, the religious authority of the mission schoolteacher was as important an influence.

Foreign identity provided power as well as status. Before Luella Miner had good control of the language, she explained that she could influence women to come to church because "if a foreign lady shows an interest in them it goes a long way toward breaking down their prejudice." Foreign

In honor of Emily Hartwell, 1915: Students from four missionary schools were summoned for group exercises to celebrate this missionary's fifty-sixth birthday.

women could inspire fear as well. A vagrant beggar woman who had been leaning in a school window at Elizabeth Perkins's school started abruptly and moved along when she was confronted by Perkins herself. "A man who was selling salt at the school kitchen of course had to put in his word," Perkins added. "He said, 'The foreigners are ugly and will kill you.' " Early fears of foreigners had arisen from their supposed supernatural powers. This nearly superstitious assumption of superior Western knowledge outlived most virulent anti-Christian sentiment. "Most of us were embarrassed that they thought we knew so much," Marjorie Steurt recalled. "It is queer the amount of different things one is called to do," Jessie Ankeny wrote, and mentioned one request she received to save the life of a dying woman.[76]

Although most missionaries were embarrassed at Chinese deference at first, they gradually adjusted to the idea that their Western training enabled them to know more and do more than the Chinese. Most missionary schoolteachers doubled as nurses and pharmacists and treated all school ailments with whatever they could acquire as medical supplies. When one Peking schoolgirl was distraught over her marital situation, for instance, Frances Wilson, the school principal, thought nothing of injecting her with a shot of morphine to calm her down. Teachers taught equally gamely subjects they knew and subjects they barely knew. In 1909 Alice Browne wrote to her sponsors at Mount Holyoke, "Miss Chapin and I have been playing we were a whole school faculty," and Luella Miner in 1899 was teaching biology, international law, physiology, geometry, and the Pauline epistles. The traditional need of every congregation for music thrust many talents judged mediocre at home into the spotlight in China. "Get the smelling salts, fan, cold water, etc.," Lucy Mead wrote home, "for if you were surprised to have me learn to float and swim, more so to have me teaching English to College graduates—I don't know what will happen when you read that today I played the organ for Sunday school at Front Chapel!"[77] Mead's glee at her China accomplishments clearly far exceeded any pretense of shame.

Like the services they performed in the work itself, many missionary avocations arose simply out of the lack of specialized service personnel that had become a part of urbanizing America. Lida Ashmore, who also filled her husband's teeth, wrote that she had "added another trade to my list. I am now a hairdresser." Members of the women's boards were frequently their own building contractors as well. Luella Miner supervised the installation of a furnace in her girls' school, and Lucy Mead in 1916 directed the first wiring for electricity in Peking's Bridgman School. Women frequently did their own carpentry because they held such low opinions of Chinese carpenters, and also mentioned sketching their own building plans. They held a similarly low opinion of the elderly men they hired as gatekeepers, and frequently kept a compound gun themselves. Jessie Ankeny had gone hunting at home, but her skill gained new significance in a community of women. If it were "noised about the country that I use a gun" she concluded, the thieves that plagued impoverished China "will never bother here." Lucy Mead, too, acquired a gun for her household and practiced shooting so she could use it.[78] The infrequency with which guns were actually needed testified to missionary women's determined self-sufficiency rather than to their vulnerability in China.

Women acquired and perfected manual skills in China, but they had even more opportunity to exercise executive skills. Running a school, hospital, or household with servants required an often rapid acquisition of managerial expertise. Christine Pickett recalled the exclamation of a visitor over her mother, who was efficiently directing both school and family: "An executive woman!" Welthy Honsinger's exacting supervision of the transfer of bricks she had purchased for the construction of her school earned a comparison with the recently deceased and tyrannical Empress Dowager. "I could not be too complimented by the remark," Honsinger wrote. Not a dominant personality like Honsinger or Pickett, Lucy Mead too was judged magisterial—too magisterial for her twenty-eight years, thought a friend who would have placed her over thirty. "Surely the way you manage things you must be," the friend told her.[79] Missionary supervision of institutions in China demanded administrative skills which missionaries developed out of necessity but exercised with growing assurance.

Missionaries did not confine their managerial activities to the construction and administration of mission properties. For both private and charitable ends, they occasionally loaned money and invested in a variety of industrial schemes. Jessie Ankeny wrote that she was continually plagued for money both by other missionaries and by Chinese and consequently had gone into the loan business. When the Caldwells, a missionary couple, told her they "had to have" $200, whe wrote:

> I loaned it to them for 6% interest and this morning one of the businessmen came in and wanted to borrow $200. at 15% interest so I told him he could have it for he is very reliable and he said he could get the security of any man in town. . . . Yesterday a woman wanted to

borrow $600. for six months—saying the least % of interest she asked was 20%. You see how scarce money is here. Some of the missionaries say we charge too much, that it is usury but the people are more than happy to pay 15%, that is less than they can get it any place else. . . . Don't you think I am getting mercenary, I feel a little mean to be asking so much interest but they would run me to death if I began on the 6% plan. Of course the Caldwells are different.

Although she eventually sent all her money home for her father to invest to avoid the complications of lending on the field, she took pride in her skill at running a profit. In 1911 she reported her affairs to her father: "I suppose I should not keep writing of money matters but I want papa to know about my interest money. I have loaned out this year in all $320. and have in $25.50 interest money." Dorothy Campbell's tribute to her missionary mother suggests that such financial investments were not uncommon. Campbell wrote that her mother was "interested in speculation (sold drawn work [a kind of emroidered linen]; invested in bonds, bo't land etc.)."[80]

Missionaries commonly ran actual businesses in which they employed impoverished women from the church who needed support. These village women worked at home to produce drawn work that would be sold in the United States by mission auxiliaries. Missionary employers provided supplies and paid wages on a local scale. Profits usually accrued to the missionary who cycled them back into the local work in some form. Lida Ashmore ran a successful drawn-work industry in Swatow, which provided funds to build a girls' school the parent board had refused to fund. She wrote several years later, however, that her next project for the drawn-work profits would be the construction of tennis courts. Lucy Lee's drawn-work business was a genuine cooperative, which she patterned on industrial experiments she had learned of in the United States. Louise Stanley corresponded with a New York banker for advice on running her industrial work.[81] As in other areas, American women who were conditioned by their experiences with Western institutions perceived the opportunities of China in Western terms; with the dearth of Western male competition, they were emboldened to seize those opportunities.

Multiple freedoms and multiple opportunities reinforced each other in missionary women's China experience, and they described themselves as fulfilled, "found," transformed, happy. "My face is so red and rosy I look like I had had an over dose of paint," Jessie Ankeny wrote soon after her arrival in Fukien. "I am feeling better and more full of vim, more rested than I have felt for four years anyway." Several years later her letters were so euphoric she had to reassure her parents that she was not going to renounce her citizenship. Lucy Mead wrote that she and Mary Vanderslice were both "*so* happy," and that Vanderslice was "satisfied as she's not been before, and sure she's right and feels so 'at home.' " "It was the best thing that ever happened to me," Louise Stanley wrote, and contrasted her early life of frailty and sickness with the vitality she found in China.[82]

Women frequently saw their China experience as a personal transformation from weakness to health, from passivity to action. Elsie Clark wrote to her parents:

> I wonder you would recognize me now as the child to whom you used to say, "Elsie, do do something else besides sitting curled up in a rocking chair with a book stuck in your hand." The people in the cottage at Peitaiho—who were, to be sure staid and middle-aged, called me the cricket, *not* on the hearth, and thought me very "brave" to be willing to go out alone to strange places, if it wasn't convenient for anyone else to go with me.

Lucy Mead did not feel that she had been a good teacher at home, and wrote of her greater feeling of accomplishment and happiness in China:

> How often I wonder why it was, that when I so failed to meet well many of the opportunities there among the girls and my pupils, God thot He could use me out here! Every week, about Fr. or Sat. I get stage struck over the thot of my S.S. [Sunday school] class and it just seems almost as tho I couldn't do it. Then Sun. I get so intensely interested with them and some of them seem so interested in my teaching that I'm just the happiest person.

As Lottie Moon of the Southern Baptist board put it, her experiences of independence in China had changed her from "a timid self-distrustful girl into a brave self-reliant woman."[83]

Women expressed this elation in their letters as best as they could. Monona Cheney wrote that though language study could be tiresome, "it's exhilarating to have a new adventure every day. And when I go to church or to a store, and find here and there a word I can really understand, I feel like shouting." Marjorie Steurt could not resist returning to China even

"The happiest person," 1919: Lucy Mead (here with two former mission school students) felt she had failed at many endeavors at home but had been successful in China.

after a bitter experience with the Presbyterian board. "I loved it!" she explained. "I wasn't thinking of the mission when I went back; I was thinking of the Chinese there trying to start a new educational system. It just fascinated me. I jumped at the chance!" Elsie Clark perhaps came closest to touching the poetic level. Recalling the "young beauty," "mental alertness," and "social bravery" of her students, she wrote to her parents, "Life is rich and full, and grandly significant. I wish I could step into your presence and enflame you with the wonder of it." She reached her highest level of eloquence in explaining to her one-time suitor why she must return to China after her furlough:

> I think I am not speaking wildly, not deceiving myself, nor forgetting what lies beyond the immediate environment, when I say that life in America would henceforth be a positive deprivation to me, unless it were clearly and unmistakeably God's will. Even so, it would still be a deprivation, and China stand to me for a closed door, a joy denied. I am not thinking only of the "work." . . . I'm thinking of a much richer term, "life." The warp and woof of living reveals so surprising and abundant a quality here that only of necessity would one leave it.[84]

The "abundant" quality of life in China was particularly available to Westerners who were not subject to the same constraints of class and economy which cramped many Chinese lives; to Western women confronting for the first time opportunities available to men at home, the quality of life was not only "abundant" but also marvelously "surprising."

This consciousness of abundant and fulfilling life provides the substance of whatever claims can be made for sexual equality on the mission fields. Not equal in station or in political rights, women missionaries were equal to men in their access to a sense of "life." The lack of the vote in many stations was insignificant next to the opportunities offered by the China field to bypass American mission hierarchies altogether. And when women did acquire the vote, as they did in Florence Manly's Methodist station in western China in 1895, like her they accepted it as only appropriate to their new existence. Manly's diary mentioned in mid-entry: "We ladies empowered to vote this year. Woman suffrage on the mission field. I never cared much about it at home, but have so much interest in mission meeting, I count it a privilege to be allowed a voice here." Like Florence Manly's, Alice Alsup's desire for equality with men emerged indirectly and mildly from her engagement with the work. Her sense of the millions who would never hear of God led her to reflect that it would be wonderful to be a preacher in China. "I think I'm not satisfied with my position," she wrote. "I want to be on a 'circuit.' "[85] Like Florence Manly and Alice Alsup, most missionary women could only consider the possibility of equality with men after the challenges and gratifications of the Chinese environment had expanded their respect for their own achievements. Only then could conservative women imagine the meaning of equality; but, ironically, by that time equality with men from home was not an issue to women intoxicated with more rewarding authority and headier pleasures.

At the core of missionary exhilaration and power was what they repeatedly referred to as their love for the Chinese. Alice Brethorst wrote on her return, "Oh, they are a wonderful race! One just can't help loving them," and Ellen Lyon returned the favor of the student who loved her teacher next to God, and "loved the Chinese next to God." May Bliss, her son wrote, treasured the memory of each of her students as if they were jewels, and Louise Campbell described the students of her Bible training school as "lovely," and went on, "I just *love* this school."[86]

The secret of endless love was the assumption of endless Chinese need. Only great weakness could provide the great opportunities missionaries enjoyed in China. Missionaries emphasized this weakness as they described their love. The "wonderful" qualities of the Chinese people, Emma Smith wrote, were "their marvellous patience," perseverence, and endurance— the great virtues of passivity. In 1902, when *Woman's Missionary Friend* published a poem entitled "China," that country emerged a supplicant to the West: "Who comes to her support? / Our lives new patterns weave with her life-strands. / Shall we not aid when she appealing stands?" Lizzie Martin wished that her parents might join her to learn for themselves why she loved the work among the Chinese. Why? she asked: "Not for ease, fame, luxury or praise, but because the people need me and the thought that 'in as much as ye have done it unto one of the least of my brethren, ye have done it unto me!' "[87] Martin's assumption that the Chinese were among the least of Christ's brethren resonated throughout missionary papers in different forms; the "loveliness" of the Chinese was a direct result of their vulnerability.

The Western infatuation with Asian people has been compared to a masculine desire for possession. Pearl Buck portrayed her father as emotionally impotent in his relations with his family, as a man who could only find enthusiasm among the Chinese he felt superior to. "I think he felt about souls very much as some people feel about eggs," Buck wrote. "He wanted them brown." Only through racial domination, Buck implied, could her father feel sexually and emotionally competent. Edward Said, too, has employed the metaphor of male sexual possession to explain the protective condescension and benign violation which French Orientalists expressed toward the supine East. Han Su-yin's account of the Belgian railroad man who befriended her as a Eurasian schoolgirl in Peking presented the metaphor most dramatically:

> Like so many Europeans in China, Joseph Hers began to "love" China, a fierce, dominating, anxious, all-conquering possessiveness, characteristic of the warped, twisted, and altogether vicious relationships miscalled "love" between the dominating and the suppressed; the powerful and the weak; the spoiler and the cheated. Like many other foreigners he expressed this "love" in sexual imagery; to all of them, China was the WOMAN, the all-enveloping, soft, weak woman, who actually welcomed rape, welcomed being invaded. "Don't worry, China is feminine, she has always ended by absorbing all her conquerors," was their favourite explanation, and Hers said this too when I spoke about the Japanese. A great part of this love for China was their attraction to Chinese women; none of them, I think, realized how much this was resented by the Chinese. Though Hers knew the cruelties inflicted upon China, this sexual explanation equating the violation of China to the defloration a woman undergoes in marriage, enhanced in them a feeling of superiority: The Great White Male seeding in the weak, moaning, submissive coloured female. And in this he was typical of nearly all the Europeans in China who declared the Chinese "forever unable to rule themselves, because they are weak, devious, volatile, timid."[88]

Han's mother was Belgian and her father, a Chinese engineer, worked for Joseph Hers. As a Chinese, Han resented Hers's power on behalf of her father; as a woman, she resented him on her own behalf as well.

Missionary women's love for China shared some of the condescension and arrogance which Han saw in Joseph Hers; yet the sexual basis of the metaphor must, at least temporarily, ally missionary women with Asia itself. Both felt, without fully knowing, the threat which Western masculine authority posed to their autonomy. Both felt without articulating it their need for unconstricted life. Before arriving in China, missionary women expressed their ambition in a conventional vocabulary of self-sacrifice and Christian service rather than in the big terms with which they celebrated their later triumphs. Those who discovered the richness of experience in China had been seeking more modest rewards. Docile and sometimes frail, missionary women anticipated a more useful life doing the Lord's work in China, but they could not imagine the way in which colonial inequalities would cancel out American sexual imbalances and help them to liberation.

Once in China, however, the balance tipped too far. The politics of fulfillment has rarely been democratic, and the richness of life afforded one group inevitably occurs at cost to another. Missionaries did offer economic opportunities and educational advantages to Chinese men and women, but these advantages often came at the expense of Chinese independence and pride. Women differed from men in the intimacy of their missionary contacts and the nature of their evangelical techniques, but they frequently shared with men a sense of the limitless reaches of their authority. An article published in 1911, the year of the Chinese revolution, explained the exhaustive responsibility of women missionaries: "What the Chinese learn to do, we must first do for them. The most startling thing to be realized back of that statement is the fact that what the Chinese *live*, we must first live for them."[89] Although there were many distinctions between men and women in turn-of-the-century America, conservative Protestant women could share with men an appreciation for personal freedom and vocational competence and also an enthusiasm for the possibilities of power.

❧ 7 ❧

CHINESE WOMEN
AND CHRISTIAN IDENTITY

American missionaries brought a broad mandate to China in the early twentieth century. They hoped to conquer China for Christ and to save the world in one generation. In line with the church's new social and moral responsibilities in the United States, the mission church also advanced instructions on how to live. Christian ambitions for empire came to include hopes that Chinese converts might demonstrate Christian personalities as well as Christian consciences.

These were mission dreams. But Christianity never made more than tenuous inroads into the vast Chinese population before the 1949 revolution. By 1920, the combined Protestant forces could optimistically number 800,000 Chinese in their Christian constituency, which included some few hundred thousands who were only registered as students in Christian schools. When considered as a proportion of a population of nearly 500 million, the Christian converts hardly constituted a conquered nation.[1]

If the missionary churches failed in their ultimate ambition to Christianize all of China, however, what about their successes along the way? Did they accomplish their goal of Christianizing and transforming the lives of those who were their converts? If not, which mission folkways did Chinese converts adopt? In particular, what was the impact of the missionary message on the lives of female converts? Is there any truth to the proposal advanced by a sociologist that because women were less rewarded in traditional Chinese hierarchies they have been more easily "Westernized" than men?[2]

Unfortunately, good evidence to answer these questions is scarce. Chinese archival material of the kind found in American missionary papers is nonexistent. Nor have Chinese Christians produced the quantity of published autobiographies which are the stock and trade of American publishing. It is particularly difficult to document the experiences of the country women who composed the primary women's board constituency in the nineteenth century. The work of anthropologists provides the best context for their lives. The daughters of the gentry who began to attend Christian schools after 1900 have left better records, which provide our only direct evidence of the meaning of Christian conversion and mission experience for Chinese women at the turn of the century.

❦❦❦❦❦

In the nineteenth century, Christian missions appealed primarily to the disadvantaged in rural areas. When missionaries moved into the countryside in the late nineteenth century, they were filled with new hope at the greater interest of country people in the Christian word. In some areas women were particularly responsive to Christian proselytizing. In 1895 Anna Hartwell wrote from rural Kwangtung describing the local anger stirred up by her success in recruiting women: "The people were hostile, i.e. the men,—for they said so many of the women and girls were 'believing Jesus' already, that if they allowed us to go on, soon the whole place would be filled with disobedient wives and daughters refusing to worship the idols when told. Therefore they came nights and stoned the house and commanded us to be turned out.[3] Women never constituted more than a third of the total Christian communicants of the Protestant church in China, but in pockets such as Hartwell described, they composed a potentially revolutionary force. Considering restrictions on women's public activities, their church participation signified greater interest than sheer numbers might convey. What did women from the countryside find in the Christian church? The appeals of Christianity emerge clearly only in the context of women's religious and social alternatives.

Women had long been considered the most earnest supporters of heterodox folk religions. Scholars have attributed female interest in such sects as the Vegetarians of Fukien as in part a response to the greater role such sects accorded women in ritual religious life. But the capricious gods of Taoist and Buddhist folk religions, who offered all Chinese grounds for fear, shared with the Confucian order a particular disdain for women. The anthropologist Emily Ahern has carefully enumerated the Buddhist folk beliefs which regarded women's procreative capacities as sources of power but also of pollution. During menstruation, she documents, women were forbidden to appear in the temples, and those who died in childbirth were said to be consigned to a hell of bloody effluvia forever after. (Some sects consigned all women who had given birth to this fate.) Women's strict adherence to the Taoist and Buddhist rites of protection and appeasement signified a special vulnerability rather than a sense of special worth. Women's pollution could offer women of all classes reason for caution in dealing with the omnipresent spirits. Women of Confucian gentry families as well as of the villages were sometimes ardent Buddhist practitioners.[4]

Understandably, women who were already trying to placate numerous gods were more receptive to the mystical message of Christ than were upholders of the one Confucian orthodoxy. Perhaps missionary Young J. Allen was referring to this occasional division along gender line when in 1867 he noted that the men were "callous and hardened" to Christ, and that "the women alone are the depositories of the good feeling and kindly sympathies that yet remain toward the truth in China." In the absence of Christianity, he wrote, the women "cling to superstition."[5] It was precisely this female openness to the mystical and the fears promoted by folk "superstition," however, which provided Christianity with some of its early hearings.

Missionaries often argued that in granting women spiritual equality with men Christianity offered Chinese women better terms than folk religion did. The descriptions of women's afterlife suggest there is some truth to that claim. Perhaps one woman's question to an evangelist—"Heaven; of course you don't mean that women go there?"—drew on her limited expectations from a Buddhist life-after-death. Missionaries, of course, liked to retell such stories—including the tale of Tang I-lien, whose childish mind was filled with fears of the ever-present demons until she went to mission school "and soon experienced the intense relief which came to her with the knowledge that the loving, protecting Jesus was Lord over the dark and dreaded demons."[6]

But Christianity had only mixed success in banishing women's special sense of horror and vulnerability. The devils of folk belief were as likely to inhabit the mission compound as other dwellings in China. Missionaries occasionally wrote home about spirit possession among their students, but perhaps the most powerful evidence of the tenacity of folk belief came from within the missionary community itself. Despite her mission service as one of the most influential members of the American women's board, Emily Hartwell, who had been raised in China by a Chinese servant, "was firmly convinced that there were devils and devil possession," her niece remembered. Her aunt's stories prompted some of the younger family members to wonder "who's converting whom," according to Christine Pickett. Pickett's own sister Nela, also raised by an amah, retained her deference for surrounding spirits well after her return to New Haven, Pickett noted, remembering that Nela took care to assuage the spirits of a room she entered by touching their dwelling places in the furniture.[7] If women from the mission community surrounded by Christian influences retained the folk beliefs of a Chinese childhood, it is likely that many mission converts did not so much surrender their beliefs as supplement them with Christianity. Perhaps Christian faith offered better terms for women than did Chinese folk religion, but faith was seldom a matter for calculated self-interest.

Therefore, Christianity especially appealed to villagers from heterodox traditions when its religious offerings were combined with needed social and economic assistance. Chinese peasants at the turn of the century did not have many resources in reserve should disaster befall them. For women the alternatives were particularly few. Among rural farm women, the anthropologist Margery Wolf has written, suicide was "not exotic" but "a part of their repertoire of threats, a conceivable course of action, and for some the pathetic finale of their existence." The range of circumstances which might inspire such an outcome has been touched on earlier. Christian missionaries sought and sometimes won converts from among these classes. "In this little village, just this past summer six women, so the Bible woman said, have commited suicide," Elizabeth Perkins wrote home in 1907 about her Diongloh station, and added their means of death, "four by opium and two by eating soap."[8] Desperate social and economic circumstances might well have encouraged a woman to consider "the Christ doctrine" as an alternative to more conclusive action.

Missionaries recruited Chinese from the margins of their society not by choice but by necessity. Most Chinese, particularly members of the gentry, were overtly hostile to the foreign presence during the entire nineteenth century. Even after the Boxer uprising, when Chinese attitudes toward many Western ideas were changing, traditional Chinese from the major cities of the hinterland continued to look down upon Christianity. Earlier, foreign associations compromised Christianity; after the Boxer uprising, its converts gave Christianity a bad reputation. Luella Miner considered running a language school in Peking in 1905 and felt "if it were not in connection with a Christian school" it would succeed; "but there are many daughters of officials who would not be willing to come into a Mission compound." One gentry father, according to his daughter, was willing to send her to a modern school for girls, but not to a mission school. "Nobody of good family goes to a mission school," he told her in 1904. K'ang Cheng, arriving in Nanchang to establish a dispensary after the turn of the century, received a delegation from the local gentry offering to sponsor her work. "It is really no credit to you to belong to the Church," they reportedly told her. "The people who belong to the Church are rather of the lower class and their object in joining the Church is to get some pecuniary good." Most Peking officials shunned the Chinese Christian community until well after the 1911 revolution. Only in 1920 could Miner write, "the most prominent Chinese in the city are now glad to work with our Christian Chinese, whereas eight years ago we Westerners had to be the ones to co-operate."[9]

Although Christianity continued to draw the skepticism of Chinese officials and landed gentry well into the twentieth century, another group, the Westernized treaty-port population, demonstrated an increased interest in Christianity and in mission schooling in the 1890s. The Chinese of this coastal region, as opposed to the hinterland of Peking and the interior, had already violated Confucian precepts by their participation in business— a low form of human activity to Confucian thinking. Their practice of Christianity served further to sever ties with the Chinese orthodoxy.

Missions rushed to accommodate the daughters of this business elite by establishing schools offering English instruction and music lessons. The Southern Methodists ran the most famous of these schools—Laura Haygood School in Soochow and McTeiyre School in Shanghai. The Northern Methodist Episcopal church also ran a finishing school in Tientsin, which Soumay Tcheng may have attended in 1908 at the age of fourteen. She described it as follows:

All the lessons were given in English. . . . It was not long before I could speak a little English. I was dressed and my hair was arranged now in European fashion. . . . With my English clothes, a hat which was the first I had ever had on my head, the skirts which I now wore instead of trousers, I felt very much "in the role.". . . I learned how to drink tea as the English take it, with sugar and milk; how to eat bread and butter and toast; how to use a knife and fork instead of chop-sticks, and how to take exercise.

Regular middle schools sometimes acknowledged class protocal by refusing boarding privileges to daughters of prominent families.[10]

The customs and student body of Anglo-Chinese mission schools were largely responsible for the reputation shared by all missions for encouraging and reinforcing the power of the Chinese elite. The disproportionate publicity which mission boards granted these schools reflected the special sense of victory felt by missionaries long abused by the Chinese ruling class. Elite Anglo-Chinese schools were most prominently represented in nationwide competitions, such as the first competition for Boxer indemnity scholarships open to women. Four out of ten students came from the Southern Methodist McTeiyre School in Shanghai.[11] Missionaries justified their efforts to win over the wealthy as a crusade for more influence throughout China. But in fact, in accord with new opportunity, the mission school system was shifting its emphasis from subsidizing the poor to receive education in the Scriptures to catering to the rich by offering courses in English.

Tsai Ling-fang, Huang Lu-yin, and Tseng Pao-sun were members of the gentry and official class which gradually began to attend Western schools after 1900. Their memoirs describe their births in the 1890s in different parts of China to non-Christian families, their conversions while in mission schools in the first decade of the century, and their future careers as an evangelist, a writer, and an educator in republican China. Tsai's account was originally published in English but has gone through twelve editions in Chinese translation. Huang's and Tseng's accounts have never been translated from Chinese.[12] In their shared class origins Huang, Tseng, and Tsai were not typical of the average Christian convert, who came from the lower- or lower-middle classes. However, their lives do suggest the ways in which mission schools adapted to the Chinese social structure, and how Christian conversion reflected and influenced relations of Chinese girls with their families and with their political culture.

Tsai Ling-fang was born the seventh in a line of girls in 1890 to a vice-governor of Nanking and his wife. Her "milk name" used in infancy was "Too Many." In a family which eventually included twenty-three children, her Christian faith provided the means for her to transcend her lowly status. Tsai's *Queen of the Dark Chamber*, the story of her life as an unfavored daughter in a privileged family and of her subsequent brief career as a mission evangelist, was first published in 1953 by the Moody Bible Institute.

Beyond her birth order, Tsai had other reasons for feeling ill-fated. Her birthdate itself was inauspicious. She was expected to be "either the very best or the very worst," and since no prospective mother-in-law would take a risk against these odds, her mother was unable to contract an engagement for her. Unlike her handsome brothers and sisters and her beautiful mother, Tsai was considered plain. Her brothers would taunt her, she remembered, with cries that "you are not our sister!" "You must have been born in a hut!" Tsai later wrote: "This made me unbearably shy and sensitive. I would run to my nursemaid and sob. . . . I became afraid of strangers. I was such an introvert that in the excitement and bustling crowds of public occasions . . . I would hide behind my nurse's apron and peek out at people." Under these circumstances, Tsai perhaps did well to consider ways to move beyond her familial lot. "Going to a school just for girls where a foreign woman would teach me English and piano was my castle in the air," she wrote. Having no other plans for her, the family was willing to indulge this interest in Western accomplishments fashionable among certain members of the elite in the post-Boxer era.[13]

Like other members of her class, at first Tsai Ling-fang strongly resisted Christian proselytizing. She flatly refused her first invitation to join an English-language Bible course, agreeing only because "though I wanted none of their Christianity, an extra English class was welcome." After her transfer to Haygood School, Tsai's resistance was more overt:

> I did not like the preaching. I thought it was very unpleasant and openly opposed it. Another girl, a Miss Wu, from a high-class family similar to my own, hated this teaching too, and we used to get together and give voice to our indignation. We even started to write a book denouncing all Christian teaching, insisting that Confucius and Buddha were our teachers, and that we did not want Christ.

Tsai brought a Chinese novel with her to the school's mandatory church services and read it while she knelt in the pew.[14]

The way for her conversion had perhaps already been prepared, however. She had always been impressed by the kindness of the missionaries, and remembered the first attentions of the Leaman sisters, in particular, who later became her lifelong companions. The "gratuitous kindness" of another woman, "a tall foreign lady with curly hair" who always bowed and smiled at her in the street, both puzzled and pleased Tsai. "We Chinese are taught to speak politely to others, but never think of smiling at strangers." "To this day," she wrote, "that winning smile is one of my treasured memories for it is the genuine evidence of God's indwelling love." Tsai was eventually converted at Soochow by an American evangelist when, as before, "God used my love for English to draw me to Himself."[15]

An early graduate from Laura Haygood, probably in 1912, Tsai received many job offers. The principal of her school invited her to become vice-principal, and the YWCA offered her a job as a general secretary. "But I had an ambition dearer than these," Tsai wrote—"to return home and lead my family to the Saviour." Using the same tactics the missionaries themselves used, Tsai returned to Nanking and began to work to convert her mother. "Her love of music was the entering wedge. . . . Her love of stories was another." The final wedge, Tsai noted, was her mother's opium habit. Following the revolution, opium had been outlawed, but her mother had not been able to break her habit. A stay in a mission hospital finally turned the tide, and along with Tsai's second and eighth brothers and their wives, she was baptized.[16]

Born in Fukien in 1898, Huang Lu-yin was also the daughter of a well-to-do official, but she led a childhood of deprivation far more severe that Tsai's. A successful writer in the 1920s, Huang wrote an autobiography in 1934 which depicted her gradual triumph over her childhood suffering. Huang's attendance at mission school and her Christian conversion took place within the context of this personal misery. Although Huang subsequently repudiated her Christian experience, she credited Christianity with relieving some of the anguish of her childhood.

Huang's grandmother had died the day of her birth, so Huang Lu-yin too was considered inauspicious. Her mother refused to nurse her, and she spent her first three years with a wet nurse, returning home to little welcome. After her father's death she accompanied her mother and siblings to live with relatives in Peking, where her sullenness grew and she was barred from family occasions. She felt that her mother's and aunt's decision to send her to the Methodist girls' school in Peking was another effort to get rid of her—like an earlier one she suspected her father of. "The tuition was cheap and also you could live at the school and return home only on holidays and for summer vacation each year. If I was willing to believe, even the tuition could be saved," she wrote. Although at barely nine years old she was too young by nearly two years, her aunt lied about her age, and in 1906 she was packed off to mission school.[17]

After the freedom or neglect of home, the life of the ordinary missionary school appeared grim even to Huang Lu-yin. Her descriptions of Mary Gamewell School in Peking were reminiscent of Dickens. She found the building gloomy and forbidding. The school principal, Charlotte Jewell, "the first long-nosed, blue eyed foreigner" she had seen, had a severe and mysterious face which made her heart pound. Her fellows students, she noticed quickly, were dispossessed paupers. "They were wearing very dilapidated clothing. Some of their coarse garments were patched, and their faces were pallid and yellow, lacking in spirit." The quality of the food was a serious affliction for Huang. After six months she wrote home begging to be removed from school, complaining, "Life is too miserable here—everyday the same old rice, corn muffins, also the unoiled old salty vegetables which I can't eat." When her well-dressed mother and aunt came to visit, they discovered that a higher quality of food could be obtained for extra payment, and they agreed to pay the higher tariff.[18]

Huang's conversion came at a time of particularly acute suffering. Bossing and bullying from the older schoolgirls aggravated a physical ailment, and Huang landed in the Methodist hospital for a back operation. When she returned to school a revival was in progress, with church attendance required three times a day. Huang wrote:

> I too was forced to go. Everyone would kneel on the floor, and out of their mouths would come the moans of prayer and repentance. Some would make noise and cry as if they were making a confession. Following their example, I too kneeled down, except I didn't believe, and I didn't pray, instead opening my eyes and glancing around. At that moment suddenly Mrs. Jewell appeared and kneeled beside me. In a sincere, trembling voice, she encouraged me, saying "Dear child, God is coming to bless you."

When Huang responded that she did not believe in God, and had never seen him, Jewell continued her prayers. Finally her energies bore fruit. Huang wrote:

> My weak and timid heart at that time was so empty. My mother didn't love me, my brothers and sisters had cast me off. My disease pained me. Because of these things, I cried.

I sobbed and sobbed, very moved. My empty heart then accepted God. Holding back tears I said to Mrs. Jewell, "I believe, I really believe." Mrs. Jewell saw I had agreed to believe, and joyfully began to cry. She kneeled and prayed for me for a long time, and then led me to the minister to enroll. When the revival was over, I became a follower.[19]

Huang's conversion followed a now classic pattern. Reduced to a state of emotional exhaustion by the oppressiveness of her circumstances, she succumbed to the beseechments of a strong and personal voice. Once converted, she began proseltyzing herself, bringing several Bibles home after her first year of school and preaching to her brothers: "I said 'God is the only savior of the world, mankind's ancestors Adam and Eve sinned and were driven by God from the happy garden, therefore all mankind is sinful at birth, and without believing in Jesus, you can't escape going to hell.' " Her brothers did not respond sympathetically. When they heard her invocation,

> they began to laugh, they laughed rolling back and forth, and I, although I was only ten and timid, the more they laughed the more ardently I proselytized, until they not only used laughter to deal with it but took the Bibles and destroyed them and threw them in the spittoon, and then beating their hands, they said in a loud voice, "What Jesus Savior? He is really a pig, a dog." They would alternate talking and laughing.
>
> Every time when the moment for grace at mealtimes arrived, they surrounded me and made jokes. This one stroked my nose, that one pulled my ear, and prevented me from saying grace. After that I could only pray secretly.

Huang wrote that she was a "true believer" as a child, and while secretly praying for them she shed many tears over her brothers' slander of Jesus.[20]

Huang eventually renounced her Christianity and attacked missionaries for raising up "slavish personalities" among their converts. But at the same time she acknowledged the important role of religion in her psychic and emotional reconstruction. "Belief in religion," she wrote, "eradicated my frequent heart ache. Whenever I experienced sorrow or fear I would pray earnestly and receive ample blessing." "Although I now think it a ridiculous thing, I am also grateful to religion," she wrote later, "for without it my crippled spirit would have been even more broken." In truth,

Huang's conversion marked the beginning of a new life for her. She did not continue in mission school, which she did not like any better after her conversion. "I really hated the gloomy life of that school and those foreigners' high-pressured domination," she wrote later. But with the aid of a brother returned home at the time of the 1911 revolution, she took and passed an entrance examination to a government school.[21] By then, she had taken her place in her family and could endure the onslaught of her brothers' mockery from her own vantage point of righteousness and compassion.

Tseng Pao-sun, great-granddaughter of the celebrated general Tseng Kuo-fan, was sponsored in mission school by a progressive uncle excited about the "New Learning," especially science and mathematics. Born in Hunan in 1894, she does not seem to have experienced the familial disfavor of Huang's and Tsai's childhoods. When her grandmother, the matriarch of the family, granted permission, Tseng attended four different schools, changing according to family circumstances, between the ages of fourteen and eighteen. Tseng eventually completed her education in England, returning to China to open an independent Christian school in Changsha in 1918. Her memoirs were written in Taiwan, where she fled in 1950.

Tseng Pao-sun was most impressed by the Christian discipline of the first mission school she attended, a Baptist school in Shanghai:

> On Sunday you had to worship six times. The morning worship undoubtedly was a kind of *chen jing* [morning watch]. After eating breakfast there were prayers again. At ten you went to the classroom for prayers. After the noon meal you would rest for a little while, and then have Sunday school. At five you would again sing hymns, and at seven back in the classroom for worship. On Sunday you weren't allowed to do anything, to read any books. You were only allowed to read the Bible.

Tseng found the classes to be less challenging than the church discipline. "The levels of the students were very different—there was no standard. There weren't any official classrooms, just a few odd rooms, and the students on their own sought the teachers catch as catch can." In particular, Tseng wrote, the standards of her classmates in Chinese literature and history were low.[22] The poor Chinese training in mission schools was to become one of the most frequent points in later charges that mission schools separated students from their culture.

Tseng Pao-sun's conversion followed a period of rebelliousness rather than degradation. Distrustful of mission education after her bad experience in Shanghai, Tseng had reluctantly agreed to the suggestion of a government schoolteacher that after graduation from Hangchow Normal School in 1909 she returned to a mission school for further study. Although the British Mary Vaughn School also required worship five times on Sunday, it was possible to go home for the weekend and avoid that unpleasant requirement. As one of the two most advanced students there, Tseng became a leader, and one day, probably in 1910, found herself leading a student strike.

The circumstances were these. With her fellow students Tseng had been punished for the unconfessed crimes of a classmate. After the students had copied exercises for an hour, a British teacher came in to assign additional punishment—mandatory outside recess for an hour—and Tseng rebelled. "Seeing her wearing a smug, self-satisfied look, with complete disregard for the opinions of the students, I suddenly stood up and said, 'I am not going out.'" Tseng was joined by six or seven other students. From that time on she bore the reputation of a troublemaker. This loss of favor encouraged Tseng's resolve and she came to consider herself the leader of a rebellion. She published a newspaper about inequalities at school and in it adopted a revolutionary perspective toward national issues.[23]

All the while Tseng was anticipating her dismissal; when she was detained in the principal's office, she presumably thought the time had arrived. Instead, to her amazement, the principal, with tears streaming from her eyes, proposed a reconciliation. "I know that *you* did not oppose the school," she said. "It was just a devil in your heart trying to hurt you." Tseng reported kneeling down and praying with Principal Barnes, and feeling her sincerity and forgiveness. The girl was deeply moved, and experienced a total transformation, she wrote. She was taken aback by the grace of kindness when she expected anger and became thereafter a believer in the power of Christian love.[24]

Tseng Pao-sun was the first convert in her distinguished family. In fact, Tseng was aware that she was violating thousands of years of familial loyalty to the Confucian order on her grandfather's side; a great grandfather on her grandmother's side had been martyred by the Taiping rebels. "All of my family were believers in Confucianism; if they did not believe in Taoism or Buddhism, how much less did they believe in Jesus?" Tseng wrote. "To stand out as a girl believing in religion" she felt, "would be to start the village laughing." But after the outbreak of the revolution, when

Tseng's uncle had conducted family members to Shanghai for temporary exile, his feelings about Christianity changed. "At this point Seventh Uncle was feeling depressed about events in the country and in the family," Tseng wrote, "and he began to talk with me about religion, especially Christianity." Tseng and her uncle were officially baptized in the church at about the same time, before Christmas in 1911.[25]

⁂

The lives of Tseng Pao-sun, Huang Lu-yin and Tsai Ling-fang raise questions about the meaning of the female mission movement that transcend individual experiences. Given the disdain with which many members of the gentry still regarded mission education, gentry decisions to allow their daughters to attend mission schools seem to have had implications for the standing of these daughters within their own families. Was mission school an option only for the unattractive, the inauspiciously born, or the disagreeably insistent? Within this context, conversion itself might have been a declaration of independence from a predetermined family identity. Huang, Tseng, and Tsai initially shared the disdain of their class for Christianity; however, at least Huang and Tsai's attendance at mission school reflected their families' disinterest in them.

What brought resistant schoolgirls to an emotional acceptance of an alien religion? In the short run the conversion experiences of Huang, Tseng, and Tsai all followed gratuitous personal attention from formerly forbidding authority figures. Tsai mentioned only surprising smiles from a strange foreigner; Tseng and Huang received the full and personalized assaults of intimate evangelism. Both the latter assaults took place when Huang and Tsai were under duress, Huang from physical pain exacerbating her longtime mental suffering, Tseng from anxiety about the consequences of her new rebelliousness.

To what extent was this duress a conscious part of missionary strategy? Huang's tale of degradation prior to conversion raises an important question about the tactics of her mission school mentors, particularly in the context of recent cult conversions. Huang's mission guardians clearly did not create her misery, although they may have contributed to it. Huang experienced humiliation well before she was packed off to school. The bad food and gloomy surroundings of the school were oppressive to her, as they were to other students of her background, but for the truly impoverished mission school student, tasteless but regular food and adequate if worn clothing must have seemed an improvement over the brutal poverty of village life. The tyranny of Huang's fellow students played a significant role in her misery, but Huang was bullied "because of her youth and size," she wrote, for which her aunt's falsification of her age by almost two years must bear some responsibility. Missionary women did not create Huang's misery, but they did know how to shape and appropriate misery for Christian purposes.

Feelings of gratitude undoubtedly contributed to many others' conversions. Tseng Pao-sun interpreted the warm feelings of relief that washed over her at her principal's forgiveness as the experience of grace. Another woman who was converted at about the same time expressed her willingness to be baptized as conscious gratitude for missionary selflessness. While a student at Eliza Yates, a Baptist school outside of Shanghai, Y. T. Zee witnessed the archetypal selflessness of Christian love. Zee recently described this experience:

> I was very much inspired by a consecrated Principal, Lottie Price who was very thin and gentle, yet so self-giving, to eradicate the *scabies*, a kind of infectious skin disease in the students compound—How she cleaned them by sulphur baths one by one, like a nurse. Only by that act, I became aware of Christian Love and when she asked me to think of Baptism by Immersion I could *not* refuse, gladly accepted.[26]

Zee agreed to be baptized more as a tribute to Lottie Price's selflessness than as an expression of a first moment of conviction. Probably this sentiment of gratitude moved others indebted to missionaries to oblige their teachers and agree to believe.

Students defying the earnest and insistent wishes of missionary authority figures undoubtedly felt some guilt at their insubordination. Hsieh Ping-ying never became a Christian and, like American youths who could not experience conversion, felt her resistance as a sin. She loved the Norwegian-run mission school she attended in Hunan but "from the day I entered the school I had a heavy weight pressing on my heart. It was that I did not believe in God, and I did not like to read the Bible. I did not like saying the Lord's Prayer before meals. . . . Wanting to avoid the prayer, I would sit in the privy and suffer every morning and evening or at meal times." Hsieh's suffering seems to have come from her sense of guilt at disappointing an important missionary expectation. Huang, Tseng, and Tsai struck stronger notes of defiance than guilt over their failure to oblige mission superiors by adopting Christian faith. But missionaries themselves frequently commented on Chinese traditions of deference which obliged students to attend with courtesy to the moral preachments of their elders.[27] Students who had consistently resisted the urgent and intimate approaches of their mission superiors might have welcomed an emotional occasion of nearly any kind to make amends for past failings of feeling.

At the same time that conversion reconciled students with missionaries, it distanced them from their families, and that sometimes seemed to be more significant. Through Christianity was held in low esteem by many members of the gentry class, it could offer a positive alternative to unwanted daughters. The stories of Huang Lu-yin, abandoned by her family, and Tsai Ling-fang, who considered herself unfavored, seem to substantiate this possibility. Both Tsai and Huang discovered distinct identities as Christians which allowed them a new, if still unfavored, role in their family. As Tsai put it: "All my sisters were good-looking, but I was considered rather plain. Yet it was I, alone, 'Too Many,' who left the big ancestral walls to enter a missionary school, crossed the ocean to America, and now have the honor of writing to you."[28] Although Tseng did not seem to share in the disregard Huang and Tsai felt from their families, her Christian conversion, too, allowed her a separate familial status. Her choice to convert to Christianity, rather than to the Western science her liberal father and uncle preferred, perhaps also demonstrated how the mission institution could grant a Chinese woman a measure of female independence from the all-embracing family unit.

As time passed, Christian identity became for some women not a negative identity, positive only in its guarantee of a measure of independence, but a positive identity in its own right. With the 1911 revolution and the destruction of the Confucian imperial order, Christianity lost its particular stigma. Indeed, some families came to rely on Christian-educated daughters or granddaughters for family support. Tsai and Tseng's alliance with a force which came to be considered modern provided their families with alternatives when many Chinese from their class needed them. Tsai Ling-fang had long felt her inferiority to her beautiful mother. But Christianity allowed her, alone of her mother's twenty-three children, to save her from the opium habit and transform her life. Tseng Pao-sun also helped family members to Jesus. For Tsai and Tseng and women like them, the journey away from tradition and into the foreign religion would lead them to a new position of influence within their own families.

But what was the relationship of Christian women to their own society? Did mission associations inevitably distance Chinese women from the problems of their people, as critics have charged? Evidence seems to indicate not. The awakening of China took place in the context of a generation of schoolmates; schools transferred crucial loyalties from family to peers. The collective experience and the living examples of mission schools brought political consciousness to female students who, if left alone, would likely have languished in family courtyards.

Chinese girls discovered each other for the first time in schools in the early century. The experience of peers, other girls at the same stage of development with similar problems, was among the most significant developments of their education. Chao Buwei did not enjoy McTyeire School in Shanghai, but she did appreciate her classmates. "If I did not quite like the school," she wrote, "I liked the friends." Hsieh Pingying especially remembered her comrades at a non-Christian girls' school at the same time. "The friendship between the schoolmates was deeper than between sisters," she wrote. When Hsieh's mother withdrew her from school she threatened to starve herself to death until her mother relented. Mission school students were sometimes reluctant to return home even over the summer. "I think the girls' friendships meant a great deal to them," Alice Reed remembered of her students. "There was always lots of weeping at the end of the school term when they had to go home, because when they got home they would have no friends, and no place to go from home. In a village you didn't go anywhere; you stayed at home.[29] Students in mission and nonmission schools shared delight over the social experience of school.

Lacking indigenous traditions to celebrate their collective identity, Chinese girls at mission schools were eager to adopt the suggestions of their American teachers about how they might celebrate. Elsie Clark wrote a school song for Hwa Nan College, and although the students themselves produced a school yell, they did so in emulation of American collegiate custom. The gratifications of collective life in fact made Christianity more palatable. "I feel more of the power of Christianity when I hear of the American college spirit," one student was reported to have said.[30]

"School spirit" in theory united all levels of the school in shared institutional loyalty. But for the female students at Christian colleges in particular, much of the spirit was a generational loyalty to each other. *The Pioneer*, a 1919 publication by the first class of women at Ginling College, revealed the gradual process of mutual discovery. At first, varying dialects and educational backgrounds posed problems for the freshman class, and each member felt isolated and alone. By the second semester of the freshman year, however, "the strain of being strangers having worn off, we were relieved from concentrating on ourselves alone." At the end of the first year, they could note "the birth of college spirit."[31] The first classes at Ginling shared in a sense of exhilaration and responsibility resulting from their uniqueness, just as had early graduates of women's colleges in the United States.

That sense of peer solidarity was the basis for the student activism of the early century. Tseng Pao-sun's 1910 rebellion was only one instance in which students in the first decade of the century resisted the political implications of Christian missions. Students at Canton Christian College had struck in 1905 in conjunction with the boycott protesting American immigration policy. And the Yale-in-China campus in Changsha was plagued by strikes, the first one significantly occurring only two weeks after it opened in 1906. Later strikes in mission schools were often simply tactical. Chinese students were the "original strikers," Alice Reed observed, for when there was a problem in the school they would protest it with collective action—perhaps encouraged by the heightened sense of community they could experience before a largely foreign hierarchy. "They very definitely depended on group action," she remembered. "You never had trouble with an individual student but if [he or she] could get a group to want something. . . ."[32]

Students exercised sufficient leverage so that before the 1920s they had assumed responsibilities for school management in some institutions. Following protests at North China Union Women's College, students took over the food service. "The girls run their own affairs now," Lucy Mead wrote in 1915, "and all we care is that they keep within the amount charged for board. They do get better food that way and cannot kick on our management so is it [sic] fine all around." Ginling's student government on its own initiative assumed authority over the college matron, to the distress of Ginling's president Matilda Thurston. "Students took liberties they would not think of taking in an American college," she wrote.[33] The collective action of mission students seemed to be less evidence of the incompatibility of Christian purposes and nationalism, than an adaptation

The birth of school spirit, 1915, 1918: As freshmen (*top*) the first class at Ginling was divided by different dialects and educational backgrounds. By their junior year (*bottom*), they had developed a sense of exhilarated solidarity. (Y. T. Zee, later a class leader, gazes off into the distance on the back right as a freshman but leans into the group from the back left as a junior. The first Chinese president of Ginling, Wu Yi-fang, joined the class late and is sitting third from the left in the junior class portrait.)

by Chinese students to insure their representation in a closed mission hierarchy.

During China's national political emergency, of course, the nature of college graduates' responsibilities was clear. College classmates worked to save their country. "Realizing our opportunities to be the first ones educated here in China," The Pioneer reported, "we decided to make the most of the preparation period and looked forward to the day when we would be privileged to have our share in the big movement." On their own, mission school students organized to demonstrate their patriotism well before the May 4 movement of 1919. Mission school students were among those who participated in the Rights Recovery Movement in the first decade of the century. "To show their patriotism the older Christian girls are going without little treats . . . in order to buy a few little shares of railroad stock," one missionary explained. Though their motive was to show the non-Christians "that being Christian does not make them disloyal to their country," this act demonstrated a keen sense of national responsibility felt in conjunction with Christian responsibility. The 1913 cheer of the Knowles School, a Bible training school for older women, was reported to be:

> Knowles School, Knowles School
> Come quickly Come quickly
> Women of China Women of China
> Save your country Save your country

Christian school graduates considering vocations remembered that, "Whatever our choice, our dominant motive was the same: we wanted to do something to help our country."[34] The Chinese mission school experience created an earnest corps of volunteers as much for national survival as for Christian soldiery.

Tseng Pao-sun's life perhaps typifies the complex interaction of mission school experience and nationalist consciousness. Tseng discovered an emotional basis for a nationalist political position while a student at Mary Vaughn School. Her resentment of missionary condescension inspired her first political action, an impromptu strike. Only then did she adopt a more general political position and edit a newspaper which addressed national as well as school issues. Missionary school experience politicized Tseng. But her rebellion was perhaps more of a strain on her than she admitted, for when the principal offered forgiveness, she immediately succumbed. She did not surrender her national concerns, though, instead avowing that the strength to act (*li hsing*) embodied in the Christian spirit would be the salvation of a China defeated by its own passivity. Like many others, she felt the force of national loyalty and Christian faith pushing her in a surprisingly consistent direction. They encouraged her overseas education and her establishment of a Christian school independent from foreign boards in 1918 in Changsha.

Like Tseng, many students were initially resistant to foreign influences and experienced national loyalty in opposition to the mission hierarchy. Like her, also, however, students gradually developed bonds with each other and their school which undermined their initial alienation from foreigners. Like her, they used the mission community as a base for vocational initiatives. Ultimately, like her also, many students expressed their new commitment to peer solidarity in equal loyalty to the Christian religion and national survival.

⁂

The overlapping forces of mission and nationalist influence proved particularly powerful in the lives of female graduates of the new women's colleges, who remained single and pursued vocations in high numbers. As of 1916, none of the seven students in the first two graduating classes from North China Union Women's College, the classes of 1910 and 1911, had married. The graduates from this Peking college, later to be known as Yenching, included five teachers, one physician, and one postgraduate student in England. Of the first five graduates from Ginling college in 1919, only one ever married, and she somewhat reluctantly. The five included two medical doctors, two academic administrators, and one evangelist, later an ordained Methodist minister. Although the proportions were more striking among college students, students in mission middle schools also considered alternatives to marriage in China's time of emergency. A survey of students in girls' schools in the late teens found that most expected to pursue some kind of outside work, only one expecting her work to be within the home. Mission school graduates were sought as appropriate brides by Chinese men who had received modern educations, and most middle-school graduates did eventually marry.[35] But the temporary dissent of even a few girls from this universal expectation is significant. Was missionary influence responsible for the professional motivation and the marital disinclination of a number of early twentieth century graduates?

Missionary schools directly or indirectly encouraged their students to engage in service for the cause. Y. T. Zee wrote of her teachers at Ginling that

> Mrs. Thurston always appealed to us with the need of science and religious teachers for all of their secondary schools. Miss Vautrin appealed to us with the urgent needs of the rural people to have their food and education. Dr. Cora D. Reeves, a Biology professor, appealed to us for the needs of medical doctors, medical workers, and more advanced Ph.D. Education work.

Not surprisingly, each teacher promoted her particular line of work. But perhaps the strongest influence of missionary women on their graduates was in their own example. Carol Chen, who attended Methodist Hwa Nan College at the same time as Zee, in the teens, remembered that her sense of career options was limited by the models available within the mission community: "There was no such thing as vocational guidance in those days. Our choice of profession was influenced by the personal examples of our teachers. As the vocations open to women were still very limited, the choice was relatively simple." Female missionaries offered the primary examples of nondomestic womanhood available to students in mission schools and undoubtedly influenced the vocations Chinese schoolgirls considered.[36]

Were the decisions of schoolgirls to delay or forego marriage likewise the result of the example of single women teachers? "We hold no antimatrimony bureau!" Luella Miner protested against accusations that missionary women were discouraging the formation of Christian families. Women's board rhetoric celebrated the Christian home. Nonetheless, the example of missionaries in girls' schools weighed largely to the contrary, for the majority were single. When Elsie Clark asked students in her English class to fantasize about what they would do if they were American girls, one student declared that if she were an American woman, "she would never marry, and many said they would be missionaries." When girl students avowed their plans to remain single, they were following in strong institutional traditions of spinsterhood.[37]

But missionary example was only one part of it. The decision to remain single, like other student actions of the early twentieth century, took place in the name of national survival and the context of peer solidarity. Even missionary reports explained the decisions of schoolgirls as decisions for China rather than for God. May Hu, who became one of the early female doctors of the Methodist board, was said to have remained unmarried "feeling her responsibility to her Chinese sisters." Frequently schoolmates made such decisions jointly. Thus Maude Wheeler reported the shared decision of three schoolgirls on a hot windy day in June—"they would never marry, but become doctors and serve their people." The high proportion of single women in the first class of Ginling graduates was not a matter of chance either, for the entire class had taken a vow not to marry. Y. T. Zee (Mrs. Way-sung New), the only one of five to break this vow, explained, "I never wanted to marry. Dr. New [her husband] didn't want to marry. . . . We thought we couldn't dedicate ourselves with a home." Before reversing her decision to satisfy her mother, she consulted her classmates. Her classmates delegated her to establish a home which would sustain the rest in service, a responsibility Zee fulfilled by maintaining a permanent Ginling guestroom in her Shanghai home. The Ginling seniors received support from one unmarried missionary teacher who "loved our idea" about not marrying, Zee reported.[38] But the inspiration for their pact derived less from missionary example than from national need.

☙❧

The girls and women of mission schools maintained some independence from mission domination, but not always as much as male students would have liked. Particularly in the 1920s, women students at Ginling and Yenching who had discovered nationalism partly from sensitivities bred in a foreign mission school, relied on girls' school identification and the support of missionary teachers to maintain some independence from marital inducements and a male-dominated political movement. Female students in Christian schools could only gain from the zealous efforts of missionary teachers and nationalist men to protect them from each other.

The debate about coeducation solidified the alliance between missionary women and women students. Both teachers and students were suspicious of the desires of parent boards and male students to see the dissolution of the separate women's colleges. Luella Miner, president of North China Union Women's College, found herself "clinging to some shreds of independence" after the Yenching merger had been decided, and wrote to the women's board in Boston, "You probably realize that the men of the University are much more keen to get Women's College money than our plans for the College." Students shared in this skepticism. The North China Women's College alumnae were dismayed at the loss of their school. A discussion at Ginling after a debate over coeducation revealed that those who had argued the pro side, as well as those who took the con, privately opposed coeducation. Wu Yi-fang, one of the first Ginling class and later its first Chinese president (and despite her missionary connections, a survivor in good standing of the cultural revolution of the 1960s), was also said to oppose coeducation.[39]

Missionary and Chinese women opposed mergers for the same reasons. Neither wanted to be absorbed and dominated by the stronger male university. Neither wanted students to be subjected to marital pressures from both university heads and students. In 1920 Luella Miner, who found herself backing up the romantic rejections of her students, wrote that she feared that the male dean and president ("who want to see some modern matches made") thought she was encouraging her students. "But the girls are some of them just getting mad in good American fashion." The evidence suggests that Ginling president Matilda Thurston may have been right in her later analysis that at Ginling "a large majority of the girls were not particularly interested in boys. Romantic love had not hitherto been featured in marriage relations in China and marriage itself had no particular attraction for the woman who had intellectual interests." Y. T. Zee's recollections of that time substantiate Thurston's conclusion. She described her admiration for a radiant "Miss, never married" who she met three years after her own marriage:

> I loved to be left alone. It was in general, the attitude of modern women of our time. We called it singleness of purpose!! It grew out of our traditional system of confinement for women at home. A wife is called, "Inner One,"—never supposed to be outdoors. I never cared for marriage, nor for home, but for school and teaching, whole of my life. Without the pressure and order from my parents, I would never get married—plenty of things in life to satisfy me.

Decisions not to marry had little of the sense of sacrifice about them for Chinese girls, who had come to think of married life in China as an oppressive burden.[40]

According to Ginling president Matilda Thurston, male students did not take lightly the resistance of Chinese women to coeducation and their withdrawal from the marital market. The University of Nanking attempted to bring about more cooperation with Ginling in the 1920s, Thurston wrote:

> They made certain demands for cooperation, but always desired to have the women fall in line with the men's program, attend their movies, take part in their social functions, and entertain their dull

lives. . . . The men resented the girls' independence and their re-
fusal to fall in behind them in their student activities, political and
otherwise. They thought the girls were under the domination of their
Western teachers, and gave them no credit for having opinions of
their own on social and political questions.

The male students also objected, Thurston wrote, because "Ginling students were foreignized and not trained to make good wives."[41] Clearly
Ginling students stood to gain from an identity which gave them additional independence within a Chinese social world, even in alliance with
missionary women.

But what of the important inequities within mission schools? What of
the implicit arrogance of certain missionaries, who defined their mandate
as instruction on how to live? The missionary enterprise must be judged for
its will to power. But at some point, it is necessary to separate an assess-
ment of missionary ambition from missionary accomplishment. Despite
their inclination to attribute changes in women's status to the missionary
influence, even some missionary women could recognize the tremendous
force of history within China itself. In 1935 Luella Miner remembered the
"wonderful changes in the independent spirit of the young women" between 1903 and 1913:

> Girls were beginning to come from other missions and provinces, and
> on their return to work in the stations which had sent them for
> training, several times reports came back to me that these young
> women were too independent and insubordinate. One of the joyous
> thrills of my life came about the end of that period during an annual
> meeting when one of my college graduates, Ting Shu-ching, rose in
> our annual meeting and made a very strong position against a pro-
> posal which I myself had made. That decade was a wonderful one
> throughout China, at least near the coast, for the liberation of
> women, especially the years following 1911.

In unclear circumstances, Miner backed Ting to be principal of Bridgman
School in 1915, but mission opposition to the appointment of a Chinese
defeated the proposal. Previous to the 1920s no major mission school had a
Chinese principal.[42] The mission schools by no means allowed their
Chinese students free access to authority. But neither was mission power
strong enough to cow mission students into "slavishness."

The life of Y. T. Zee demonstrates how Chinese results bedeviled
mission intent. Like Ting Shu-ching, Y. T. Zee was an early graduate of a

Independent spirit, 1922: Since missionary schools paid less, Y. T. Zee took a job as a teacher in a government school. "We did not think it was very fair to work on only a service level."

Filial marriage, 1924: Y. T. Zee and her husband agreed to marry to satisfy their parents. "I never wanted to marry. Dr. New didn't want to marry. . . . We thought we couldn't dedicate ourselves with a home."

Christian college and exercised considerable influence during her student days. From two generations of Chinese Baptists, Zee was a leader of the first Ginling class, the class of 1919, and an instigator of its May 4 activities. With her four other classmates, she coauthored *The Pioneer*, the class yearbook, which demonstrated a loyalty both to Ginling's proud female independence and to the currents of nationalism sweeping the country. *The Pioneer* voiced "the earnest hope of the students" that the new missionary faculty "will forever belong to Ginling" and added their hope for its stable autonomy, "that their title will ever be 'Miss.' " At the same time, *The Pioneer* presented a utopian visit to a more patriotic future Ginling. At this Ginling, the teaching of Chinese history made students "conscious of their desire to bear a part in the making of present history." Y. T. Zee loved Ginling as a student and as an alumna. Upon graduation, however, she was unwilling to take the low salary offered her to return there to work. "They wanted us to accept a lower scale of salary because they said our work is from the heart," she remembered. Instead she and Wu Yi-fang both accepted better-paid positions with government schools. "We did not think it was very fair to work on only a service level. Both of us had financial burdens to take care of."[43]

Y. T. Zee ultimately decided for herself how to apply the lessons of Christian love which she had learned in her missionary education. In the United States, where she lived until her recent death, she felt that she was returning "the gifts of love and mercy" she had received from missionaries, giving her "best to the West." In this she was fulfilling the wishes of her mother, a Christian with mission affiliations, who urged her "to go and work for the Americans." "You carry so much from the missionary sacrifice that we must return."[44] Missionary women did not anticipate this interpretation of their message of Christian love. They loved China with the love of the bounteous for the deprived, or the superior for the inferior. Zee's American missionary work revealed a pride which defied these narrower missionary assumptions. Her missionary drama played itself out in an international setting rather than in the China she cared about. But for Zee, this was only the final act of a Chinese life rich in national commitment.

The mission work of Y. T. Zee in the United States and the contrasting political role of her classmate and friend Wu Yi-fang as a Communist party functionary in the People's Republic demonstrate the range of Chinese applications of their missionary training.[45] Chinese Christians who fled to the United States in 1949, such as Y. T. Zee and Tsai Ling-fang, shared a lingering sense of "school spirit" with many of those who remained behind, as recent acknowledgments of mission-school ties in China testify. The missionary enterprise must be judged for its ambitions to cultural domination at the turn of the century, but these ambitions failed both in absolute terms and in the lives of individual converts. Chinese women put missionary offerings to their own uses and retained independence from missionary as well as Chinese social expectations.

Despite their differences in status and authority, Chinese Christians and American missionary women held common fond memories of the China mission experiment in international sisterhood. Both students and teachers had ventured beyond strict conventions and away from easy traditions. Both were poised on a cultural interface, both engaged in creating feasible lives for themselves from an amalgam of feminine expectation, religious conviction, national affiliation, and newfound opportunity. If American single women were more easily absorbed into Chinese society than American men, and Chinese women more readily attracted to Western customs (as nationalist students argued), it was because the frontier where East met West offered them escape from home hierarchies. In remarkably similar ways, both Chinese women and their foreign mentors found mission institutions useful oases beyond the deserts of conventional familial expectation. Both Chinese and American women discovered that the margins of others' societies could encourage collective pride, nationalist consciousness, and female autonomy discouraged at the center of their own.

❧ AFTERWORD ☙

AMAZONS IN CATHAY

In 1912, the year after the republican revolution, Ida Kahn or K'ang Cheng, adopted daughter of missionary Gertrude Howe, wrote a story published in English by the Methodist women's board. Entitled *An Amazon in Cathay*, K'ang's didactic tale contrasted the patriotic service of two female cousins, a Chinese Christian who served her country in a "womanly" way and a pagan who volunteered as a soldier to fight for her country. K'ang's story aimed to criticize the actual military service of radical female revolutionaries during the previous year and to reaffirm the central notion of woman's sphere, that woman's contributions to the public world must be determined by her sex.[1] *An Amazon in Cathay* contrasted two concepts: an evangelical Christian concept of gender as destiny, and a "pagan" Chinese concept of gender as role. Its simple moral belied the discrepancy between missionaries' message and their experience in China.

The cousins of K'ang's story came from an old country family of declining fortune. The Christian cousin, Hoying ("Harmonious Sound"), had attended mission school and had a "decidedly spiritual face." She dressed in gowns "exquisite in their soft tints," and her entire demeanor radiated "beauty and culture." During China's time of need, she was serving her country modestly as an "assistant" in a hospital for women and children. Hoying typified evangelical womanhood by bringing women's special gifts of feeling, charity, and refinement into the public world.

The other cousin, Pearl, was a heathen who "delighted to wear the brightest hues and used trimmings as lavishly as possible" prior to her service. When she heard about the national emergency, she resolved to join a military band of women who were "going to give their lives for their country and form themselves into 'Dare-to-Die' bands." She disregarded advice "that it was not modest to put on men's attire" and suppressed her sorrow when her beautiful tresses were cut. "Forthwith she prepared to join the Amazon Corps," comforting herself "with the thought that her country's cause called for sacrifices." Unlike her cousin, Pearl had cast off her sex to serve her nation.

The figure of Pearl drew on both mythic and historic Chinese precedents. The story of Mu-lan, the legendary woman warrior of the Six Dynasties period, was particularly popular at the time of the republican revolution. Mu-lan had posed as a man to spare her father from conscription, and had led a heroic military career. The female radicals of the republican revolution sometimes dressed as men, and though they drew their contemporary inspiration from such Western women as the Russian anarchist Sophia Perovskaya, they seem to have taken their cultural style from Mu-lan. Most famous among these revolutionaries was Ch'iu Chin, who during her student days in Japan practiced bomb-making, carried a short sword, and dressed in men's clothing, taking the *tzu*, or honorific name, *Ching-hsiung* (Challenger of Men). Although Ch'iu was executed in 1906, in 1911 her corevolutionists formed women's armies such as the Women's Army of Chekiang, the Women's National Army, and the unit of K'ang's story, the Women's Dare-to-Die Corps.[2] The Mu-lan myth and the actions of female radicals during the Chinese Revolution suggested that under extreme conditions women could set aside the defining characteristics of their sex and act as if they were men.

An Amazon in Cathay demonstrated both the unseemliness and the impossibility of this female divorce from gender. Although Pearl marched bravely off to war "to the music of the band and the cheering of the crowd," she discovered that as a woman she could not be a soldier. The other soldiers offered her "flesh stripped from decapitated bodies; and when she declined, and fairly fainted at the sight, they scoffed and told her that she was no patriot." Worse yet, she "began to suffer personal persecutions. Unchaperoned and unprotected, how was she to withstand such attacks?" Pearl attempted escape and then suicide. When she dosed herself with opium, she awoke to find herself in her cousin's hospital. The virtuous Hoying was grieving over her cousin's bed, crying, "Believe in the true God and He will teach you to serve your country in a way that is worthy." Pearl survived, believed, and it was arranged that "she too might be a nurse in the hospital and help to ease the sufferings of women and children." The story ended with the message of evangelical womanhood: "How better could she serve her country?"

Pearl's mistake was her failure to acknowledge the primacy of her sex. As a woman she had women's feelings (which were also the feelings of true virtue), which would ultimately render her unable to fight and serve like a man. Undermined by her female identity, which allowed her to be sexually assaulted on the field of battle, Pearl discovered the folly of her way and accepted the lesson that woman's "true service" is womanly service. Pearl, too, learned to dress in pastels and to perform her public function from within a woman's sphere. *An Amazon in Cathay* illuminates the contrast between two strategies for female accomplishment; one based on glorious self-sacrifice, another on more subtle self-abnegation; one based on the assumption of male roles, the other on the expansion of womanly ones; one based on a transcendence of sex, the other on the submission to sex; one based on heroic, nearly theatrical action, the other on womanly feeling.

This fictionalized account of two women's responses to a national emergency would be a mere curiosity were it not for other evidence supporting its contrast of Chinese and Christian patterns for female initiative. Other data, too, suggest that in China gender could occasionally be adopted as a role rather than simply inherited as a sex. It is true that Chinese custom rigidly segregated women from men, barring women from the streets and from all manner of public life. The depths of these proscriptions even for working-class women in northern China are validated by Ida Pruitt's account of Ning Lao T'ai-t'ai ("Old Mrs. Ning"), who ate crumbs of brick rather than disgrace herself as a woman by emerging into the streets to look for food.[3]

But a reading of Chinese women's autobiographies from the republican era suggests that, at least as children, a few girls favored by fond fathers acquired their freedom simply by dressing, being presented, and passing as boys. When she was an infant, for instance, Chao Buwei's father deeded her to his childless brother, and she was raised substantially as a boy until the age of twelve. "To be called 'Little Master Three' and to be dressed as 'Little Master Three' also made me feel and behave as 'Little Master Three,' " she wrote. "I was privileged to do things which none of my sisters or female cousins would dream of doing." Chao went on:

My life as a boy reached full manhood when I went pleasure-boating on the Ch'inhuai River inside Nanking city with Fifth Uncle and elder brothers, engaging singsong girls, one girl to each gentle-man. . . . I was very proud to be old enough to go bad by having a 12-year-old sing song girl to sit with me and eat melon seeds at the bow of the boat, while Fifth Uncle and elder brothers drank noisily inside with the older girls.

Soumay Tcheng's father also brought her into the streets as a "favorite son." In order to avoid attracting attention, "it was decided that I should have my hair cut short and thrown back from my forehead, and that I should be dressed in a long silk coat, trousers such as the little boys of my age wore, and boots of soft leather which came part way up the leg and then turned over at the top. I was eleven years old at this time." Members of classes other than the elite were known to disguise daughters as sons to allow them outside freedom. Before the establishment of a local girls' school, the Christian parents of at least one young girl also dressed their daughter in boys' clothes so she could gain an education.[4]

In these accounts, girl children generally once again dressed as girls at puberty. Chao Buwei, however, wrote that although she had ceased to attend a boy's school at the age of twelve, it was only at the age of nineteen that she began to consider herself female. A "Miss Chi," was taken as a son by her father into her late twenties and was prominent among the Chinese women reformers in Peking in the early century. Missionary Luella Miner described her as "the most remarkable woman I have met in China," and gave her history as follows:

Her father held high offices in central China and Manchuria and was very fond of this child, bringing her up as his son, dressing her in boys' clothes (which are long robes here you know), giving her a fine education at home, and keeping her always with him. This continued until his death not long ago. She isn't at all what you would imagine her to be. She has a man's breadth of vision with a woman's refine-ment, and since her father's death she dresses as a woman.

Sarah Goodrich noted that Miss Chi's father had left his daughter his property and the care of his two secondary wives. She "performs the rites at the grave as if she were a son."[5]

The practice of passing daughters off as sons was uncommon and was perhaps in part a response to the overwhelming importance attached to a male heir in the Chinese family. At the same time, it reveals a perspective on gender substantially different from the sexual determinism at the heart

of American evangelical thinking. American evangelicals, perhaps Westerners in general, considered sex not as a function of role, which in
extreme circumstances could be shed, but as the essence of identity itself,
which must permeate self and determine a person's entire temperament.
The discomfort which Westerners experienced at the idea of women
posing as men is revealed in missionary assurances that Miss Chi "isn't at
all what you would imagine her to be," and in dressing as a man had after
all worn only long robes.

❦❦❦

The contrast in American and Chinese theories of gender was only part
of a deeper cultural opposition which lay at the root of the relationship
between missionaries and Chinese women. The struggle of evangelical
intimacy to penetrate Chinese face was the struggle of a Protestant culture
of feeling with a Chinese culture of role.[6] As documented in chapter 6,
missionary women deplored the tendency of Chinese students to act only
appropriately toward each other rather than emotionally and intimately.
Missionary complaints about empty Chinese formalism proved a consistent
refrain throughout many missionary writings.

But in one area American women were filled with admiration for the
capacity of Chinese students to fill roles, transcend self-consciousness, and
conquer feeling. American missionaries applauded the extraordinary accomplishments of their students either at the podium or on the stage.
Missionary praise for the theatrical skills and speaking talents of their
students suggests an awareness on some level that the American female
ethos of feeling was not always an asset to women's accomplishments. The
greater self-control and "presence" of Chinese women perhaps had implications for the comparative performance of Western and American women
on broader stages.

Missionaries overwhelmingly agreed that their shy Chinese students
outshone American schoolgirls in both oratorical and acting skills. Alice
Reed expressed the view as common wisdom in 1917. "The girls spoke
easily and forcefully without any notes," she wrote of a middle school
debate. "It is recognized that they speak more fluently and easily than
Western women." A 1910 note by Charlotte Jewell, principal of Huang
Lu-yin's Peking school, made the same point: "In our weekly rhetoricals,
when an American girl would stammer and hesitate, Miss China reels off
her sentences as glibly as possible in dialogues and debates." When Ameri-

can and Chinese appeared on the same podium the difference was most apparent. Lucy Mead wrote of a 1910 nursing school graduation, "Two girls and they gave their speeches so well. [sic] The American lady who gave (read) the address was the most scared person I've ever seen." As a rule, missionary women themselves abhorred public speaking, which they did not feel they did well. [7]

Missionaries were proud of the skill and self-control of their students in public speaking, but they were unabashedly delighted with their spontaneous theatrical talents. Jessie Ankeny wrote of one student entertainment: "It truly was the funniest thing I ever saw and I laughed until I was sore. Everything was so original and as for acting, the Chinese are born actors." Writing of another drama seven months later, she asked, "Do you think a class of girls at home four in numbers could do it? I am convinced they could not—These girls are inventive." Elsie Clark was more definitive. "The girls surpass Americans ten times over in ease and abandon in reproducing other characters, and as for the dialog—they improvise as they go, never being put out by a word too many or too few." Luella Miner, too, noted that the "histrionic talent is very liberally bestowed upon the Chinese," and described the successful production of the story of Mu-lan in 1909 as evidence. [8] The frequency and enthusiasm with which missionaries described Chinese theatricals suggests that they were not merely repeating a cliché but offering testimony about an important cultural distinction.

When missionaries attempted to explain the ease of their students in playing roles, they mentioned their lack of self-consciousness. Jessie Ankeny remembered that her students' improvisations were done "all unconsciously," and recently a former missionary has suggested that Chinese "lack the self-consciousness of Americans."[9] A Chinese lack of self-consciousness, which explained the liveliness, spontaneity, and assurance of schoolgirls "in character," might also have explained the lack of feeling that missionaries perceived in Chinese personal relationships. Chinese did not need the constant visual reassurances of emotion that evangelical female culture had come to expect.

Originally, American evangelical culture had demanded self-consciousness as a religious responsibility. Potential believers monitored their emotions as evidence of the state of their souls. But during the course of the nineteenth century, evangelical feeling also acquired a social dimension that was formalized in an etiquette of the emotions. Believers were expected not only to *feel* benevolence, but to communicate it through a benign or loving countenance. Evangelical etiquette demanded that the face transparently reflect the goodness and grace of the heart. (The irony, of course, is that for missionary women a display of sentiment was itself expected behavior.)[10] For Chinese students, though, the appearance of true feeling was never as important as the performance of appropriate action.

What does this say about the means by which Chinese and American women made their way into the public world? The evidence of course is only suggestive. It does tend to corroborate the theory that Chinese women were more able to adapt themselves to the demands of different roles than were evangelical American women. American women's redefinition of the public world as an arena in need of feminine nurture could not accommodate all the challenges the public world presented. The demand for harmony between inner and outer selves, however incompletely realized, undoubtedly interfered with the efforts of missionary women to adopt conscious roles and to perform assumed parts which required that they be something they had not learned to feel. The need for congruence between self and action hampered the performance of evangelical women, particularly in "unnatural" settings,—settings in which women's qualities of self-effacement and modesty were detrimental to success. The stage or the podium were two such settings, but evangelical sincerity could not help but interfere with the appropriate role behavior of American women in other areas as well.[11]

Armed with different notions of the relationship between sex and self, Chinese women were not so encumbered. In fact, the remarkable advances of certain Chinese women at the turn of the century have been explained in terms of successful role behavior. Historian Mary Rankin uses this theory to illuminate the career of Ch'iu Chin, who moved from secluded female intellectual, to wife and mother, and finally to martyred revolutionary. As Rankin argues:

> A woman who succeeded in breaking away from family bonds and becoming a teacher, doctor, revolutionary, etc., was . . . expected to act in accord with well-defined concepts of behavior, and others often gave her the recognition accorded a person in that role. . . . When a woman did enter one of these roles, she also assumed their normally male characteristics, a factor that may in part account for the sexual neutrality that Witke has noted in twentieth-century Chinese women.

The Chinese "rectification of names" helped to facilitate this role movement, Rankin argues. A named position brought its own rules for appropriate behavior and its own nearly automatic status; expectations shared by all governed the relationship of mother and son, general and foot soldier, teacher and student.[12]

The initial stages of rebellion for a woman shedding one role to adopt another were clearly filled with more tension than the gentle expansion of responsibilities within the evangelical woman's sphere. The movement of a Chinese woman from one role to another brought enormous strains, particularly to women with children. The decision of patriotic women in both the Christian and the non-Christian communities to remain single might well have emerged from the sense that the roles of national martyr and devoted mother were not complementary. Y. T. Zee's phrasing of her attraction to the single life tends to corroborate this possibility. "I loved to be left alone," she wrote. "It was in general, the attitude of modern woman of our time. We called it singleness of purpose!!"[13] Indeed, the virtue of the American woman's sphere was also its liability; as it gradually broadened to include all areas of life susceptible to the improvement of a woman's hand, it also burdened American women with multiple overlapping responsibilities which other cultures subdivided into distinct, single-minded roles.

American women arrived in China with a traditional evangelical mandate for womanly service that remained their official interpretation of their lives and work. However, their experience qualified the lessons K'ang Cheng hoped to teach in An Amazon in Cathay. Unlike Hoying, missionary women were doctors and teachers, not simply "assistants" in hospitals. Missionary women traveled freely among men in China, and, unlike Pearl, they were not assaulted. Nor did their womanly feelings undermine their efforts to perform men's jobs. In fact, the Chinese scarcely regarded these large independent women as women at all and saw little resemblance between them and the dutiful wives and mothers with whom they shared the American woman's sphere. Chinese observers of American missionary women considered them women who had already forsworn their sex to assume roles as teachers, doctors, or preachers, to become "neither one nor the other," or the unfeminine women historian Roxane Witke has termed a "third sex."

A former male student and colleague of missionary Luella Miner, for instance, memorialized her at the time of her death in 1937 as a nü chang-fu, variously translated a "woman among men," an "upright and fearless woman," or even "a manly woman." She was one who had sworn not to marry, he wrote; she walked alone throughout the Chinese country-side even in times of trouble. And as for her friends, "she most liked to have contact with those of proud bearing, talent and tenacity regardless of sex."[14] Ts'ui Yi's tribute to Miner depicted her far more within the Chinese tradition of Mu-lan, the woman warrior, than as the womanly emissary of female culture she had set out to be.

China had offered Luella Miner free passage beyond her American possibilities. Evangelical women at home lived in a society which rein-forced their limited expectations. The evangelical insistence that demeanor communicate feelings meant that women who felt uncomfortable on a podium, in a classroom, or in the streets would appear unsure in their journeys through American life. Lacking the attribution of power that missionary women found in China, women at home remained confined in a cycle in which the feeling of uncertainty produced the appearance of vulnerability, which in turn provoked the domination accorded the weak.

Coming from this tradition, Luella Miner and women like her initially expressed discomfort at the extra authority bestowed freely upon them in China. At first they were troubled by the discrepancy between their expected demeanor of modesty and self-effacement, and their experience of authority. Gradually, however, the experience of authority transformed self-expectations, and missionary women came to discover inner certain-ties to match their circumstances. Gradually, they developed colonial temperaments to accord with their colonial status. And when colonial power destroyed the instincts of self-deprecation, it destroyed with them the habits of gender. Western women in turn-of-the-century China were no longer a second sex, because, as others have argued, only the powerless are the second sex.[15]

Power in China may have transformed missionary women but it did not educate them. This was the paradox of the missionary experience, embod-ied in the life of Luella Miner. Miner never acknowledged that she had been transformed into a *nü chang-fu*, "a woman among men." Instead, she consistently applied American standards of womanliness to her coworkers and to the Chinese, and applauded the suppression of the Chinese suffrag-ist "Amazons" who, she felt, had "offended against the laws of the land and the humanitarian nature of womanhood."[16] Other missionary women shared Miner's genteel vision and extolled the virtues of the evangelical woman's sphere at the same time that their lives were celebrating their surprising and abundant liberation from its bonds.

ABBREVIATIONS

ABCFM   American Board of Commissioners for Foreign Missions Papers, Houghton Library, Harvard University, Cambridge, Massachusetts

CRP   China Records Project, Day Missions Library, Yale Divinity School, New Haven, Connecticut

"Calendar"   "Calendar to the Correspondence of the Board of Foreign Missions," Presbyterian Board of Foreign Missions, Presbyterian Historical Society, Philadelphia, Pennsylvania (microfilm copy in CRP)

COH   China Missionaries Oral History Project, Claremont Colleges, Claremont, California (typescript in CRP)

DFMC   Decreased File of the Woman's Foreign Missionary Society, The General Commission on Archives and History, United Methodist Church, Madison, New Jersey

SCUO   Special Collections, University of Oregon Library, Eugene, Oregon

UBCHE   United Board for Christian Higher Education in Asia (now part of CRP)

WMF   *Woman's Missionary Friend*

NOTES

Preface

1. Helen Barrett Montgomery, *Western Women in Eastern Lands: An Outline Study of 50 Years of Woman's Work in Foreign Missions* (New York: Macmillan, 1911), p. 143.

2. Rachel Benn, Deceased File, Woman's Foreign Missionary Society, Commission on Archives and History, United Methodist Church, Madison, New Jersey (hereafter DFMC).

3. Karl E. Tauber and James A. Sweet, "Family and Work: The Social Life Cycle of Women," in The American Assembly, *Women and the American Economy: A Look to the 1980s* (Englewood Cliffs, N.J.: Prentice-Hall, 1976), p. 42; Mary Ryan, *Womanhood in America* (New York: Watts, 1979), p. 142. For men as well as women, mission service sometimes represented an opportunity for prestige that exceeded home offerings. Valentin Rabe argues that missions "lent a sense of importance and participation in an international crusade to average men." *Men and Missions*, a Protestant periodical, supported Rabe's formulation in an article in 1917, which noted, "There is wider opportunity today than ever before for an ordinary life to touch world issues. Big things are not restricted to big men." "The American Protestant Foreign Mission Movement, 1880–1920" (Ph.D. diss., Harvard University, 1965), pp. 167, 827.

Chapter 1

1. Elsie Clark to Andrew Krug, 8 March 1913, China Records Project, Yale Divinity School (hereafter CRP); Martha Wiley, interview, 1969, China Missionaries Oral History Project, Honnold Library, Claremont, Calif. (hereafter COH); Lucy Lee, "An American Sojourn in China" (printed memoir), CRP: Clark to Krug, 31 December 1916, CRP; Marjorie Rankin, interview, 1970, COH, recalled cemeteries and blue clothes as her first impression of China.

2. Elsie Clark, diary, 24 September 1913, CRP; Lucile Jones, interview, 1970, COH; Guilelma Alsop, *My Chinese Days* (Boston: Little, Brown, 1918), p. 84.

3. Ruth White to family, 29 March 1918, CRP; Emma Martin, diary, 27 April 1900, CRP; Mildred Rowland to family, 19 September 1911, CRP.

4. Ning Lao T'ai-t'ai, *A Daughter of Han: The Autobiography of a Chinese Working Woman*, as told to Ida Pruitt (Stanford, Calif.: Stanford University Press, 1967), p. 143; Arthur Waley, *The Opium War through Chinese Eyes* (Stanford, Calif.: Stanford University Press, 1958), pp. 68–69.

5. Mary Clabaugh Wright, "Introduction: The Rising Tide of Change," *China in Revolution: The First Phase, 1900–1913*, ed. Wright (New Haven, Conn.: Yale University Press, 1968), p. 38, argues the paramount significance of the year 1900 in Chinese history.

6. Kenneth Scott Latourette, *The History of Christian Missions in China* (New York: Macmillan, 1929), p. 517; John King Fairbank, *East Asia: Tradition and Transformation* (Boston: Houghton Mifflin, 1973), p. 635.

7. Paul Varg, *Missionaries, Chinese, and Diplomats* (Princeton, N.J.: Princeton University Press, 1958), p. 89.

8. Latourette, *History of Christian Missions*, p. 533; Luella Miner to family, 12 April 1912, Papers of the American Board of Commissioners for Foreign Missions, Houghton Library, Harvard University (hereafter ABCFM); Sarah Goodrich to family, 20 October 1912, CRP; Philip West, *Yenching University and Sino-Western Relations, 1916–1952* (Cambridge, Mass.: Harvard University Press, 1976), p. 19.

9. Jessie Lutz, *China and the Christian Colleges* (Ithaca, N.Y.: Cornell University Press, 1971), pp. 220–22.

10. For these statistics, see Milton T. Stauffer, ed., China Continuation Committee, *The Christian Occupation of China: A General Survey of the Numerical Strength and Geographical Distribution of the Christian Forces in China, Made by the Special Committee on Survey and Occupation* (Shanghai, 1922), p. 346. This exhaustive atlas, published by an interdenominational Protestant committee, is the single most valuable research tool for the study of China missions. In 1889 the American mission force numbered 513; in 1905, 1,304; and in 1919, 3,305.

11. J. B. Jeter, *A Memoir of Mrs. Henrietta Shuck: The First American Female Missionary to China* (Boston, 1846), p. 38.

12. Lee Chew, "The Biography of a Chinaman," reprinted in *Chinese Recorder*, May 1903; Ellsworth C. Carlson, *The Foochow Missionaries 1847–1880* (Cambridge, Mass.: Harvard University Press, 1974), p. 68.

13. Carlson, *Foochow Missionaries*, p. 169.

14. Mission supporters at home, too, were also some of the strongest voices for political empire. Josiah Strong's *Our Country*, published in 1895, was one of the strongest arguments for Anglo-Saxon mission and empire published in the nineteenth century. A 1900 survey by the *Boston Herald* found more clergymen in favor of empire than representatives of any other profession surveyed. (Marilyn Young, *Rhetoric of Empire: American China Policy, 1895–1901* [Cambridge, Mass.: Harvard University Press, 1968], p. 143.) For scholarly analysis of the Ament and Tewksbury raids, see Young, *Rhetoric of Empire*, pp. 187–97; Stuart Creighton Miller, "Ends and Means: Missionary Justification of Force in Nineteenth Century China," in John Fairbank, ed., *The Missionary Enterprise in China and America* (Cambridge, Mass.: Harvard University Press, 1974).

15. Michael H. Hunt, *Making of a Special Relationship: The United States and China to 1914* (New York: Columbia University Press, 1983), pp. 161–62.

16. Hunt, *Special Relationship*, p. 165. Marilyn Young explores fully this American flirtation with empire. She reports that Minister Edwin Conger suggested from Peking in 1899 that the United States seize a foothold in the province of Chihli (*Rhetoric of Empire*, pp. 99). In an article, she quotes John Hay to Henry Adams in 1900: "The ideal policy

is . . . to do nothing, and yet be around when the watermelon is cut. Not that we want any watermelon, but it is always pleasant to be seen in smart colored circles on occasions of festivity" (Young, "American Expansionism, 1870–1900: The Far East," in Young, ed., *American Expansionism: The Critical Issues* [Boston: Little, Brown, 1973], p. 96). Michael Hunt quotes McKinley pondering the China question: "May we not want a slice, if it is to be divided?" (*Special Relationship*, p. 182).

17. *Woman's Missionary Friend*, February 1900, p. 271, (hereafter WMF). For the argument on Harrison's opposition to annexation, see Robert Beisner, *Twelve against Empire: The Anti-Imperialists 1898–1900* (New York: McGraw-Hill, 1968), pp. 9, 192. Republican, anti-imperialist Mugwumps such as James B. Angell, a former minister to China, were frequently also promoters of mission. Even William Jennings Bryan supported missions, and sent a contribution to a Methodist girls' school following a trip to Peking in 1906. Bryan's letter was published in *WMF*, January 1907, p. 13. Valentin Rabe also makes the point that both expansionists and anti-imperialists could find something to support in missions, ("The American Protestant Foreign Mission Movement, 1880–1920" [Ph.D. diss., Harvard University, 1965], p. 695). Young (*Rhetoric of Empire*, p. 87) notes the 1898 upswing in mission contributions. John Lindbeck demonstrates that missionaries themselves were invariably Republicans and tended to favor expansionists for office. "American Missionaries and Policies of the United States in China 1898–1901" (Ph.D. diss., Yale University, 1948), p. 88).

18. Theodore Roosevelt, "The Awakening of China," *Outlook* 28 (November 1908): 665–67.

19. Paul Varg, *Missionaries, Chinese and Diplomats*, p. 80; Woodrow Wilson, "An Address in Nashville on Behalf of the Y.M.C.A.," *The Papers of Woodrow Wilson*, ed. Arthur S. Link (Princeton, N.J.: Princeton University Press, 1978), 24:208. Wilson's reputation as a church man earned him the support of China missionaries. "We are watching politics and rather hoping that Wilson gets the presidency in spite of the fact that we are all republicans," wrote Ida Lewis to family 9 July 1912, Special Collections, University of Oregon, Eugene (hereafter SCUO).

20. Alice Gregg, *China and Educational Autonomy: The Changing Role of the Protestant Educational Mission in China, 1807–1937* (Syracuse, N.Y.: Syracuse University Press, 1946), pp. 45–46, 55–56; (Gregg quotes *China Centenary Mission Conference Records*, 1907, p. 519); Rabe, "The American Protestant Foreign Mission Movement," p. 86. American missionaries in China were the leading practitioners of the social gospel, partly as a result of the increasing American involvement in such youth organizations as the Student Volunteer Movement, an offshoot of the Y.M.C.A. The Student Volunteers were evangelical in spirit but practical in tactics. As their historian has explained, their rhetoric was clearly changing at the turn of the century, "away from the older emphasis on saved individual souls to a 'social gospel' for the mission field." Americans were deprecated as activists by German and sometimes British missionaries. See M. Searle Bates, "The Theology of American Missionaries in China, 1900, 1950," in Fairbank, ed., *The Missionary Enterprise*, pp. 136, 150; Clifton J. Phillips, "The Student Volunteer Movement and Its Role In China Missions, 1886–1920," in Fairbank, *The Missionary Enterprise*, p. 102.

21. William Hutchinson, "Modernism and Missions," in Fairbank, *The Missionary Enterprise*, p. 121; Paul Varg also documents this change, with missionaries no longer interpreting acts of imperialism as acts of God. *Missionaries, Chinese and Diplomats*, p. 84.

22. R. Pierce Beaver, *All Loves Excelling: American Protestant Women in World Mission* (Grand Rapids, Mich.: Wm. B. Eerdmans, 1968), pp. 51–52.

23. For some reason the boards excepted service to American Indians from their proscription on posting single women. By 1860, 108 single women had worked in the American West. Beaver, *All Loves*, p. 71.

24. Helen B. Montgomery, *Western Women in Eastern Lands: An Outline Study of Fifty Years of Woman's Work in Foreign Missions* (New York: Macmillan, 1911), p. 8; Beaver, *All Loves*, pp. 91–94, 109.

25. Beaver, *All Loves*, p. 138.

26. Mary Isham, *Valorous Adventures: A Record of Sixty and Six Years of the Woman's Foreign Missionary Society, Methodist Episcopal* (Boston: WFMS, 1936), p. 17.

27. Beaver, *All Loves*, p. 98; Sara Haskin, *Women and Missions in the Methodist Episcopal Church South* (Nashville, Tenn.: Publishing House M.E. Church, 1923), p. 239.

28. Beaver, *All Loves*, pp. 86, 91.

29. *Christian Occupation*, p. 307; Beaver, *All Loves*, p. 112.

30. On declining interest of men in mission work and its consequences for women, see Barbara Welter, "She Hath Done What She Could: Protestant Women's Missionary Careers in Nineteenth Century America," *American Quarterly*, Spring 1979, p. 624. For Laymen's Missionary Movement, see Valentin Rabe, "Evangelical Logistics: Mission Support and Resources to 1920," in Fairbank, *The Missionary Enterprise*, pp. 64–65. For "real boys" and "he-men," see E. C. Ford, "Chinese Chapel Chimes," pamphlet about Emery Ellis, ABCFM; Roy Chapman Andrews, introduction to Harry Caldwell, *Blue Tiger* (New York: Abington, 1924).

31. Ellen C. Parsons, "History of Organized Missionary Work as Presented by American Women," in *Women in Missions* (Chicago, 1893), p. 107.

32. *Christian Occupation*, p. 346. According to the 17th Census, 1940, *Comparative Occupation Statistics for the United States 1879–1940*, pp. 135–36, in 1900 women represented 7,387 out of the 132,102 total of physicians, surgeons, and healers, or about 6 percent.

33. *Ruth V. Hemenway, M.D.; A Memoir of Revolutionary China 1924–1941*, ed. with an intro. by Fred Drake (Amherst: University of Massachusetts Press, 1977), p. 30; Varg, *Missionaries, Diplomats, and Chinese*, p. 93.

34. Ida Belle Lewis, *The Education of Girls in China* (New York: Teachers College, Columbia University, 1919), p. 24.

35. Luella Miner to family, 6 February 1888, ABCFM.

36. Ibid., 4 July 1889, ABCFM.

37. For Shuck quotation, see Mary Anderson, *Protestant Mission Schools for Girls in South China 1887 to the Japanese Invasion: A Cycle in the Celestial Kingdom* (Mobile, Ala.: Heiter-Starke Printing Co., 1943), p. 46; United States, Department of State, *Papers Relating to the Foreign Relations of the United States*, 1871, p. 102.

38. *Foreign Relations*, 1871, p. 102. For an analysis of antimissionary propaganda, see Paul Cohen, *China and Christianity 1860–1870* (Cambridge, Mass.: Harvard University Press, 1963).

39. Anderson, *Protestant Mission Schools*, pp. 62, 303; Rev. W. N. Brewster, *Chinese Recorder*, December 1903, p. 590; Lewis, *Education of Girls in China*, p. 24.

40. Daniel H. Bays, "The Missionary Audience: Chinese Christian Converts in the Nineteenth Century," paper presented at the AHA, December 1978, commented on the significance of the sizeable minority of female converts. Chen Tung-yuan, *Chung-kuo fu-nu sheng-huo shih* (Shanghai, 1926), p. 333, quotes a 1903 pamphleteer, Jin Yi, who argues that women must be educated in order to free China from the religious superstitions which they particularly supported. The consequences of Christian identity for female converts will be considered in chapter 7.

41. Anderson, *Protestant Mission Schools for Girls*, p. 242. Chen Tung-yuan argues that missionaries waited until the founding of the Chinese movement to oppose footbinding (*Chung-kuo fu-nu*, p. 319). Charlotte Beahan's definitive "The Women's Movement and

Nationalism in Late Ch'ing China" (Ph.D. diss., Columbia University, 1976), p. 51, refers to a debate in mission circles about the wisdom of attacking footbinding prior to the 1890s. The social custom was considered to be too entrenched. One missionary report, however, notes a first anti-footbinding society in Amoy in 1873.

42. Chen, *Chung-kuo fu-nu*, p. 316.

43. Ibid., pp. 316, 326; Lewis, *Education of Girls in China*, p. 24; Margaret Burton, *Notable Women of Modern China* (Chicago: Fleming H. Revell, 1925), p. 131; Luella Miner Papers, passim, esp. 1906, ABCFM.

44. Roxane H. Witke, "Transformation of Attitudes Towards Women during the May 4th Era of Modern China" (Ph.D. diss., University of California, Berkeley, 1970), p. 28. Witke notes that nineteenth-century reformers could look to Manchus as models for the anti-footbinding movement (pp. 22–23). In 1888, Luella Miner observed that in Peking, "We saw many more women on the streets than in Paotingfu, for there are many Manchus here, and they have not the Chinese idea of seclusion" (Letter to Carrie, 28 May 1888, ABCFM).

45. Theodore E. Hsiao, *The History of Modern Education in China* (Peiping, China: Peiping University Press, 1932), p. 51; Beahan, "The Women's Movement and Nationalism," pp. 326, 192; Lewis, *Education of Girls in China*, p. 27.

46. Chen, *Chung-kuo fu-nu*, p. 343; Ida Lewis, *Education of Girls in China*, pp. 24, 34, gives the following statistics for enrollments in mission and government schools:

	In Mission Schools		In Government Schools
1860	196		
1869	556		
1896	6,798	1906	5,945
1910	16,190	1908	18,202
1915	45,168	1912	141,130
1916	50,173	1917	170,789

47. China Educational Commission, *Christian Education in China; A Study Made by an Educational Commission Representing the Mission Boards and Societies Conducting Work in China* (New York: Foreign Missions Conference of North America, 1922), pp. 68, 259; Anderson, *Protestant Mission Schools for Girls*, p. 210.

48. Luella Miner, pencil fragment, n.d., ABCFM; Charlotte Beahan, "The Women's Movement and Nationalism," p. 48, notes that Liang Ou-ti and Kiang K'ang-hu, both 1930s nationalist critics of the missionary presence, credited missionaries for their educational work—Kiang, for "the introduction of public school education for women." Luella Miner quoted "Princess Kalachin" in a general letter, 6 January 1906, ABCFM. Beahan concurs that "The real significance of the missionaries lay not in the limited success of their nineteenth century reforms and conversions, but in their steady injection of new ideas, information, practices and role models into Chinese society" "Women's Movement," p. 59.

Chapter 2

1. Emma Martin, diary, 20 March, 5 April 1900, CRP.

2. This chapter draws on the partial biographical records of two of the largest American boards represented in China, the Methodist Episcopal Board and the American Board of Commissioners for Foreign Missions. These boards were, respectively, the second and the third largest American boards in China, with the total number of women in the Methodist

Episcopal mission during the first twenty years of this century at 247, and the total American Board female representation at 187. Some background material is available for all of the 187 women of the American Board in the biographical file, ABCFM. The biographical files of the Methodist Episcopal church are far less complete, biographical information of any kind being available only for the largely single women of the women's board, the Woman's Foreign Missionary Society. This material itself is far from complete, with information available on 56 percent of the WFMS representatives in China between 1900 and 1920, DFMC. Birthplaces are available for 94 percent of the American Board women and for 53 percent of the Methodist WFMS. Percentages for other information will be given as they pertain.

3. U.S., Department of the Interior, Census Office, *Eleventh Census: 1890*, pp. ixv, ixviii, provides this profile, defining a city as a community of 8,000 or more residents. By this definition, 60 percent of the ABCFM volunteers in China between 1900 and 1920 were born in areas that were nonurban in 1890. The median population for communities of origin was 2,889 for Massachusetts and 1,977 for Ohio. In Ohio, less settled than Massachusetts, the pattern of missionary birthplaces mirrored the demography of the state as a whole, with 68 percent from nonurban areas. Allen Davis, *Spearheads for Reform: The Social Settlements and the Progressive Movement 1890–1917* (New York: Oxford University Press, 1967), pp. 33–34, provides this profile of the settlement worker. Over 90 percent, a substantially higher percentage than in the missionary movement, had attended college.

4. Lida Ashmore, autobiography, p. 1, SCUO; Jennie Campbell, autobiography, p. 9, CRP; Emily Hartwell, autobiography, ABCFM. When there were no boys in the family, farm work for girls might be a necessity. Sarah Seymour [DeHaan] wrote that because she had only one brother on her big family farm, "we girls often had to play the part of boys in helping about the lighter work" (letter, 1908, candidate files, ABCFM). John Mack Faragher, *Women and Men on the Overland Trail* (New Haven, Conn.: Yale University Press, 1979), notes that the movement westward did not bring women greater freedoms than they had had in the East.

5. Emma Martin, dedication to dairy, CRP.

6. Only 48 percent of the American Board files contained information on father's occupation. Of these 88, 24 were farmers, 22 home and foreign missionaries, 16 clergymen, 12 small businessmen and skilled tradesmen, 5 lawyers, 4 teachers, 2 newspapermen, 1 doctor, 1 banker, and 1 millworker. Blanche T. Search, DFMC.

7. Jessie Ankeny to home family, 31 January 1909, 30 September 1910, SCUO; Frederica Mead to family, 7 February 1919 CRP.

8. Clara Collier, Phoebe Wells, DFMC.

9. Pearl Buck, *The Exile* (New York: John Day, 1936), p. 71. Catharine Beecher, earlier in the nineteenth century, also experienced great suffering because she could not feel God's love. See Kathryn Kish Sklar, *Catharine Beecher: A Study in American Domesticity* (New Haven, Conn.: Yale University Press, 1973), pp. 28–42.

10. Joan Jacobs Brumberg persuasively argues that missionary heroines made better copy in the popular press than did missionary heroes. *Mission for Life: The Story of the Family of Adoniram Judson, the Dramatic Events of the First American Foreign Mission, and the Course of Evangelical Religion in the Nineteenth Century* (New York: Free Press, 1980), pp. 13–15, 63, 77.

11. Carrie Jewell, Anna Gloss, Ruth Stahl, DFMC; "Miss Godfrey," *Woman's Missionary Friend*, May 1919; Carolyn Sewell, autobiography, ABCFM. For childhood ambition, see also Estie T. Boddy, Elizabeth E. Varney, DFMC.

12. The health papers in the candidate files of the American Board contain information about siblings and sibling order. The sample represents 68 percent of the total.

13. Susan Skinner, autobiographical statement; Clara Skinner, MS biography of James E. Skinner, SCUO; Carrie M. Dubois to Alice Frame, 4 May 1936, about Luella Miner, ABCFM; Welthy Honsinger, DFMC.

14. S. J. Humphrey [re. Mary Porter], 3 May 1867, Bertha Reed, 18 May 1902, candidate files, ABCFM.

15. Marjorie Rankin Steurt, interview, 1970, COH; Edna Terry, DFMC; Grace Rowley, interview, 1970, COH; Alice Powell, DFMC.

16. Sarah DeHaan, letter 1908, Mabel Daniels, Lucy Bement, letter 1898, candidate files, ABCFM.

17. L. Ethel Wallace to board, 1949, DFMC; Jeanie Graham [McClure] to mother, 22 November 1911, CRP; Jeanie Graham [McClure], life sketch, candidate papers, ABCFM.

18. Of those whose prior occupations are known, 75 percent of the American Board women and 72 percent of the Methodist women had had teaching experience prior to their China enlistment. Ten percent (ME) and 25 percent (AB) had had experience in paid church work, and 19 percent (ME) and 8 percent (AB) had had experience either as clerks, stenographers, or assistants in "business."

19. For teaching as "way station," see Robert Wiebe, *Search for Order* (New York: Hill & Wang, 1967), p. 118; Carrie Bartlett, Agnes Edmonds, Ellen Lyon, DFMC.

20. Mabel Craig, Mathilde Goertz, Evelyn Worthley, candidate files, ABCFM.

21. Isabelle Phelps, Adelaide Thomson, Eunice Thomas, candidate files, ABCFM.

22. Katherine Crane, autobiographical sketch, Elizabeth Perkins, candidate files, Mary Ledyard, biographical file, Alice Huggins, candidate files, ABCFM.

23. Dee Garrison, *Apostles of Culture: The Public Library and American Society 1876–1920* (New York: Macmillan, 1979), pp. 192, 188.

24. Welthy Honsinger, *Beyond the Moon Gate: Being a Diary of Ten Years in the Interior of the Middle Kingdom* (New York: Abington, 1924), p. 15; Elsie Clark, diary, August 1912 passim, CRP.

25. Elsie Clark, diary, 20 April 1912, CRP.

26. Carrie M. Dubois, "Family Information for Alice Browne Frame," 4 May 1936.

27. Luella Miner to family, 17 March 1884, 22 March 1887, 6 April 1887, ACBFM.

28. Mary Thomas, Lela Lybarger, DFMC. Sixty-five percent of the American Board is represented in these calculations of family situation at the time of departure. Since the absence of one or both parents was more likely to find its way into the record than their presence, it would probably be a mistake to generalize that half of the pool of all missionary volunteers lacked one or both parents. However, even including those volunteers for whom there is no family information, the percentage is still significant. Nineteen percent of this total population lacked one or both parents at the time of enlistment—a figure which is undoubtedly low. Katherine Crane, autobiographical sketch, ABCFM.

29. Mabel Craig, candidate files, ABCFM; Ruth Pyke Breece, "Mary Davis," *China Christian Advocate*, April 1938, p. 5, CRP; Mabel Hartford, DFMC.

30. Dora Foster, "Thirty-four Years as a Missionary," *Colorado Springs News*, 28 August 1954, in Marbel Thompson, DFMC; Charlotte Jewell, Susan Tippett, Clara Pearl Dyer, personal statement, DFMC.

31. Vera Holmes, Grace McConnaughey, Myra Sawyer, Katie Myers, candidate files, ABCFM.

32. The marital information on the women of the American Board is nearly complete, with the marriage dates unknown for only six out of the sixty-five women who entered service married. A third of the women of the American Board came to the China field married, and a quarter of the women who came to the field single eventually married. Marion Wells, Margaret Gillette, candidate files, ABCFM.

33. Jennie Campbell, autobiography, as retyped by Dorothy Campbell, p. 8, Jennie Wortman [Campbell], diary, April 1881, 5 June 1881, March 1881, autobiography, p. 6, CRP. For other women for whom marriage facilitated a prior commitment, see Erma Kline [Heininger], Ruth Yeoman [St. Clair], Grace Howe [Roberts], candidate files, ABCFM.

34. Jennie Campbell, autobiography, p. 6; diary, March 1881, CRP.

35. Jennie Wortman [Campbell], diary, 22 February 1882, CRP. Wortman's ambivalence about sex and service resembles Martha Foster Crawford's, as discussed by Irwin T. Hyatt, Jr., *Our Ordered Lives Confess: Three Nineteenth Century American Missionaries in East Shantung* (Cambridge, Mass.: Harvard University Press, 1976), p. 7. According to Hyatt, Martha Foster "had always wanted to do something important in life on her own." She had rejected a number of suitors because she feared sex, but could not completely forget about men, Hyatt concludes. Her decision to marry a missionary, like Jennie Wortman's, allowed her to compromise between surrender and vocational assertion.

36. Agnes Scott, interview, 1972, COH; Lida Ashmore, autobiography, p. 25, SCUO. For other women's disclaimers of missionary ambition, see: Mildred Rowland to family, 15 June 1912, CRP; Lillian Dudley Porter, Mary Robinson, candidate files, ABCFM.

37. Martha Wiley, interview, 1969, COH; Caroline Chittenden, letter 1891, candidate file, ABCFM; Mabel Allen, DFMC; Mary Porter, candidate file, ABCFM; Sarah Goodrich to Grace, 18 September 1910, CRP; Grace Wyckoff, candidate file, ABCFM. For a particular category of volunteer, those who had been professional workers as deaconnesses in the Methodist church, "recruitments" could be closer to directives. Deaconness Martha Nicolaisson received this communication from her bishop: "I want you to go to China to be with Miss Lebeus. Will you go?" (DFMC).

38. Clifton J. Phillips, "The Student Volunteer Movement and Its Role in China Missions, 1886–1920," in John K. Fairbank, ed., *The Missionary Enterprise in China and America* (Cambridge, Mass.: Harvard University Press, 1974), p. 101, notes that the SVM's executive director John R. Mott claimed to have sent 70 to 75 percent of the turn-of-the-century force to the field, a figure Phillips feels is too high.

39. Grace Turkington, "College Girls in Missions," WMF, May 1902, p. 155; Lucy Mead to family, 1 September 1911, ABCFM; Jessie Ankeny to family, 10 July 1909, SCUO; Luella Miner to father, 1 March 1899, ABCFM.

40. Phillips, "The Student Volunteer Movement," in Fairbank, ed., *The Missionary Enterprise in China and America*, pp. 91–98.

41. Myra Jaquet, DFMC; Welthy Honsinger Fisher, personal interview, 20 October 1978. For another pledge at missionary meeting, May Thompson, DFMC.

42. Pamphlet, "Roll Call, 1869–1896," Minnie Wilson, DFMC; Rose Lombard, candidate file, ABCFM.

43. Reuben Holden, *Yale in China; The Mainland, 1901–1951* (New Haven, Conn.: Yale in China Association, 1964), p. 10.

44. Lucia Lyons to parents, 23 March 1902, candidate files, ABCFM.

45. Alice Reed to Rev. Arie B. DeHaan, 16 March 1916, DeHaan to Reed, 29 March 1916, candidate file, ABCFM; Alice Reed, introduction to letters, CRP.

46. Olin White to parents, 20 June 1917, Ruth White to parents, 13 June 1917, CRP.

47. Ruth White to parents, 13 February 1918, 17 April 1918, CRP.

48. Simone de Beauvoir's classic study *The Second Sex* argues that women have historically been confined to the mundane, to "immanence," and have been denied access to the liberation of transcendent purpose.

49. Jeanie Graham [McClure] to family, 4 October 1912, 19 March 1911, CRP.

Chapter 3

1. Married women and men were always somewhat better represented than single women. In 1898 there were 256 single women out of a total American Protestant force of 968, or 26 percent of the total, with married women at 34 percent (Page Smith, *Daughters of the Promised Land* [Boston: Little, Brown, 1970, p. 192). At the turn of the century a greater proportion of women were single than at any other time in American history, with 14 percent of all women over the age of twenty-five single, or roughly 7 percent of the total population over twenty-five. Setting aside the age factor, the density of single women in the American China mission community was nearly four times greater than this high figure. For American statistics, see Karen Sue Johnson, "Single Women and Men in the United States since the Turn of the Century," as abstracted in *Dissertation Abstracts International* 37 (1976): 633–634A. In 1919, the total Protestant foreign force consisted of 29 percent single women, 33 percent married women, 33 percent married men, and 5 percent single men. Milton Stauffer, ed., *The Christian Occupation of China* (Shanghai: China Continuation Committee, 1922), pp. 287, 297.

2. Jeanie McClure to mother, 22 January 1917, CRP; Lida Ashmore to Edith Ashmore, 28 August 1915, SCUO. For examples of the use of "old maid" and "spinster" by single women, see: Luella Miner to Stella Miner, 17 June 1891, ABCFM; Frederica Mead to parents, 3 November 1918, CRP. Ida Belle Lewis to her mother, 16 April 1922, SCUO.

3. Sarah Goodrich to Grace Goodrich, 28 November 1909, CRP.

4. Goodrich to Grace Goodrich, 7 February 1908, CRP. Nancy Cott demonstrates the connection between women's identification "in relation to" others and her dependent status. Single missionary women decided not to partake of conventional dependencies and hence were left without conventional sources of identity. For them in particular, "affiliative motives" remained central in their efforts to discover alternative groups by which to define themselves. Nancy Cott, *The Bonds of Womanhood: "Woman's Sphere" in New England, 1780–1835* (New Haven, Conn.: Yale University Press, 1978), pp. 165–67.

5. Jane Addams, *Twenty Years at Hull House* (New York: Macmillan, 1910), p. 49; Prof. H. S. Pope, recommendation for Mabel Daniels, candidate file, ABCFM; Agnes Meebold memorial service pamphlet, biographical file, ABCFM.

6. Lida Ashmore, "Autobiography" (printed), p. 38, Ashmore to Edith, 20 November 1919, SCUO; Marjorie Rankin Steurt, interview, 1970, COH; Dorothea Smith Coryell, "The Dragon Charms and Seduces" (unpublished typescript), CRP.

7. Elsie Clark to mother, 26 August 1914, CRP; Monona Cheney to family, 30 July 1919, SCUO; Elizabeth Perkins to mother, 26 July 1908, CRP.

8. Jessie Ankeny to parents, 17 July 1911, Lida Ashmore to Edith, 1 March 1908, SCUO.

8. Elsie Clark to family, 25 April 1915, CRP; Luella Miner to Carrie (sister), 25 January 1892, ABCFM.

10. Elizabeth Perkins to family, 26 January 1908, CRP; Monona Cheney to family, 26 October 1918, Jessie Ankeny to family, 22 February 1910, 27 July 1912, SCUO.

11. Ruth White to mother, 5 January 1918, CRP. Missionary mothers were the principal correspondents of their sons as well as their daughters. Cf. Lida Ashmore to Frank Ashmore, 23 March 1897, SCUO, telling him to "just keep on expecting" letters from his father, because he ought "to write even if he didn't." Elsie Clark, diary, 15 November 1913, CRP; Monona Cheney to family, 4 October 1919, SCUO.

12. Cheney to family, 26 October 1918, SCUO; Jeanie McClure to family, 1 December 1918, CRP; Jessie Ankeny to Louise (sister), 23 August 1911, 24 November 1911, SCUO; William Brown to Florence and W. Edward Manly, 18 March 1895, CRP.

13. Jessie Ankeny to family, 24 November 1911, SCUO. Elsie Clark's father, a supporter of women's suffrage, told a friend he could not understand "how it is that I like it here." Clark to family, 10 December 1916, CRP. Mothers were frequently more enthusiastic at enlistment. See chapter 2 above, and Edna Deahl, Mary Stambaugh (Robinson), candidate files, ABCFM.

14. Clark to family, 7 March 1916, CRP; Jessie Ankeny to mother, 2 September, to father, 15 October 1910, SCUO; Jeanie McClure to family, 16 March 1919, CRP.

15. Emma Martin to family, 20 October 1917, CRP; Monona Cheney to family, 4 January 1920, SCUO; Luella Miner to family, 30 October 1890, ABCFM.

16. Miner to family, 4 October 1887, ABCFM; Elsie Clark to family, 1 September 1917, CRP.

17. Emma Martin to family, 6 October 1912, CRP; Emily Hobart to mother, 30 March 1905, SCUO; Clark to family, February 1916, CRP; see also Lucile Jones, interview, 1970, COH.

18. Elizabeth Perkins to family, 15 May 1903, CRP.

19. Luella Miner to father, 20 October 1906, ABCFM.

20. Bessie Ewing to Aunt Myra, 26 January 1896, ABCFM.

21. Luella Miner to family, 29 November 1889, 7 December 1889, ABCFM. Other women besides Miner came close to breaking down over the impermanence of their dwellings. Elizabeth Perkins wrote to her family of Helen Crane, who was unsettled a long time before finding a home "at last." She did not recover from her "unsettled time of it," and was "all worn out nervously." Perkins to family, 28 November, 12 December 1915, CRP.

22. John Faragher writes that in an earlier period at least, "the worst fate for a midwestern woman was to live out the life of an old maid, confined to the house of her father." *Women and Men on the Overland Trail* (New Haven, Conn.: Yale University Press, 1979), p. 35.

23. The right of single women to their own housing was not a matter of codified policy, but rather of changing practice. Problems continued to arise, as in 1920 when Anna Hartwell wrote in her notebook her concerns about a friend's loss of her house to a family: "I do feel that something is due every *single* woman (as well as the married). For Clifforde to come back and find herself without a home convenient to her school, her home with the furnishings she left in the hands of a single women, occupied by a family with little children,—I don't know,—may be it is all right . . . but it seems to me she ought to find enough room there upon her return to be comfortable in, until her new place is built." Hartwell, 4 February 1920, CRP.

24. Luella Miner to mother, 17 May 1891, to Edith (sister), 6 April 1896, ABCFM.

25. Monona Cheney to family, 22 September 1918, 7 December 1919, 28 December 1920, SCUO; Ruth White to family, 10 November 1917, CRP.

26. The emergence of the cultural type, the "New Woman," is associated with the 1890s in the United States. See John Higham, "The Reorientation of American Culture in the 1890's," in *Writing American History* (Bloomington: Indiana University Press, 1970), esp. pp. 82–83. Once the term entered the language, it remained and has undergone variations to accommodate new developments in American mores. Welthy Honsinger, *Beyond the Moon Gate: Being a Diary of Ten Years in the Interior of the Middle Kingdom* (New York: Abington, 1924), pp. 22.

27. Monona Cheney to family, 22 March 1919, SCUO.

28. Cheney to family, 22 March 1919, SCUO; Luella Miner to Mary Matthews, 27 February 1915, to family, 10 October 1917, Lucy Mead to family, 1 January 1910, ABCFM; Monona Cheney to family, 30 September 1918, SCUO; "Some ins and outs in China," *WMF*, February 1919, 48.

29. Mead to family, 20 June 1910, ABCFM.

30. Alice Reed to family, 19 January 1919, CRP; Mead to family, 6 January 1910, 15 December 1915, ABCFM.

31. Elsie Clark to family, 7 February 1914, 14 July 1915, CRP.

32. See Clark, diary, 5 June 1914, 2 April, 8 August, 15, 27, September 1913, CRP. Elsie Clark's focus on the hardships of the interior was based on its material discomforts, but also on its isolation from European society. Though in fact many women in the interior had close Chinese associations, Chinese friends did not seem to provide the reassurance that relationships which other Europeans would have provided. One could argue, as O. Mannoni does in his brilliant study of colonialism, *Prospero and Caliban: The Psychology of Colonization*, trans. Pamela Powesland (New York: Praeger, 1964), that among Europeans and Americans at this time, people of other races were not considered genuine "others."

33. Clark to family, 25 December 1912, 22 March 1914, to mother 21 May 1914, CRP. Clark wrote that her associates manifested little knowledge of or interest in politics "because we get the papers late, and live in a household of women who have no direct connection with the government." She found the conversation in the women's house lacking in substance and concluded that, for this reason among others, "a house is always more interesting when it has a man in it." (Clark to family, 9 July 1916, CRP). William James would have applauded Elsie Clark's efforts at self-expression and considered them normal and healthy. This instance indicates the inadequacy of James's standard of self-submission or assertion to measure nineteenth-century *female* norms. Self-denial was such an accepted part of feminine ideology, and so crucial to the logic of missionary service, that no one besides Elsie Clark, a James disciple, found it worthy of comment. For James on the abnormality but saintliness of extreme self-denial, see his *Varieties of Religious Experience*, lecture 1.

34. Lulu Golisch to Jessie Ankeny, 21 July 1909, Lacy Papers, SCUO.

35. Nancy Cott argues that female friendships in the early nineteenth century were significant partly as "peer relationships" in an age when relationships between equals were replacing hierarchical relationships as desirable forms of human interaction. Nevertheless, the language of hierarchical male–female relationships was often used to describe relationships between single women in the late century. Perhaps women without a dominant masculine "other" lacked the compelling need to emphasize a counterbalancing equality (Cott, *The Bonds of Womanhood*, p. 187). Emma Martin to family, 19 June 1900, Lizzie Martin to family, 6 October 1900, CRP; "Dr. Kate Woodhull," pamphlet, biographical file, Grace and Gertrude Wyckoff biographical file, ABCFM.

36. Evelyn Worthley, 1 July 1901, Harriet Osborne, [1901?], candidate file, ABCFM; for information on Harriet Osborne when working alone, see Elizabeth Perkins to family, 4 February 1908, CRP.

37. Janet Junker, "Valiant Women Still Inseparable after Working Together 40 Years as Early Missionaries for China," news clipping, Althea Todd file, DFMC.

38. "Extract from Mrs. Bagnell's letter," 27 June 1920, Jennie Hughes file, DFMC.

39. Sarah Goodrich to Carrrington Goodrich, 20 May 1914, CRP; Bethel Mission of China, newsletter, January 1952, Hughes file, DFMC.

40. An important context for this discussion is supplied by Carroll Smith-Rosenberg, "The Female World of Love and Ritual: Relatons between Women in Nineteenth-Century America," in Michael Gordon, ed., *The American Family in Social-Historical*

Perspective, 2d ed. (New York: St. Martin's, 1978), pp. 334–59. Smith-Rosenberg argues that a pre-Freudian age did not make the distinctions made today between emotional and physical love among women. The strict segregation of male and female spheres, she argues, tended to render the female sphere the natural arena for uninhibited female emotion. Particular female friendships survived throughout the married lives of their participants, abating only slightly in intensity and immediacy through successive years and the rearing of children.

41. Jeanie Graham [McClure] to parents, 6 January 1910, CRP.

42. Lucy Mead to family, 18 May 1911, ABCFM.

43. For semimaternal relationships as promoters of generational harmony the Cheney-Jewell friendship is illustrative. Monona Cheney, who had earlier chafed at being chaperoned by elder missionary Charlotte Jewell, later accompanied her on a summer rest retreat and wrote that she especially appreciated her spiritual knowledge and maternal habits. Of Jewell's spiritual counsel she wrote: she "is as frank as mother would be about things. So you see, since *I can't* have my own mother, she is a pretty good substitute, and since I'm pretty much of a mother-baby, it is much more really restful to me to be with her than it would be to be with someone my own age" (letter to family, 11 July 1921, SCUO); Lucy Mead to family ("my dear teddies"), 29 December 1909, 12 June 1910, ABCFM.

44. Mead to family, 17 July 1910, ABCFM.

45. Mead to family, 11 January 1911, ABCFM. Blanche Wiesen Cook argues importantly against previous tendencies among historians to regard participants in female love relationships as "repressed" or "unfulfilled." In Cook's view, the unwillingness of historians to acknowledge the sexuality and power of such relationships represents a "historical denial of lesbianism." Since the term *lesbian* came into use in the context of the modern preoccupation with genitality, though, it seems inappropriate as a descriptive term for the preconscious, "special friendships" of the nineteenth and early twentieth centuries, whatever the nature of their sexuality. "The Historical Denial of Lesbianism," *Radical History Review*, Spring/Summer, 1979.

Nancy Sahli argues that women's self-consciousness about intense female friendships began as early as the 1880s, accompanied by a growing literature which described love between women as a perversion. Undoubtedly the urban college women Sahli describes were more sensitive to a changing climate of popular scientific opinion than older or less sophisticated women on the mission field. Sahli sees Ellis's *Sexual Inversion* as the culmination of this trend. Ellis used the terms *homosexuality* and *lesbianism* "inter-changeably to describe women's love relationships that did not necessarily include either physical involvement or actual genital contact," Sahli demonstrates. "Smashing: Women's Relationships before the Fall," *Chrysalis* (Summer 1974), p. 24.

46. The significance of these particular names is unclear. Saint Dorothea was a virgin martyr celebrated for her grace and tenderness, but Dorothea was also the name of George Eliot's discerning heroine in *Middlemarch*. Longfellow's Evangeline, a young girl parted from her lover, is perhaps a clearer reference. Clarence L. Barnhart, ed., *The New Century Cyclopedia of Names* (New York: Appleton-Century, 1954); Anna Hartwell to Leila Watson, 25 October 1919, notebook, CRP.

47. Bessie Hartwell to Anna, 16 April 1921, in ABH notebook, CRP.

48. Hartwell to Anna, 7 May 1921, in ABH notebook, CRP.

49. For Hunt, Search, Seek, and Rob: Maude Russell, personal interview, 15 April 1978; Jessie Ankeny to family, 10 August 1910, SCUO; Elizabeth Perkins to family, 31 January 1915, CRP.

50. Elsie Clark diary, 24 July 1913, CRP; Stella Flagg to Alice Frame, 7 September

1936; Luella Miner papers, ABCFM; Miner to sister Carrie, 7 June 1892, ABCFM. For Lewis's sensitivities, see: Ida Lewis journal, 11 September 1910, letter to her mother, 16 April 1922; for quote, Lewis to her mother and Clara, 1920, SCUO.

51. Lida Ashmore to Edith, 20 July 1907, SCUO; Bessie Ewing to family, 11 May 1900, ABCFM.

52. Welthy Honsinger Fisher, *To Light a Candle* (New York: McGraw-Hill, p. 153.) Valentin Rabe argues for the analogy between entering a Catholic order and joining mission service: "To a greater extent than the ordained, male missionary . . . she cut herself off from a familiar way of life and surrendered herself to spinsterhood in an environment where eligible males were rare. Her commitment was more difficult to revoke than her male counterparts' and took on aspects of entering a Catholic order." Valentin Rabe, "Evangelical Logistics: Mission Support and Resources to 1920," in John K. Fairbank, ed., *The Missionary Enterprise in China and America* (Cambridge, Mass.: Harvard University Press, 1974), p. 77.

53. Lucy Mead to family, 29 January, 28 August 1910, 14 June 1914.

54. Corda Gracey to Mrs. Lucius Perkins, 29 October 1907, Perkins papers, CRP; Mary Gamewell to Jessie Ankeny, 29 October 1910, Lacy papers; Ankeny to mother, 5 November 1911, SCUO.

55. Alice Alsup to family, 3 September 1921, CRP.

56. Alice Reed to family, 9 September 1917, CRP; Jessie Ankeny to mother, 25 October 1910, to Helen, 1 May 1909, SCUO; E. L. Bliss to family, in Edward Bliss, Jr., "Yankee in Fu-kien," clipping, biographical file, ABCFM; Ida Lewis to family, 29 January 1911, SCUO. Invariably there were exceptions—men who were neither "decent" nor "nice." Majorie Rankin Steurt told of a station lecher: "Every one of his sermons was against sex. And that man! We single women didn't dare go out at night" (interview, COH, p. 60). Pearl Buck's *Fighting Angel* (New York: John Day-Reynal & Hitchcock, 1936), pp. 77–81, told of the repressions and secret sins which pervaded the missionary communities she knew: "And what incredible stories, what pathetic, human, inevitable stories! They are hushed, guarded against, kept secret, for the sake of the Work, for the sake of the 'home church,' for shame's sake, for God's sake—but what stories!"

57. Smith, *Daughters of the Promised Land*, p. 181, writes that "the missionary field was, in fact, the first area of American life where women achieved a more or less equal professional status with men," a statement which is accepted uncritically by Sandra C. Taylor, "The Sisterhood of Salvation and the Sunrise Kingdom: Congregational Missionaries in Meiji Japan," *Pacific Historical Review*, February 1979, p. 27.

58. *The Relative Place of Women in the Church: A Tentative Report of the Joint Committee Appointed by the Council of Women for Home Missions, the Federation of Women's Boards of Foreign Missions of North America and the Federated Council of the Churches of Christ in America, to Study the Place of Women's Organized Work in the Church* (New York, 1927), p. 53; on crocheting, Luella Miner to mother, 19 May 1888, ABCFM; Rabe, "Evangelical Logistics," fn. 35, p. 385; China Continuation Committee, "Findings of the National Conference Held in Shanghai March 11 to 14th, 1913," pamphlet, CRP.

59. Elizabeth Wilson, "The American Situation," introduction to Charles E. Raven, *Women and the Ministry* (New York: Doubleday, Doran & Co., 1929), pp. 9–10, 22.

60. Isabelle Phelps, candidate file, ABCFM; Woman's Board of Missions, Constitution, as reprinted in *Annual Report*, 1910.

61. R. Pierce Beaver, *All Loves Excelling: American Protestant Women in World Mission* (Grand Rapids, Mich.: William B. Eerdmans, 1968), p. 178. The Methodist Episcopal Church, South, for instance, which merged much of its administration during the 1920s,

found that the men's wages were substantially higher than the women's of comparable rank. The women agreed to several small increases, "although they refused to consent to equal salaries," according to *The Relative Place of Women in the Church*, p. 46.

62. Anna Hartwell "to myself," notebook, 5 June 1921; on financial embarrassment, letter to Blanche Walker, 16 July 1921, CRP; Luella Miner to sister Carrie, 30 October 1903, letter to Mrs. Lee, secretary of Woman's Board of Missions of the Interior, 13 September 1922. Miner's financial conservatism was reflected in her management of North China Union Women's College. In 1922 she wrote: "In the 17 year history of the college we have never had a debt, either for current expenses or for building, larger than the treasurer could carry over in to the next year on her personal account" (to Mrs. Lee of WBM, 30 September). Miner herself realized that such abstemiousness brought its own problems, as indicated by her fears in 1919, "that the necessity for working within narrow limitations so long may have shortened my vision and diminished my courage for large things" (to Alice Frame, 9 September, ABCFM).

63. Jessie Ankeny to mother, 10 November 1912, SCUO; Miner to Mrs. Clark, WBMI, 28 February 1915, ABCFM; Sarah Goodrich to Mrs. Clark and Mrs. Moore, 20 March 1916; James Barton to Goodrich, 29, April 1915, CRP.

64. Emma Martin to family, 18 January 1903, CRP.

65. Luella Miner to father, 16 May 1894, general letter, 1 March 1905, ABCFM; Emma Martin to parents, 4 May 1902, 6 October 1912, CRP; Beaver, *All Loves Excelling*, p. 106.

66. Beaver, *All Loves Excelling*, p. 104; Valentin Rabe, "The American Protestant Foreign Mission Movement 1880–1920" (Ph.D. diss., Harvard University, 1965), p. 278.

67. Methodist women's organizations in the field, though not advocates of individual rights like the home boards, tended to protect women's independent initiatives. Luella Miner wrote of the Methodist Woman's Union Medical College: "The lady doctors . . . haven't the courage to put their institution under this board of managers, which of course is made up mostly of men, but if it works well with our woman's college, I think they will be willing to come into the union later" (general letter, 15 September 1905, ABCFM). Elsie Clark diary, 18 October 1913, CRP; Miner general letter, 28 August 1912, ABCFM.

68. Barbara Welter, "She Hath Done What She Could: Protestant Women's Missionary Careers in Nineteenth-Century America," *American Quarterly*, Spring 1979.

69. Elsie Clark diary, 14 October 1914. Clark wrote about a YWCA conference two years later: "I should like to be able to be present invisibly among a similar gathering arranged by men to see how their methods would differ from those of women. Some of us go too much upon our nerves, and perhaps magnify the importance of details" (letter to family, 7 September 1916, CRP).

70. For "honor," Elizabeth Perkins to family, March 1918, CRP; for lack of protection for single women, Edward Bliss," "Yankee in Fu-kien," ABCFM; for "esprit de corps," Clark diary, 2 April 1913, CRP.

71. *Relative Place of Women in the Church*, p. 36. These efforts were doomed to ultimate failure, as the general boards gradually did abolish the institutional autonomy of the women's boards. L. Pierce Beaver notes that this process was in general complete by the 1920s but not accomplished within the United Methodist Church until 1964, where there still remains a strong Woman's Division (*All Loves Excelling*, p. 182).

Chapter 4

1. Pearl S. Buck, *The Exile* (New York: John Day, 1936), pp. 71, 83; Jeanie Graham [McClure] to Kittie Graham, 20 January 1911, to parents, 26 September 1912, 11 February 1913, CRP.

2. Missionary work was opening up for women partly as a result of declining interest in it among men. Until the revitalization of the mission movement in the early twentieth century, missionary service, for women, was a decision for public activity but, for men, a form of dignified withdrawal. Like the alliance Ann Douglas found between ministers and female writers earlier in the nineteenth century, missionary marriages joined men and women from opposite ends of the spectrum of career options for their respective sexes. Perhaps this explains the personality configurations that emerged in some missionary marriages. Pearl Buck remembered her mother as a practical, vibrant woman, her father as cerebral and withdrawn: "a secret doubt of himself as a man was always mingled with his certainty of himself as God's messenger." Dorothy Campbell's memory of her parents stressed their contrasting temperaments. She wrote: "I fear I was early infected with my mother's attitude of superiority to men. She was the dominant figure in our family life, a very active, capable, enthusiastic type of person. My father was a scholar and a man of fine character but cautious and retiring." Visitors to Sarah and Chauncey Goodrich remembered Chauncey as a "saint," and Sarah as "very aggressive and outspoken," "concerned about living today rather than going to Heaven." Ann Douglas, *The Feminization of American Culture* (New York: Knopf, 1977); Pearl S. Buck, *Fighting Angel* (New York: John Day, 1936); (Buck's *Exile* and *Fighting Angel* are portraits of her parents which elaborate this comparison throughout); Dorothy Campbell, autobiographical sketch, Campbell Family Papers, CRP. For material on Sarah and Chauncey Goodrich, see Maude Hunter, "Sarah Boardman Goodrich"; Dorothea Smith Coryell, "The Dragon Charms and Seduces," Sarah Goodrich to Carrington Goodrich, 28 August 1910, 22 August 1915, CRP. For the significance of declining male interest in encouraging female missionary participation, see Barbara Welter, "She Hath Done What She Could: Prostestant Women's Missionary Careers in Nineteenth-Century America," *American Quarterly* (Spring 1979), p. 264.

3. Buck, *The Exile*, p. 109; Jennie Campbell to sister Lyda, 7 August 1890, CRP. Earlier in the nineteenth century, in a more secular context, abolitionist Abby Kelly Foster made the same assumption: "If I am not mistaken in physiological facts, I can never be a mother while I work so hard in this cause." Abby Kelley Foster to Lucy Stone, 15 August [1846], as quoted in Joel Bernard, "Authority, Autonomy and Radical Commitment: Stephen and Abby Kelley Foster," *Proceedings of the American Antiquarian Society*, vol. 90, pt. 2 (October 1980), p. 368. Sarah Stage discusses the use of biology in the late-nineteenth-century fight against higher education for women. One argument held that serious study would cause a woman's womb to atrophy (*Female Complaints: Lydia Pinkham and the Business of Women's Medicine* [New York: Norton, 1979], p. 84). See also Barbara Ehrenreich and Deirdre English, *For Her Own Good: 150 Years of the Experts' Advice to Women* (Garden City, N.Y.: Anchor, 1978), pp. 125–31.

4. Florence Brown to W. Edward Manly, 16 June 1893, CRP; Lida Ashmore to Edith Ashmore, 31 July 1908, SCUO.

5. Jeanie McClure to parents, 7 January 1919, CRP; Grace Smith to family, 8 August 1903, CRP.

6. Lida Ashmore to Edith Ashmore, 3 November 1907, 7 March 1913, SCUO. For a discussion of some of the literature on culture shock, including reference to the alien as a child, see John Schumann, "Affective Factors and the Problem of Age in Second Language Acquisition," *Language Learning* 25 (1975): 209–35, esp. 210–14.

7. See McClure to parents, 24 September 1917, 7 May 1918, CRP; Bessie Ewing to mother, 17 August 1905, personal papers, ABCFM; Edward Bliss, Jr., "Yankee in Fukien," newspaper clippings, biographical file, ABCFM; W. Edward Manly diary, 19 April 1893, CRP.

8. Emily Hobart to family, 25 January 1889, SCUO.

9. Jessie Ankeny Lacy to Louise Ankeny, 4 February 1914, 6 December 1913, SCUO; Jeanie McClure to family, 16 December 1919, CRP.

10. W. E. Manly to Manly family, 6 April 1894, CRP.

11. Bessie Ewing to "Aunt Myra," 9 September 1896, ABCFM; Netta Allen, interview, 1971, COH.

12. Eleanor Frances Lewis, *Beads of Jade* (New York: Vantage Press, 1958), p. 23; Schumann, "Second Language Acquisition," pp. 210–14.

13. Monona Cheney to family, 21 May 1920, SCUO. "The use of a new language may cause a sense of shame which results from feelings of insufficiency." For this and a summary of the literature, see Schumann, "Second Language Acquisition," pp. 210–14.

14. Irwin T. Hyatt, Jr., *Our Ordered Lives Confess: Three Nineteenth-Century American Missionaries in East Shantung* (Cambridge, Mass.: Harvard University Press, 1976), p. 8. Hyatt's eloquent treatment of the Crawford relationship indicates that Martha's preeminence in other areas of mission life was to cause her lasting problems. Consistently jealous of his wife's time and her success, T. P. Crawford demanded that she close down her flourishing boys' school; when she resisted, he adopted two orphans to try to restrain the public activities of his childless wife. Martha Crawford ultimately agreed to her husband's request to close her school and immersed herself instead in village itinerating. On Sydenstricker, see Buck, *The Exile*, p. 107.

15. Jeanie McClure to parents, 28 October 1917, 29 April 1917, 20 January 1919, CRP.

16. McClure to parents, 16 February 1919, CRP. Married women at least occasionally pressured each other to limit language study. Lida Ashmore wrote of a woman who "tries to get all the married ladies to give up studying after they have passed their year's exams" (to Edith Ashmore, 2 May 1915, SCUO).

17. Sarah Goodrich to Lucy Beach, 30 April 1904, Goodrich to Rev. Smith, of ABCFM, 12 July 1903, Goodrich to Chauncey Goodrich, 23 July 1905, CRP. The particular personal quality of women's board aid is revealed in Susan Skinner's complaint about not receiving Christmas boxes. "The WFMS workers always have boxes of things from home to use at Christmas-time, but the rest of us usually have to buy out of our own pockets whatever we want to give. For example, we have used about five dollars, gold, this year for pencils alone, for the students in our Yungan boys' schools" (to Mrs. Hydon, 10 January 1923, SCUO).

18. Goodrich to Mrs. Clark and Mrs. Moore, of women's board, 20 March 1916, CRP.

19. Ibid.

20. Lida Ashmore to Edith Ashmore, 6 August 1905, SCUO; Goodrich to Mrs. Clark and Mrs. Moore, 20 March 1916. Married women's expressions of pity for the single women conveyed their resentment less directly. Mildred Rowland ended up undermining her pity by her acknowledgment of single women's contentment: "It's all right for a man to come out and bring his family but it seems to me it is pretty hard on the WFMSers. Perhaps they don't mind it and I am wasting my pity but I'm glad I'm not one. They are doing a fine work and all that but to live out here with people you never knew before and none of your family—I couldn't do it. Now don't read this or tell it to anyone because the ladies all seem happy" (to family, 10 December 1912, CRP).

21. Lucy Mead to parents, 1 September 1913, ABCFM; Luella Miner to Mrs. Clark of women's board, 28 February 1915, ABCFM.

22. Sarah Goodrich to Rev. Smith of ABCFM, 12 July 1903, CRP.

23. Lida Ashmore discussed the Episcopal Protestant policy of sending widows home in relation to a Mrs. Riddel, who had returned and was "so sad and lonely and says she wishes she had made her permanent home in Thai yong!" (to Edith Ashmore, 8 June 1913,

SCUO); Pearl Buck on knitting, *Fighting Angel*, p. 190. Luella Miner's memory of American Board station meetings before women could vote emphasized the crocheting: "We ladies, who are not allowed to vote, and are not expected to lift up our voices in the meetings, take our crochetting" (letter to her mother, 19 May 1888). For Pearl Buck's feminism, see her curse of Saint Paul: "Since these days when I saw all her [her mother's] nature dimmed I have hated St. Paul with all my heart and so must all true women hate him, I think, because of what he has done in the past to women like Carie, proud free-born women yet damned by their very womanhood" (*The Exile*, p. 283).

24. Lida Ashmore to Edith and Frank Ashmore, 5 October 1897, February 1905, 22 February 1912, SCUO.

25. Ashmore to Edith, 8 September 1907, SCUO. Jeanie McClure's challenge to the women's board candidate for the second auditor of her tiny station lined up parent board against women's board in a passionately fought election (14 January 1919, 1 June 1920, CRP).

26. Mildred Rowland to aunts, 14 March 1912, 15 November 1912, CRP.

27. Rowland to aunts, 15 November 1912, CRP.

28. Jennie Campbell to Mrs. Fife, 17 June 1890; to Elia Campbell, 12 August 1890, CRP.

29. Buck, *The Exile*, p. 184; Lucy Chaplin Lee, "An American Sojourn in China" (printed memoir), CRP.

30. On hairstyles, Bessie Ewing to Aunt Mira, 21 January 1910, ABCFM; on child care, Edith Trimble to family, 27 December 1918, SCUO; on student mothers, Bertha Allen to parents, 22 July 1917, ABCFM; on dreading teaching, Emily Hobart to home family, 25 May 1896, SCUO; on Lacy's gratitude, Elsie Clark Krug, personal interview, Baltimore, Md., 20 June 1979.

31. For emphasis on American child care, see Mildred Rowland to aunts, 6 October 1919, CRP; Jeanie McClure to parents, 15 December 1918, CRP; Lucile Jones, interview, 1970, COH.

32. Jones, interview, 1970, COH.

33. Jeanie McClure to parents, 23 July 1919, CRP; for "degenerate offspring," Emily Hobart to James (brother?), 19 March 1899; Sarah Goodrich to parents, 19 December 1892, CRP.

34. Emily Hobart to Henry (brother?), 9 November 1893, SCUO; Jennie Campbell to Ella (sister), 18 June 1890, CRP; Florence Manly to sister-in-law, 26 July 1898, CRP; Margaret Smythe, interview, 1971, 1972, COH. For another example, see Marjorie Rankin Steurt's memories of the Luce family, interview, 1970, COH.

35. For evidence on community attitudes toward Chinese care of missionary children, see Sarah Goodrich to Carrington, 29 October 1916, CRP; Lida Ashmore to Edith Ashmore, 8 December 1907, 1 January 1908, SCUO; Alice Williams to Goodrich, 13 March 1894, CRP; Emily Hobart to brothers, 1 November 1893, SCUO; Jessie Ankeny Lacy to parents, 7 October 1920, SCUO.

36. Ida Pruitt, personal interview, Philadelphia, 18 June 1979.

37. Lewis, *Beads of Jade*, p. 40.

38. Buck, *The Exile*, p. 186; Bessie Ewing to Aunt Mira, 8 January 1907, ABCFM.

39. Ida Pruitt, *Chinese Childhood* (San Francisco: China Materials Center, 1978), p. 77; Margery Wolf, "Child Training and the Chinese Family," in Maurice Freedman, ed., *Family and Kinship in Chinese Society* (Stanford, Calif.: Stanford University Press, 1970), pp. 40–41.

40. Dorothy Campbell, autobiographical sketch, ca. 1946, Campbell Family Papers, CRP; Bessie Ewing to family, 15 December 1897, ABCFM. Perhaps part of the imperious-

ness of American children, and also parents' unwillingness to have them play with Chinese, resulted from their minority status. Bessie Ewing described the reaction of her children to their experience as racial oddities: "They dislike being fingered and questioned and hearing anyone remark on their looks and size and manners. . . . Edward pays no attention. He goes outdoors and all around as usual. Then a crowd of children surround him. He acts as though no one was there unless they get in his way, then beware! Once I caught him throwing sand at boys who teased him, again it was bricks and a third time I discovered about a dozen big boys admiring him from a safe distance while he brandished the ax at them" (to Aunt Mira, 1 November 1906), ABCFM.

41. Lucy Lee, "An American Sojourn in China"; Gertrude Wilder, "Random Jottings" (xerox typescript), March 1959, p. 6, CRP; Sarah Goodrich, "The Relationship of Foreign Children to the Chinese" (typescript), 1904, CRP. Goodrich suggested that American children might learn courtesy and respect for elders from the Chinese.

42. Florence Manly to Martha Johnson, 14 August 1896, CRP; Clara Foster to mother-in-law, 6 November 1890, 26 October 1892, CRP. Missionary mothers frequently came to the conclusion that work must give way to family responsibilities—for example, Buck, *The Exile*, p. 111; Jeanie McClure to parents, 3 April 1920, CRP.

43. McClure to parents, 3 December 1917, CRP; Sarah Goodrich to parents, 6 February 1894, CRP.

44. Emily Hobart to mother, 24 July 1896, SCUO; Elsie Clark to mother, 18 November 1917, CRP; Jessie Lacy to mother, 12 February 1914, SCUO; McClure to Margaret (sister), 5 September 1918, CRP. The difficulties married women had in participating in the work have been commented on by other mission historians: L. Pierce Beaver, *All Loves Excelling: American Protestant Women in World Mission* (Grand Rapids, Mich.: Wm. Eerdman, 1968), p. 59; Welter, "She Hath Done What She Could," pp. 632–34.

45. Mary Williams Hemingway, "Mrs. Annette W. Atwood," *Missionary Herald*, May 1912, biographical file, ABCFM.

46. Margaret Burton, *Women Workers of the Orient* (West Medford, Mass., 1918), p. 35.

47. Pearl Buck, *Of Men and Women* (New York: John Day, 1941), p. 33; Ida Pruitt, *Chinese Childhood*, p. 125.

48. On missionary home as object lesson, see Luella Miner, "Preparation of Women Missionaries," ABCFM; Jeanie McClure to Margaret (sister), 5 September 1918, CRP.

49. Clara Foster to mother-in-law, 4 December 1891, CRP; Emily Hobart to mother, 10 February 1895, SCUO.

50. This discussion is heavily indebted to John Mack Faragher, *Women and Men on the Overland Trail* (New Haven, Conn.: Yale University Press, 1979), esp. p. 87.

51. Sarah Goodrich to sisters, 21 February 1908, Goodrich to mother, 10 December 1891, 6 February 1892, CRP.

52. Goodrich to father, 18 October 1892; Goodrich to mother, 7 September 1893; Bessie Ewing to family, June 1898, ABCFM.

53. Jennie Campbell to aunts, 23 June 1890; to Elia Campbell, 4 August 1890, CRP.

54. Buck, *The Exile*, p. 207; Emily Hobart to sister, 8 February 1896, SCUO.

55. Sarah Goodrich, "Reasoning with myself over my problem," May 1919, CRP; Jennie Campbell to sister Ella, 18 June 1890, CRP.

56. Bessie Ewing to family, July 1898, ABCFM.

57. Minnie Bliss, general letter to supporters, 1 March 1920, in McClure collection, CRP; Lida Ashmore, "Autobiography" (printed), SCUO; Lewis, *Beads of Jade*, p. 173.

58. Sarah Goodrich to Rev. Smith of ABCFM, 12 July 1903, CRP; Ashmore to Edith, 8 August 1898, SCUO.

59. Ashmore to children, 15 July 1898, SCUO; Jeanie McClure to mother, 30 October 1919, CRP.

60. Pickett, *From the Rising of the Sun*, p. 9; Ashmore to Edith, 27 October 1912, SCUO; Clara Foster to mother-in-law, 22 July 1897, CRP.

61. Buck, *The Exile*, p. 279.

62. Coryell, "The Dragon Charms"; for description of summer without work, see Sarah Goodrich to Grace Goodrich, 23 August 1908, CRP.

63. Clara Foster to mother-in-law, 31 March 1890, CRP.

64. Foster journal, 13 January 1916; letter to mother-in-law, 4 May 1893, CRP; for description of Mary Ament, see Luella Miner, general letter, 23 February 1906, ABCFM.

65. Foster journal, 11 January 1916, 25 December 1915, 12 July 1916, 28 May 1916, CRP.

66. Elsie Clark to mother, 28 January 1917, CRP; Clark, personal interview, 20 June 1979; Hyatt, *Our Ordered Lives Confess*, p. 171.

Chapter 5

1. Elizabeth Perkins to mother, 18 November 1907, CRP.

2. Ida Pruitt, *Chinese Childhood* (San Francisco: China Materials Center, 1978), p. 15; Monona Cheney to family, 30 June 1919, SCUO; for appreciation of open spaces, see Jeanie McClure to family, 7 February 1920, CRP.

3. Jane Field Bashford, "The Foochow Woman's Conference," WMF, February 1905, p. 50; Elsie Clark to family, 27 January 1915, Lizzie Martin to family, 2 August 1902, CRP; see also Mamie Glassburner, general letter, 26 July 1909, in Jessie Ankeny Lacy Papers, SCUO.

4. Lida Ashmore to Edith Ashmore, 20 April 1918, Clark, diary, June 1913, CRP; Ashmore to Edith, April 1897, SCUO. For more on gardens, see Margaret Campbell Burket to Dorothy Campbell, 1 March 1919, CRP; Edward J. Bliss, "Yankee in Fu-kien," clipping, biographical file, ABCFM; Louise Stanley, interview, 1971, COH; Clara Hess to John Foster's mother, 1 January 1889, Foster Family Papers, CRP.

5. Elizabeth Perkins to family, 21 October 1907, Clark to family, 4 February 1917, CRP; Pruitt, *Chinese Childhood*, p. 10; Evelyn Sites, "Real Christmas at Abiding Joy," n.d., CRP; Jessie Ankeny to family, 3 March 1911, SCUO; Lucy Mead to family, 1 January 1910, ABCFM. Passe-partout is a method of framing in which picture, glass, and mat are held together by paper or cloth pasted over the edges.

6. Clark to mother, 12 January 1913, CRP; for description of conference preparations, Alice Alsup to family, 20 October 1919, CRP; Luella Miner to Carrie Miner, 2 June 1980, ABCFM.

7. Grace Smith to family, 2 November 1902, Sarah Goodrich to mother, 29 February 1892, to father, 9 June 1892, Smith to husband's family, 18 October 1907, CRP.

8. Elsie Smith to family, 14 December 1912, CRP. Clark did collect Chinese artifacts, which she arranged around her room: "As I gradually get one pretty thing after another to show you in America of China's art, I put it around me in some appropriate place, until my eyes fairly revel in the glow of brass, the distinction of cloisonné, the never dimmed lustre of lacquer, and the richness of carved wood. You shall see some of these things soon in your own hands, but you'll never see them altogether in the beautiful combination they make now" (20 February 1918, CRP).

9. Elizabeth Perkins to family, 24 May 1908, Mildred Rowland to family, 9 October 1911, Sarah Goodrich to Carrington Goodrich, 11 November 1913, CRP. The Chinese, of course, found knives and forks equally offensive. Helena Kuo considered them "worse than

barbarous. Knives were used for killing animals and people, and it seemed exceedingly impolite to use them at table. I knew that the Chinese had used knives and forks thousands of years ago, but had given them up in the interest of being civilized." *I've Come A Long Way* (New York: Appleton Century, 1942), p. 75.

10. Bertha Allen to family, 17 December 1916, Perkins to mother, 9 November 1907, CRP.

11. Clara Foster to husband's parents, 17 May 1889, CRP. Pruitt, *Chinese Childhood*, p. 45, wrote of her mother, who had her own vegetable garden: "Chinese vegetables in their almost endless variety she never knew. The ones she used were, to her substitutes only." On getting fat, Luella Miner to mother, 15 November 1887, CRP; Clara Pearl Dyer, *WMF*, November 1914, 394.

12. Luella Miner to family, 28 March 1891, ABCFM; Jessie Ankeny to mother, 27 June 1912, SCUO; Foster to husband's parents, 7 August 1889, CRP. See also Elsie Clark to family, 28 December 1915, CRP.

13. Frederica Mead to family, 15 August 1919, Clark, diary, 17 January 1913, CRP; Ankeny to family, 1 January 1911, SCUO.

14. Luella Miner to mother, 11 June 1888, to Mary Vanderslice, 12 October 1913, ABCFM.

15. Elsie Clark, diary, 18 May 1913, CRP.

16. Lottie Moon, "Advantages and Disadvantages of Wearing the Native Dress in Missionary Work," *Woman's Work in China*, November 1881, pp. 14–22.

17. Alfred Street, 21 April 1894, Frank Chalfont, 22 March 1891, A. Beattie, 11 December 1893, R. E. Abbey, 9 May 1887, E. C. Lobenstine, 15 July 1899—all to the Presbyterian Board of Foreign Missions, as excerpted in "Calendar to the Correspondence of the Board of Foreign Missions," microfilm, CRP (hereafter "Calendar").

18. Grace Smith to family, 8 August 1903, Mildred Rowland to family, 9 October 1911, Elsie N. Garretson to Elizabeth Perkins, 28 February 1907, CRP. For reference to Nanchang riot, see Fred Drake, ed., *Ruth V. Hemenway, M.D.: A Memoir of Revolutionary China, 1924–1941* (Amherst: University of Massachusetts Press, 1977), p. 154.

19. Elsie Clark, 6 December 1914, CRP; Lida Ashmore to Edith Ashmore, 24 October 1897, SCUO. Male and female members of the British China Inland Mission and certain minor evangelical sects sometimes wore Chinese dress even after 1900. This divergence between the major American denominations and the evagelical sects reflected a trend in the prominent American boards away from village itinerating and toward secular work and secular life-styles.

20. Clark to family, 30 April 1913, Jeanie McClure to family, 17 June 1917, 25 October 1920, CRP.

21. Clark to family, 18 April 1915, CRP.

22. For a colorful description of the besieged community, see Peter Fleming, *The Siege at Peking* (London: Harper & Brothers, 1959), esp. p. 145; Emma Martin, siege diary, typescript, 18 August 1900, CRP; Luella Miner to family, 25 December 1900; ABCFM. For discussion of turn-of-the-century newsmen and of the problem of "overcivilization," see Larzer Ziff, *The American 1890s* (New York: Viking, 1966).

23. Lucy Mead to family, 4 June 1911, ABCFM.

24. Gertrude Wilder, "Random Jottings," p. 11, CRP.

25. Emma Martin to family, 8 April 1901, CRP; Monona Cheney to family, 3 May 1919, Lida Ashmore to Edith Ashmore, 2 May 1915, SCUO.

26. Sarah Goodrich to Emma, 18 May 1894, Ruth White to family, 25 November 1917, CRP.

27. Bessie Ewing to Aunt Myra, 13 October 1894, 21 March 1895, ABCFM; Monona Cheney to family, 16 November 1918, SCUO.

28. Jessie Ankeny to family, 31 January 1909, SCUO; Elsie Clark to family, 12 November 1915, CRP.

29. Ruth White to family, 25 November 1917, CRP; Myra Jaquet papers, SCUO; on Past-time Club, Lucy Mead to family, 3 November 1913, ABCFM; on Nanking Association, Margaret Lillian Smythe, interview, 1971, COH; Monona Cheney to family, 22 February 1920, SCUO.

30. The Presbyterian Board of Foreign Missions in 1889 proposed six weeks as a reasonable summer vacation for Peking workers, but local doctors insisted that women and children needed to be out of the city heat for at least two months. Charles Leaman of Nanking wrote to the board after the death of Robert Abbey of the choice the church must make (1 December 1890, "Calendar"). For Peking debate, I. Dudgeon to board, 1889, missionaries of Peking to board, 13 February 1889, "Calendar." For information on China-wide summer resorts, see Kenneth Scott Latourette, *History of Christian Missions in China* (New York: Macmillan, 1929), p. 627.

31. Jessie Ankeny Lacy to father, 26 April 1914, CRP. Lacy explained her summer trip to Shanghai as the necessity to be "with our own kind." Such arguments also justified summer resorts.

32. For Kuliang routine, see Elizabeth Perkins to family, 16 August 1908, CRP; for immigrant party, Elsie Clark to family, 14 August 1915, CRP; Welthy Honsinger, *Beyond the Moon Gate: Being a Diary of Ten Years in the Interior of the Middle Kingdom* (New York: Abington, 1924), p. 50.

33. Alice Reed to family, 6 May 1917, CRP; Monona Cheney to family, 14 March 1921, SCUO; Elsie Clark, diary, 23 May 1913, CRP.

34. Lucy Mead to family, 20 November 1919, 16 April 1911, ABCFM; Cheney to family, 14 March 1921, SCUO.

35. Cheney to family, 30 November 1918, Sarah Goodrich to Mary, 18 August 1891, Elsie Clark, diary, 26 October, 1912, CRP; Mead to family, 22 July 1913, ABCFM; Leonard Christian, biographical file, Irma Davis, "Edna Terry," a memorial pamphlet, DFMC.

36. Alice Reed to family, 14 July 1918, Clark to family, 7 July 1913, 9 July 1916, CRP.

37. Luella Miner to "college family," 13 October 1919, Lucy Mead to family, 6 January 1910, 26 September 1911, ABCFM; Jeanie McClure to family, 15 July 1919, Elizabeth Perkins to family, 4 October 1907, CRP.

38. Mead to family, 18 November 1913, ABCFM; Perkins to family, 3 September 1907, CRP; Monona Cheney to family, 5 June 1920, SCUO.

39. W. H. Lingel wrote in 1897 that although the Presbyterian board stipulated that missionaries should receive a salary of $1,000, at the current rate of exchange it worked out to $2,000 per year. "I am not able to satisfy my conscience," he wrote the board, 12 August 1897, "Calendar"; Jeanie McClure to family, 11 February 1917, Elsie Clark to Andrew H. Krug, 13 March 1913, CRP; Christine Pickett, *From the Rising of the Sun* (Frankfort, Ohio: Privately printed, 1978), pp. 10, 23; Valentin Rabe, "The American Protestant Foreign Mission Movement, 1880–1920" (Ph.D. diss., Harvard University, 1965), p. 823.

40. Jessie Ankeny to parents, 11 October 1910, SCUO; "Take your ease," Ruth White to family, 27 May 1919, CRP. For other examples of desire to share servants with home families, see Elizabeth Perkins to family, 10 September 1908, Elsie Clark to family, 8 February 1914, CRP.

41. Luella Miner to sister Stella, 15 October 1894, ABCFM. For further examples of English obedience: Florence Manly to family, 4 October 1898, Sarah Goodrich to Carrington Goodrich, 24 November 1913, Ruth White to family, 12 September 1917, Emma Martin, siege diary, 6 August 1900, CRP.

42. Martin, siege diary, 17 July 1900, 17 August 1900; Goodrich, siege journal, 3 June 1900, CRP. The British in China may well have been more rigid than other nationalities. Englishman Robert Hart, Insepector General of Chinese Customs, seemed to think so: "I am not in favor of bringing out any experienced English hand," he wrote of customs recruitment in 1893. "English are not properly accommodating and they have not enough india-rubber in their composition, and for success native wants and native conditions must be studied and allowed for—too parishional, too provincial, too insular are our country-men." *The I.G. in Peking: Letters of Robert Hart, Chinese Maritime Customs 1868–1907* (Cambridge, Mass.: Harvard University Press, 1975), 2:956.

43. Matilda Thurston to family, 1 February 1914, "Letters from Nanking," United Board for Christian Higher Education in Asia (hereafter UBCHE).

44. Eleanor Lewis, *Beads of Jade* (New York: Vintage, 1958), p. 100; Emma Martin to family, 10 April 1905, CRP.

45. Sarah Goodrich to Carrington Goodrich, 16 October 1916, to Grace Goodrich, 26 September 1910, CRP; on need for French and music lessons, Lida Ashmore to Edith, 24 October 1897, 12 March 1898, SCUO; Goodrich to Carrington, 24 August 1913, CRP.

46. Charles Denby, *China and Her People* (Boston: L. C. Page & Co., 1906), pp. 60–61; for biographical material on Denby, see the *Dictionary of American Biography*; Lewis, *Beads of Jade*, p. 102; Lottie Hartwell to family, 26 June 1897, Hartwell Family Papers; Agnes McClure Alden, letter about Jeanie McClure, 23 August 1977, CRP.

47. Elsie Clark, diary, 7 August 1913, 25 August 1914, letter to family, 23 March 1918. Evidence of Clark's interest in the British community emerges from her response to an invitation from a British missionary: "The invitation was an attractive one because of the opportunity it held out of closer acquaintance with our British friends" (to mother, 10 May 1914). Clark's Anglophilia extended to a strong attraction to the ritual and formality of the Anglican church, which she frequently contrasted favorably with her own, plainer Method-ism (diary, 2 November 1913, 5 April 1914, letter to family, April 1918, CRP).

48. Sarah Goodrich to Emma, 14 April 1891, CRP; Christine Pickett referred to the prevailing sense that "Great Britain was holding 'dominion over palm and pine' . . . and on Kuliang we Americans were definitely second rate" (*From the Rising of the Sun*, p. 15); Dorothy Campbell, autobiographical sketch, 1946, p. 2, CRP.

49. Lida Ashmore, autobiography, p. 44, SCUO; Elsie Clark to family, 9 February 1913, 13 March 1913, CRP.

50. Mildred Rowland to aunts, 13 November 1911, CRP; Ashmore to Edith, 11 February 1912, "Extracts," Monona Cheney to family, 3 May 1919, 5 July 1919, SCUO; Rowland to family, 4 November 1911, CRP.

51. Elizabeth Perkins to family, 2 December 1907, Sarah Goodrich to children, 24 October 1915, Rowland to family, 3 December 1912, CRP.

52. Rowland to family, 3 December 1912, CRP; Marjorie Rankin Steurt, interview, 1970, COH; W. E. Manly to family, 4 December 1893, Elsie Clark to family, 9 February 1913, CRP.

53. Lizzie Martin to family, 26 May 1900, Elizabeth Perkins to father, 16 June 1908, CRP; Jessie Ankeny to mother, 18 February 1911, SCUO.

54. Monona Cheney, general letter, 8 January 1919, SCUO; Ankeny to father, 26 February 1912, CRP. For further examples of denial of race, see: Lucy Mead to family, 29 October 1911, Luella Miner, general letter, 8 February 1890, ABCFM; Alice Reed, interview, 1969, COH.

55. Sarah Goodrich to Carrington, 17 February 1920, CRP; Luella Miner, "The Relationships of Chinese Workers and Missionaries," n.d., ABCFM.

56. Lizzie Martin to family [1901], Elsie Clark to family, 22 December 1913, CRP.

57. Ruth White to family, 25 November 1917, CRP; Ellen H. Suffern, letter, *WMF*, December 1918, p. 531; Jeanie McClure to family, 27 January 1918, CRP; Grace Rowley, interview, 1970, COH; McClure to family, 11 March 1918, CRP. Marjorie Steurt mentioned another missionary woman skilled at Chinese strategies for manipulating servants. When she found that her cook was charging her for twelve dozen eggs a week, she told him, "I went to the doctor yesterday and he said my whole trouble is that I am eating too many eggs. You don't want me to get sick do you?" Her egg bills went down, the message having been communicated without loss of face to the cook (interview, COH).

58. Jessie Ankeny to family, 4 February 1912, SCUO; Mildred Rowland to family, 9 September 1912, Sarah Goodrich to family, 2 October 1893, Clara Foster, journal for children, 30 May 1916, Elizabeth Perkins to father, 16 June 1908, CRP.

59. Florence Manly to family, 7 June 1899, CRP; Luella Miner to Carrie Miner, 15 May 1889, ABCFM; Ruth White to family, 25 November 1917, CRP; for Chinese as ideal servants, see also Bessie Ewing to cousin Frank, 29 September 1894, ABCFM; Mary Burns, 23 December 1907, DFMC; Goodrich to Carrington, 27 February 1910, CRP.

60. Ewing to Aunt Mira, 26 July 1899, ABCFM; Mrs. Arthur H. [Emma] Smith, "Our Duties to Our Servants," *Chinese Recorder*, September 1902, pp. 445–53; Lida Ashmore to Edith, 3 October 1908, "Extracts," SCUO; for more on relationship between Christian faith and quality of servants, see Evelyn Sites, "A Savior Who Is Christ the Lord," mimeograph, CRP; Jessie Ankeny to Louise, 16 April 1909, SCUO.

61. Ruth White to family, 16 June 1918, CRP.

62. In their acceptance of racial hierarchies, missionary women mirrored trends in other areas of American women's history. The women's suffrage movement, which in the mid-nineteenth century had advocated equal rights for women, by the turn of the century was basing its request for the vote on the need for a genteel influence to counter the dangerous immigrant vote. See Aileen Kraditor, *The Ideas of the Woman Suffrage Movement 1890–1920* (New York: Norton, 1965), and Christopher Lasch, "The Woman Reformer's Rebuke," in Lasch, *The World of Nations* (New York: Random House), pp. 54–55.

63. Alice Tisdale Hobart, *By the City of the Long Sand* (New York: Macmillan, 1926), p. 84; for house as fortress, see also pp. 97, 106, 112.

64. For the Woolson quote, Esther B. Aresty, *The Best Behavior* (New York: Simon & Schuster, 1970), p. 259. There are many analogies between the Southern and the missionary household. Anne Firor Scott, *The Southern Lady: From Pedestal to Politics 1830–1930* (Chicago: University of Chicago Press, 1970), pp. 16, 46, discusses the administrative skill required of planter women and the paternal modes of authority they exercised. Col. Charles Denby compared the Shanghai foreign concession to the antebellum South in terms of both the grace of life and the racial burden (*China and Her People*, pp. 7–8). It could be argued that the seeds for the hierarchical developments of domestic ideology were present from the beginning in Catharine Beecher's thought. Beecher opposed slavery and excoriated its abuses, but her *Essay on Slavery and Abolitionism* accepted the inevitability of human hierarchies (Philadelphia, 1837, p. 98). "It is the grand feature of the Divine economy, that there should be different stations of superiority and subordination," she wrote, "and it is impossible to annihilate this beneficent and immutable law." Although she was here justifying the subordination of women to men, her logic loaned itself to other uses. Her personal decision to remain inactive on the issue of slavery presented fewer inconsistencies than did the silences of earlier architects of American union who proclaimed the equality of all mankind. Kathryn Sklar's *Catharine Beecher: A Study in American Domesticity* (New Haven, Conn.: Yale University Press, 1973) traces the development in Beecher's thought from mid-century egalitarianism to an increasing attraction to hierarchies, perhaps best embodied in Beecher's conversion to Episcopalianism. Sklar's

work on domestic ideology remains the most impressive theoretical framework we have. For Beecher's early emphasis on the separation of the spheres as a counterforce to other social divisions, see pp. 132, 156, 160.

65. Sarah Goodrich to family, 5 June 1891, CRP; Jessie Ankeny to family, 24 October 1911, SCUO; Goodrich to Grace Goodrich, 3 July 1910, CRP. This evidence runs parallel to Eugene Genovese's in *Roll, Jordan, Roll* (New York: Random House, 1976), p. 344, where he argues that while slaves needed masters and mistresses they could depend on, masters and mistresses needed slaves who loved them. Missionaries, too, needed to believe that their servants loved them.

66. Jeanie McClure to family, 15 September 1919, CRP; Lucy Mead to family, 6 August 1910, ABCFM; Lida Ashmore to Edith, 14 November 1915, "Extracts," SCUO; Matilda Thurston to family, 2 November 1913, UBCHE.

67. McClure to family, 13 March 1917, CRP. For evidence of community drinking, see: Sarah Goodrich to family, 12 March 1916; McClure to family, 17 August 1920, Emma Martin to family, 27 December 1910, CRP.

68. Monona Cheney to family, 22 December 1918, SCUO; Goodrich to friends, 31 January 1910, CRP. The intimate connection between moral reform and missionary work can be seen in the opinion expressed by one missionary writer that the American drinking habit was the greatest hindrance to Christian work abroad as well as at home. Mrs. C. W. Scott, "Patriotism a Factor in Missionary Endeavor," *WMF*, April 1903, p. 134.

69. Stuart Creighton Miller, "Ends and Means: Missionary Justification of Force in Nineteenth-Century China," in John K. Fairbank, ed, *The Missionary Enterprise in China and America* (Cambridge, Mass: Harvard University Press, 1974), p. 268; Mrs. J. L. Nevius to Presbyterian Board of Foreign Missions, 5 December 1900, "Calendar."

70. Ellen N. LaMotte, *Peking Dust* (New York: Century, 1919), p. 119; Harriet V. Noyes to Presbyterian Board, 24 December 1895, "Calendar"; Luella Miner, general letter, 24 September 1894, ABCFM; Sarah Goodrich to Emma and Mary, 19 November 1894, Jeanie McClure to family, 11 July 1917, CRP; Edward Said, *Orientalism* (New York: Random House, 1979).

71. For good accounts of missionary involvement in Boxer retaliation, see Miller, "Ends and Means," or Marilyn Blatt Young, *The Rhetoric of Empire* (Cambridge, Mass.: Harvard University Press, 1968). Articles in the *Woman's Missionary Friend* took issue with the news coverage of these episodes and with Mark Twain's essay ("Affairs in China," June 1901, p. 192, March 1901, p. 86.)

72. Emma Martin to family, 12 January 1901; Sarah Conger, *Letters from China* (Chicago: A. C. McClurg, 1909), pp. 176, 188, 189; Young, *Rhetoric of Empire*, p. 88.

73. Lida Ashmore to Edith, 4 January 1908, SCUO; Lucy Mead to family, 27 February 1916, ABCFM.

74. Luella Miner to family, 27 January 1904, ABCFM; Elsie Clark, diary, 5 April 1913, CRP.

75. George Miller, *China Inside Out* (New York: Abington, 1917), p. 21; Roy Chapman Andrews refers to Caldwell as a "he-man" in his introduction to Caldwell's *Blue Tiger* (New York: Abington, 1924); for quotation, see p. 19. Eugene Genovese's evidence that "white ladies" often exercised a mediating force over the harshness of plantation relations supports the idea that genteel feminine values were not simply a matter of style (*Roll, Jordan, Roll*, pp. 81–82).

Chapter 6

1. Laura M. White noted that "we women" were called "Western She-Tigers" ("China in Transition," *WMF*, October 1900, p. 188).

2. Luella Miner, general letter, February 1913, ABCFM; Mary Swail Taft, "Present-Day China," WMF, January 1915, p. 8; Miner, "Higher Education in China," n.d., ABCFM; Sarah Goodrich, "Mary E. Andrews," n.d., CRP.

3. Sarah Goodrich to Grace, 28 January 1908, 5 October 1913, Elsie Clark to family, 18 April 1915, 14 March 1917, CRP; Goodrich also worried about gossip (to mother, 10 January 1895, CRP).

4. Goodrich, "Young Woman's Societies," n.d., CRP.

5. Ella Glover, letters, WMF, December 1917, p. 438; Althea Todd, "A Vacation Letter," WMF, June 1915, p. 194; Mamie Glassburner to "laborers together," 23 July 1914, SCUO; Northeast China Conference Report, "The Day of Opportunity," WMF, February 1913, p. 60.

6. Kate Ogborn, "Itinerating, Wuhu District, 1911–12," printed letter, DFMC.

7. Jessie Ankeny to Henry, 11 October 1911, 5 May 1911, Emma Martin to family, 29 April 1911, Mildred Rowland to family, 26 April 1912, CRP.

8. Monona Cheney to family, 10 September 1922, SCUO.

9. Louise Campbell, diary, 15 April 1913, CRP; Martha Wiley, interview, 1969, COH.

10. Lida Ashmore to Edith, "Extracts," 4 January 1908, 5 March 1905, SCUO.

11. Sarah Goodrich to "Professor Hu," 24 April 1920, to Carrington, 25 April 1920, Evelyn Dewey to Sarah Goodrich, n.d., CRP.

12. Lydia Wilkinson, "May Hu," DFMC; Lucy Mead to family, 19 June 1916, ABCFM.

13. For varying occupations and means of support, see: Lida Ashmore to Edith, "Extracts," 1 December 1912, SCUO; Sarah Goodrich to Carrington, 20 May 1914, Clara Foster to husband's mother, 4 October 1890, CRP; Jessie Ankeny to family, 27 April 1912, SCUO; from "Chinese sister of the Congregational church" to "The church I love in America," 1892, ABCFM; Mrs. Sherwood Eddy, "Days with a Chinese Lady Doctor," The Classmate, 15 July 1916; Goodrich to family, 24 September 1891, CRP.

14. Emily Hartwell, "Story of Beacon Hill Farm Assoication Work," pp. 2–5, CRP; Ashmore to Edith, "Extracts," 25 May 1924, SCUO; Luella Miner, general letter, 4 January 1904, ABCFM; Ankeny to Louise, 24 April 1910, SCUO.

15. Anna Kauffman, candidate papers, Miner to Carrie, 21 February 1893, ABCFM.

16. Rebecca Miller to the Presbyterian Board of Foreign Missions, 12 December 1896, in "Calendar."

17. Sarah Goodrich described the attributes of Julia Pickett: "When Miss Julia beams on the Chinese boys I should suppose she would thrill them through and through, she has such beautiful soft black eyes, eyes that can snap, eyes that can look love" (to family, 6 April 1913, CRP). "Looking love" was a missionary strategy practiced equally by those without beautiful eyes. See Ann Douglas, The Feminization of American Culture (New York: Knopf, 1977).

18. Evelyn Sites, "The Real Essence," n.d., CRP; Paul Johnson, A Shopkeeper's Millennium (New York: Hill & Wang, 1978), pp. 98–99; Ruth White to mother, 6 December 1917, CRP.

19. White to family, 21 January 1918, Sarah Goodrich to Carrington, 1 August 1920, CRP; Lida Ashmore to Edith, "Extracts," 16 February 1919, SCUO; Anna Hartwell to Carrie, notebook, 16 July 1919, 4 June 1907, 1907, CRP.

20. Goodrich to children, 17 August 1914, CRP; Irwin Hyatt, Our Ordered Lives Confess (Cambridge, Mass.: Harvard University Press, 1977), p. 170; Ida Pruitt, personal interview, 18 June 1979.

21. Anna Hartwell wrote that a woman the mission had been praying for four years had finally "yielded her will" (to Leila Watson, notebook, 25 October 1919, CRP); Luella Huelster, "Following the Gleam," WMF, June 1913, p. 194.

22. Luella Miner, general letter, 5 April 1909, ABCFM; Matilda Thurston to family, 15 February 1914, UBCHE; Anna Hartwell was of the "sentimental" school of evangelists and relayed the sick woman's story as a beautiful example of spiritual transcendance (to Brother Willingham, 22 October 1895, CRP).

23. For material on the feminization of the teaching profession, see R. S. Sugg, Jr., "Pedagogy of Love," *Virginia Quarterly Review* (Summer 1978): 411–26; Lucy Mead to family, 11 June 1912, ABCFM; Ruth White to family, 5 May 1919, CRP; Alice Reed, interview, 1969, COH; White to family, 4 November 1917, CRP.

24. Lulu Golisch to Jessie Ankeny, 25 July 1910, SCUO; Frederica Mead to family, 13 October 1918, CRP.

25. Alice Reed, interview, COH; Matilda Thurston to family, 13 December, UBCHE; Monona Cheney to family, 3 November 1919, CRP. For other accounts of unresponsive students, see: Louise Campbell, diary, 30 March 1914, Elizabeth Perkins to family, 9 November 1913, CRP; Alice Browne to Mount Holyoke, 23 March 1907, ABCFM.

26. Ruth White to family, 28 April 1918, Elsie Clark, diary, 9 May 1913, CRP; Monona Cheney to family, 4 September 1920, SCUO; Clark, diary, 10 April 1914, Clara Foster to husband's parents, 7 August 1889, CRP.

27. Alice Reed to family, 10 April 1917, CRP; Agnes Scott, interview, 1969, COH; Luella Miner to mother, 3 May 1894, ABCFM; Frederica Mead to family, 17 October 1915, CRP.

28. Florence B. Manly, diary, 9 March 1898, CRP; Lucy Mead to family, 4 April 1916, ABCFM.

29. Jessie Ankeny to Helen, 1 May 1909, to dear ones, 20 June 1909, SCUO.

30. Luella Miner to family, 15 June 1890, to father, 30 September 1892, ABCFM; Margaret Campbell Burket to Dorothy Campbell, 16 January 1917, CRP. Sydney Forsythe's sociological study of the American Board in North China at the turn of the century concludes that single women followed married women as the most "mission-centric" members of the mission community. It concludes that men were the most knowledgeable about Chinese society. A knowledge of public affairs could and did frequently coexist for missionary men with a largely foreign social existence. Single women were less likely to be well-schooled in Chinese subjects, but more likely to count their closest relationships within the Chinese community. *An American Missionary Community in China, 1895–1905* (Cambridge, Mass.: East Asian Research Center, Harvard University, 1971).

31. Jessie Ankeny to family, 11 January 1913, SCUO.

32. [Louise] Johnston, 23 July 1894, "Calendar"; Agnes Scott on Martha Wiley, interview, 1972, COH; "Lucy Hoag," memorial, DFMC; Dorothy Campbell, "Writing," n.d., CRP; Luella Miner to mother, 30 December 1904, ABCFM; Irma Davis, "Edna Terry," n.d., "Martha Lebeus," biographical material, DFMC; on Lora Dyer, see Mildred Rowland, 13 June 1912, CRP. For additional material on single women who took China as their world: on Lida Trimble, Elsie Clark to family, 13 January 1917, CRP; Miner to Carrie, 28 May 1891, ABCFM.

33. [Mary Porter Gamewell, obituary], "A Beautiful Life," *WMF*, February 1907, p. 47; Alice Browne to Mount Holyoke, 10 October 1906, ABCFM. Methodist Welthy Honsinger's adoption of "Precious Pearl," for instance, prompted an angry protest from the Methodist board (personal interview, 20 October 1978). The practice of childhood adoption of girls was the norm in at least some Chinese cultures. Arthur Wolf reports that in several districts on Taiwan in the early twentieth century, 70 percent of all daughters would have been given out in adoption, customarily into the families of their future husbands. "The Women of Hai-shen," in Margery Wolf and Roxane Witke, eds., *Women in Chinese Society* (Stanford, Calif.: Stanford University Press, 1975), p. 95.

34. Jessie Ankeny to family, 18 June 1911, April 1911, 8 January 1911, SCUO; W. E. Manly to family, 6 April 1894, CRP. For circumstances of children before adoption, see: Luella Miner to Edith, 14 February 1895, ABCFM; Frances Hitchcock, *WMF*, September 1906, p. 329; untitled article, *WMF*, May 1908, p. 188; Agnes Edmonds, *WMF*, November 1919, p. 322; Ruth V. Hemenway, M.D., *A Memoir of Revolutionary China, 1924–1941* (Amherst: University of Massachusetts Press, 1977), p. 71. For individual provisions for children's schooling, see Irma Davis, "Edna Terry," memorial, 30 September 1912, ABCFM.

35. Bessie Ewing to Aunt Mira, 28 August 1897, 19 March 1896, 14 June 1900, 23 July 1900, ABCFM; Hemenway, *Memoir*, p. 129.

36. Emma Martin to family, 3 February 1901, Mildred Rowland to family, 11 May 1912, CRP.

37. Ida Lewis to mama and papa, [1912?], SCUO; Luella Miner to Alice Frame, 9 May 1919, Myra Sawyer, "Little Devil," story, 1925, ABCFM.

38. Katherine Boeye, "Anna Lulu Golisch," n.d., DFMC.

39. Fletcher Brockman, "A Daughter of Confucius," *Christian Advocate*, 15 October 1914, p. 11, "The Story of Dr. Kahn and Her Adoption by an American," newspaper clipping, both DFMC.

40. Bessie Merrill, "Adventures in Faith under Ida Kahn," DFMC; Evelyn Riley Nicholson, "Coronation," *WMF*, April 1929; Mary Stone, "Miss Gertrude Howe," pamphlet, DFMC.

41. Stone, "Miss Gertrude Howe," DFMC; Liang Ch'i-chao, "Chi Chiang-hsi K'ang nu-shih" [Miss K'ang of Kiangsi] in *Yin-ping shih ho-chi* (Shanghai: Chung-hau shu-chu, 1932), 1:1, 119. When Kahn and Stone returned to Kiukiang, Stone wrote, "Miss Howe left the beautiful home to the mission and came to live in a little Chinese home she built for us out of her own money" ("Kiangsi People Honor Gertrude Howe in Death," DFMC). Experienced missionaries made no secret of the fact that they considered their converts partly in terms of their money-raising potential. Ida Lewis wrote of another adoption which was likely to be profitable "Cant you see the great appeal Miss Hughes can make with this girl?" (to mother, 29 April 1922, SCUO).

42. The story of the relationship of Methodist missionary Nora Dillenbeck to her convert Ching T'un-ying in the 1920s and 1930s demonstrates that as political balances changed, interpersonal relations were likely to take different forms as well. Ching had been a Buddhist before Dillenbeck converted him to Christianity while he was teaching her Chinese. For a while a dutiful convert in the Methodist hierarchy, in 1922 Ching left the Methodist church and founded his own fundamentalist sect, known as the "Yeh-su chia-t'ing" or the Family of Jesus. His sect preached communal living, the distribution of property, and the simple life. Nora Dillenbeck increasingly came under its sway. In an age of liberalization, she refused to teach anything but the Bible and disregarded the curricular requirements made by the board. According to a letter from a fellow missionary at the time of her death, she said "that she had her orders from God and did not need to listen to others. The loud weeping and shouting in their meetings was like a Chinese funeral." Dillenbeck eventually withdrew from the Methodist board and moved to the communal "Yeh-su chia-t'ing," where she lived for two years before falling ill and dying. Dillenbeck's surrender demonstrated that cultural compromises did not always leave the balance of power with the West. Theodore Romig, "Yeh-su chia-t'ing," *Missionary Research Library Occasional Bulletin*, no. 11 (23 October 1950); Perry Hanson to Methodist Board of Foreign Missions, 27 July 1938, DFMC.

43. Luella Miner to family, 28 March 1891; "Relationship of Chinese Workers and Missionaries," n.d., both ABCFM; Sarah Goodrich to Carrington Goodrich, 9 July 1913.

44. Anna Hartwell to Jane Lide, 4 February 1920, notebook, CRP. This same argument was sometimes used in regard to adoptions. "It is never very wise in China to take a Chinese child into a foreigner's home because of the jealousy it is liable to stir up in the hearts of those whose Christian development has not yet reached the point of perfect charity," Clara Dyer wrote in "The Story of Golden Pearl," WMF, August 1913, p. 310.

45. Jessie Ankeny to Louise, 5 July 1910, to Henry, 9 June 1909, to Louise, 5 July 1910, to family, 24 February 1911, to family, 21 June 1910, to mother, 5 January 1910, SCUO. Althea Todd lived alone in a provincial city for three years at the turn of the century, but "a precious little Bible woman was with me," she wrote (DFMC).

46. Ankeny to mother, 20 April 1912, to Florence, 2 December 1911, to mother, 11 March 1911, SCUO.

47. Ankeny to family, 22 January 1910, 23 January 1911, SCUO.

48. Ankeny to family, 15 April 1910, fragment [fall 1912?], to mother, 2 December 1910, to father, 13 December 1910, SCUO.

49. Ankeny to mother, 27 September 1912, 25 March 1910, to family, 20 January 1912, Ding Miduang to Mrs. Ankeny [Mama], September 1912, Jessie Ankeny Lacy, fragment [1914?], SCUO.

50. Ankeny to family, 15 April 1910, CRP.

51. Louise Campbell, diary, 16, 20, 21, 22, 26 April 1916, 12 March 1916, 8 February 1920, 19 November 1920, CRP.

52. Campbell, diary, 15, 23 May, 18 June, 2 November 1916, 13 May 1921, 18 October 1921, CRP.

53. Campbell, diary, 1 July, 1 September 1916, Margaret Campbell Burket to Dorothy Campbell, 16 January 1917, Louise Campbell, diary, 23 May 1919, 26 July 1920, 15 November 1916, CRP.

54. Lucy Mead to family, 30 November 1909, ABCFM; Ruth White to family, 13 September 1917, CRP; Alice Browne to Mount Holyoke, 24 November 1905, ABCFM; Elsie Clark to Anabel, 18 January 1913, CRP.

55. Clark to family, 27 February 1913, diary, 21 October 1913, CRP; Monona Cheney, general letter, 8 January 1919, SCUO.

56. Ruth White to family, 13 September 1917, Mildred Rowland to family, 25 April 1912, Sarah Goodrich to family, 3 October 1898, CRP; Mary Carleton, letter, WMF, February 1915, p. 67; Rowland to family, 9 June 1914, Elizabeth Perkins, scrapbook, n.d., CRP.

57. White to family, 16 June 1918, CRP; Jessie Ankeny to "kids," 26 January 1909, SCUO; Hemenway, Memoir, p. 45; Ida Lewis to Standard Bearers, "Notes from Tientsin," 20 March 1915, SCUO; Luella Miner to mother, 21 August 1889, ABCFM.

58. Miner to family, 30 May 1889, ABCFM; Elsie Clark to family 3 August 1913, Alice Reed to family, 10 April 1917, CRP.

59. Nina Stollings, personal interview, 18 May 1978; Florence Manly, diary, 21 July 1898, CRP. In the later period of the Second World War, Grace Boynton arranged for a university student to serve as an interpreter for the American fliers stationed in western China. She told a journalist of her reservations about how her "modest, quiet student, formal in manner and elegant in tastes," would get along with "my he-man compatriots," ([interview with Grace Boynton], Dorothy Cushing, "Medford Woman Aids 'Flying Tigers' in Free China," Boston Sunday Post, 7 June 1942, ABCFM).

Agnes Smedley, who covered the early stages of the Chinese revolution in Yenan from a sympathetic viewpoint, revealed the two sides to Western women's attitudes. Smedley was a feminist and an acute observer of the suffering within many Western marriages. She appreciated her anomalous role as a Westerner in China and her ability to be "good friends" with Chinese patrician intellectuals. "To them I was not man, woman, concubine, or courtesan. I was a foreigner who was no longer young, was not beautiful, earned her own living, and associated with men as an equal. Neither wifehood nor love was my profession." But at the same time Smedley had a visceral negative reaction to Chinese manhood. Her description of her first meeting with Mao focused on a disconcerning femininity. His voice was "high-pitched," his hands "as long and sensitive as a woman's," his mouth "feminine." "Whatever else he might be, he was an aesthete. I was in fact repelled by the feminine in him and by the gloom of the setting." Despite herself, she missed the Western chivalry in male-female relations, as she confessed to a friend in 1939. "Though I have never liked to be treated as bourgeois women are treated, still the foreign men from England, America, and perhaps France, have a deep and unconscious attitude of protection for women; of helping a woman; and a kind of gentleness toward her. Often this kindness blended a bit with tenderness or a breath of romance. It is difficult to explain, because it is there as an atmosphere. In the Chinese man this is totally lacking in all respects. There is not even friendship and comradeship between man and woman in China. The foreign word 'romance' has been taken into the Chinese language and means promiscuous sexual relations. . . . For a Chinese man to even touch a woman's arm or hand means something sexual and arouses shock." To be treated as an equal meant not to be treated as a woman; the mediation offered by Western chivalry exerted a pull on even such a staunch revolutionary as Agnes Smedley. *The Battle Hymn of China* (New York: Knopf, 1943, p. 52; letter to Freda Utley, June 1939, quoted in Jan Mackinnon and Steve Mackinnon, introduction to Smedley, *Portraits of Chinese Women in Revolution* (Old Westbury, N.Y.: Feminist Press, 1976), p. xxix.) See also Susan Sontag, *Trip to Hanoi* (New York: Farrar, Straus and Giroux, 1969), for a fascinating contemporary analysis along similar lines.

60. Sarah Goodrich to Waumatosa Sunday School, 10 November 1894, Alice Reed to family, 10 April 1917, Ruth White to family, 3 February 1918, CRP.

61. White to family, 24 February 1918, Luella Miner, "The Relationships of Chinese Workers and Missionaries," ABCFM. On Miner's admiration for Chinese morality and Chinese male-female etiquette, see also: general letter, 27 July 1905; "The Chinese Education of Christian Women," printed pamphlet; general letter, 22 September 1905; "Higher Education in China," n.d. [1915 or 1916?] letter to family and Alice Frame, 3 October 1920, ABCFM.

62. Miner to mother, 8 July, 22 October 1888, ABCFM.

63. Alice Reed to family, 22 April 1917, Jeanie McClure to family, 27 April 1919, CRP; Monona Cheney to family, 21 July 1919, SCUO; "First Experiences in China," WMF, December 1918, p. 425.

64. Miner to mother, 22 October 1888, ABCFM; Sarah Goodrich to "Mary," 10 November 1894, Elsie Clark to family, 22 July 1917, Ruth White to family, 17 March 1918, CRP. For more on safety in China, see: Evelyn Sites, "A Savior Who Is Christ the Lord," n.d., mimeo, Alice Alsup to family, 4 December [1920?], CRP.

65. For absence of drunks, see: Alice Reed to family, 23 October 1916, Jeanie McClure to family, 26 January 1916, Clark to family, 10 February 1916, 14 April 1913, 10 February 1916, CRP; on nudity, Clara Foster, journal, 4 May 1916, CRP. Jonathan Spence suggests that opium smoking "for Chinese humiliated by their positions under barbarian conquerers, [may] have been a surrogate for withdrawal, a form of erematism in one's own home" "Opium Smoking in Ch'ing China," in Frederic Wakeman, ed., *Conflict and Control in Late Imperial China* (Berkeley: University of California Press, 1975), p. 143.

66. For examples of travels accompanied only by a Chinese man, see: J. Nellie Nevitt, testimonial about Edna Jones, 2 September 1965, DFMC; Luella Miner, "Relationship of Chinese Workers and Missionaries," n.d., to family, 4 July 1889, ABCFM; Jessie Ankeny

to family, 12 December 1910, CRP; Lucy Mead to family, 13 April 1912, ABCFM; Sarah Goodrich to Carrington, 28 September 1913, CRP.

67. Ruth White to family, 9 September 1917, CRP.

68. Luella Miner to Carrie, 26 July 1894, ABCFM; Elizabeth Perkins to family, 23 January 1915, 16 January 1908, CRP; Miner to family, 13 December 1914, ABCFM.

69. Ida Pruitt, *Chinese Childhood* (San Francisco: China Materials Center, 1978), p. 95.

70. Clara Foster, journal, 13 March 1916, Elsie Clark, diary, 21 December 1912, CRP; Jessie Ankeny to father, 22 February 1910, SCUO; Gertrude Wyckoff, "How the Battle Went at Lintsing," ABCFM. For other episodes of gender confusion, see: Pruitt, *Chinese Childhood*, p. 180; Hemenway, *Memoir*, p. 40; Louise Campbell, tape transcript, p. 2, CRP.

71. W. Edward Manly to "Manly family budget," 16 February 1893, CRP; "Why One Wife," *WMF*, April 1913, p. 135.

72. Luella Miner to family, 9 January 1900, to Carrie, 13 January 1890, ABCFM.

73. Mary Seely White, an early missionary to Foochow, wrote, "it is evident that I am 'the elephant' with these people, being the first foreign female . . . they have ever seen." Ellsworth C. Carlson, *The Foochow Missionaries, 1847–1880* (Cambridge, Mass.: Harvard University Press, 1974), p. 18.

74. Monona Cheney to family, November 1919, 4 September 1920, SCUO; Inez Marks, *WMF*, June 1918, p. 221; Mary Gamewell, "History of the Methodist Peking Work," p. 13, CRP.

75. Elizabeth Perkins to family, 11 December 1907, CRP; Alice Browne to Mount Holyoke, 13 August 1909, ABCFM.

76. Luella Miner to Hayward Ladies Missionary Society, 5 March 1888, ABCFM; Elizabeth Perkins to family, 23 October 1909, CRP; Marjorie Steurt, interview, 1970, COH; Jessie Ankeny to family, 1 January 1910, SCUO.

77. Alice Browne to Mount Holyoke, 25 October 1909, Miner, general letter, 3 November 1899, Lucy Mead to family, 28 September 1910, ABCFM.

78. Lida Ashmore to Edith Ashmore, 23 August 1905, 12 March 1898, SCUO; Mead to family, 24 June 1912, 12 January 1916, ABCFM; Louise Stanley, interview, 1971, COH; Dorothy Campbell, autobiographical sketch, Elizabeth Perkins to family, 15 July 1908, CRP; Jessie Ankeny to family, 1 March 1909, 23 January 1911, SCUO.

79. Christine Pickett, *From the Rising of the Sun* (Frankfurt, Ohio: Privately printed, 1978), p. 12; Welthy Honsinger, *Beyond the Moon Gate* (New York: Abington, 1924), p. 141; Mead to family, 16 September 1912, ABCFM.

80. Jessie Ankeny to family, 5 March 1910, to mama, 7 April 1911, to family, 7 March 1912, SCUO; Dorothy Campbell, writings on family, n.d., CRP.

81. Lida Ashmore to Edith, "Extracts," 5 October 1897, 11 March 1899, 3 January 1898, SCUO; Louise Stanley, interview, COH; Lucy Lee, "An American Sojourn in China," memoirs, CRP.

82. Jessie Ankeny to family, 31 January 1909, SCUO; Lucy Mead to family, 24 March 1910, ABCFM; Stanley, interview, COH.

83. Elsie Clark to family, 22 July 1917, CRP; Mead to family, 5 May 1912, ABCFM; Hyatt, *Ordered Lives*, p. 105.

84. Monona Cheney to family, 26 October 1918, SCUO; Marjorie Steurt, interview, COH; Clark to family, 15 October 1916, to Andrew Krug, 31 December 1916, CRP.

85. Florence Manly, diary, 1 April 1895, Alice Alsup to family, 23 October 1919, CRP.

86. Alice Brethorst, "The Voyage of the Twenty-Seven," *WMF*, March 1914, p. 86; *Kiukiang Register*, [Ellen Lyon], 1919, DFMC; Edward Bliss, "Yankee in Fu-kien," newspaper clipping, ABCFM; Louise Campbell, diary, 20 July 1913, CRP.

87. Emma Smith, recollection of 50th wedding anniversary, ABCFM; Margaretta A. Karr, "China," *WMF*, May 1902, p. 156; Lizzie Martin to family, 8 January 1905, CRP.

88. Pearl Buck, *The Fighting Angel* (New York: John Day, 1936), p. 118; Edward Said, *Orientalism* (New York: Random, 1979), pp. 92, 146, 182; Han Su-yin, *A Mortal Flower* (New York: Putnam's, 1965), pp. 216–17.

89. "After a Year's Experience," *WMF*, November 1911, p. 398.

Chapter 7

1. John D. Durand, "Population Statistics of China," *Population Studies* 13 (March 1960): 247.

2. Chin Ai-li, "Mainland China," in Raphael Patai, ed., *Women in the Modern World* (New York: Free Press, 1967), p. 418.

3. Anna Hartwell to "Evangeline," 25 April 1895, CRP.

4. Emily M. Ahern, "The Power and Pollution of Chinese Women," in *Women in Chinese Society*, ed. Margery Wolf and Roxane Witke (Stanford, Calif.: Stanford University Press, 1975), p. 206; Marjorie Topley, "Marriage Resistance in Rural Kwangtung," describes the extreme case, in which all women who had given birth were consigned to hell (in Wolf and Witke, p. 75). For women of Confucian gentry, see H. H. Ts'ui, Biographical file, ABCFM. Ts'ui wrote: "My grandfather and father were Confucian scholars but my grandmother and mother were ardent Buddhists. My grandmother chanted as many as 7,000 passages of Buddhist scriptures in a year." Helena Kuo, *I've Come A Long Way* (New York: Appleton-Century, 1942), p. 22, also noted that her father was a Confucian, interested in progressive education, her mother "a devout Buddhist."

5. Adrian A. Bennett and Kwang-Ching Liu, "Christianity in the Chinese Idiom: Young J. Allen and the Early *Chiao-hui hsin-pao*, 1868–1870," in John K. Fairbank, ed., *The Missionary Enterprise in China and America* (Cambridge, Mass: Harvard University Press, 1974), p. 167.

6. Elsie Clark to family, 22 May 1915, CRP; newspaper clipping, Minneapolis, October 1906, in Grace Howe, DFMC.

7. Alice Reed to family, 8 June 1919, CRP; personal interview with Christine Hubbard Pickett, Hamden, Conn., 27 February 1979. Maxine Hong Kingston's contemporary tale of her mother's battles with the Taoist Fox Spirit took place while her mother was a student at Hackett Medical School, a Presbyterian missionary school. Although this episode may have been fictionalized, the relationship of her mission-trained mother with ghosts undoubtedly was not. *Woman Warrior: Memoirs of a Girlhood among Ghosts* (New York: Knopf, 1975), pp. 64–65.

8. Margery Wolf, "Women and Suicide in China," in Wolf and Witke, eds., *Women in Chinese Society*, p. 112; Elizabeth Perkins to family, 21 October 1907, CRP.

9. Luella Miner, general letter, 4 September 1905, 10 July 1920, ABCFM; Buwei Chao, *Autobiography of a Chinese Woman*, as told to Yeunren Chao (New York: John Day, 1947), p. 62; Fletcher Brockman, "A Daughter of Confucius," *Christian Advocate*, 15 October 1914, p. 11, DFMC.

10. Ida Lewis, "Bits from Days in Tientsin," n.d., SCUO; Soumay Tcheng [Cheng Yu-hsiu, Mme. Wei Tao-ming], *A Girl from China*, as told to Bessie VanVorst (New York: Fred A. Stokes, 1926), pp. 77–79; Tsai Ling-fang was not allowed to board at a Presbyterian school in Nanking because of the coarse food, student work requirement, and poverty of the student body. Instead she enrolled as a day student. Later Tsai went to Soochow to Laura Haygood School, run "especially for girls from wealthy homes, so better food and service

were provided," Christiana Tsai [Tsai Ling-fang], *Queen of the Dark Chamber*, as told to Ellen L. Drummond (Chicago: Moody Press, 1953), p. 53.

11. *WMF*, November 1916, p. 393.

12. Tsai, *Queen*; Huang Lu-yin [Huang Ying], *Tzu chuan* [Autobiography] (Shanghai: First Publishing Co., 1934); Tseng Pao-sun, *Hui-i lu* [Memoirs] (Hong Kong: Chinese Christian Literature Council, 1970).

13. Tsai, *Queen*, pp. 15, 33, 35.

14. Ibid., pp. 54–57.

15. Ibid., pp. 54–55, 57–59.

16. Ibid., pp. 64–66. Between 1914 and 1920 Tsai traveled around China preaching and interpreting for such evangelists as Ruth Paxson, a frequent visitor to mission stations. Tsai's health deteriorated during subsequent years and she became bedridden in 1931 and increasingly blind. She lived with Mary Leaman of the Presbyterian women's board during these years, returning with her to the United States in 1949. Since Leaman's death in 1970, Tsai has continued to live in Pennsylvania, pursuing her relentless evangelism by correspondence. The Moody Bible Institute has published thirty-six editions of *Queen of the Dark Chamber* since 1953, and in 1978 published another volume of Tsai's memoirs, *Christiana Tsai* (Chicago: Moody Press).

17. Huang, *Tzu chuan*, p. 16.

18. Ibid., p. 17. The food seemed often to be an affliction. Helena Kuo, *I've Come A Long Way* (New York: Appleton-Century, 1942), p. 59, remembered that the watery rice and tasteless side dishes contributed to her initial unhappiness at Lingnan, a Christian college in Canton. "Having always respected my stomach as an essential part of my well-being, I hated to have it ill-treated."

19. Huang, *Tzu chuan*, pp. 26–28.

20. Ibid., p. 28.

21. Ibid., pp. 28–31. Huang's life began to gather momentum from that time forward. She attended school from 1912 to 1917, thereafter teaching for a few years prior to enrolling at a Peking normal school in 1919 in time for the May 4 movement. By then she had completely lost the habits of shyness which accompanied her earlier life, because soon after her arrival she was elected head of the student association. During the 1920s she was active in various reform movements, including James Yen's literacy campaign. At this same time she began to write increasingly popular novels, often about women in a changing China. She was married twice and in 1934 died at the age of thirty-seven in childbirth. Her autobiography was published the same year. For biographical material on Huang, see Howard L. Boorman, ed., *Biographical Dictionary of Republican China* (New York: Columbia University Press, 1970).

22. Tseng, *Hui-i-lu*, pp. 26–27.

23. Ibid., p. 33.

24. Ibid., pp. 32–34.

25. Ibid., pp. 34–36.

26. Y. T. Zee [Mrs. Way-sung New], personal letter, 26 July 1978.

27. Hsieh Pingying, *Girl Rebel: The Autobiography of Hsieh Pingying*, trans. Adet and Anor Lin (New York: John Day, 1940), p. 41. Jessie Ankeny wrote home about Chinese students' "great sense of respect for their Superiors. If they are corrected they nearly always come and apologize afterwards" (to father, 30 April 1910, SCUO).

28. Tsai, *Queen*, p. 15.

29. Chao, *Autobiography*, p. 75; Hsieh, *Girl Rebel*, pp. 30, 33; Alice Reed, interview, COH. Huang Lu-yin was one who did not make friends during her Christian school years,

perhaps because she was younger than the other students, perhaps because of the class differences between her and other students.

30. Elsie Clark to family, 20 November 1916, 4 June 1916, CRP; "Student Work," WMF, March 1919, p. 97.

31. *The Pioneer* (Shanghai: Presbyterian Mission Press, 1919), pp. 20–21, UBCHE; Matilda Thurston and Ruth Chester, *Ginling College* (New York: United Board of Christian Colleges in China, 1955), p. 20.

32. Jessie Lutz, *China and the Christian Colleges 1850–1950* (Ithaca, N.Y.: Cornell University Press, 1971), pp. 170–73; Alice Reed to family, 25 January 1920, CRP, interview, 1969, COH.

33. Lucy Mead to family, 12 October 1915, ABCFM; Thurston and Chester, *Ginling*, p. 31. Y. T. Zee noted that the May 4 movement caused a temporary rift between the Western faculty and the student body at Ginling: "We also wanted to join the outside students movement in spirit, but not in a negative way. . . . Wu Yi Fang and I proposed to join one march to petition the Government not to recognize the three traitors treaty but to punish them." Eventually, however, the faculty "gave us sympathetic support, and respected our proposals and trusted us," Zee recalled (personal letter, 26 July 1978).

34. *The Pioneer*, p. 22; Elsie Sites, letter, WMF, November 1908, p. 417; Mary Ninde Gamewell, WMF, August 1913, p. 273; Carol Chen, "Progressive Education in the Days of Old: Hwa Nan College, 1915–1918," *World Outlook*, November 1947, in Elsie Clark [Krug] Papers, CRP.

35. Luella Miner to family, 15 February 1916, ABCFM; Y. T. Zee, personal letter, 26 July 1978; Ida Belle Lewis, *The Education of Girls in China* (New York: Teacher's College, Columbia University Press, 1919), p. 54; Alice Reed, interview, COH.

36. Y. T. Zee, personal letter, 26 July 1978, Carol Chen, "Progressive Education," CRP.

37. Luella Miner to family, 15 February 1916, ABCFM; Thurston and Chester, *Ginling*, p. 76; Elsie Clark to family, 28 February 1917, CRP. Charlotte Beahan, "The Women's Movement and Nationalism in Late Ch'ing China" (Ph.D. diss., Columbia University, 1976), p. 60, argues the significance of the missionary role model to Chinese women.

38. "May Hu," *Missionaries of the Des Moines Branch* (printed pamphlet), p. 123; Maude Wheeler, "Here and There; Now and Then" (typed MS), DFMC; Y. T. Zee, personal interview, Saint Petersburg, Fla., 25 May 1978; Zee, personal letter, 26 July 1978.

39. Luella Miner to Mrs. Clark, Woman's Board, 14 January 1921, 12 July 1921, general letter, 17 March 1920, ABCFM; Frederica Mead, untitled essay, 1919, CRP; Y. T. Zee, personal interview, 25 May 1978.

40. Luella Miner to Stella (sister), 15 May 1921, ABCFM; Thurston and Chester, *Ginling*, p. 70; Y. T. Zee to Mary Lou Dixon, 16 March 1974, biography, p. 32, CRP. Hsieh Pingying's autobiography substantiates that this attitude was not limited to mission students and in fact was a feature of much nationalist thinking in the 1920s. "To those who are willing to devote their lives to the people and who have a firm faith in their social mission, love is only a little game for the rich sons and daughters of the leisure class" (*Girl Rebel*, p. 74).

41. Thurston and Chester, *Ginling*, pp. 70–71. The experience at Yenching was perhaps even more bitter. Grace Boynton saw the union as a bitter experience for the women, particularly under the presidency of Leighton Stuart. She reported that Luella Miner, who became the first dean under the merger, was forced to resign. Alice Frame, her successor, was said to have suffered a nervous breakdown in her "effort to get Leighton to observe the conditions of the merger" (Philip West, *Yenching University and Sino-Western Relations*,

1916–1952 [Cambridge, Mass.: Harvard University Press, 1976], pp. 129–130). Men students at Yenching also protested the independent posture of the women's college. According to Boynton, the "anger of excitable men students against the 'proud Women's College' subjected the Dean [Alice Browne Frame] to cruel attacks. Some reached the threat of personal violence" MS, ABCFM.

42. Luella Miner, "Social gospel," misc. notes, [1935?], ABCFM. The exact circumstances of the Ting appointment are unclear. Sarah Goodrich wrote to Luella Miner: "Many of us were aghast at the wrong we felt was being done to place Miss Ting in a position for which she was not qualified. Surely there was no attempt to discover the opinion of those who know the inner workings of the Academy" (28 May 1916, CRP). Lucy Mead wrote home that there was a crisis over whether Jessie Payne or Ting Shu-ching would be the head of Bridgman. "We never thot of their putting in a Chinese, but she would be only a figure head, so 'twould be all right in that way" (25 May 1916, ABCFM). Miner appears to have had doubts about Payne's qualifications, but little is clear about the nature of her support for Ting. See letters to Sarah Goodrich, [May?] 1916, 29 July 1914, in Goodrich Papers, CRP; Miner to family, 10 October 1917, ABCFM.

43. *The Pioneer,* p. 27; Y. T. Zee, personal letter, 26 July 1978.

44. Zee, personal letter.

45. One article about a mission school gathering in China is Thomas B. Gold, "The Shanghai-Ming Hsien Connection," *Oberlin Alumni Magazine,* Autumn 1980, pp. 9–10. For a biography of Wu Yi-fang, see Boorman, ed., *Biographical Dictionary.*

Afterword

1. Ida Kahn, M.D. [K'ang Cheng], *An Amazon in Cathay* (Boston: Woman's Foreign Missionary Society, 1912), DFMC.

2. Mary Rankin, "The Emergence of Women at the End of the Ch'ing: The Case of Ch'iu Chin," in Margery Wolf and Roxane Witke, eds., *Women in Chinese Society* (Stanford, Calif.: Stanford University Press, 1975), p. 52; Roxane H. Witke, "Transformation of Attitudes Towards Women during the May 4th Era of Modern China" (Ph.D. diss., University of California, Berkeley, 1970), pp. 14–15, 45–46, 62–64, 143.

3. Ning Lao T'ai-t'ai, *A Daughter of Han: The Autobiography of a Chinese Working Woman,* as told to Ida Pruitt (Stanford, Calif.: Stanford University Press, 1967), p. 55. Ning said, "Day after day I sat at home. Hunger gnawed. What could I do? My mother was dead. My brother had gone away. When my husband brought home food I ate it and my children ate with me. A woman could not go out of the court. If a woman went out to service the neighbors all laughed. . . . I did not know enough even to beg. So I sat at home and starved. I was so hungry one day that I took a brick, pounded it to bits, and ate it. It made me feel better."

4. Buwei Chao, *Autobiography of a Chinese Woman,* as told to Yeunren Chao (New York: John Day, 1947), pp. 32–34; Mme. Wei Tao-ming [Soumay Tcheng, Cheng Yu-hsiu], *My Revolutionary Years: The Autobiography of Madame Wei Tao-Ming* (New York: Scribner's 1943), p. 15; Soumay Tcheng [Cheng Yu-hsiu, Mme. Wei Tao-ming], *A Girl from China,* as told to Bessie VanVorst (New York: Fred A. Stokes, 1926), p. 50; Ella Shaw, "Autobiography," CRP.

5. Chao, *Autobiography,* p. 45; Luella Miner to family, 19 January, 1907, 2 March, 1907, ABCFM; Sarah Goodrich to Grace and Carrington Goodrich, 1910, CRP.

6. These terms might be considered analogues to Francis Hsu's "individual-centered" and "situation-centered" cultural types. Hsu argues that Chinese culture expects people to act according to the demands of the situation they find themselves in; American culture expects people to act on the basis of their inherent, individual characteristics, of which sex

is one of the most significant. As Hsu put it, "for Americans, sex differences tend to overshadow situation. For Chinese, situation tends to overshadow sex." *Americans and Chinese: Reflections on Two Cultures* (Garden City, N.Y.: Natural History Press, 1970), pp. 10–11, 56. This discussion is indebted to Hsu's original formulation but attempts to place it within a more specific historical context.

7. Alice Reed to family, 27 May 1917, CRP; Reed, interview, 1969, COH; Charlotte Jewell, letter, *WMF*, May 1910, p. 158; Lucy Mead to family, 21 January 1910, ABCFM. Missionary Elsie Clark was one woman who did enjoy public speaking, but she was pronounced "queer" and "odd" by her fellows for this taste (see chap. 3).

8. Jessie Ankeny to Homer, 6 May 1909, to mother, 30 December 1910, SCUO; Elsie Clark to family, 1 May 1917, CRP; Luella Miner to family, 31 December 1909, ABCFM. For more descriptions of Chinese acting ability, see: Dr. O. L. Baldwin, *Light and Life*, January 1899, p. 21; Miner to Edith, 7 May 1898, to family, 11 February 1904, Bessie Ewing to family, February 1899, Lucy Mead to family, 26 December 1909, 14 May 1910, 13 January 1914, 4 June 1916, ABCFM; Sarah Goodrich to Grace, 1 August 1915, CRP; Monona Cheney to family, 5 October 1918, SCUO; Clark, diary, 4 June 1913, [letter to family, 11 October 1915], Jeanie McClure to family, 11 November 1917, 19 May 1917, CRP.

9. Jessie Ankeny to Homer, 16 May 1909; Alice Reed mentioned this statement of a friend, interview, 1969, COH.

10. This discussion of emotional etiquette in evangelical culture is indebted to Karen Halttunen, *Confidence Men and Painted Women: A Study of Middle-Class Culture in America, 1830–1870* (New Haven, Conn.: Yale University Press, 1982). Halttunen argues that in late Victorian America a bourgeois culture came to terms with the inherent theatricality of social life and no longer felt the same obsessive concern about hypocrisy felt by midcentury evangelicals. In contrast with Chinese, however, American evangelicals at the turn of the century were still particularly concerned with congruence between self and demeanor.

11. Nancy Chodorow's theory of the learning of male and female role behavior is interesting here. Girls have traditionally grown up without having to make the radical break from identification with mother that boys have to make, she argues. For them, gender has not been a role, but the only conceivable mode of action. But because fathers have generally been away, boys usually have come to gender identity without a constant, personalized male model. They therefore have had to break with their mother and adopt an abstract role which they frequently have not identified with emotionally ("Family Structure and Feminine Personality," in Michelle Zimbalist Rosaldo and Louise Lamphere, eds., *Women, Culture and Society* [Stanford, Calif.: Stanford University Press, 1974], pp. 43–66). This theory of role behavior might even indicate, within evangelical culture, a greater role flexibility among men than among women.

12. Rankin, "Emergence of Women," pp. 63–64.

13. Y. T. New [Y. T. Zee] to Mary Lou Dixon, 16 March 1974, biography, p. 32, CRP. A brilliant argument for the adverse psychological effects of Asian role behavior is Reed Ueda, "The Americanization and Education of Japanese-Americans: A Psychodramatic and Dramaturgical Perspective," *Cultural Pluralism*, ed. Edgar Epps (Berkeley: University of California Press, 1974), pp. 71–90.

14. T'sui Yi, "Mai Mei-de jiao-shi lai hua hsing-hsu hsiao-ji" [a short account of the career of Luella Miner since coming to China], ABCFM.

15. Rosabeth Moss Kanter, *Men and Women of the Corporation* (New York: Basic, 1977), p. 205; Kanter refers to Elizabeth Janeway, "The *Weak* are the Second Sex," *Atlantic Monthly*, December 1973.

16. Luella Miner, "Higher Education in China" (1915?), ABCFM.

NOTE ON SOURCES

The following manuscript sources figured most prominently in this study. For a discussion of printed materials, see my dissertation, "Imperial Evangelism: American Women Missionaries in Turn-of-the-Century China" (Ph.D., Yale University, 1981), and for a complete bibliography on the women's missionary movement, see R. Pierce Beaver, *All Loves Excelling: American Protestant Women in World Mission* (Grand Rapids, Mich.: William B. Eerdmans, 1968).

Personal Documents

Over the past twenty years, several archives have been actively seeking the private papers of former Protestant missionaries in China. The collections gathered by the China Records Project at the Yale Divinity School, the University of Oregon Library, and as part of the American Board of Commissioners for Foreign Missions Papers, constitute the core of this study. These collections include extensive personal and family papers, sometimes extending over several decades.

The China Records Project at Yale Divinity School in New Haven, Connecticut, was originally inherited from the National Council of Churches, and has since been greatly augmented and fully indexed. Its private papers collection contains 1,213 boxes, or about 560 linear feet, of correspondence, diaries, memorabilia, and photographs, dating from 1834 to 1978. It includes the papers of missionaries from a number of denominations, with particularly strong holdings of Congregationalists, Northern Baptists, and Methodists. A few remarkable sets of family papers span several generations. Particularly noteworthy for this project are the letters, diaries, and notebooks of Elsie Clark, a woman suffragist and an eloquent commentator on China mission life. Jeanie Graham McClure's papers document the transformation of a college leader and spirited missionary volunteer into a contented missionary housewife, while Sarah Goodrich's describe her enlistment as a single woman, her subsequent marriage, her depression during child-rearing years, and her emergence as a prominent mission lecturer thereafter. Other important papers of married women missionaries within large family collections are the papers of Jennie Wortman Campbell and Florence Manly. The Campbell and Manly Papers include letters of missionary daughters Louise and Dorothy Campbell and Marian Manly, all of whom also served as missionaries in China. In addition, the Manly collection includes extensive photographs of Szechwan taken by Edward Manly and others. Anna Hartwell's copybooks are part of a large Baptist family collection.

The papers at the Special Collections, University of Oregon Library, in Eugene, are virtually unindexed and roughly sorted. They include the Lacy family papers, however, which feature the remarkable letters of Jessie Ankeny prior to her marriage. This collection also contains the papers of the William Ashmore family, including those of Lida Ashmore which present a sour picture of missionary life useful as a corrective to other more positive perspectives. The Monona Cheney Papers are a good source on Peking colonial life.

The private papers connected with the ABCFM papers at Houghton Library, Harvard University, in Cambridge, Massachusetts, can be easily overlooked in that vast collection. They are extensive, however, and several collections proved particularly useful for this project. The extraordinary papers of Sarah Luella Miner touch on five decades and include regular "general" letters sent to mission supporters, which comment extensively on the changing political climate of Peking. Her private letters are rich accounts of the challenges of life for a single woman in late-nineteenth-century China.

The China Missionaries Oral History Project, located at the Honnold Library of the Claremont Colleges in Claremont, California, offers valuable contemporary oral history. Between 1969 and 1972 interviewers for this project talked with forty-three former China missionaries then living in the Claremont area. The typed transcripts from these interviews, which were conducted with an eye to current historical interests, have been deposited in a number of libraries and contain material which might be useful to students of American–Chinese relations and Chinese history, as well as mission history.

Mission Board Papers

The papers of two mission boards, the Methodist Episcopal Woman's Foreign Missionary Society and the American Board of Commissioners for Foreign Missions, figure significantly in this study. The material in these collections varies greatly in strength. The most useful collection in the WFMS papers, which have been moved to the Archives of the United Methodist Church in Madison, New Jersey, is a deceased file of former missionaries, which contains biographical material in the form of letters, pamphlets, and clippings on many China missionaries. The board's correspondence with the field, and the papers of the general Board of Foreign Missions, along with the papers of the Southern Methodist mission boards, disappeared during the merger of the United Methodist Church in 1939.

In contrast, the ABCFM papers are voluminous. They include full candidate papers, extensive correspondence of the board with virtually every missionary, and a biographical file for each missionary or missionary couple. The biographical and candidate files provide the demographic information discussed in chapter 2.

Recently fully indexed and deposited at the China Records Project in New Haven, the United Board for Christian Higher Education in Asia papers are extensive, representing 206 manuscript feet. This interdenominational body inherited the American archives of Ginling, Yenching, and the other Christian colleges in China, and its papers still constitute a largely unexploited resource.

One other source is worth noting. A "Calendar to the Correspondence of the Board of Foreign Missions" provides a convenient summary of the correspondence of the Presbyterian Board of Foreign Missions with the field at the turn of the century. This typescript on microfilm is located at the Presbyterian Historical Society in Philadelphia and consists of an item-by-item digest, with liberal quotation of particularly significant parts. The originals from which the microfilm calendar was made have subsequently been destroyed, and the accuracy of the digest is open to question. Nonetheless, it provides an easy device for quickly sampling the concerns which missionaries discussed with their board.

INDEX

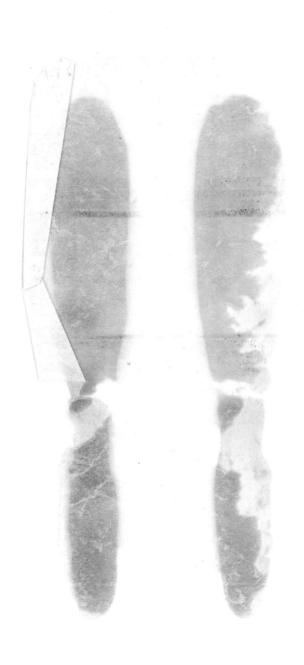